Extended Realities, Virtual Environment, and Interactive Experiences

Editors

Özge Cordan
Istanbul Technical University, Turkey

Mehmet İlker Berkman
Bahçeşehir University, Turkey

Demet Arslan Dinçay
Istanbul Technical University, Turkey

Güven Çatak
BUG Lab TEKMER, Turkey

CRC Press
Taylor & Francis Group
Boca Raton London New York

CRC Press is an imprint of the
Taylor & Francis Group, an **informa** business
A SCIENCE PUBLISHERS BOOK

Cover credit: **Cover Art by Can Büyükberber**

First edition published 2026
by CRC Press
2385 NW Executive Center Drive, Suite 320, Boca Raton FL 33431

and by CRC Press
4 Park Square, Milton Park, Abingdon, Oxon, OX14 4RN

CRC Press is an imprint of Taylor & Francis Group, LLC

Library of Congress Cataloging-in-Publication Data (applied for)

ISBN: 978-1-032-94110-3 (hbk)
ISBN: 978-1-032-94760-0 (pbk)
ISBN: 978-1-003-58164-2 (ebk)

DOI: 10.1201/9781003581642

Typeset in Palatino
by Prime Publishing Services

Preface

Technologies, applications, and practices for virtual environments create interactive and immersive experiences and blend the transitions and permeabilities between the virtual and physical world. In a world rapidly embracing technological innovation, *Extended Realities, Virtual Environment, and Interactive Experiences* serves as an illuminating guide to the dynamic and multifaceted landscapes of Extended Reality (XR) and immersive technologies. The chapters in this book is a compilation to explore a wide array of topics at the intersection of virtual and physical realms offering readers an in-depth understanding of the potential of XR in various fields, education, and training to entertainment and beyond. The book delves into the intricacies of augmented reality (AR), virtual reality (VR), mixed reality (MR), assisted reality (AsR), and the ever-expanding metaverse, with a keen focus on real-world applications and case studies, with a focus on user experience.

This book gathers 15 chapters from different disciplines such as game design, graphic design, architecture, interior architecture, and planning, robotics and cobotics, computer and computing, civil and systems engineering, digital and interactive media, art, and education with a common interest for extended realities.

The first chapter, written by Berkman, is an introduction to the book, explaining terminology, describing the technology, and providing a brief history, followed by an examination of methods for evaluating user experience in XR as an umbrella term encompassing AR and VR.

Wiik, Suovuo, Kähkönen, and Smed explore the interactive experiences of social virtual realities with a particular focus on how transgender individuals navigate gender identity through customizable avatars. By analyzing current VR avatar creation interfaces, the chapter provides insights into making these technologies more inclusive and supportive for all users. Authors delve into how to develop customizable visual, auditory, and behavioral aspects of virtual reality avatars that can better serve diverse audiences, particularly concerning gender diversity. They also emphasize the transformative capacity of XR technologies for transgender and gender non-conforming individuals, suggesting that they can provide beneficial psychosocial experiences.

Skult, Piispanen, and Smed present two case studies regarding VR projects that demonstrate how immersive VR can make complex topics more accessible and engaging for students, explaining quantum physics phenomena of superposition and entanglement to students. The chapter focuses on the design challenges of creating interactive experiences that meet a variety of learning needs and provides insights into how VR can be used for error detection, user behavior analysis, and continuous design improvement.

Tüker, Başer Nejat, and Ürkmez focus on the use of a mechanical printing simulator to teach typography concepts to graphic design students. Examining the usability and teaching value of the VR simulator, the chapter provides a concrete example of how XR can bridge the gap between traditional methods and innovative, immersive learning experiences.

Şengün and Bezgin explore the incorporation of XR technologies in the aviation industry, contributing to the book's broader theme of exploring the intersection between virtual and physical realities. Their meta-study approach highlights recent advancements in XR and underscores its potential for cost savings, improved security, and efficiency focusing on how XR can transform aviation processes such as pilot training, maintenance, and air traffic control, with showcases of real-world applications.

Nyyssönen, Lehtonen, and Smed discuss interaction possibilities of virtual reality via gameplay mechanics design. Their chapter explains several possible interaction methods in virtual reality and contemplates on when and how they should be utilized, taking into account their limitations. The main topics relate to whether controller-based interaction or hand-tracking is better in certain scenarios, with in-depth discussion on both including example studies. Furthermore, they showcase more experimental mechanics, such as utilizing eye-openness and pulse to control movement, in addition to scraping the surface on context-awareness in virtual reality applications.

Teixeria Belek and Teixeria employ a research-by-design methodology to explore how virtual art can facilitate learning by integrating intellectual contemplation and empirical experience. Their analysis of the exhibition "The One and the Multiple" highlights the role of spatial experiences in knowledge construction, emphasizing that knowledge is not static but evolves through interaction and engagement with digital environments. The chapter's exploration of spatial education and didactic systems underscores the potential of virtual reality to provide new dimensions of interaction and perception, fostering creativity and critical thinking.

Karatas and Surer examine the opportunities for VR and MR use in systems engineering from a more technical perspective. They define a system design framework and develop modeling application prototypes, one for VR and MR devices and the other for desktop computers. By testing the compatibility of VR and MR technologies with model-based systems engineering methodology with users, they reveal that VR and MR prototypes are neither better nor worse than desktop prototypes, but they have advantages and disadvantages.

Franzè, Caldwell, Belek Teixeira, and Rittenbruch analyzed ten international case studies of small- and medium-sized enterprises in architecture, engineering, and construction industries, developing a taxonomy of AR-enhanced workflows that emphasize the important role the technology can play in enhancing fabricators' application of tacit knowledge and problem-solving skills. AR's blending of digital and physical realms transforms traditional manufacturing processes, providing fabricators with insights into complex materializations and newfound morphological possibilities. The chapter underscores the role AR can play in addressing production challenges, highlighting the need for concerted efforts between academia and industry.

Shafiei, Teixeira, Mashaly, and Karlovsek depict a workflow in the use of AR for design and manufacturing with an emphasis on architectural entities, leading to robotic assembly of parametric prototypes. They report on their four-part process beginning with free-hand drawing or sketching, continuing with form-finding through parametric design script, resolved into a design optimization step to end up in robotic assembly. Their AR-integrated process allows less-computationally skilled educators, scholars, or industry workers to be involved in parametric design in collaboration with robots.

Liu, Caldwell, Belek Teixeira, Rittenbruch, Burden, and Guertler further explore the human-robot collaboration and XR technologies, through a systematic literature review and horizon scan review which emerged 59 studies between 2019 to 2024, revealing that XR technologies mentioned in these studies are mainly intended as an interface for human-robot interaction, but also the researchers benefited XR as development environment, learning environment, design platform, visualization, simulation, instruction and guidance, task and motion planning. By examining how XR improves cognitive workload, safety, and decision-making in HRC, the chapter reinforces the book's focus on practical case studies and cutting-edge research.

Globa, Lyu, Yildirim, and Gocer report their comparative findings on low-immersion and highly immersive VR environments created for enabling virtual architectural site visits, interactive site analysis, and immersive evaluation of design proposals, which are used in an educational context by the participants. The VR development pipeline they propose, which combines 360° videos and 3D objects using relatively simpler technologies, but capable of letting the students create virtual site visits, site evaluations, and project presentations in architectural practice and education.

Sezen and Sezen examine how science fiction has shaped public perceptions of extended reality technologies, followed by an analysis of the representation XR technologies within the context of table-top roleplaying game the "Shadowrun", discussing how these provide a unique space for exploring societal perceptions and expectations surrounding the evolution of extended reality technologies, fostering both speculation and critical reflection.

Öksüz, Cordan, and Çatak introduce a beta version of a single-player VR serious game which aims to enhance earthquake preparedness and awareness to prevent and reduce deaths, injuries, and property loss. Their simulation demonstrates proper and improper practices in organizing interior spaces and selecting and arranging non-structural elements, such as furniture, equipment, and lighting with a focus on experiential learning exemplifies the integration of virtual technologies into real-world applications.

Arslan Dinçay takes both a conventional and critical standpoint of using XR technologies as virtual memory spaces, and explores user perceptions and expectations of a VR representation of a monumental architectural artefact, the Taşkışla building. Through a comparative analysis, the research discusses how people perceive and experience physical and virtual memory spaces, particularly regarding user experience and sense of presence.

Combining these studies in different fields which employ XR technologies, this book presents new perspectives and emphasizes recent studies in disciplinary and interdisciplinary domains in the realm of extended realities and interactive experiences related to the virtual environment. By doing so, it is aimed to increase collaboration, convergence, and communication between different fields. Whether the reader is a seasoned professional, a curious enthusiast, or an academic seeking insights into the future of human-computer interaction, *Extended Realities, Virtual Environment, and Interactive Experiences* is your guide for captivating realm where digital and physical realities converge.

Editors:
Özge Cordan
Mehmet İlker Berkman
Demet Arslan Dinçay
Güven Çatak

Acknowledgement

This collection would not exist without the help of many contributors. First of all, we would like to thank Dr. Barbaros Bostan, who was introduced as an associate editor at the beginning of this journey and who made valuable contributions to the initial ideas of this collection. The editors would also like to thank Vijay Primliani at the CRC Press for his guidance and support throughout this process.

This collection gained meaning and value thanks to the scholars who contributed to it. Without them, this work could not have been done. We thank all of them for their contributions to the theme of the book and the literature with their research and new ideas. As editors, we have learned a lot from all of you, and we hope that readers will similarly acquire a lot from your research and ideas.

We also thank our families for supporting us in this process.

Contents

Preface .... *iii*
Acknowledgement .... *vii*

1. **Introduction: Experience in Extended Realities** **1**
2. **Navigating Identities: Avatar Customization and Transgender Experiences in Social VR** **40**
3. **Exploring Interactive Storytelling in Virtual Reality for Teaching Quantum Physics and Computation: A Comparative Analysis of Qwiz and Qplayground** **60**
4. **Using VR Technology for Teaching Letterpress** **80**
5. **A Survey of the Use of Extended Reality and Spatial Computing in the Aviation Industry** **103**
6. **Non-Conventional Virtual Reality Mechanics** **124**
7. **Knowledge through Virtual Art Systems of Didactic Communication** **148**
8. **Development of a Systems Modeling Language Framework in Virtual Reality and Mixed Reality Environments: A Comparative Analysis** **170**
9. **Custom Manufacturing 4.0: Identifying Emerging Augmented Fabrication Workflows to Support SME Advancement in the AEC Industry** **192**
10. **Workflow for Augmented Reality Aided Design to Advanced Manufacturing: From Sketch to Robotic Assembly of Parametric Prototypes** **217**
11. **Extended Reality in Human-Robot Collaboration: Present and Future** **243**

12. VR Environments for Architectural Education: Feasibility, Development, Integration, and Evaluation of VR Prototypes 270

13. I Like Your New Eyes: Representation of Extended Reality Technologies in Tabletop Roleplaying Games 298

14. Enhancing Earthquake Preparedness and Awareness: A Virtual Reality Serious Game for Residential Interiors 317

15. Regenerating a Memory Place in the Virtual World: Taşkışla 339

Index *355*

About the Editors *359*

Chapter **1**

Introduction: Experience in Extended Realities

Mehmet İlker Berkman
Department of Visual Communication Design,
Faculty of Communication, Bahcesehir University (TR)

INTRODUCTION

Nowadays, when we hear about "journeys through cyberspace", we tend to think about world wide web and social media, which are structured as interlinked blocks of text with embedded two dimensional visuals. McLuhan's (1962) *Gutenberg Galaxy* did not vanish, but dematerialized as a digital medium dominated by typography. Meanwhile, the real universe that we perceive in three dimensions has also been reconstructed or altered within the binary digits of spatial computing. These virtual realms, which are subject to our spatial cognition, offer us new galaxies in the 'metaverse', i.e., extended reality (XR).

From a metaphysical perspective, there are binary approaches towards our experiences through these technologies. The fictional or virtual is taken opposed to the real. However, our experiences in VR can be explained through a theory of pictorial seeing familiar from the philosophy of the arts, as a form of egocentric and interactive picturing (Tavinor 2023),

For Correspondence: ilker.berkman@bau.edu.tr

DOI: 10.1201/9781003581642-1

which leads to a type of experience unique to XR environment: a perceptual illusion of "self being there" for telepresence, or "things being here" for local presence. A conceptualization for presence from this perspective would be helpful to understand the terminology around the term XR.

TERMINOLOGY

While the abbreviation XR sometimes unpacked as "cross-reality", "extended reality" is more common. The term has been adopted quite recently as an umbrella term covering virtual, augmented, and mixed reality (VR, AR, MR), and delineation between these terms necessarily remains fuzzy. (Çöltekin et al. 2020). It is easier to distinguish VR from the other two, since the "VR experiences can be conceptualized on a telepresence-continuum", while the other's experiences are on a local-presence continuum (Rauschnabel et al. 2022).

However, it is also a little bit tricky to distinguish VR from other immersive media. The Burdeau Triangle (Burdeau and Coiffet 2003, based on Burdeau's earlier work) of immersion-interaction-imagination may help us to understand the pillars of VR experience, which is later expanded to four key factors of "Immersion, Interactivity, Information Intensity, and Intelligence of Objects" (MacEachren et al. 1999). While there are some other forms of immersive media, such as 3D movies or Norton Heilig's (1960) infamous head-mounted television set; these do not provide an essential factor for VR: the interaction. Although the PC games and the mobile games are highly interactive, it is arguable that they provide an extensive experience of immersion. In this sense, a complete or a partial barrier that isolates the users from their surroundings, with the aim of occluding the reality, can be a keypoint of distinguishing virtual reality from other interactive media as well as with AR and MR (Peddie 2017).

Contrastively, the MR technologies do not have the aim to separate the users from their surroundings, either they are in a virtual or in a real environment. The seminal work of Milgram and Kishino (1994) defines the "mixed reality" as a continuum lying between the real environment and virtual environment, where the "augmented reality" is situated closely to the real environment. On the other side of the continuum, there is augmented virtuality. Authors who embrace this approach are said to have an "MR-dominant view" depicted in Figure 1.1, one of the four views identified in the literature by Rauschnabel et al. (2022) through expert interviews and focus group study. The others are the "VR-dominant view", the "MR-centered view", and the "extended reality view", which are also schematized in Figure 1.1.

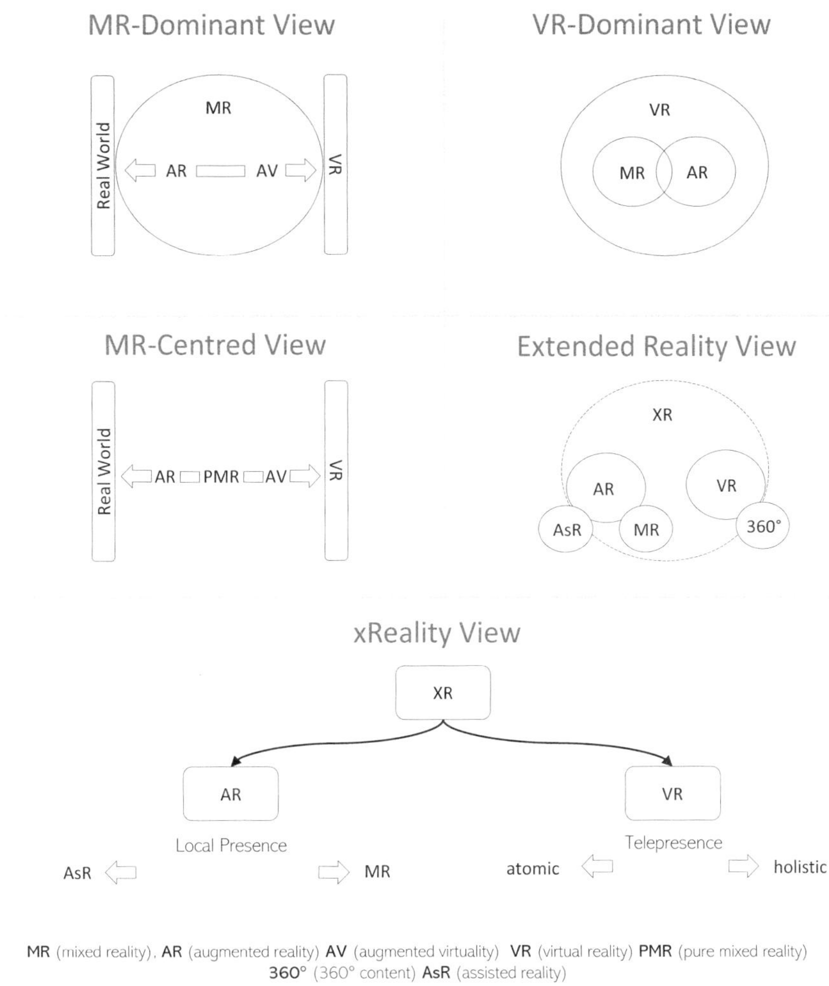

Figure 1.1 Explanations of terminology based on different views. Adapted from Rauschnabel et al. (2022).

Advocates of the "MR-dominant view" consider AR and VR as subclasses of MR. Within this perspective, another way to distinguish AR and AV (augmented virtuality) is the proportion of real vs. the virtual content. A further dichotomous distinction depends on whether virtual elements are superimposed onto the real world (i.e., AR) or real objects are integrated into virtual environments (i.e., AV).

VR-dominant view suggests that VR stands above all other formats, i.e., AR and MR are subsets of VR. From the perspective of the MR-centered view, there is something called PMR ('pure' mixed reality) in between the AR and AV, where AR is closer to the real world and AV is closer to the VR which lies at the opposite end. However, dichotomous structure does not leave a territory for extended reality.

The extended reality view suggests that AR and VR are unrelated domains and both are covered by XR, with partial exceptions. Related to the VR domain, there are the 360 videos. These media are interactive, as the view angle depends on user input, but they mostly reflect the real world as it is, so that it is arguable how they extend the reality. Similarly, there is the assisted reality domain in relation to AR, in which virtual objects are used to enhance the users' understanding of the real environment, rather than being simply merged into.

Based on their study, Rauschnabel et al. (2022) suggest a novel framework approach to define the terminology. They propose to use the term XR for xReality, an umbrella term that covers VR and AR, as given in Figure 1.1. To distinguish AR from VR through a user experience point of view, they suggest that it should be asked whether the real environment, at least visually, is a part of the user's experience or not. If it is, then the user is having a local presence experience in the AR continuum that lies in between the two ends: assisted reality and mixed reality. Local presence is experienced at a lower level in assisted reality, where virtual objects are not intended to be a part of real space. On the contrary, it is higher in MR experiences where designers aim to blend the virtual objects with the real world. For VR, there is a telepresence continuum that lies between the atomistic and holistic virtual reality. The term holistic VR is proposed for applications in which designers intend to reproduce a user experience that does highly resemble real world experiences, not just in terms of visual realism, but also by providing a wide range of possible actions. There is a much lesser priority on the real-world resemblance of content representation and user action in atomic VR, where there is some other primary goal of the VR application.

Throughout this chapter, we would embrace the Rauschnabel et al. (2022) "xReality" dichotomy for VR and AR as they lead to different user experiences regarding presence as mentioned above: a perceptual illusion of "self being there" or "things being here".

TECHNOLOGY

There are a variety of devices used to explore XR experiences. Muhanna (2015) proposed a simple taxonomy for VR devices. Excluding the monitors and handheld devices which he categorizes as simple VR devices, the proposed category of enhanced VR devices are explored according to their level of immersion. The fully immersive technologies are separated as "room-based" and "binocular head-based". Room-based devices are CAVE (Cave Automatic Virtual Environment) systems and vehicle simulators, while head-based systems are stereoscopic HMDs (head-mounted displays).

There is more diversity in AR technologies. Peddie (2017) proposed a taxonomy for AR technologies depending on their wearability, but he also recommended using another taxonomy that he cites to Ron Padzensky since it covers a further variety of devices. This taxonomy depends on mobility of the devices, since the main three branches are 'head-mounted', "mobile non-wearable", and 'projected'.

Head-mounted devices can be categorized as 'tethered', 'self-contained', and 'smartphone viewer' devices for their design. Form factor is another possible taxonomy where spectacle, visor, goggle, helmet, and headset are possible subcategories. Monocular, binocular, stereoscopic, and holographic are other classification dimensions for head-mounted devices. Furthermore, the sensing capabilities in terms motion, spatial depth, and geo position; and control capabilities through gesture, voice, motion sensors, and controllers are proposed as other taxonomies to classify not only head-mounted, but also mobile non-wearable and projected devices. For their form factors, mobile non-wearable devices are simply divided as tablets and smartphones, while the projected devices are categorized into three as surfaces, vehicular windscreens, and retro-reflective devices. The very basic visualization for classifying AR technologies had been made by Bimber and Raskar (2005), where they categorize the devices as head-mounted, hand-held, optical see-through, and spatial projection. Their simple visualization is very helpful in understanding AR technologies, as seen in recreation of their diagram in Figure 1.2.

The AR hardware has mainly three components (Arena et al. 2022). The sensors, such as cameras, GPS locators, ultrasound or laser beam-scanning technologies are required to determine the users' and objects' position in the real world. The display, which could be in the form of the aforementioned devices, such as an HMD or a retinal projection, is required to let the users perceive content where virtual objects are merged into the real-world vision. Finally, there are input devices to let the user manipulate virtual objects. There is a large variety of interfaces, from data gloves to voice-command input. Similarly, VR hardware also has sensors, which are mainly required to locate the user, a display which may provide stereoscopic images; and controllers which are essential for user input.

While hardware was evolving, there was a need to standardize the data structures used for AR y. The Open Geospatial Consortium (2015) approved the ARML (Augmented Reality Markup Language) for adoption (Liao 2020). Furthermore, the ISO/IEC 3721 (ISO 2023) is released as an international standard to describe the core objects and their attributes for XR applications. The standardization efforts for VR development started much earlier, with the VRML (VR modeling language) (ISO 1997) as an effort of a consortium of several organizations (Carson 1999), with the goal of developing 3D (three-dimensional) media on the World Wide Web. These efforts later evolved into X3D, which is an open standard of "file format and run-time architecture to represent and communicate 3D scenes and objects" (Web3D Consortium 2024).

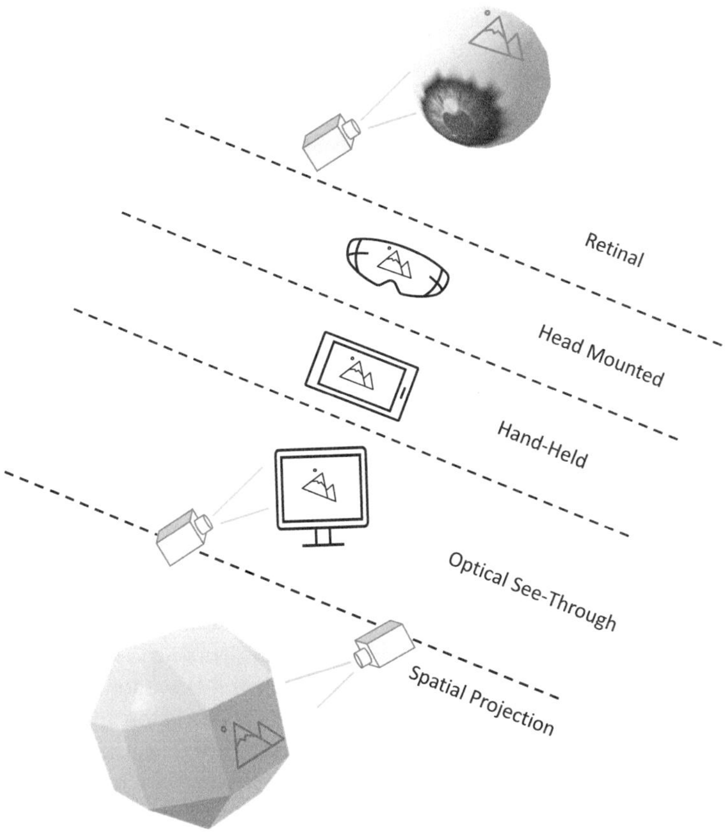

Figure 1.2 Simplified classification of AR technologies. Adapted from Bimber and Raskar (2005).

A BRIEF HISTORY

The idea of creating an artificial environment that cannot be distinguished from reality, or altering reality with visual artifice was present long before mankind developed the technology to achieve it almost perfectly. Stereoscopic projections could have been used as early as 17th century, and anaglyph stereoscopic magic lanterns are known to be used by entertainers in the late 18th and 19th century, as in Etienne Gaspard's smoke reflecting projected 'Phantasmagoria' illusions in Paris, 1798; or Pepper's Ghost illusions reflected on tilted glass panels, an invention by John Henry Pepper which had been used in theaters starting in 1862 (Zone 2014, Peddie 2017). In 1793, Robert Barker was displaying his panoramic paintings at the rotunda in Leicester Square, London (Benosman and Kang 2001). This rotunda was the world's first purpose-built building designed specifically for viewing panorama paintings, which were situated on the inner surface of circular walls. In Barker's memoir, it is reported that King George III and Queen Charlotte had a special tour before the day of opening. As the queen had 'seasickness' while viewing the "Grand Fleet at Spithead in 1791" (Brewer 2007), she might have been the first person ever reported to have experienced cybersickness.

These and some other mechanical precursors, such as Wheatstone and Brewster stereoscopes, d'Almeida, du Hauron and Anderton's efforts on stereoscopic projection are some early technical milestones in reaching the modern day XR (Zone 2014). However, the XR, which requires it to be interactive, could only have been possible with the digital computer.

The concept of establishing and altering reality using a digital computer was envisioned as the "ultimate display" (Sutherland 1965), where a computer is suggested to be used to emulate real-life physics. Surprisingly, the realization of this idea emerged not as a completely immersive virtual environment, but rather as a system where computer-generated geometric forms interact with the real world. With his system which he called the "Sword of Damocles", Sutherland showcased his concepts through a prototype. This head-mounted 3D display could present computer-generated images to users, adjusting the perspective as they moved. The system utilized a specialized display with two miniature cathode ray tube screens for stereoscopic vision. Additionally, it featured two head position sensors—one mechanical and the other ultrasonic—to track the user's head position. The name "Sword of Damocles" originated from the mechanical head-positioning sensor, resembling a heavy, uncomfortable arm hanging from the ceiling. Interestingly, this display system fell into the category of AR rather than VR, because the cathode ray tube images were reflected on half-silvered mirrors, allowing users to simultaneously see real-world objects in the room. These images appeared as transparent 'wireframe' line drawings due to the computational challenges of rendering solid objects in real time. Despite the simplicity of the objects (such as a cubical room), Sutherland (1968) reported positive user responses on stereographic vision.

An extensive chronological list of inventions regarding AR and partially VR can be seen in Peddie (2017: 56–80), including military HUD (head-up display) technologies. For a detailed historical review of VR-related technologies, please see Berkman (2018) or (Burdea and Coiffet 2017) which also include information on locomotion and interaction appliances.

VR HMDs

The XR technologies are not limited to stereoscopic HMDs, but most people think of a large goggle covering one's face, when they hear about VR. We owe the term VR to Jaron Lanier, one of the pioneering personalities of the commercial VR HMDs in the 1990s. Commercial VR in the 1990s ended up to a "VR winter" since the VR companies naively acted in terms of commerce, while academic centers of excellence could not deliver valuable and usable intellectual properties. The hardware was expensive and unreliable, limitations and requirements of the users were not considered, in case studies and cost-benefit analysis (Stone 2009). There was not any public interest in commercial VR for almost a decade, until the world's dominating technology companies, Google and Meta (which was known as Facebook back then) showed an interest in the development of HMDs as a consumer product. This was largely based on the efforts of Palmer Luckey, the founder of the company Oculus. Using smartphone technologies such as small high-resolution screens with low energy consumption, sensors such as gyroscopes, accelerometers, magnetometers, Luckey prototyped an affordable and well-functioning HMD in his family's garage at the age of 18 in 2011, which led to manufacturing of Oculus Rift Development Kit series devices in 2012 and 2013 (Harley 2020). While Luckey's company Oculus was acquired by Facebook founder Mark Zuckerberg in 2014, Google was investing in projects like Cardboard and Daydream, which are VR headset boxes in which users can insert a smartphone. Companies such as HTC in collaboration with Valve Software Inc. came up with their own device in 2016, the HTC Vive, which is targeting a gaming audience by providing support for VR gaming on the Steam game repository platform. In the same year, Sony also started to sell their VR headset for the Playstation gaming consoles. With the interest of these international companies and their efforts to incent content creators to develop VR content, the HMD-based VR technologies became a profitable industry. Apple Inc. was the last to develop and sell a VR HMD, with their Vision Pro released in 2024. Although the commercial development of the VR headsets was mainly mobilized by the gaming community and industry from the beginning, current uses of VR technology is broadening towards research and industry. As of 2021, The Valve and HTC do not mass-produce low-cost gaming headsets; they are focused on high-end products with enhanced hardware, targeting the enterprise and professional market.

Currently, VR is embraced in several industries such as healthcare, in which VRis used for medical training and surgery simulation, where Osso VR is one of the leading companies. The aviation industry uses immersive technologies for training for a long time, and there is support for VR HMDs in many systems (Marron et al. 2024, Trinon 2019). Real-estate companies are reported to be employing VR technologies for property viewing, while retail companies are known to be using VR for personnel training (Raji et al. 2024). In Ford Motor Company, VR technologies are used for prototyping vehicles as well as designing the manufacturing line (Remondino 2017). Boletsis and Karahasanovic (2020) provide a case study of companies who used VR as a sales channel or for virtual try-on of their products as well as branding and marketing their products, mentioning Alibaba, Carrefour, Nike, North Face, Tesco, Volvo, and Walmart.

AR HEADSETS

Keeping in mind that Sutherland's "Sword of Damocles" (1968) mentioned above is augmenting graphics on real-world view, Stephen W.G. Mann's EyeTap is suggested to be an example of pioneering AR systems, as early as 1984 (Vertucci et al. 2023). The history of AR goes hand-in-hand with mobile computing, digital cameras, and sensors used in handheld devices. Arth et al. (2015) report a chronological list of those devices that they acquire as a milestone for wearable AR systems. The term "augmented reality" was used for the first time to refer to a concept of providing "a 'see-thru' virtual reality goggle to the factory worker" (Caudell and Mizell 1992). Even before the mobile computers became available sufficiently, researchers (Rekimoto and Nagao 1995, Fitzmaurice 1993) contributed to the future mobile AR with their efforts using stationary computers, which led to the very first mobile AR system (Feiner et al. 1997), where the users need to carry a backpack computer along with a handheld device. The total weight of the system was a little bit less than 20 kilograms, including a rechargeable battery belt. Sony Glasstron (1998), which was originally marketed as a TV viewing device, did not get a lot of attention from the consumers but researchers employed this device for many studies of human-computer interaction in wearable AR scenarios until the late 2000s. During this era, the AR research was focused on handheld screens with cameras, especially the smartphones and tablets with cameras became largely available for consumers. Thanks to the popularity of these devices for social media use, the commercial AR applications reached a wider audience. Announced in 2012, Google Glass was also promised to become a daily-use device for regular users (Starner 2013), but similarly to Sony Glasstron, it acquired higher attention from the researchers rather than consumers.

OTHER VR AND AR DEVICES

While head-mounted stereoscopic devices are the most popular way of experiencing XR, there are other ways of reconstructing and altering reality.

The earliest digital VR systems that were commercially available were the flight simulators. While the mechanical Link Simulators dated back to the 1930s, their first digital system, the Mark-I, was developed in the early 1960s (Page 2000), which employs parallel processors to handle arithmetic operations, generate functions, and select radio stations. These systems later became furnished with CGI (computer-generated images), which made them provide an immersive experience for trainees. McDonnell-Douglas Electronics Corporation initially developed and marketed VITAL, while Evans and Sutherland/Redifon introduced NOVOVIEW, followed by Link's IMAGE Visual Systems. Along with flight simulators, driving simulators also followed a similar technological evolution, leading to CGU visualizations (Allen et al. 2011).

The CAVE (Cave Automatic Virtual Environment) with a recursive acronym, reminiscent of Plato's allegory of cave (Cruz-Neira et al. 1992), is a room with walls, ceiling, and floor surrounding a viewer with projected images and a method to track user movements and direction. Located in universities to be used for 3D scientific data visualizations, virtual prototyping, or simply as virtual environments; most common instances have three walls. Since the users are not completely detached from the real environment, CAVE systems have the potential to support collaborative activities.

Mirror worlds offer a second-person experience by augmenting the viewer's video-captured image onto a virtual environment, where the computer analyzes features like position, movement, and finger count (McLellan 2004). A very early example is dated back to 1974, the Videoplace system of computer artist Myron Krueger (Krueger and Wilson 1985). The Mandala VR is an early commercial system developed by a group of Canadian performance artists (Wyshynski and Vincent, 1993). In a sense, these technologies can be identified as "augmented virtuality", where the subject's real-world image overlays on a digital surrounding. Mirror worlds also may employ a virtual avatar in third-person view, reflecting the user's movements. For the readers of this chapter, several applications in Nintendo Wii (Jones and Thiruvathukal 2012), Playstation Eyetoy and Microsoft Kinect can be more familiar examples for mirror worlds as they are "controller free" (Vöhringer 2011), in which the avatar's movements are controlled with the corresponding body movements of the player.

Many popular AR applications run on mobile phones. With their large screens and sensors, consumer mobile devices have been a practical platform for AR developers. Fitzmaurice's Chameleon (1993) is suggested to be the very first handheld instance of AR technologies, but the first mobile handheld AR on a consumer cell phone had to wait more than a decade (Mohring et al. 2004), when the cameras became a common component of mobile phones, enabling tracking and registration of the surroundings. The modern-day smartphones and tablets, standardized after Apple's first I-phone released in 2007, have geographical sensors and advanced IMUs (inertial measurement units) that make them highly capable for tracking and registration.

A relatively less popular technique for AR is projection, creating spatial AR. Although this type of AR system is not as many as mobile and HMD applications, the field of application for these are plenty; such as manufacturing (Zhang et al. 2022), medicine (Cutolo 2024), and education (Hidayat and Wardat 2024).

The retinal displays, also called Maxwellian displays are not practically applicable for commercial applications yet, but they are promising especially for AR applications, as they deliver all the light from the image source into viewers' eyes, without being affected by the environmental light (Xiong et al. 2021).

USER EXPERIENCE IN EXTENDED REALITY

There are many methods to assess user experience, especially regarding the use of a product. Vlahovic et al. (2022) provided an extended review of Quality of Experience assessment for VR applications. Simões-Marques (2024) ran a systematic literature review for categorizing those state-of-the-art usability assessment methods that are applicable to the XR spectrum, which are frequently used in VR or AR studies. Furthermore, there are several novel methods that are proposed for assessment of XR applications, which are not embraced by the research community yet. Some of these methods are intended to measure anticipated use of XR artifacts.

Similar to other interactive digital artifacts, usability is a key aspect of experience in XR. Based on ISO-9241-11 (2018), it is defined as "Extent to which a product can be used by specified users to achieve specified goals with effectiveness, efficiency, and satisfaction in a specified context of use". It is required to conduct a usability test to measure usability either for comparison to quantitative objectives or for comparing products (Lewis and Sauro 2021). User experience is a broader concept that involves usability, mainly referring to the perceptions and responses of users regarding the use of digital artifacts, as in the definition given in ISO 9241-210 (2010): "a person's perceptions and responses that result from the use and/or anticipated use of a product, system or service". XR artifacts can be related to all three. The hardware is obviously a product. The software, whether it is a game, a 360° video, or a simple AR tool for length measurement, can be considered either as a product or a system. Furthermore, there are services integrated with AR applications, such as AR navigation aids, or repositories for downloading software and games.

Technology Acceptance, which focuses on "Perceived Usefulness" and "Perceived Ease of Use" of a technological artifact, is another perspective that is taken in XR studies. For researchers who study XR in games user research context, player experience is the key aspect in evaluation. Similarly, many XR applications are developed for educational purposes, which lead to development of specific assessment methods in learning context.

As a technology-mediated phenomenon of inaccurate perception of technology involvement, presence is the most frequently explored user experience element, especially for VR applications (Zheleva et al. 2024). By its nature, spatial presence is triggered through immersion, which refers to the technological quality of a system, objectively measuring how effectively it creates a vivid virtual environment while excluding physical reality. As a result, presence is a very important aspect of user experience in VR applications, rather than other types of XR artifacts. However, along with spatial presence, there are other interests of measurement in terms of presence, such as social presence, engagement, and realism, which could be applied to other domains of XR.

Furthermore, cybersickness, which is a special kind of visually induced motion sickness, also referred to as VRISE (VR-induced symptoms and effects) are some negative side effects such as nausea, dizziness, disorientation, fatigue, and instability; frequently observed while using highly immersive VR technologies. These effects are widely studied in terms of hardware, content, and human factors (Chang et al. 2020) in VR. There is evidence that similar adverse effects emerge during AR simulations (Kaufeld et al. 2022, Hughes et al. 2020).

There are also methods that can be used in XR studies that do not directly assess the user experience but could be required to understand the user attributes regarding their use of XR. Choosing the proper participants for the sample would affect the generalizability and replicability of the results. Furthermore, some studies may require diverse groups of participants, in terms of their prior experience with technology or perception of technology. Still being a niche technology, i.e., not adopted by large populations yet, use of XR may lead to a halo effect due to the novelty of the technology for the participants and this may affect the results. Furthermore, some participants should not be subjected to XR technologies due to health, safety or ethical issues. For these reasons (Vlahovic et al. 2022), pre-screening methods are required to evaluate and report the participants of XR studies. These types of methods will also be explored in this chapter, along with the methods used to evaluate use or anticipated use.

Halbig and Latoschik (2021) mention a classification for methods mainly as explicit methods and implicit, depicted in Figure 1.3. In explicit

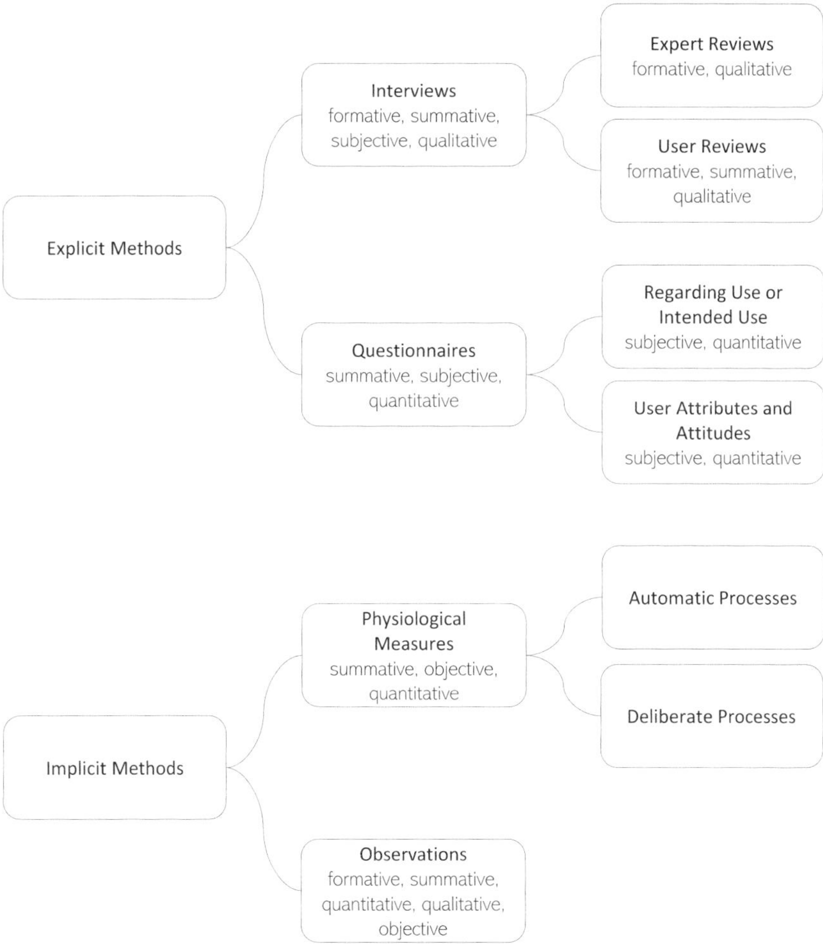

Figure 1.3 Methods classification regarding users' activity. Adapted from Halbig and Latoschik (2021).

methods, users express their own experience actively and explicitly, leading these methods to be subjective. Interviews, including user and expert reviews, provide qualitative information on users, which can either be employed for formative purposes, that is, to make changes in the following versions of the system, or as a summative method, to illustrate users' attitude towards the system. On the other hand, questionnaire methods provide quantitative data but can be used for summative purposes rather than being formative. They are usually used for summative purposes, i.e., to illustrate qualities of the final design.

Implicit methods are based on the users' behavior in response to certain stimulus or event. Some data can be acquired by simply observing users' activities, such as counting clicks on each menu item or recording their path of choices to navigate in a virtual world. While the first is quantitative, the latter is qualitative. Both can be used in a formative manner, such as re-ordering the menu items by click frequency or removing the game rewards out of the most frequently used path areas.

The physiological measures can seek the users' automatic processes which cannot be controlled by the user, such as heart rate or sweating. The physical actions of the users which they are in control, such as smiling, or head rotations can also be a rich source of data to understand the experience of the users in XR.

Although the above categorization depends on users' perception and awareness of their participation in the evaluation process, the rest of this chapter is organized according to the concepts related to experience in XR, i.e. what the researchers aim to measure, regardless of their method being implicit or explicit. As mentioned above, the researchers explore usability, user experience, technology acceptance, presence and cybersickness in terms of experience in XR studies, along with learning related issues. They also need to understand the users and report the attributes and attitudes of the participants.

Each subsection regarding these topics will start with quantitative explicit methods, which are standardized questionnaires that rely on the users' responses regarding their experience with the system. After quantitative explicit methods, some implicit methods will be explored which rely on measurements executed by the researcher, that are mainly related to the observed performance and behavior of the user. In addition, biometrics are employed as implicitly collected indicators, based on physiological responses of the users. According to their technology and correspondence of the physiological systems, they can be categorized as cardiovascular system, brain-computer interface measures, facial and muscular measures, electrodermal activity, and eye-related measures (Akan and Berkman 2020). Moreno-Arjonilla (2024) gives an overall survey of eye-related methods and metrics. Some qualitative methods will be mentioned at the end of every subsection, which are usually formative methods that could be more beneficial at the earlier phases of design, as they make it easier to see the design problems and offer solutions.

USABILITY

There are several questionnaires to assess usability and user experience in a subjective manner, and some of them were employed in XR studies. The first set of methods listed below assess usability, mainly regarding the definition given in ISO-9241-11 (2018).

System Usability Scale (SUS) (Brooke 1996, 2013) was clearly in first place among the other methods that measure usability (Simões-Marques 2024). With its alternating 10 items that point out effectiveness, efficiency, satisfaction, ease of use and learnability, SUS has been applied not only to XR but also in a wide range of other technologies and became an industry standard over the decades. An extended version of SUS, with four additional items (Harper and Dortin 2021) was also employed in XR studies.

As an alternative to SUS, researchers used Computer System Usability Scales (CSUQ), which is one of the IBM usability scales developed by Lewis (1995) in the 1980s. It has 16 items that measure usability in three dimensions: System Quality, Information Quality, and Interface Quality. It is criticized to have a blend of system centric questions along with the experience centric questions (Berkman and Şahin 2022), instead of focusing on the users' experience. Some of its system-centric items may not be suitable for spatial experiences, as they query about "the screens" in the system.

Although it is not used in the studies that are inspected by Simões-Marques (2024), UMUX (Usability Metric for User Experience) (Finstad 2010) is a relatively novel and shorter alternative for subjective evaluation of usability, with conformance to ISO-9241-11 (2018) definition. There are several recent studies using UMUX to assess XR systems, e.g., Varela-Aldás et al. (2023) for VR, Kim and Kim (2024) for AR.

There is also a usability scale specified for VR applications: The Virtual Reality System Usability Questionnaire (VRSUQ) (Kim and Rhiu 2024). Its nine items query the users on compatibility, feedback and error prevention of the VR systems regarding effectiveness; understandability, learnability and error recovery regarding efficiency; pleasure, physical discomfort (motion sickness), and emotional discomfort regarding satisfaction.

In addition, there is a usability scale specialized for handheld AR systems (Santos et al. 2014). With its 16 items, HARUS (Handheld Augmented Reality Usability Scale) measures Manipulability and

Comprehensibility. Unfortunately, it is not completely applicable for head-mounted AR systems since some of its items refer to comfort of holding the handheld AR device. Some other items refer to the clarity of the screen, and can be applicable to AR systems other than the handheld devices.

The objective methods of assessing usability depend on observations on the behavior of the participants. For a detailed inspection of user activities, video recording is a valuable method. In addition, the software that is assessed may include hooks to collect measures of user behavior, such as keystrokes or object interactions.

Goal achievement indicators (such as success rate and accuracy) and operability indicators (such as error rate and function usage) refer to effectiveness; work rate indicators (such as speed and time) refer to efficiency; knowledge acquisition indicators (such as learnability and learning rate) can be taken as a specific case of efficiency for novice users.

For example, the completion of the task is a primary measure for effectiveness and can be taken as a simple binary indicator for 'completed' or "not completed", as in Berkman et al. (2020). In terms of completeness, it could also be taken as the number of correctly executed tasks, such as the number of correctly executed soccer drills in a VR training environment (Wood et al. 2021). Furthermore, accuracy of the completeness can be a measure of effectiveness, as the distance of the golf ball from the hole (Harris et al. 2021). The percentage of the visual targets that are not detected by the participants in an AR enhanced driving task (Maag et al. 2023) is an example of error rate. The distance traveled in a virtual environment can be an example of function usage, as in Lin et al. (2020).

For measuring efficiency, the time-on-task can be used such as a games completion time in Berkman et al. (2020) or time to evacuate as in Lin et al. (2020). The amount of work in a certain amount of time can also be employed as a measure of efficiency. For example, Kobayashi et al. (2001) assessed the feed rate of welding electrodes before and after the virtual welding training session.

The gaze-tracking methods determining where a person is looking in their environment or on a screen, are valuable tools as formative methods, to determine area of interest for the users. By understanding problems in users' identification of areas of interest regarding their task, designers can make improvements in the visual qualities of XR environments.

Think-aloud is also useful as a qualitative method to understand the users' intentions and thoughts regarding their actions (Zhang and Simeone 2023). When think-aloud methods and semi-structured interviews are used along with the RITE (Rapid Iterative Testing and Evaluation) methods (Medlock et al. 2005), a rich source of qualitative information can be gathered from the users to identify issues in an XR system, as in Pentangelo et al. (2024).

Heuristic evaluation method, which depends on reviews of a group of experts based on a set of principles, has been used for a long time for formative evaluation. Nielsen's Heuristics (Nielsen and Molich 1990) are employed for mobile AR applications (Labrie and Cheng 2020). Nishchyk et al. (2024) proposed 55 heuristics for the AR systems developed for elderly users. Endsley et al. (2017) proposed some heuristics for designing dynamic interactions in AR. Murtza et al. (2017) attempted to define a set of heuristics for VR. Oliveira et al. (2017) explored the applicability of heuristics of Sutcliffe and Gault (2004) and Rusu et al. (2011) on modern day mobile phone VR HMD systems. There are 52 heuristics with a detailed 156 sub-heuristics proposed for all XR applications, named as Heuristics for Metaverse (Omar et al. 2024).

Cognitive walkthrough is also a review method that links the interface walkthrough to a cognitive model. The method has a long history and there have been many variants proposed (Mahatody et al. 2010). A group of designers, experts or users conduct a review of a single task and its related interfaces, as in Liu and Steed (2021) where several social VR applications were inspected with a group of participants using their method named as guided "group walkthrough".

USER EXPERIENCE

User Experience Questionnaire (UEQ) has 26 items in a semantic differential format (Laugwitz et al. 2008). The subscales of Perspicuity, Efficiency, Dependability can be grouped into a Pragmatic Quality measure that represents task-related aspects. Stimulation and Originality dimensions can be summed-up as Hedonic Quality, which are the aspects that are not related to the task. In addition, there is an Attractiveness dimension, which refers to the overall impression of the product. There is also a shorter form with eight items, UEQ-S (Schrepp et al. 2017), which provides scores for Pragmatic Quality and Hedonic Quality of the assessed artifact. Another alternative to UEQ could be AttrakDiff (Hassenzahl et al. 2003), with a similar structure with a slightly different set of items.

Alternatively, Modular Evaluation of Key Components of User Experience (meCUE) also focuses on UX in its five modules (Minge et al. 2016). In terms of product perceptions, Module I measures usefulness and usability while Module II is for assessing visual aesthetics, status, and commitment. Module III includes subscales for negative and positive emotions separately. Module IV has items for product loyalty and international to use dimensions, which are conceptualized as consequences of the assessed product. Unlike the other modules that have 7-step Likert scale responses, Module V consists of a single 11-step semantic differential item that queries on their experience of the product as a whole.

Specialized for AR holographic applications, the Usability and User Experience Evaluation in Touchable Holograms (UUXE-ToH) questionnaire (Prado de Campos et al. 2024) is a novel addition to the XR researchers' toolkit. The 50 items proposed intend to measure many aspects of holograms integrated in the real world through AR technologies: effectiveness, efficiency, learnability, memorability, controllability, error prevention and recovery, overall usability, immersion, usefulness, trustworthiness, value, creativity and novelty, stimulation, beauty and aesthetics. However, it cannot be considered as a complete tool, since it was only validated for its content through an expert review. There is no statistical evidence on its psychometric properties at the time this chapter is written.

To detect the changes in users' emotional state, researchers employed many physiological metrics. Halbig and Latoschik (2021) provide a broad review of the use of biometrics in VR studies, and they listed out that most studies use EEG (electroencephalogram, measuring electrical activity in the brain) as indicators of arousal and valence. PPG (photoplethysmography, measuring the blood volume in veins) is also employed along with ECG (electrocardiography, measuring electrical activity of the heart) and EDA (electrodermal activity, measuring the electrical activity on the skin, sometimes mentioned as GSR - galvanic skin response) as indicators of emotional changes, which are also mentioned by Moinnereau et al. (2022).

TECHNOLOGY ACCEPTANCE

Some of the measures used in XR studies focus on a broader concept of technology acceptance, which is highly related to usability (Lah et al. 2020). Measures regarding the technology acceptance are grounded on "Technology Acceptance Model" (Davis 1989) which proposes a measure to assess "Perceived Usefulness" and "Perceived Ease of Use", but could cover further concepts such as "curiosity, anxiety, interest, user-friendliness, immersion, usefulness, skepticism and accessibility" in addition to "intention to use", assessed in Technology Usage Inventory (Kothgassner et al. 2012). The "Usefulness, Satisfaction, and Ease of Use" (USE) questionnaire (Lund 2001) also has a focus on concepts regarding technology acceptance, but also includes items to evaluate learnability and satisfaction. On the other hand, since technology acceptance is built upon ease of use and usefulness that is perceived by the user, these methods can be used regarding the anticipated use of artifacts.

Unified Theory of Acceptance and Use of Technology (UTAUT) is another approach that was used in VR user research. The model was originally developed to explore the use of technology in an organizational setting, but also can be applied to individuals (Marikyan and Papagiannidis 2023). There are several extensions for UTAUT (Venkatesh et al. 2016), where a number of dimensions are measured regarding the technology acceptance including attributes of participants; age, gender and experience.

PLAYER EXPERIENCE

Considering that many XR applications are games, the surveys standardized for games user research are highly valued in XR. Game Engagement Questionnaire (GEQ) (Brockmyer et al. 2009) and Game User Experience Satisfaction Scale (GUESS) (Phan et al. 2016) were reported (Simões-Marques 2024) to be used in some XR studies. With its four dimensions of Absorption, Flow, Presence, and Immersion, GEQ measures players' experience from a "psychological state attainment" perspective (Abeele et al. 2020).

GUESS also has some dimensions regarding the psychological states of the player such as Enjoyment, Creative Freedom, Player Engrossment and Personal Gratification, along with items querying the player about their opinion of about game elements; Audio Aesthetics, Narratives, Social Connectivity, Visual Aesthetics and Usability/Playability. The Usability/Playability dimension is criticized since usability and playability are not conceptually similar. Berkman et al. (2022) provided evidence that players have a different understanding of these concepts while they evaluated the games using GUESS items translated into Turkish, resulting in separate Usability and Playability dimensions. GUESS subscales can be used independently. Since 55-question survey is cumbersome to administer repeatedly and frequently, shorter versions are available in English (Keebler et al. 2020), German (Mittmann et al. 2024) and Turkish (Berkman and Aker 2023), with two items per subscale.

Player Experience Inventory (PXI) (Abeele et al. 2020) is a more economical tool that has 10 dimensions with 3 items each. Meaning, Mastery, Immersion, Autonomy, and Curiosity are Psychosocial Consequences that are second order emotional responses regarding gameplay, while Eease of Control, Challenge, Progress Feedback, Audio-visual Appeal, and Goals and Rules are immediate responses to game design elements as Functional Consequences; devised on Means-End theory. An 11-item shorter form of PXI is available (Haider et al. 2022).

PXI and GUESS are the most recent tools that are well-acknowledged in the research community, as they evaluate the games for players psychological state and response to the game elements, resonate with the Mechanics-Dynamics-Aesthetics (MDA) framework (Hunicke et al. 2004). However, there are many more standardized questionnaires for assessing experience within the gaming context. The famous PENS (Player Experience of Need Satisfaction Questionnaire) is devised from a self-determination theory perspective, assessing Competence, Autonomy and Relatedness as well as Presence and Intuitive Controls. UPEQ (Ubisoft Perceived Experience Questionnaire) (Azadvar and Canossa 2018) also queries the participants for the same constructs, but the Relatedness construct has a broader understanding regarding the engagements with other players. The Basic Needs in Games Scale (BANGS) (Ballou et al. 2024) is a recent addition to tools based on self-determination theory, as it includes items to assess "needs frustration" as well as "needs satisfaction".

As objective measures, physiological measures which are used to assess arousal, and valence could also be employed for player experience. Akan and Berkman (2020) provide a review of the studies that utilize these measures in a gaming context. Furthermore, in-game achievements such as points, level grades, and total time spent on the game can be quantitative measures for quality of playing experience, where achievements such as items in the players' inventory or quests selected by the player can be used as quantitative indicators.

A qualitative assessment for XR environments could also be made with an expert review approach, using the heuristics suggested for assessing games (Korhonen 2016) although they are proposed as a framework for evaluating mobile games. Those heuristics can also be used as a structure to categorize findings in user interviews (Aker et al. 2020).

WORKLOAD

Perceived workload is the subjective measurement of effort used on a task. Although the After-Scenario Questionnaire (Lewis 1991) simply queries the user about the ease of a task with a few items, many studies require a more thorough assessment of perceived workload. NASA-TLX (National Aeronautics and Space Administration—Task Load Index) (Hart and Staveland 1988) had been widely used for this purpose so that it can serve as a benchmark (Hertzum 2021), NASA-TLX assesses workload in terms of Physical, Temporal and Mental demand required for the task from the participants perspective. It also provides measures for the participants to assess their Performance, Frustration and Effort they spent. The scoring of NASA-TLX can be difficult to use for its weighted scoring method, but the raw scoring method is also widely used.

Harris et al. (2020) proposed SIM-TLX (Simulation Task Load Index) based on NASA-TLX, which is tailored to the specific demands on users of simulated environments, using a simpler scoring of 10-items to measure mental, physical and temporal demands; frustration, task complexity, situational stress, distraction, perceptual strain, task control, and presence.

Several physio-psychological measures are employed in XR studies. As an objective measure of physical workload, EMG (electromyography —electrical activity of muscles) can be used to detect the activity of several muscle groups, as in Stone et al. (2011). Eye tracking measures are also used as indicators of cognitive workload, such as task-evoked pupillary response in Cowan et al. (2021). EDA (Kosch et al. 2019) and EEG (Tremmel et al. 2019) are also used as indicators of mental workload although they are more commonly used as an indicator of users' emotional state. PD, EDA, and EEG frequency band power are reported to be affected by cognitive load in physically active VR stimuli (Ahmadi et al. 2023).

PRESENCE

There are many standardized tools that were proposed to assess presence as a multidimensional construct. Witmer and Singer's (1998) Presence Questionnaire is the earliest attempt in developing a multi-dimensional assessment tool; but there are earlier measures of presence as a unidimensional construct (see Berkman and Akan 2019). For VR applications, spatial presence is a primary concern for researchers. The Spatial Presence Experience Scale (SPES) (Hartmann et al. 2016) measures users' perception of being in the mediated environment with Self-location items, while Possible Actions items query for carrying out actions in the environment and manipulating it. The same items for the same two constructs are also employed in MEC-SPQ (Measurement, Effects, Condition - Spatial Presence Questionnaire) (Vorderer et al. 2004), in which Higher Level of Involvement and Suspension of Disbelief influences the construction of Spatial Presence, where other dimensions are Spatial Situation Model driven by Attention Allocation. Visual Spatial Imagery and Domain Specific Interest are suggested to affect these two factors. MEC-SPQ can be used with four, six, or eight items for each of its dimensions. IPQ (I-Group Presence Questionnaire) (Schubert et al. 2001) also includes Spatial Presence dimension besides items for measuring Realism and Involvement, which was originally developed in German and translated into several languages. The Temple Presence Inventory (Lombard et al. 2009) also has similar dimensions for assessing spatial presence engagement and perceptual realism, but its real strength is

Mechanics, and In-Game Assistance. The VRISE section evolved into Cybersickness in Virtual Reality Questionnaire (Kourtesis et al. 2023).

Based on a set of 9-items isolated from SSQ, Hussain et al. (2023) proposed the Augmented Reality Sickness Questionnaire, where the Nause dimension is omitted, although the "stomach awareness" item is kept. On the other hand, Hughes et al. (2020) reported that higher scores on Nausea dimension of SSQ observed after a relatively longer period of using see-through AR on a HMD.

Postural sway, ECG, Electrogastrogram (EGG), eye-related measures, EDA, EEG, PPG, respiration pneumogram (RSP), skin temperature, and blood pressure are objective behavioral and physiological measures of cybersickness listed in the studies reviewed by Chang et al. (2020). The saccade mean speed and average heart rate were reported to be highest when cybersickness symptoms occurred, and blink count is found to be correlated with nausea and oculomotor discomfort (Cebeci et al. 2019).

PRE-SCREENING METHODS: PARTICIPANT'S ATTITUDES AND ATTRIBUTES

The methods mentioned in this part are not mainly resulting from the users' engagement with the assessed artifact. Some of these methods can be used to explore the users' anticipations on the use of a system. Other methods are used to explore the attributes of users regarding their technology use.

Media and Technology Usage and Attitudes Scale (Rosen et al. 2013) include subdimensions to assess the participants' usage habits of media technologies such as smartphone, general social media, Internet, e-mailing, media sharing, text messaging, video gaming, online friendships, Facebook friendships, phone calling, and watching television. It also has items to assess positive attitudes, negative attitudes, technological anxiety/dependence, and attitudes toward task-switching, in general towards media technologies.

Bunz et al. (2021) developed Attitudes toward Virtual Reality Technology Scale (AVRTS) to assess the attitudes of people towards VR use from a technology acceptance perspective regarding enjoyment in addition to ease of use and usefulness.

The Educational Virtual Reality Attitude Scale (Karaoglan-Yilmaz et al. 2023) is a tool specialized to assess students' opinions about using VR in an educational context, focusing on the positive aspects. Many studies need to classify users according to the amount of their prior experience with XR technologies. For this purpose, a modified version of the Lifetime Television Exposure Scale (Riddle 2010) can be used (Berkman et al. 2020) to query the users for a special time span, e.g., last month or last 3 months, for their engagement with the media queried by the researcher, such as mobile games or HMD 360° videos. The scale provides a score over 100 through the questions on 10 different day parts, regarding the weekdays with a weight of 71.4 and weekends weight of 28.6. Such a method is easier for the participants to tell the absolute number of hours they have engaged with the given medium in the given time span.

In the gaming context, researchers need to understand the motivations of players for playing. Hughes et al. (2023) provides a critical analysis for standardized player motivation assessment tools. Questionnaires such as Digital Motivations for Play in Online Games (Yee 2006), Video Game Uses and Gratifications Instrument (Sherry et al. 2012), Games Motives Scale (De Grove et al. 2016), Videogaming Motives Questionnaire (López-Fernández et al. 2020) are some examples. Similarly, BrainHex (Nacke et al. 2014) aims to describe players within 7 player archetypes, each characterizing a specific playing style. In that sense, the Video Game Challenge Inventory (Vahlo and Karhulahti 2020) can also be used to identify the levels of players' preference on four different types of challenges in gameplay: Physical, analytical, socio-emotional, and insight challenges.

In studies that presence is a primary aspect regarding the research questions, it may be required to evaluate the participants for their propensity to experience presence. Immersive Tendencies Questionnaire (Witmer and Singer 1998) and Tendency towards Presence Inventory (Thornson et al. 2009) are developed for this purpose. In a similar manner, the Visual Spatial Imagery module of MEC-SPQ (Vorderer et al. 2004) can also be used as a predictor for participants' experience of spatial presence.

When participants' vulnerability to symptoms and adverse effects is a critical issue, researchers may need to use Motion Sickness Susceptibility Questionnaire (Golding 2006) or Visually Induced Motion Sickness Susceptibility Questionnaire (Golding et al. 2021). The Virtual Environment Performance Assessment Battery (VEPAB) (Lampton et al. 1994), which is a set of tasks that are suggested for evaluation of VR training, can be used as a pre-test module to determine the participants' vulnerability to cybersickness as well as their skill level to perform in VR.

The age and sex of participants are reported as objective attributes of users in almost all studies, which can also be used as an inclusion criteria and dependent variable. In research on cybersickness where oculomotor discomfort is evaluated, the participants can be selected based on their visual acuity (Xu et al. 2019). Research on therapeutic uses of XR technologies (Rodríguez-Almagro et al. 2024; Emmelkamp and Meyerbröker 2021) focus on user groups selected for their diseases, impairments, or disabilities. Physical attributes of the participants, for example height (Pfeil et al. 2020) can be devised in the research as an objective attribute of participants.

REMARKS

The XR technologies, which pave the road to a metaverse have not only been embraced by a larger user community, but also utilized by many researchers studying in different domains. Either it is conducted to assess the players' involvement with a VR shooter game or instrumentalizing a see-through HMD in medical imaging, evaluating the user experience is critical in VR research. However, user experience is a complex concept with multiple components, which may vary according to the purpose of the software, context of use and intended users. As researchers should consider the purpose of the evaluated application in the first place, the local presence for AR/telepresence for VR distinction can be a useful approach to explore an application's purpose. AR applications lie within the continuum between low local presence assisted reality and high local presence mixed reality experiences. VR applications are within the continuum of low telepresence atomistic applications and high telepresence holistic virtual reality. Regarding the applications' purpose and the research question, suitable measures can be selected. For example, for VR applications that are close to the holistic end of the continuum, presence should be measured with tools that have higher precision, such as scales with multiple items and Likert points. Furthermore, such an application may require an inspection on cybersickness. For an AR application close to the assisted reality end of the continuum, usability should be explored thoroughly, especially in terms of legibility of user interface elements. However, it is not likely that such an application can yield to emotional effects that can be detected using physiological measures.

Furthermore, XR technology can determine the methodology, especially in the case of physiological measures. It is difficult to run an fMRI study with HMDs since the magnetic field of the measurement device interferes with electronics. Devices for measuring EDA and PPG mostly need to be attached to the fingers of participants which makes it difficult to use handheld devices and controllers. Besides, questionnaire items should be inspected by the researchers for their applicability in the evaluated use case.

The context of use for a system can be interfering with the evaluation method. A VR- based sports activity may trigger sweating due to physical effort, which is also queried as a symptom of cybersickness in some questionnaires. For a social VR application, not only a spatial presence scale, but also a survey that emphasizes the social presence should be utilized. There could be many further examples for the effect of the context of use in XR research. The researchers should anticipate the context clearly, even if they are designing an experiment in a controlled laboratory setting.

Definitely, the participants should be capable of representing the intended users of the evaluated application. Unavoidably, students in higher education dominate the participants in XR research, similar to many other research domains, since they are highly available for the researchers' access. Furthermore, male participants are more likely to be overrepresented in technology research, particularly in gaming studies. Researchers should put extra effort in recruiting participants for a clear representation of intended users for the evaluated system. Another issue specific to XR is that it is a novel technology that many people are not acquainted with, which leads to cognitive bias in research participants. To avoid this, participants can be introduced to the XR technologies by trying something other than the evaluated artifact.

Ultimately, there is not a one-fit-to-all research design and evaluation framework for XR studies. It is not even possible to claim that there is a best collection of methods for VR or AR studies, separately. Researchers need to follow the studies in their domain and related areas to determine the best methodological solutions based on weakness and strength of the previous work.

REFERENCES

Abeele, V.V., Spiel, K., Nacke, L., Johnson, D. and Gerling, K. 2020. Development and validation of the player experience inventory: A scale to measure player experiences at the level of functional and psychosocial consequences. International Journal of Human-Computer Studies. 135: 102370.

Ahmadi, M., Michalka, S.W., Lenzoni, S., Ahmadi Najafabadi, M., Bai, H., Sumich, A., et al. 2023. Cognitive load measurement with physiological sensors in virtual reality during physical activity. *In*: Proceedings of the 29th ACM Symposium on Virtual Reality Software and Technology. 1–11.

Akan, E. and Berkman, M.İ. 2020. Physiological measures in game user research. pp. 231–249. *In*: Bostan, B. (ed.). Game User Experience And Player-Centered Design. International Series on Computer Entertainment and Media Technology. Springer, Cham. https://doi.org/10.1007/978-3-030-37643-7_10.

Aker, Ç., Rızvanoğlu, K. and İnal, Y. 2020. Revisiting heuristics for evaluating player experience in different gaming platforms: A multi-modal approach. pp. 123–161. *In*: Bostan, B. (ed.). Game User Experience And Player-Centered Design. International Series on Computer Entertainment and Media Technology. Springer, Cham. https://doi.org/10.1007/978-3-030-37643-7_6.

Allen, R.W., Rosenthal, T.J. and Cook, M.L. 2011. A Short History of Driving Simulation. ResearchGate.

Arena, F., Collotta, M., Pau, G. and Termine, F. 2022. An overview of augmented reality. Computers. 11(2): 28.

Arth, C., Grasset, R., Gruber, L., Langlotz, T., Mulloni, A. and Wagner, D. 2015. The history of mobile augmented reality. Technical Report. ICG–TR–2015-001. arXiv preprint arXiv:1505.01319.

Assaf, N. and Morán-Mirabal, L.F. 2023. Instructional usability and learner-user experience assessment in a virtual reality educational milieu: A deductive tech-instructionality model from EdTech. *In*: 2023 Future of Educational Innovation-Workshop Series Data in Action. 1–8. IEEE.

Azadvar, A. and Canossa, A. 2018. UPEQ: Ibisoft perceived experience questionnaire: A self-determination evaluation tool for video games. *In*: Proceedings of the 13th International Conference on the Foundations of Digital Games. 1–7.

Ballou, N., Denisova, A., Ryan, R., Rigby, C.S. and Deterding, S. 2024. The Basic Needs in Games Scale (BANGS): A new tool for investigating positive and negative video game experiences. International Journal of Human-Computer Studies. 188: 103289.

Balog, A. and Pribeanu, C. 2010. The role of perceived enjoyment in the students' acceptance of an augmented reality teaching platform: A structural equation modelling approach. Studies in Informatics and Control. 19(3): 319–330.

Barbieri, L., Angilica, A., Bruno, F. and Muzzupappa, M. 2013. Mixed prototyping with configurable physical archetype for usability evaluation of product interfaces. Computers in Industry. 64(3): 310–323.

Benosman, R. and Kang, S.B. 2001. A brief historical perspective on panorama. pp. 5–20. *In*: Benosman, R., Kang, S.B. (eds). Panoramic Vision. Monographs in Computer Science. Springer, New York.

Berkman, M.I. 2018. History of virtual reality. pp. 1–9. *In*: Lee, N. (ed.). Encyclopedia of Computer Graphics and Games. Springer, Cham. https://doi.org/10.1007/978-3-319-08234-9_169-1.

Berkman, M.I. and Akan, E. 2019. Presence and immersion in virtual reality. pp. 1461–1470. *In*: Lee, N. (ed.). Encyclopedia of Computer Graphics and Games. Springer, Cham. https://doi.org/10.1007/978-3-319-08234-9_162-1.

Berkman, M.İ., Çatak, G. and Eremektar, M. 2020. Comparison of vr and desktop game user experience in a puzzle game: "Keep talking and nobody explodes". AJIT-e: Academic Journal of Information Technology. 11(42): 180–204.

Berkman, M.İ. and Şahin, Ş. 2022. Exploring usability as a formative construct through UMUX: A multi-language approach for Turkish adaptation. International Journal of Human–Computer Interaction. 40(2): 457–481.

Berkman, M.I., Bostan, B. and Şenyer, S. 2022. Turkish adaptation study of the game user experience satisfaction scale: GUESS-TR. International Journal of Human–Computer Interaction. 38(11): 1081–1093.

Berkman, M.İ. and Aker, Ç. 2023. A shorter form of the game user experience satisfaction scale in Turkish: GUESS-20-TR. Acta Infologica. 7(2): 229–242.

Bimber, O. and Raskar, R. 2005. Spatial Augmented Reality: Merging Real and Virtual Worlds. AK Peters.

Boletsis, C. and Karahasanovic, A. 2020. Immersive technologies in retail: Practices of augmented and virtual reality. *In*: Proceedings of the 4th International

Conference on Computer-Human Interaction Research and Applications. SciTePress.

Bouchard, S., Robillard, G. and Renaud, P. 2007. Revising the factor structure of the simulator sickness questionnaire. Annual Review of Cybertherapy and Telemedicine. 5(Summer): 128–137.

Brewer, J. 2007. Sensibility and the urban panorama. Huntington Library Quarterly. 70(2): 229–249.

Brockmyer, J.H., Fox, C.M., Curtiss, K.A., McBroom, E., Burkhart, K.M. and Pidruzny, J.N. 2009. The development of the game engagement questionnaire: A measure of engagement in video game-playing. Journal of Experimental Social Psychology. 45(4): 624–634.

Brooke, J. 1996. SUS-A quick and dirty usability scale. Usability Evaluation in Industry. 189(194): 4–7.

Brooke, J. 2013. SUS: A retrospective. Journal of Usability Studies. 8(2): pp. 29–40.

Bunz, U., Seibert, J. and Hendrickse, J. 2021. From TAM to AVRTS: Development and validation of the attitudes toward virtual reality technology scale. Virtual Reality. 25: 31–41. doi: 2131/10.1007/s10055-020-00437-7.

Burdea, G.C. and Coiffet, P. 2003. Virtual Reality Technology. John Wiley & Sons Inc. Hoboken, New Jersey. ISBN 0-471-36089-9.

Carson, G.S., Puk, R.F. and Carey, R. 1999. Developing the VRML 97 international standard. IEEE Computer Graphics and Applications. 19(2): 52–58.

Caudell T. and Mizell, D. 1992. Augmented reality: An application of heads-up display technology to manual manufacturing processes. *In*: System Sciences, 1992. Proceedings of the Twenty-Fifth Hawaii International Conference. 2: 659–669.

Cebeci, B., Celikcan, U. and Capin, T.K. 2019. A comprehensive study of the affective and physiological responses induced by dynamic virtual reality environments. Computer Animation and Virtual Worlds. 30: e1893. doi:10.1002/cav.1893.

Chang, E., Kim, H.T. and Yoo, B. 2020. Virtual reality sickness: A review of causes and measurements. International Journal of Human–Computer Interaction. 36(17): 1658–1682.

Çöltekin, A., Lochhead, I., Madden, M., Christophe, S., Devaux, A., Pettit, C., et al. 2020. Extended reality in spatial sciences: A review of research challenges and future directions. ISPRS International Journal of Geo-Information. 9: 439. doi: 10.3390/ijgi9070439.

Corrales-Serrano, M., Merchán, P., Merchán, M.J. and Pérez, E. 2024. Virtual reality applied to heritage in higher education: Validation of a questionnaire to evaluate usability, learning, and emotions. Heritage. 7(6): 2792–2810.

Cowan, A., Chen, J., Mingo, S., Reddy, S.S., Ma, R., Marshall, S., et al. 2021. Virtual reality vs dry laboratory models: Comparing automated performance metrics and cognitive workload during robotic simulation training. Journal of Endourology. 35(10): 1571–1576.

Cruz-Neira, C., Sandin, D.J., DeFanti, T.A., Kenyon, R.V. and Hart, J.C. 1992. The CAVE: Audio visual experience automatic virtual environment. Communications ACM. 35(6): 64–73.

Cutolo, F. 2024. Augmented reality in image-guided surgery. pp. 182–192. *In*: Lee, N. (ed.). Encyclopedia of Computer Graphics and Games. Springer, Cham. https://doi.org/10.1007/978-3-031-23161-2_78.

Davis, F.D. 1989. Perceived usefulness, perceived ease of use, and user acceptance of information technology. MIS Quarterly. 319–340.

De Grove, F., Cauberghe, V. and Van Looy, J. 2016. Development and validation of an instrument for measuring individual motives for playing digital games. Media Psychology. 19(1): 101–125.

Emmelkamp, P.M. and Meyerbröker, K. 2021. Virtual reality therapy in mental health. Annual Review of Clinical Psychology. 17(1): 495–519.

Endsley, T.C., Sprehn, K.A., Brill, R.M., Ryan, K.J., Vincent, E.C. and Martin, J.M. 2017. Augmented reality design heuristics: Designing for dynamic interactions. *In*: Proceedings of the Human Factors and Ergonomics Society Annual Meeting. 61(1): 2100–2104. Sage CA: Los Angeles, CA: Sage Publications.

Feiner, S., MacIntyre, B., Höllerer, T. and Webster, A. 1997. A touring machine: Prototyping 3D mobile augmented reality systems for exploring the urban environment. *In*: IEEE International Symposium on Wearable Computers. 74–81.

Finstad, K. 2010. The usability metric for user experience. Interacting with Computers. 22(5): 323–327.

Fitzmaurice, G.W. 1993. Situated information spaces and spatially aware palmtop computers. Communications of the ACM. 36(7): 39–49.

Georgiou, Y. and Kyza, E.A. 2017. The development and validation of the ARI questionnaire: An instrument for measuring immersion in location-based augmented reality settings. International Journal of Human-Computer Studies. 98: 24–37.

Gianaros, P.J., Muth, E.R., Mordkoff, J.T., Levine, M.E. and Stern, R.M. 2001. A questionnaire for the assessment of the multiple dimensions of motion sickness. Aviation, Space, and Environmental Medicine. 72(2): 115–119. https://www.ncbi.nlm.nih.gov/pubmed/11211.

Golding, J.F. 2006. Predicting individual differences in motion sickness susceptibility by questionnaire. Personality and Individual Differences. 41(2): 237–248.

Golding, J.F., Rafiq, A. and Keshavarz, B. 2021. Predicting individual susceptibility to visually induced motion sickness by questionnaire. Frontiers in Virtual Reality. 2: 576871.

Grassini, S. and Laumann, K. 2020. Questionnaire measures and physiological correlates of presence: A systematic review. Frontiers in Psychology. 11: 349.

Haider, A., Harteveld, C., Johnson, D., Birk, M.V., Mandryk, R.L., Seif El-Nasr, M., et al. 2022. miniPXI: Development and validation of an eleven-item measure of the player experience inventory. *In*: Proceedings of the ACM on Human-Computer Interaction. 6(CHI PLAY): 1–26.

Halbig, A. and Latoschik, M.E. 2021. A systematic review of physiological measurements, factors, methods, and applications in virtual reality. Frontiers in Virtual Reality. 2: 694567.

Hamilton, D., McKechnie, J., Edgerton, E. and Wilson, C. 2021. Immersive virtual reality as a pedagogical tool in education: A systematic literature review of quantitative learning outcomes and experimental design. Journal of Computers in Education. 8(1): 1–32.

Harley, D. 2020. Palmer luckey and the rise of contemporary virtual reality. Convergence. 26(5–6): 1144–1158.

Harper, S.B. and Dorton, S.L. 2021. A pilot study on extending the sus survey: Early results. *In*: Proceedings of the Human Factors and Ergonomics Society Annual Meeting. 65(1): 447–451. Sage CA: Los Angeles, CA: SAGE Publications.

Harris, D., Wilson, M. and Vine, S. 2020. Development and validation of a simulation workload measure: The simulation task load index (SIM-TLX). Virtual Reality. 24(4): 557–566.

Harris, D.J., Buckingham, G., Wilson, M.R., Brookes, J., Mushtaq, F., Mon-Williams, M., et al. 2021. Exploring sensorimotor performance and user experience within a virtual reality golf putting simulator. Virtual Reality. 25: 647–654.

Hart, S.G. and Staveland, L.E. 1988. Development of NASA-TLX (Task Load Index): Results of empirical and theoretical research. *In*: Advances in Psychology. 52: 139–183. North-Holland. doi: 10.1016/S0166-4115(08)62386-9.

Hartmann, T., Wirth, W., Schramm, H., Klimmt, C., Vorderer, P.A., Gysbers, A., et al. 2016. The spatial presence experience scale (SPES): A short self- report measure for diverse media settings. Journal of Media Psychology. 28: 1–15. doi: /10.1027/18641105/a000137.

Hassenzahl, M., Burmester, M. and Koller, F. 2003. AttrakDiff: Ein Fragebogen zur Messung wahrgenommener hedonischer und pragmatischer Qualität. Mensch & Computer 2003: Interaktion in Bewegung. 187–196.

Heilig, M.L. 1960. U.S. Patent No. 2,955,156. Washington, DC: U.S. Patent and Trademark Office.

Hertzum, M. 2021. Reference values and subscale patterns for the task load index (TLX): A meta-analytic review. Ergonomics. 64(7): 869–878. doi: 10.1080/00140139.2021.1876927.

Hidayat, R. and Wardat, Y. 2024. A systematic review of augmented reality in science, technology, engineering and mathematics education. Educational Information Technology. 29: 9257–9282. https://doi.org/10.1007/s10639-023-12157-x. http://doi.org/10.54941/ahfe1005373.

Hughes, C.L., Fidopiastis, C., Stanney, K.M., Bailey, P.S. and Ruiz, E. 2020. The psychometrics of cybersickness in augmented reality. Frontiers in Virtual Reality. 1: 602954.

Hughes, N.G., Flockton, J.R. and Cairns, P. 2023. Growing together: An analysis of measurement transparency across 15 years of player motivation questionnaires. International Journal of Human-Computer Studies. 169: 102940.

Hunicke, R., LeBlanc, M. and Zubek, R. 2004. MDA: A formal approach to game design and game research. *In*: Proceedings of the AAAI Workshop on Challenges in Game AI. 4(1): 1722.

Hussain, M., Park, J. and Kim, H.K. 2023. Augmented Reality Sickness Questionnaire (ARSQ): A refined questionnaire for augmented reality environment. International Journal of Industrial Ergonomics. 97: 103495.

International Organization for Standardization. 1997. Information technology—Computer graphics and image processing—The Virtual Reality Modeling Language. (ISO/IEC 14772). https://www.iso.org/standard/25508.html.

International Organization for Standardization. 2010. Ergonomics of Human-System Interaction—Part 210: Human-Centred Design for Interactive Systems (ISO 9241-210). https://www.iso.org/standard/52075.html.

International Organization for Standardization. 2018. Ergonomics of Human-System Interaction—Part 11: Usability: Definitions and Concepts (ISO 9241-11). https://www.iso.org/standard/63500.html.

International Organization for Standardization. 2023. Information technology—Computer graphics, image processing, and environmental data representation—Information model for mixed and augmented reality content—Core objects and attributes (ISO/IEC 3721:2023). https://www.iso.org/standard/81207.html.

Jones, S.E. and Thiruvathukal, G.K. 2012. Codename Revolution: The Nintendo Wii platform. MIT Press.

Karaoglan-Yilmaz, F.G., Yilmaz, R., Zhang, K. and Ustun, A.B. 2023. Development of educational virtual reality attitude scale: A validity and reliability study. Virtual Reality. 27: 1875–1885. doi: 10.1007/s10055-023-00778-z.

Kaufeld, M., Mundt, M., Forst, S. and Hecht, H. 2022. Optical see-through augmented reality can induce severe motion sickness. Displays. 74: 102283.

Keebler, J.R., Shelstad, W.J., Smith, D.C., Chaparro, B.S. and Phan, M.H. 2020. Validation of the GUESS-18: A short version of the Game User Experience Satisfaction Scale (GUESS). Journal of Usability Studies. 16(1): 49.

Kennedy, R.S., Lane, N.E., Berbaum, K.S. and Lilienthal, M.G. 1993. Simulator sickness questionnaire: An enhanced method for quantifying simulator sickness. The International Journal of Aviation Psychology. 3(3): 203–220.

Keshavarz, B. and Hecht, H. 2011. Validating an efficient method to quantify motion sickness. Human Factors. 53(4): 415–426.

Kim, H.K., Park, J., Choi, Y. and Choe, M. 2018. Virtual Reality Sickness Questionnaire (VRSQ): Motion sickness measurement index in a virtual reality environment. Applied Ergonomics. 69: 66–73.

Kim, K.S. and Kim, C.S. 2024. Development and usability evaluation of augmented reality content for light maintenance training of air spring for electric multiple unit. Applied Sciences. 14(17): 7702.

Kim, Y.M. and Rhiu, I. 2024. Development of a Virtual Reality System Usability Questionnaire (VRSUQ). Applied Ergonomics. 119: 104319.

Kobayashi, K., Ishigame, S. and Kato, H. 2003. Skill training system of manual arc welding: By means of face-shield-like HMD and virtual electrode. Entertainment Computing: Technologies and Application. 389–396.

Korhonen, H. 2016. Evaluating Playability of Mobile Games with the Expert Review Method. Published PhD Thesis. Dissertations in Interactive

Technology, Number 24 Acta Electronica Universitatis Tamperensis 1701. ISBN 978-952-03-0205-4. Tampere University Press. Finland.

Kosch, T., Karolus, J., Ha, H. and Schmidt, A. 2019. Your skin resists: Exploring electrodermal activity as workload indicator during manual assembly. *In*: Proceedings of the ACM SIGCHI Symposium on Engineering Interactive Computing Systems. 1–5.

Kothgassner, O.D., Felnhofer, A., Hauk, N., Kastenhofer, E., Gomm, J. and Kryspin-Exner, I. 2012. TUI. Technology Usage Inventory: Manual. Icarus Research Team. White Paper. Austrian Research Promotion Agency (FFG), Federal Ministry for Transport, Innovation and Technology (BMVIT). Wien.

Kourtesis, P., Collina, S., Doumas, L.A. and MacPherson, S.E. 2019. Validation of the virtual reality neuroscience questionnaire: Maximum duration of immersive virtual reality sessions without the presence of pertinent adverse symptomatology. Frontiers in Human Neuroscience. 13: 417.

Kourtesis, P., Linnell, J., Amir, R., Argelaguet, F. and MacPherson, S.E. 2023. Cybersickness in Virtual Reality Questionnaire (CSQ-VR): A validation and comparison against SSQ and VRSQ. Virtual Worlds. 2(1): 16–35. MDPI.

Krueger, M.W. and Wilson, S. 1985. VIDEOPLACE: A report from the ARTIFICIAL REALITY laboratory. Leonardo. 18(3): 145–151.

Krüger, J.M. and Bodemer, D. 2022. Work-in-Progress—Measuring learners' subjective experience in augmented reality: First evaluation of the ARcis questionnaire. *In*: 2022 8th International Conference of the Immersive Learning Research Network (iLRN). 1–3. IEEE.

Labrie, A. and Cheng, J. 2020. Adapting usability heuristics to the context of mobile augmented reality. *In*: Adjunct Proceedings of the 33rd Annual ACM Symposium on User Interface Software and Technology. 4–6.

Lah, U., Lewis, J.R. and Šumak, B. 2020. Perceived usability and the modified technology acceptance model. International Journal of Human–Computer Interaction. 36(13): 1216–1230.

Lampton, D.R., Knerr, B.W., Goldberg, S.L., Bliss, J.P., Moshell, J.M. and Blau, B.S. 1994. The Virtual Environment Performance Assessment Battery (VEPAB): Development and evaluation. Presence: Teleoperators and Virtual Environments. 3(2): 145–157.

Laugwitz, B., Schrepp, M. and Held, T. 2008. Construction and evaluation of a user experience questionnaire. pp. 63–76. *In*: Holzinger, A. (ed.). HCI and Usability for Education and Work. USAB 2008. Lecture Notes in Computer Science, vol 5298. Springer, Berlin, Heidelberg. https://doi.org/10.1007/978-3-540-89350-9_6.

Lessiter, J., Freeman, J., Keogh, E. and Davidoff, J. 2001. A cross-media presence questionnaire: The ITC-Sense of Presence Inventory. Presence: Teleoperators and Virtual Environments. 10(3): 282–297.

Lewis, J.R. 1991. Psychometric evaluation of an after-scenario questionnaire for computer usability studies: The ASQ. ACM SIGCHI Bulletin. 23(1): 78–81.

Lewis, J.R. 1995. IBM computer usability satisfaction questionnaires: Psychometric evaluation and instructions for use. International Journal of Human–Computer Interaction. 7(1): 57–78. doi: 10.1080/10447319509526110.

Lewis, J.R. and Sauro, J. 2021. Usability and user experience: Design and evaluation. Handbook of Human Factors and Ergonomics. 972–1015.

Liao, T. 2020. Standards and their (Recurring) stories: How augmented reality markup language was built on stories of past standards. Science, Technology and Human Values. 45(4): 712–737.

Lin, J., Cao, L. and Li, N. 2020. How the completeness of spatial knowledge influences the evacuation behavior of passengers in metro stations: A VR-based experimental study. Automation in Construction. 113: 103136.

Liu, Q. and Steed, A. 2021. Social virtual reality platform comparison and evaluation using a guided group walkthrough method. Frontiers in Virtual Reality. 2: 668181.

Lombard, M., Ditton, T.B. and Weinstein, L. 2009. Measuring presence: The temple presence inventory. *In*: Proceedings of the 12th Annual International Workshop on Presence. 1–15. Los Angeles, CA: International Society for Presence Research.

López-Fernández, F.J., Mezquita, L., Griffiths, M.D., Ortet, G. and Ibáñez, M.I. 2020. The development and validation of the video gaming motives questionnaire (VMQ). PLoS One. 15(10): e0240726.

Lund, A.M. 2001. Measuring usability with the use questionnaire. Usability Interface. 8(2): 3–6.

Maag, C., Schömig, N., Naujoks, F., Karl, I., Keinath, A. and Neukum, A. 2023. Measuring workload effects of augmented reality head-up displays using detection response task. Transportation Research Part F: Traffic Psychology and Behaviour. 92: 201–219.

MacEachren, A.M., Edsall, R., Haug, D., Baxter, R., Otto, G., Masters, R., et al. 1999. Virtual environments for geographic visualization. *In*: Proceedings of the Workshop on New Paradigms in Information Visualization and Manipulation in Conjunction with the 8th ACM Conference on Information and Knowledge Management—NPIVM'99, Kansas City, MO, USA, 2–6 November. 35–40.

Mahatody, T., Sagar, M. and Kolski, C. 2010. State of the art on the cognitive walkthrough method, its variants and evolutions. International Journal of Human–Computer Interaction. 26(8): 741–785.

Makransky, G., Lilleholt, L. and Aaby, A. 2017. Development and validation of the Multimodal Presence Scale for virtual reality environments: A confirmatory factor analysis and item response theory approach. Computers in Human Behavior. 72: 276–285.

Marikyan, D. and Papagiannidis, S. 2023. Unified theory of acceptance and use of technology: A review. *In*: Papagiannidis, S. (ed.). TheoryHub Book. Available at https://open.ncl.ac.uk/ ISBN: 9781739604400.

Marron, T., Captain, N., Mac Namee, B. and O'Hagan, A.D. 2024. Virtual reality and pilot training: Existing technologies, challenges, and opportunities. Journal of Aviation/Aerospace Education and Research. 33(1): 1.

Marto, A. and Gonçalves, A. 2022. Augmented reality games and presence: A systematic review. Journal of Imaging. 8(4): 91.

McLellan, H. 2004. Virtual realities. pp. 461–498. *In*: Jonassen, D.H. (ed.). Handbook of Research for Educational Communications and Technology, Lawrence Erlbaum Associates, London.

McLuhan, M. 1962. The Gutenberg Galaxy: The Making of Typographic Man. University of Toronto Press. ISBN 978-0-8020-6041-9.

Medlock, M.C., Wixon, D., McGee, M. and Welsh, D. 2005. The rapid iterative test and evaluation method: Better products in less time. pp. 489–517. *In*: Bias, R.G. and Mayhew, D.J. (eds). Cost-justifying Usability. Morgan Kaufmann.

Milgram, P. and Kishino, F. 1994. A taxonomy of mixed reality visual displays. IEICE Transactions on Information and Systems. 77(12): 1321–1329.

Minge, M., Thüring, M. and Wagner, I. 2016. Developing and validating an English version of the meCUE questionnaire for measuring user experience. *In*: Proceedings of the Human Factors and Ergonomics Society Annual Meeting. 60(1): 2063–2067. Sage CA: Los Angeles, CA: SAGE Publications.

Mittmann, G., Zehetner, V., Krammer, I. and Schrank, B. 2024. Translation, adaptation, and validation of the German version of the Game User Experience Satisfaction Scale (GUESS-GA-18) for adolescents. Behaviour and Information Technology. 43(7): 1401–1415.

Mohring, M., Lessig, C. and Bimber, O. 2004). Video see-through AR on consumer cell-phones. *In*: Third IEEE and ACM international Symposium on Mixed and Augmented Reality. 252–253. IEEE.

Moinnereau, M.A., de Oliveira Jr., A.A. and Falk, T.H. 2022. Immersive media experience: A survey of existing methods and tools for human influential factors assessment. Quality and User Experience. 7(1): 5.

Moreno-Arjonilla, J., López-Ruiz, A., Jiménez-Pérez, J.R., Callejas-Aguilera, J.E. and Jurado, J.M. 2024. Eye-tracking on virtual reality: A survey. Virtual Reality. 28(1): 38.

Muhanna, M.A. 2015. Virtual reality and the CAVE: Taxonomy, interaction challenges, and research directions. Journal of King Saud University-Computer and Information Sciences. 27(3): 344–361.

Murtza, R., Monroe, S. and Youmans, R.J. 2017. Heuristic evaluation for virtual reality systems. *In*: Proceedings of the Human Factors and Ergonomics Society Annual Meeting. 61(1): 2067–2071. Sage CA: Los Angeles, CA: SAGE Publications.

Nacke, L.E., Bateman, C. and Mandryk, R.L. 2014. BrainHex: A neurobiological gamer typology survey. Entertainment Computing. 5(1): 55–62.

Nielsen, J. and Molich, R. 1990. Heuristic evaluation of user interfaces. *In*: Proceedings of the SIGCHI Conference on Human Factors in Computing Systems. 249–256.

Nishchyk, A., Sanderson, N.C. and Chen, W. 2024. Elderly-centered usability heuristics for augmented reality design and development. Universal Access in the Information Society. 1–21.

Oliveira, E., Simões, F.P. and Correia, W.F. 2017. Heuristics evaluation and improvements for low-cost virtual reality. *In*: 2017 19th Symposium on Virtual and Augmented Reality (SVR). 178–187. IEEE.

Omar, K., Fakhouri, H., Zraqou, J. and Marx Gómez, J. 2024. Usability Heuristics for Metaverse. Computers. 13(9): 222.

Open Geospatial Consortium 2015. OGC Augmented Reality Markup Language 2.0 (ARML 2.0) (OGC 12–132r4) http://www.opengis.net/doc/IS/arml/2.0.

Page, R.L. 2000. Brief history of flight simulation. *In*: SimTecT 2000 Proceedings. 11–17.

Peddie, J. 2017. Augmented Reality: Where We Will All Live. Springer International Publishing AG. Gewerbestrasse 11, 6330 Cham, Switzerland. ISBN: 9783319545011; 3319545019; 9783319545028; 3319545027.

Pentangelo, V., Di Dario, D., Lambiase, S., Ferrucci, F., Gravino, C. and Palomba, F. 2024. SENEM: A software engineering-enabled educational metaverse. Information and Software Technology. 174: 107512.

Petukhov, I.V., Glazyrin, A.E., Gorokhov, A.V., Steshina, L.A. and Tanryverdiev, I.O. 2020. Being present in a real or virtual world: An EEG study. International Journal of Medical Informatics. 136: 103977.

Pfeil, K., Wisniewski, P.J. and Laviola Jr., J.J. 2020. The effects of gender and the presence of third-party humans on telepresence camera height preferences. ACM Symposium on Applied Perception. 2020: 1–10.

Prado de Campos, T., Damasceno, E.F. and Valentim, N.M.C. 2024. Evaluating usability and UX in touchable holographic solutions: A validation study of the UUXE-ToH questionnaire. International Journal of Human-Computer Interaction. 1–21.

Raji, M.A., Olodo, H.B., Oke, T.T., Addy, W.A., Ofodile, O.C. and Oyewole, A.T. 2024. Business strategies in virtual reality: A review of market opportunities and consumer experience. International Journal of Management and Entrepreneurship Research. 6(3): 722–736.

Ratan, R.A. and Hasler, B. 2009. Self-presence standardized: Introducing the self-presence questionnaire (SPQ). *In*: Proceedings of the 12th Annual International Workshop on Presence (Vol. 81).

Rauschnabel, P.A., Felix, R., Hinsch, C., Shahab, H. and Alt, F. 2022. What is XR? Towards a framework for augmented and virtual reality. Computers in Human Behavior. 133: 107289.

Regenbrecht, H. and Schubert, T. 2002. Measuring presence in augmented reality environments: Design and a first test of a questionnaire. *In*: Proceedings of the Fifth Annual International Workshop Presence, 2002, Porto, Portugal–October 9–11.

Rekimoto, J. and Nagao, K. 1995. The world through the computer: Computer augmented interaction with real world environments. *In*: Proceedings of the 8th Annual ACM Symposium on User Interface and Software Technology. 29–36.

Remondino, M. 2017. Virtual reality and immersive simulation technology outside video gaming: Enterprise applications and potential implications. International Journal of Simulation: Systems, Science & Technology. 18(2): 11.1–11.12.

Rodríguez-Almagro, D., Achalandabaso-Ochoa, A., Ibáñez-Vera, A.J., Góngora-Rodríguez, J. and Rodríguez-Huguet, M. 2024. Effectiveness of virtual reality therapy on balance and gait in the elderly: A systematic review. Healthcare. 12(2): 158. MDPI.

Rosen, L.D., Whaling, K., Carrier, L.M., Cheever, N.A. and Rokkum, J. 2013. The media and technology usage and attitudes scale: An empirical investigation. Computers in Human Behavior. 29(6): 2501–2511.

Rusu, C., Muñoz, R., Roncagliolo, S., Rudloff, S., Rusu, V. and Figueroa, A. 2011. Usability heuristics for virtual worlds. *In*: Proceedings of the Third International Conference on Advances in Future Internet. 16–19.

Ryan, R.M., Rigby, C.S. and Przybylski, A. 2006. The motivational pull of video games: A self-determination theory approach. Motivation and Emotion. 30: 344–360.

Santos, M.E.C., Taketomi, T., Sandor, C., Polvi, J., Yamamoto, G. and Kato, H. 2014. A usability scale for handheld augmented reality. *In*: Proceedings of the 20th ACM Symposium on Virtual Reality Software and Technology. 167–176.

Schrepp, M., Hinderks, A. and Thomaschewski, J. 2017. Design and evaluation of a short version of the User Experience Questionnaire (UEQ-S). The International Journal of Interactive Multimedia and Artificial Intelligence. 4(6): 103–108.

Schubert, T., Friedmann, F. and Regenbrecht, H. 2001. The experience of presence: Factor analytic insights. Presence: Teleoperators & Virtual Environments. 10(3): 266–281.

Sevinc, V. and Berkman, M.I. 2020. Psychometric evaluation of simulator sickness questionnaire and its variants as a measure of cybersickness in consumer virtual environments. Applied Ergonomics. 82: 102958. https://doi.org/10.1016/j.apergo.2019.102958.

Sherry, J.L., Greenberg, B.S., Lucas, K. and Lachlan, K. 2012. Video game uses and gratifications as predictors of use and game preference. *In*: Playing Video Games. 248–262. Routledge.

Simões-Marques, M. 2024. Usability assessment of extended reality applications. A review. *In*: Isabel L. Nunes (ed.). Human Factors and Systems Interaction International Conference AHFE Open Access (Vol. 154).

Sony Corporation. 1998. Personal LCD Monitor Glasstron Operating Instructions. https://www.sony.com/electronics/support/res/manuals/W000/W0009025M.pdf.

Starner, T. 2013. Project Glass: An Extension of the Self. *In*: IEEE Pervasive Computing. 12(2): 14–16. doi: 10.1109/MPRV.2013.35.

Stone, R. 2009. Serious games: Virtual reality's second coming? Virtual Reality. 13(1): 1–2.

Stone, R.T., Watts, K.P., Zhong, P. and Wei, C.S. 2011. Physical and cognitive effects of virtual reality integrated training. Human Factors. 53(5): 558–572.

Stone III, W.B. 2017. Psychometric Evaluation of the Simulator Sickness Questionnaire as a Measure of Cybersickness (Doctoral dissertation, Iowa State University).

Sutcliffe, A. and Gault, B. 2004. Heuristic evaluation of virtual reality applications. Interacting with Computers. 16(4): 831–849.

Sutherland, I.E. 1965. The ultimate display. *In*: Proceeding of IFIPS Congress. 2: 506–508.

Sutherland, I.E. 1968. A head-mounted three dimensional display. *In*: Proceedings of the AFIPS '68 Fall Joint Computer Conference, Part I, San Francisco, California, December 09 –11. 757–764.

Tavinor, G. 2023. Against Metaphysical Interpretations of VR. pp. 40–56. *In*: A. Kissel and E.J. Ramirez (eds). Exploring Extended Realities. New York. Routledge. ISBN: 9781003359494.

Thornson, C.A., Goldiez, B.F. and Le, H. 2009. Predicting presence: Constructing the tendency toward presence inventory. International Journal of Human-Computer Studies. 67(1): 62–78.

Tremmel, C., Herff, C., Sato, T., Rechowicz, K., Yamani, Y. and Krusienski, D.J. 2019. Estimating cognitive workload in an interactive virtual reality environment using EEG. Frontiers in Human Neuroscience. 13. doi:10.3389/fnhum.2019.00401.

Trinon, H. 2019. Immersive Technologies for Virtual Reality-Case Study: Flight Simulator for Pilot Training. HEC-Ecole de gestion de l'Universite de Liege. Master en ingenieur de gestion, a finalite specialisee en Supply Chain Management and Business Analytics.

Uzunboylu, H. and Tugun, V. 2016. Validity and reliability of tablet supported education attitude and usability scale. Journal of Universal Computer Science. 22(1): 82–93.

Vahlo, J. and Karhulahti, V.M. 2020. Challenge types in gaming validation of video game challenge inventory (CHA). International Journal of Human-Computer Studies. 143: 102473.

Varela-Aldás, J., Buele, J., López, I. and Palacios-Navarro, G. 2023. Influence of hand tracking in immersive virtual reality for memory assessment. International Journal of Environmental Research and Public Health. 20(5): 4609.

Venkatesh, V., Thong, J.Y. and Xu, X. 2016. Unified theory of acceptance and use of technology: A synthesis and the road ahead. Journal of the Association for Information Systems. 17(5): 328–376.

Vertucci, R., D'Onofrio, S., Ricciardi, S. and De Nino, M. 2023. History of augmented reality. *In*: Nee, A.Y.C. and Ong, S.K. (eds). Springer Handbook of Augmented Reality. Springer Handbooks. Springer, Cham. doi: 10.1007/978-3-030-67822-7_2.

Vlahovic, S., Suznjevic, M. and Skorin-Kapov, L. 2022. A survey of challenges and methods for quality of experience assessment of interactive VR applications. Journal on Multimodal User Interfaces. 16(3): 257–291.

Vöhringer, S. 2011. Controller-Free Gaming. Institute of Media Informatics Ulm University. 29.

Vorderer, P., Wirth, W., Gouveia, F.R., Biocca, F., Saari, T., Jäncke, F., et al. 2004. MEC Spatial Presence Questionnaire (MEC-SPQ): Short Documentation and Instructions for Application. Report to the European Community, Project Presence: MEC (IS T-2001-37661).

Web3D Consortium. 2024. Recommended standards. https://www.web3d.org/standards reached on Oct. 7, 2024.

Wertheim, A.H., Bos, J.E. and Krul, A.J. 2001. Predicting Motion Induced Vomiting from Subjective Misery (MISC) Ratings Obtained in 12 Experimental Studies. Report TNO-TM-01-A066. TNO Human Factors Research Institute, Soesterberg, NL.

Witmer, B.G. and Singer, M.J. 1998. Measuring presence in virtual environments: A presence questionnaire. Presence. 7(3): 225–240.

Wood, G., Wright, D.J., Harris, D., Pal, A., Franklin, Z.C. and Vine, S.J. 2021. Testing the construct validity of a soccer-specific virtual reality simulator using novice, academy, and professional soccer players. Virtual Reality. 25: 43–51.

Wyshynski, S. and Vincent, J.V. 1993. Full-body unencumbered immersion in virtual worlds (the vivid approach and the Mandala® VR system). pp. 46–65. *In*: Wexelblat, A. (ed.). Virtual Reality: Applications and Explorations. Academic Press, New York.

Xiong, J., Hsiang, E.L., He, Z., Zhan, T. and Wu, S.T. 2021. Augmented reality and virtual reality displays: Emerging technologies and future perspectives. Light: Science and Applications. 10(1): 1–30. doi: 10.1038/s41377-021-00658-8.

Xu, L., Huang, M., Lan, J., Huang, W., Wang, X., Zhang, G., et al. 2019. Assessment of binocular imbalance with an augmented virtual reality platform in a normal population. Cyberpsychology, Behavior, and Social Networking. 22(2): 127–131. doi:10.1089/cyber.2019.0020.

Yee, N. 2006. Motivations for play in online games. Cyberpsychology and Behavior. 9(6): 772–775.

Zhang, J., Wang, S., He, W., Li, J., Cao, Z. and Wei, B. 2022. Projected augmented reality assembly assistance system supporting multi-modal interaction. The International Journal of Advanced Manufacturing Technology. 123(3): 1353–1367. doi: 10.1007/s00170-022-10113-6.

Zhang, X. and Simeone, A.L. 2023. Using think-aloud protocol in immersive VR evaluations. *In*: Simeone, A., Weyers, B., Bialkova, S. and Lindeman, R.W. (eds). Everyday Virtual and Augmented Reality. Human–Computer Interaction Series. Springer, Cham. doi: 0.1007/978-3-031-05804-2_8.

Zheleva, A., De Marez, L., Talsma, D. and Bombeke, K. 2024. Intersecting realms: A cross-disciplinary examination of VR quality of experience research. Virtual Reality. 28(3): 135.

Zone, R. 2014. Stereoscopic Cinema and the Origins of 3-D Film. 1838–1952. University Press of Kentucky, Lexington.

Chapter 2

Navigating Identities: Avatar Customization and Transgender Experiences in Social VR

Joona Wiik*[1], Tomi "bgt" Suovuo[1], Lotta Kähkönen[2] and Jouni Smed[1]
[1]Department of Computing, University of Turku (FI)
[2]Department of Art History, Musicology and Media Studies, University of Turku (FI)

INTRODUCTION

The possibilities of social virtual reality (social VR) have become a widely discussed topic with the progression of VR's capabilities, graphics, and distribution. Social VR refers to virtual spaces where multiple human users can interact with each other through HMDs (head-mounted displays (McVeigh-Schultz et al. 2019). This has also led to various studies focused on the effects of VR avatars on players' enjoyment, engagement, identities, and social interaction with each other (e.g., Trepte and Reinecke 2010, Freeman et al. 2020, Lin and Latoschik 2022). Furthermore, some research has been directed towards the formation of individual social

*For Correspondence: joona.e.wiik@utu.fi

DOI: 10.1201/9781003581642-2

identities with the assistance of customizable avatars (e.g., Neustaedter and Fedorovskaya 2009, Waggoner 2009). The question of social identity formation has become increasingly relevant, especially in the case of transgender experiences in social virtual environments. Transgender people represent a relatively significant and active segment of the queer gamer and social VR communities. However, their experiences remain largely under-researched.

Transgender and gender nonconforming people refer to individuals with gender identities that are not fully aligned with their sex assigned at birth. While an individual's sex refers to their biological status (male/female) determined at birth, gender refers to the socially constructed roles, behaviors, and attributes considered appropriate for men and women—which are further reflected on an individual's actions, interactions, and feelings about themselves (APA 2023). Within this chapter, transgender and trans* are used as inclusive umbrella terms for people whose gender identities, gender expressions, and/or behaviors do not conform to those typically associated with expectations of their sex assigned at birth. However, the terminology and its usages vary according to cultural contexts—with the transgender umbrella term having been used especially in the Western and Anglo-American world since the 1990s (Stryker 2017).

While some transgender people choose to medically transition, others prefer to only transition socially. The transitional process of every trans* individual is unique, as it is determined by multiple factors including the individual's personal wishes and socially and legally available options. Despite the chosen transitional path of a transgender individual, extended realities and virtual environments have enabled and simplified the process of (temporarily) embodying an avatar conforming or differing from the individual's physical body and characteristics according to the individual's choices. This enables transgender people to experience identity affirmation and exploration, strengthening their understanding of their gender identity, and feeling empowered by it.

The following chapter is divided into three distinct parts. First, theoretical background is given to the concepts of identity and avatar. After discussing the basics of identity theory and how gender identities are formed, we move on to discuss how virtual avatars reflect an individual's existing identities and allow exploration with completely new ones. This discussion will revolve around attempts to create avatars with varying degrees of self-similarity (similarity to the physical body an individual experiences the world through). Although these topics are discussed in connection with transgender individuals, questions of identity, self-exploration through avatars with self-similarities or self-dissimilarities, and identity affirmation through embodiment are correspondingly central topics in all human experiences.

Second, the discussion moves towards the psychosocial effects that social VR avatar creation and customization can provide for transgender experiences. This topic is approached by providing an overview of the previously published literature on psychological effects of VR avatar creation and customization on the self-awareness, self-expression, and self-affirmation of transgender and gender nonconforming individuals. The study reflects on the potential effects of VR avatar customization by intertwining the following three themes:

1. Social VR avatars are discussed for their potential to experiment and explore gender identities in a low-stake environment.
2. Avatar customization and embodiment are analyzed as tools for alleviating gender dysphoria. This includes providing possibilities for escapism from real-life (offline) body dysmorphia and dysphoria.
3. Avatar creation and customization are discussed in terms of inducing gender euphoria as transgender individuals receive internal and external validation on their gender identity and transition goals by embodying an avatar with their idealized body in a social VR environment.

The final focus of the chapter is in analyzing a popular and widely used VR avatar creator with a transgender perspective and focus on the customizability of gendered features to accommodate transgender individuals. Reyes and Fisher (2022) propose design guidelines for virtual reality avatar creation interfaces to better take transgender experiences into consideration. The chapter concludes with an analysis on the avatar customization provided by Ready Player Me roughly based on the design guidelines by Reyes and Fisher. Ready Player Me is a cross-game avatar customization platform for the metaverse, and one of the leading avatar creator systems for the social VRChat platform (Ready Player Me 2024a, VRChat 2024). This analysis will discuss the customizability of the visual, auditory, and behavioral aspects of avatars with the main focus being on body shapes and sizes, voice and communication options, movement styles, pronouns, and the inclusion of gender neutral and/or gender mixing possibilities

IDENTITY AND AVATAR

An interest in identity theory stems from the importance of understanding individuals located in social interaction and embedded within society (Stets and Serpe 2013). Therefore, questions of identity are inherently interconnected with social human experiences. Generally, an identity is defined as a set of meanings that are attached to individuals in certain *roles* occupied in the social structure (Stryker [1980] 2002), as members of specific *groups*, and as *persons* with specific unique characteristics (Stets and Serpe 2013). When discussing identities in the context of virtual realities, it becomes even clearer how an individual can inhabit multiple separate and even contradictory identities, as not only can there be a clear distinction between an individual's online and offline identity, but also the roles, groups, and persons attached to the individual can be determined and redefined within virtual worlds.

The ways that an individual can inhabit multiple separate and redefinable identities in offline and online worlds seems to suggest that identities are, in a manner of speaking, performances put on by individuals in certain social settings. When our focus is directed towards gender and gender identities, we find similar implications discussed by Butler (1999). Butler highlights gender as a performative identity that does not remain stable but is rather a continuous process of doing gendered acts, gestures, and language that constitutes an individual's gender. Furthermore, Butler discusses the constitution of an identity as a non-singular and culturally constructed entity that is heavily shaped by "class, race, ethnicity, and other axes of power relations". Although Butler's theory has received criticism for overlooking the materiality of the body, and not considering the complexity of embodiment and lived experiences of transgender people (Stryker 2017), the theory of gender performativity serves as a basis for the constitution of gender identities within virtual spaces and realities.

Due to the culturally imposed identity signifiers accepted by the majority, gender identities and presentations falling outside the cisgender binary expectations face many hardships socially (Marciano 2014) and incongruence between one's sex, gender, and sexuality are generally disparaged (Butler 1999). Nonetheless, transgender individuals have been found to experience an overwhelming urge to express their gender identity (Gagné et al. 1997). To satisfy this urge, trans* individuals have often turned to virtual worlds, especially when presenting one's identity in public offline settings can be dangerous and sanctioned (Whittle 1998). At its best, social VR can provide a private space to satisfy this social urge by allowing an identity performance that can be a fully anonymous rehearsal of an identity performance while participating in social interaction within public spaces.

Another concept that can be applied to studies focused on individual gender identities is identity verification from *Identity Theory* by Stets and Serpe (2013). Identity verification is the process of an individual receiving confirmation that others see them similarly to the way they see themselves in a certain situation (Stets and Serpe 2013). This verification can be considered to get formed by the perceptual control model introduced by Burke and Stets (2009). In a simplified form, this model consists of a feedback loop that evaluates the dynamics between the *identity standard* (i.e. the meanings that individuals associate with their own identities), and the *perceptual input* (i.e,. the input an individual receives about their identities both by seeing themselves and by receiving feedback from others). This interaction might result either in mutual correspondence that produces positive emotions, or non-correspondence and discrepancies, which produce negative emotions and a greater compulsion to enact corrections/modification to the way an individual performs. In the case of negative emotions, the output, which consists of, e.g., behaviors consistent with the identity standard, is modified in order to match the perceptual inputs with the identity standard. Burke and Stets (2009) conclude that behaviorally, this feedback loop will result in individual determination to work harder to resolve possible discrepancies as long as "there are no significant situational constraints".

These situational constraints mentioned by Burke and Stets (2009) can be a significant obstructing factor especially for trans* individuals in the offline world, depending on the opportunities an individual is equipped with. However, providing online digital spaces to create and construct an individual online identity affords novel forms of identity practices and embodiment of the self (Freeman and Maloney 2020). The internet provides a tool for the expression of gender identities as it allows identities to cross boundaries instantaneously, regardless of physical space (Hegland and Nelson 2002). Social VR has managed to transform the scope of possibilities even further. To reluctantly quote transphobic communities satirically claiming to "identify as attack helicopters" (Blake et al. 2020), in VR there are no situational constraints prohibiting or obstructing individuals from convincingly performing even as a helicopter. As the significant situational constraints are practically removed, this brings forth new possibilities for individuals who struggle with discrepancies between their identity standard and perceptual input, whether forced by definitive or temporal situational constraints.

When social interactions happen within a VR, the identity performance requires the creation of an avatar. Avatars are proxies for users and their interactions conducted in virtual environments (Manninen and Kujanpää 2007). While an avatar serves as the user's interface to approach other human users and navigate the virtual world, it also represents the user's second self—with its unique appearance, behavior, and sense of personality (Friedl 2002, Ducheneaut et al. 2009, Schroeder 2012). Avatars take a central part in the communicative dynamics of virtual worlds (Manninen and Kujanpää 2007) and integrate different social values (Ducheneaut et al. 2009, Nowak and Rauh 2005, Yee et al. 2007). Furthermore, avatars provide possibilities for experimenting with new identities (e.g., cross-gender play) and reaffirming existing identities (e.g., queer play) (Freeman et al. 2020, Huh and Williams 2010, Ruberg and Shaw 2017).

In contrast to traditional virtual experiences and worlds that are experienced through avatars, VR platforms provide a more intimate connection between the user and their avatar. Studies focused on discovering emerging themes in user perceptions and experiences with their avatars have found that participants feel more present, engaged, intimate, and personal interacting with their VR avatars (Freeman et al. 2020). As the user's body becomes the immediate and sole interface to experience an avatar, participants have expressed experiences of immersion and realism. Utilizing full-body tracking and one's own voice creates interactions that are experienced in a manner similar to offline face-to-face interaction (Acena and Freeman 2021). While avatars in traditional games were "simply characters", in social VR they became "real life" and "truly an extension" of oneself (Freeman et al. 2020). These experiences of strong embodiment, agency, and ownership of the virtual body (body ownership illusions or BOIs) (Mottelson et al. 2023) highlight the unique and powerful relationship between the user and their avatar, which further allows for embracing VRs as social spheres. While the social aspects of online spaces are valuable to versatile user demographics, the sociability is exceedingly valuable for users subject to social marginalization (Marciano 2014) such as gender minorities. Furthermore, as argued by Whittle (1998), for many transgender people, their gender identity can be experienced and expressed solely through the virtual self, as in the offline world this identity might need to be hidden.

In social VR, users can physically express themselves through avatars with varying degrees of self-similarity. Kim et al. (2023) suggest that avatars with high levels of similarity both exhibit morphological and conceptual congruence with the user and mirror the user's behavior (reflecting the user's "genuine identity"), while low levels of similarity only mirror the user's behavior (reflecting "an alternative persona/ fictional identity"). While studies focused mainly on cisgender VR users suggest that participants wish to create a virtual avatar based on their real-life body or with a strong self-similarity to their physical appearance (Freeman et al. 2020, Lin and Latoschik 2022, Kim et al. 2023), other studies suggest that the majority of trans* users prefer to embody their idealized body or something closer to that end of the spectrum (e.g., a realistically achievable version of their idealized body) (Baldwin 2018, Reyes and Fisher 2022, Morgan et al. 2020, van Aller 2018). Furthermore, trans* and genderqueer users view gender-aligned avatars to be more representative of their genuine selves (Whitehouse et al. 2023). It has also been suggested that particularly those users that are satisfied with their real lives and appearances opt for self-similar avatars regardless of their gender identity (Trepte and Reinecke 2010).

Previous studies have found that self-similarity not only improves users' performance, engagement, and presence in virtual environments (Rahill and Sebrechts 2021), but also enjoyment, intrinsic motivation, and identification with their avatars (Birk et al. 2016, Midha and Nandedkar 2012). In the case of transgender users, we however argue that an avatar with a low degree of morphological self-similarity might result in similarly positive effects as physically self-similar avatars do for cisgender users. This is corroborated by findings displaying how encouraging it is for trans* users to customize their avatar to reflect their own identities rather than physical bodies (Freeman and Maloney 2021) and suggesting that for some users, avatar's reflecting an ideal self can actually stimulate higher interactions, increase engagement, and enhance intrinsic motivation more effectively than avatars accurately resembling the user's body (Jin 2009, Przybylski et al. 2012). This brings forth the question of what positive psychosocial effects could be evoked within the transgender community through social VR, and how these effects could be pursued.

EXPERIENCES OF GENDER IN SOCIAL VR

Case studies by Griffiths et al. (2016) suggest that video games can be a functional way of dealing with gender. The evidence indicates that virtual experiences can have multiple various functions for transgender individuals ranging from allowing feelings of pleasure, happiness, and relaxation, to fostering harmful addictions, as some prefer the secure online world over a more oppressive offline reality (Griffiths et al. 2016). Some of these experiences are interlocked with the transgender individual's gender identity, while others find VR to have very limited effects on their gender experiences. In this chapter, we focus on the anterior cases, that pertain specifically to the experiences of trans individuals. These experiences can roughly be divided into three topics that circle themes of gender dysphoria relief, induction of gender euphoria, and gender experimentation and exploration. As the themes are often interdependent, they are discussed interconnectedly in the following paragraphs.

Gender dysphoria can be defined as distress that arises from conflicts between an individual's gender identity or expression and their assigned sex (Beischel et al. 2022). Another definition describes gender dysphoria as a negatively perceived mismatch of an individual's biological sex and experienced gender (Schwind et al. 2017). Various studies have found VR to relieve gender dysphoria of trans and genderqueer individuals (Reyes and Fisher 2022, Acena and Freeman 2021, van Aller 2018) and help people with gender dysphoria come to terms with their gender identities (Griffiths et al. 2016). In social VR, the direct and immersive connection established between the user's physical body and their self-created avatar provides an influential change from other social online platforms and avatar-based games (Freeman and Maloney 2021).

Contrastingly, gender euphoria serves as a positive counterpart to gender dysphoria. The term is mainly used by trans* individuals to describe powerfully positive experiences and emotions concerning their gender (Jacobsen and Devor 2022, Beischel et al. 2022). This might consist of experiences during which an individual gets affirmation of their gender identity or expression from their peers or feels content and happy within their own skin. Within a social VR environment, gender euphoria can be induced by gender affirming situations (Reyes and Fisher 2022) as social support is considered to be a vital part of the formation of gender identities (Acena and Freeman 2021). For example, Morgan et al. (2020) find that positive emotions are experienced by trans* users when their avatars are acknowledged and accepted in their gender through game dialogue or communication with other players. When the social environment and a community of peers accepts and affirms the gender of the avatar, by extension they are also affirming the player.

Therefore, it can be established that similarly to physical spaces, in social VR environments, one of the biggest factors defining whether an individual feels accepted depends on the reactions of the community and received social affirmations and/or rejections they receive (Reyes and Fisher 2022). By enabling trans and genderqueer individuals to create virtual representations that correspond with their gender identity and expression, social VR platforms foster valuable acceptance and validation for individuals who might not be able to feel fully accepted or understood in physical spaces. The ability to use gender-affirming avatars in VR have been found to provide benefits for the player's self-perception even in situations when the same results would not realistically be possible or available in real life (Reyes and Fisher 2022).

Furthermore, virtual experiences can be used as psychological tools to increase one's self-awareness of gender identity as a part of the self (Griffiths et al. 2016). Results collected by van Aller (2018) indicate that the most frequently mentioned benefits of versatile character customization for trans* individuals are allowing self-expression and experimentation, which have also been found to enhance feelings of gender euphoria (Reyes and Fisher 2022). Similarly, research focused on social VR platforms has found that they offer trans* users an immersive and embodied way to explore, express, and experiment with their gender (Freeman et al. 2020, Freeman and Maloney 2021). This exploration of an individual's experienced gender was described by trans and gender diverse young people as an ongoing process of experimentation, refinement, and finally consolidation of their identity (Morgan et al. 2020).

Experimentation and exploration are also mentioned in various other sources. Marciano's (2014) analysis suggests a recurring motif of trans* users employing cyberspace as a preliminary sphere to virtually go through various transitional experiences before "entering the real world". In a study by Cantrell and Zhu (2022), all participants discussed using character creation for self-exploration of their gender identity. Similarly, van Aller (2018) found that the majority of respondents report using character customization as a way to experiment with their gender expression and gender identity—with 52.8% of respondents strongly agreeing that they use character customization for these purposes. In these cases, when experimentation and exploration are considered to be a central theme for the user, the process often begins before the individual gradually comes out in the offline world. Customizable avatars function as a tool for testing and preparing for more public representations of the self (Griffiths et al. 2016). In these situations, trans* people often embody an avatar in order to take their first steps into conceptualizing and actualizing their gender identity (Morgan et al. 2020). Contrastingly, transgender individuals who have already publicized their gender identity and begun forms of medical transition are less likely to participate in gender experimentation (Baldwin 2018).

Ideally, the online world offers a safe, non-threatening, non-alienating, non-stigmatizing, and non-critical environment for explorations and expressions of one's experienced gender identity (Griffiths et al. 2016). While preparing for public representations of the self, the first formative step of embodying an avatar with the desired gender identity and expression is deemed a safe and anonymous tool for exploration and identity consolidation (Morgan et al. 2020, Whitehouse et al. 2023). Social VR as an anonymized space is continually mentioned as a beneficial factor for boosting confidence during the discovery phases of LGBTQ identities (Lucero 2017, Craig and McInroy 2014, Acena and Freeman 2021).

Young trans and genderqueer individuals have been found to use customizable avatars to explore their experienced gender identities (Baldwin 2018, Morgan et al. 2020). This exploration consists of trying out different things, developing and refining a personal gender identity, and experimenting with varying gender expressions. Individuals often find freedom of choice and a greater agency within an ACI (avatar creation interface) empowering (Reyes and Fisher 2022). The findings by Morgan et al. (2020) indicate that customizability and diverse options are widely considered vital to be incorporated into the ACI design to avoid evoking negative experiences and feelings of exclusion. Especially non-customizable or exclusively binary avatar options are considered alienating, with negative emotions particularly appearing as the user is forced to perform within a gender they desire to distance themselves from and not to be identified as (Whitehouse et al. 2023). Furthermore, removing or restricting the user's control of their avatar's body configurations have been found to increase dysphoria, as it removes feelings of validation (Reyes and Fisher 2022).

Accordingly, customization capabilities incorporating versatile body shapes, hair styles, facial features, outfits and accessories, voice options, pronouns, and styles have been considered to promote positive and gender euphoric experiences. Providing diverse gender choices with gender-neutral options and a wide variety of expressions and mutable characteristics within those choices can assist in inducing gender euphoria. Furthermore, abilities to select and mix conventionally binary gendered features in untraditional ways was found to have a positive emotional impact on the respondents' well-being. (Reyes and Fisher 2022, Morgan et al. 2020). Especially nonbinary and genderqueer individuals have been found to prefer customization capabilities that allow for deconstruction and transgression of arbitrary gender roles and boundaries associated within them to more closely reflect their lived experiences (Baldwin 2018, Cantrell and Zhu 2022).

However, defining which customizable features are most vital for evoking feelings of empowerment and euphoria is rarely straightforward. While some feel euphoria due to being allowed to choose the perceived gender of an avatar, others find these options limiting and would rather wish to be allowed choices of different aesthetic representations associated with certain genders without needing to define the gender of their avatar (Reyes and Fisher 2022). Furthermore, voice and pronoun options are found to be causes of gender dysphoria more often than the body customization capabilities of an avatar (Reyes and Fisher 2022). Therefore, providing a wide range of customizable characteristics to support feelings of gender euphoria requires paying attention to various different defining features of an avatar that are culturally linked or assumed to relate to a certain gender.

Furthermore, social VR platforms are not necessarily always the safe and non-stigmatizing arena they are often depicted as. Harassment, abuse, and hate speech directed towards marginalized communities have not only been found to have more intense and destructive consequences within social VR due to the increased levels of presence and embodiment, but also to be difficult to monitor and mitigate (Freeman et al. 2022, Blackwell et al. 2019). However, moving the social interaction into a virtual sphere can also allow an individual to find a supportive community regardless of geographic distances. Acena and Freeman (2021) find that a central benefit stemming from social VR is its immersive and realistic methods for creating safe communities and connecting diverse users with each other in interactions much like offline face-to-face communications. Therefore, most users utilize social VR as a tool supporting the creation of a safe space to build close interpersonal relationships (Acena and Freeman 2021). Marciano (2014) categorizes these patterns of trans* users existing in cyberspace as a complementary sphere that functions as a supplemental part of the offline world and serves as a fulfilling social arena in the user's life.

VRs can also provide other psychological benefits and a sense of escapism to alleviate feelings of gender dysphoria (Griffiths et al. 2016). Marciano (2014) suggests a recurring pattern of trans* users utilizing cyberspace as an alternative sphere—a parallel world that offers varying and sometimes contradictory experiences from those in the offline world—to contribute to the user's well-being. Anonymous online communities may offer trans individuals the power to modify and reshape their experiences of themselves and their bodies. Therefore, the embodiment of a VR avatar might even pose a therapeutic role to the trans user during an emotionally challenging period, during which the rapid physical and social transitional changes are not possible or accessible (Morgan et al. 2020). Furthermore, McKenna et al. (2024) suggest that especially gender diverse adolescents—who rarely have access to extensive gender affirming treatment—find video games, VR, and customizable avatars a beneficial source of immersion and escapism to divert gender dysphoria and enact aspirational appearance goals.

EVALUATION OF READY PLAYER ME

In this section, a closer look will be taken at a widely used ACI from a transgender perspective. Ready Player Me is one of two VRChat compatible VR avatar creators that require no Unity or 3D modeling skills (Ready Player Me 2024a). The second option provided by VRChat at the time of writing is the mobile application MakeAvatar (Gugenka 2019). While Ready Player Me offers more realistic avatars, MakeAvatar provides easily accessible options for cartoon- and anime-themed avatars. The main focus of this evaluation will be on Ready Player Me as the provided avatar options relate more closely with real-life human proportions and body shapes.

Freeman et al. (2020) discuss the technical challenges of avatar crafting as one of the key themes appearing in experiences of social VR users. The creation and customization of a social VR avatar is a difficult and time-consuming process that requires technical skills. This results in tensions between the high demand for avatar personalization and the limited features provided (Freeman et al. 2020). Many existing social VR platforms are yet to offer simple customization interfaces allowing for personalization beyond generic avatar designs and limited features. However, often VR platforms and ACIs allow capabilities for versatile avatar and asset customization as long as the user has the required proficiencies in 3D modeling. The same goes for both VRChat and Ready Player Me, as they allow personalized customization of avatars through Unity. However, the main focus of the following section is on evaluating the capabilities and features provided by a ready-made ACI that can also be used with limited technical skills.

Reyes and Fisher (2022) propose tentative design guidelines to help develop more inclusive and diverse ACIs. These guidelines consist of three principles. First, ACI design should favor the inclusion of greater gender diversity and offer options for gender neutrality. According to interviews conducted by Reyes and Fisher, allowing agency regarding aesthetic decisions in avatar creation was found to induce feelings of gender euphoria. Second, designs should promote a larger number of voice and pronoun options that should not be connected with the body type and shape of the avatar. Furthermore, in social VR environments, the platform should offer the option for the user to communicate through text chat and/or emotes instead of verbal communication. Agency relating to the communicative aspects of social VR experiences has been found to help especially individuals with voice dysphoria. Furthermore, the ability to choose specific pronouns used for them is often a big part in inducing feelings of social acceptance and gender euphoria in transgender individuals (Reyes and Fisher 2022).

Finally, the platform should provide the users with opportunities to experience mundane gender affirming interactions and situations. A sense of normalcy can be experienced through social VR when transgender people receive social validation through mundane and familiar experiences and interactions and are treated during those interactions "like any other person" regardless of their transgender identity. This has been found to relieve social dysphoria and induce gender euphoria especially when combined with agency to customize the aesthetic and social aspects of the avatar according to the users' preferences (Reyes and Fisher 2022).

In addition to the guidelines introduced above, other studies have found that participants often wish for the incorporation of similar features into ACIs. Wide customizability (especially concerning body types, shapes and sizes, facial features, accessories, and hair styles) (Morgan et al. 2020, van Aller 2018, Freeman et al. 2020), diverse pronoun options (Morgan et al. 2020, van Aller 2018), non-binary options (Morgan et al. 2020), non-normative options (van Aller 2018), and abilities to mix and match conventionally binary gendered features with each other (Cantrell and Zhu 2022, Morgan et al. 2020) were mentioned repeatedly. Furthermore, abilities to customize an avatar with both a wide variety of different voice and communication options—but also with versatile movement styles, poses, and gaits (especially when full-body tracking is not used to accurately mimic a user's movements) are considered meaningful in shaping an avatar's perceived gender.

When evaluating an ACI from a transgender perspective, the main attention should be directed towards the customizability of gendered features and how well these design decisions accommodate transgender individuals. The analysis will discuss the customizability of the visual, auditory, and behavioral aspects of VR avatars. Providing concrete examples of VR avatar creation interfaces can help improve more inclusive and diverse avatar customization platforms. As the evaluative focus is directed towards a commercial ACI, it must be noted that ACIs are continually updated and new customization features are regularly added. Therefore, the analysis quickly becomes outdated in its description of the customization capabilities provided by Ready Player Me, and its main contribution, therefore, is in providing a framework for researchers and designers to evaluate future ACIs for social VR platforms.

The creation of an avatar with Ready Player Me begins with an option to either automatically create a personal avatar from a photo or to customize an avatar from scratch. In both cases, the user can opt for either a male or female avatar, although avatars created from photos are first automatically assigned one of the options by the facial recognition system. The avatars have armatures based on either a feminine- or a masculine-shaped skeleton (Ready Player Me 2024b). In the ACI, these options are depicted with the standard symbols used in biology to depict sex. Choosing one of the provided options results in the avatar being assigned with a masculine or feminine body type which cannot be altered or adapted. Both options include four body size options ranging from slim to athletic/muscular, and two slightly larger body types. The range of these options is limited, and the user cannot make changes to the physical measurements created automatically depending on the chosen sex (Figure 2.1). These measurements include for example shoulder width, chest size, waist and hip width, definition of muscles, and the placement of body fat. Also, the pose and slight movement of the avatar differs according to the chosen gender, with the male avatar taking a wider and more assertive stance while the female avatar has a narrower and friendlier pose while leaning slightly on one foot. The pose and movement style of the avatar are only visible within the ACI. After importing the avatar into VRChat, full-body tracking can be used to detect and imitate the movement style of the user.

Similarly, as in many virtual worlds (Blodgett et al. 2007), binary gender and limitations concerning gender and gender presentation are hard coded into the software. As of August 2024, the option to choose a nonbinary avatar has not been implemented despite being mentioned as an upcoming feature (Ready Player Me 2024a). Therefore, choosing a gender-neutral avatar is currently not possible. This contradicts the first design guideline proposed by Reyes and Fisher (2022) directly. In addition, customization options for body shapes, skin tones, and body dimensions and measurements remain limited.

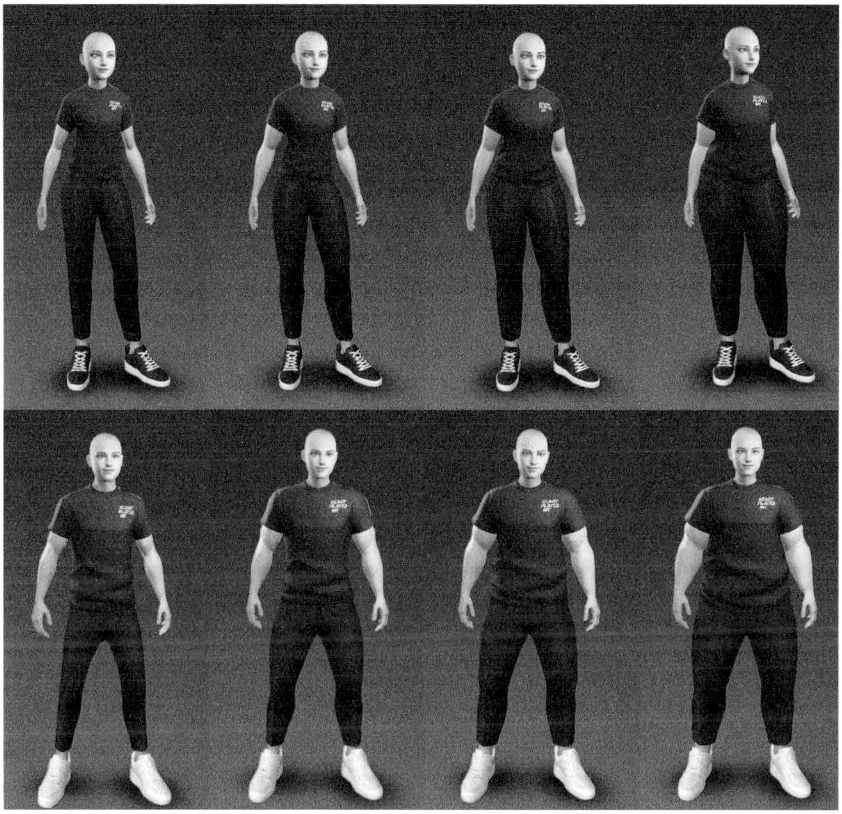

Figure 2.1 All female and male body shape and size options provided by Ready Player Me 2024a.

The majority of further bodily customization options provided by Ready Player Me are not gender-specific. Customizable options for facial features, hairstyles and accessories are almost identical—although they appear slightly differently depending on whether the masculine or feminine skeleton is used. Some traditionally feminine attributes (e.g., feminine makeup) and traditionally masculine attributes (e.g., facial hair) can be applied to either avatar. These possibilities provide agency for the user to "mix and match" gendered features quite freely. However, there are some limitations. For example, the male avatar can be clothed with a black hijab, but the female avatar has six additional color and style choices that do not appear as options for the male avatar. Similarly, the male avatar has three facial hair options that do not exist for feminine avatars. Although the majority of headgear can be equipped with either avatar, there are a few exceptions. The male avatar has a top hat and a Santa hat that are not available for female avatars. Correspondingly, the female avatar has two options for "female Santa hats" both of which include long hair.

These differences are not clearly stated or explained, suggesting they are likely unintentional remnants of an older version of the ACI. According to the Ready Player Me documentation, the gender-specific asset entity properties are stored within each entity as an enumeration with a string value of either 'male' , 'female' , or 'neutral' (Ready Player Me 2024b). For assets such as outfits or accessories, a neutral value indicates that the asset can be equipped by both male and female avatars. Discrepancies suggest that although the majority of accessory assets are valued as neutral, some still have specific male or female values.

Although the majority of accessories are not gender-specific, the biggest discrepancies between available assets for male and female avatar options are found in available outfits. Various outfits are clearly gendered in a way that choosing the same outfit will result in dramatically different outcomes depending on the chosen sex of the character (illustrated in Figure 2.2). The feminine clothing options are often more revealing and show more skin, while the masculine options are more loosely fitted. The user cannot equip an avatar with clothing of the opposite sex. Most notably, it is impossible for male avatars to wear a dress or a skirt. Conversely, female avatars are not provided with similar suit and dress shirt options as their male counterparts. In doing so, the ACI once again directly contradicts the first design guideline favoring user agency. However, it is expected that with the upcoming

Figure 2.2 Examples of gendered outfit options. All avatars are also equipped with gender-specific headwear (Ready Player Me 2024a).

release of a gender-neutral nonbinary option, all clothing options will have to become available to each avatar regardless of the chosen gender.

Ready Player Me does not offer built-in options for voice changers. However, the platform provides an integration to the Oculus Lipsync plugin (Meta 2021) that can be used to sync avatar lip movements to pre-recorded audio or live microphone input (Ready Player Me 2024b). VRChat further recommends utilizing viseme blend shapes to create detailed animations for speaking, although this requires that the used avatar model has the required blend shapes, making the process technically challenging for custom-built avatars. However, all Ready Player Me avatars are automatically created with 14 animatable visemes. Furthermore, VRChat supports voice-changing software, allowing users to switch between different voices and apply voice filters to modify the microphone input. As voice-changing technologies advance, they might prove a more engaging means of interaction for users experiencing voice dysphoria, compared to relying solely on gestures and text chat options. However, some trans* users have reported that using their own voice and engaging in voice training within social VR is a liberating experience (Acena and Freeman 2021). As voice and communication training is often an important part of a transgender individual's transition journey (Smith et al. 2023), VR allows for a training platform to independently undertake regular practice to align one's voice with their gender identity.

Regarding pronoun options, Ready Player Me (2024 a, b) and VRChat (2024) do not provide any in-built capabilities for defining or customizing avatar pronouns. In social environments, users typically inform others of their preferred pronouns directly or through a profile bio. Therefore, Reyes and Fisher's discussion (2022) concerning the importance of customizable pronouns primarily applies to VR experiences, where the player can also interact with pre-scripted NPCs that refer to the avatar with certain pronouns.

CONCLUSION

In this chapter, the primary goal was to establish how social VR can have a direct positive impact on the well-being of transgender individuals by enabling experimentation, exploration, verification, and consolidation of one's gender identity in an anonymous and ideally safe environment. VR avatar customization and embodiment are also found to function as practical tools to relieve experiences of gender dysphoria, allow for escapism, and ideally induce feelings of gender euphoria as a consequence of both internal and external validation of one's gender identity.

Although the majority of highlighted transgender experiences with social VR are positive, negative effects and undesired experiences of exclusion, alienation, and gender dysphoria can be evoked in the user by inadequate customization capabilities or a lack of self-determination during VR avatar creation. It is important to recognize that the positive experiences are directly influenced by the features available on social VR platforms and ACIs. Although full customizability is often allowed if the individual has the required technical skills, it is also vital to highlight the deficiencies of current social VR ACIs. Addressing these shortcomings can assist developers in making informed decisions while considering which customizable features could enhance beneficial experiences in social VR users.

REFERENCES

Acena, D. and Freeman, G. 2021. "In My Safe Space": Social support for LGBTQ users in social virtual reality. *In*: Extended Abstracts of the 2021 CHI Conference on Human Factors in Computing Systems (CHI EA '21). ACM, New York, NY, USA.

American Psychological Association (APA). 2023. Understanding Transgender People, Gender Identity and Gender Expression. Retrieved from https://www.apa.org/topics/lgbtq/transgender-people-gender-identity-gender-expression.

Baldwin, K. 2018. Virtual avatars: Trans Experiences of ideal selves through gaming. Markets, Globalization and Development Review. 3(3): Article 4.

Beischel, W.J., Gauvin, S.E.M. and van Anders, S.M. 2022. "A little shiny gender breakthrough": Community understandings of gender euphoria. International Journal of Transgender Health. 23(3): 274–294.

Birk, M.V., Atkins, C., Bowey, J.T. and Mandryk, R.L. 2016. Fostering intrinsic motivation through avatar identification in digital games. *In*: Proceedings of the 2016 CHI Conference on Human Factors in Computing Systems. 2982–2995.

Blackwell, L., Ellison, N., Elliott-Deflo, N. and Schwartz, R. 2019. Harassment in social virtual reality: Challenges for platform governance. *In*: Proceedings of the ACM on Human-Computer Interaction. 3(CSCW): Article 100: 1–25.

Blake, K., Godwin, M. and Whyte, S. 2020. "I sexually identify as an Attack Helicopter": Incels, trolls, and non binary gender politics online. First Monday. 25(9).

Blodgett, B.M., Xu, H. and Trauth, E.M. 2007. Lesbian, Gay, Bisexual, and Transgender (LGBT) issues in virtual worlds. ACM SIGMIS Database: The DATABASE for Advances in Information Systems. 38(4): 97–99.

Burke, P.J. and Stets, J.E. 2009. Identity Theory. New York: Oxford University Press.

Butler, J. 1999. Gender Trouble: Feminism and the Subversion of Identity. Routledge.

Cantrell, Y. and Zhu, X.A. 2022. Choice-based games and resilience building of gender nonconforming individuals: A phenomenological study. Digital Transformation and Society. 1(2): 198–218.

Craig, S.L. and McInroy, L. 2014. You can form a part of yourself online: The influence of new media on identity development and coming out for LGBTQ youth. Journal of Gay and Lesbian Mental Health. 18(1): 95–109.

Ducheneaut, N., Wen, M.-H., Yee, N. and Wadley, G. 2009. Body and mind: A study of avatar personalization in three virtual worlds. *In*: Proceedings of the SIGCHI Conference on Human Factors in Computing Systems. ACM.

Freeman, G., Zamanifard, S., Maloney, D. and Adkins, A. 2020. My body, my avatar: How people perceive their avatars in social virtual reality. *In*: Extended Abstracts of the 2020 CHI Conference on Human Factors in Computing Systems (CHI EA '20). Association for Computing Machinery, New York, NY, USA, 1–8. https://doi.org/10.1145/3334480.3382923.

Freeman, G. and Maloney, D. 2021. Body, avatar, and me: The presentation and perception of self in social virtual reality. *In*: Proceedings of the ACM on Human-Computer Interaction. 4(CSCW3): 1–27.

Freeman, G., Zamanifard, S., Maloney, D. and Acena, D. 2022. Disturbing the peace: Experiencing and mitigating emerging harassment in social virtual reality. *In*: Proceedings of the ACM on Human-Computer Interaction. 6(CSCW1): Article 85: 1–30.

Friedl, M. 2002. Online Game Interactivity Theory with Cdrom. Charles River Media.

Gagné, P., Tewksbury, R. and McGaughey, D. 1997. Coming out and crossing over: Identity formation and proclamation in a transgender community. Gender and Society. 11(4): 478–508.

Griffiths, M.D., Arcelus, J. and Bouman, W.P. 2016. Video gaming and gender dysphoria: Some case study evidence. Aloma. 34(2): 59–66.

Gugenka. 2019. MakeAvatar [Computer software]. Retrieved from https://makeavatar.jp/en.

Hegland, J.E. and Nelson, N.J. 2002. Cross-dressers in cyber-space: Exploring the internet as a tool for expressing gendered identity. International Journal of Sexuality and Gender Studies. 7(2): 139–161.

Huh, S. and Williams, D. 2010. Dude looks like a lady: Gender swapping in an online game. pp. 161–174. *In*: Bainbridge, W. (ed.). Online Worlds: Convergence of the Real and the Virtual. Human-Computer Interaction Series. Springer, London. https://doi.org/10.1007/978-1-84882-825-4_13.

Jacobsen, K. and Devor, A. 2022. Moving from gender dysphoria to gender euphoria: Trans experiences of positive gender-related emotions. Bulletin of Applied Transgender Studies. 1(1–2): 119–143.

Jin, S.-A. A. 2009. Avatars mirroring the actual self versus projecting the ideal self: The effects of self-priming on interactivity and immersion in an exergame, Wii Fit. Cyberpsychology and Behavior. 12(6): 761–765.

Kim, H., Park, J. and Lee, I.-K. 2023. "To be or Not to be Me?": Exploration of self-similar effects of avatars on social virtual reality experiences. IEEE Transactions on Visualization and Computer Graphics. 29(11): 4794–4804.

Lin, J. and Latoschik, M.E. 2022. Digital body, identity, and privacy in social virtual reality: A systematic review. Frontiers in Virtual Reality. 3: 974652.

Lucero, L. 2017. Safe spaces in online places: Social media and LGBTQ youth. Multicultural Education Review. 9(2): 117–128.

Manninen, T. and Kujanpää, T. 2007. The value of virtual assets: The role of game characters in MMOGs. International Journal of Business Science and Applied Management (IJBSAM). 2, 1: 21–33.

Marciano, A. 2014. Living the virtureal: Negotiating transgender identity in cyberspace. Journal of Computer-Mediated Communication. 19(4): 824–838.

McKenna, J.L., Wang, Y.-C., Williams, C.R., McGregor, K. and Boskey, E.R. 2024. "You can't be dead-named in a video game": Transgender and gender diverse adolescents' use of video game avatar creation for gender-affirmation and exploration. Journal of LGBT Youth. 21(1): 29–49.

McVeigh-Schultz, J., Kolesnichenko, A. and Isbister, K. 2019. Shaping pro-social interaction in VR: An emerging design framework. *In*: Proceedings of the 2019 CHI Conference on Human Factors in Computing Systems. ACM. 564.

Meta. 2021. Oculus Lipsync [API]. Retrieved from https://developer.oculus.com/downloads/package/oculus-lipsync-unity/.

Midha, V. and Nandedkar, A. 2012. Impact of similarity between avatar and their users on their perceived identifiability: Evidence from virtual teams in second life platform. Computers in Human Behavior. 28(3): 929–932.

Morgan, H., O'Donovan, A., Almeida, R., Lin, A. and Perry, Y. 2020. The role of the avatar in gaming for trans and gender diverse young people. International Journal of Environmental Research and Public Health. 17(22).

Mottelson, A., Muresan, A., Hornbæk, K. and Makransky, G. 2023. A systematic review and meta-analysis of the effectiveness of body ownership illusions in virtual reality. ACM Transactions on Computer-Human Interaction. 30(5): Article 76.

Neustaedter, C. and Fedorovskaya, E. 2009. Presenting identity in a virtual world through avatar appearances. *In*: Proceedings of Graphics Interface 2009 (GI '09). Canadian Information Processing Society, CAN. 183–190.

Nowak, K.L. and Rauh, C. 2005. The influence of the avatar on online perceptions of anthropomorphism, androgyny, credibility, homophily, and attraction. Journal of Computer-Mediated Communication. 11(1): 153–178.

Przybylski, A.K., Weinstein, N., Murayama, K., Lynch, M.F. and Ryan, R.M. 2012. The ideal self at play: The appeal of video games that let you be all you can be. Psychological Science. 23(1): 69–76.

Rahill, K.M. and Sebrechts, M.M. 2021. Effects of avatar player-similarity and player-construction on gaming performance. Computers in Human Behavior Reports. 4: 100131.

Ready Player Me [Computer software]. 2024a. Retrieved from https://readyplayer.me/.

Ready Player Me. 2024b. Ready Player Me Documentation. Retrieved from https://docs.readyplayer.me/.

Reyes, Z. and Fisher, J. 2022. The impacts of virtual reality avatar creation and embodiment on transgender and genderqueer individuals in games. *In*: FDG '22: Proceedings of the International Conference on the Foundations of Digital Games. No. 25.

Ruberg, B. and Shaw, A. 2017. Queer Game Studies. University of Minnesota Press.

Schroeder, R. 2012. The Social Life of Avatars: Presence and Interaction in Shared Virtual Environments. Springer Science & Business Media.

Schwind, V., Knierim, P., Tasci, C., Franczak, P., Haas, N. and Henze, N. 2017. "These are not my hands!" Effect of gender on the perception of avatar hands in virtual reality. *In*: Proceedings of the 2017 CHI Conference on Human Factors in Computing Systems. 1577–1582.

Smith, C., Gregory, C. and Bryant, L. 2023. Utilizing virtual reality for gender-affirming voice training: Surveying the attitudes and perspectives of potential consumers. International Journal of Language and Communication Disorders. 59: 976–990. https://doi.org/10.1111/1460-6984.12968.

Stets, J.E. and Serpe, R.T. 2013. Identity theory. pp. 31–60. *In*: DeLamater, J. and Ward, A. (eds). Handbook of Social Psychology. Springer Dordrecht.

Stryker, S. [1980]. 2002. Symbolic Interactionism: A Social Structural Version. Caldwell, NJ: Blackburn Press.

Stryker, S. 2017. Transgender History: The Roots of Today's Revolution. New York: Seal Press. 36–37.

Trepte, S. and Reinecke, L. 2010. Avatar creation and video game enjoyment: Effects of life-satisfaction, game competitiveness, and identification with the avatar. Journal of Media Psychology: Theories, Methods, and Applications. 22(4): 171–184.

van Aller, M. 2018. Transgender and Genderqueer Experiences of Avatar Creation in Games. University of Uppsala.

VRChat Inc. 2024. I [Computer software]. Retrieved from https://hello.vrchat.com/.

Waggoner, Z. 2009. My Avatar, My Self: Identity in Video Role-Playing Games. McFarland.

Whitehouse, K., Hitchens, M. and Matthews, N. 2023. Trans* and gender diverse players: Avatars and gender-alignment. Entertainment Computing. 47: 100584.

Whittle, S. 1998. The trans—Cyberian mail way. Social and Legal Studies. 7(3): 389–408.

Yee, N., Ducheneaut, N., Yao, M. and Nelson, L. 2007. Do men heal more when in drag?: Conflicting identity cues between user and avatar. *In*: Proceedings of the SIGCHI Conference on Human Factors in Computing Systems. ACM. 773–776.

and we will discuss some of these challenges in the sections dedicated to the selected case studies.

VR aims to simulate real-world interactions within a fully abstracted digital world. Worldbuilding can be aesthetically simplified or hyper-realistic compared to the real world. However, interaction and content are only available within the digitally represented world, while the user is physically placed in a dedicated area free of any obstacles to prevent possible accidents. The limits of the selected area are typically presented in the digital world with a visual grid, which the player is recommended not to move beyond. If the player moves beyond the boundaries, the headset activates built-in cameras that show the actual surroundings to prevent possible accidents. The grid is only visible in VR when the player is too close to the edges of the gameplay area, while in-game movement can be done by various interactions, the most common being a teleportation from spot to spot within the game world. Here lies the first set of challenges for the experienced designers, more commonly called game designers. The initial challenge is integrating the player, with their physical specifications such as height and movement abilities, into the game world. The world needs to adapt to the players' physical specifications and the preference of play, for example in case they prefer to sit on a chair while playing. This means that no matter where the player looks or turns, there is a 360-degree space in which they can observe, move, and interact. Their movement is based on their natural way of moving, especially if using a hand-tracking feature that does not require controllers as input devices. Some players, even if fully able-bodied, may prefer to use controllers instead of hand movements, as it provides more sensory stimulation by pressing buttons compared to interacting with a digital world that lacks haptic feedback. There are more devices on the market that support this feature, such as haptic gloves and other tools, but most headsets are equipped with the standard controllers. Haptic devices are advancing rapidly but are not commonly used outside of industrial VR training. Therefore, designing a coherent experience, especially for learning purposes, requires clear guidelines and limited content provided to the player at specific times and conditions, e.g. completing a task not only gives a reward but also more content to experience. Learning methods are specific to each individual—some learn better by consuming content at their own pace through reading or listening, others by immediately applying guidelines into practice, and some by combining various activities that build lasting memories and preserve knowledge (Sugiarto et al. 2024). Considering this, gamification allows designers to present learning content in various forms, including videos and practical tasks, which can be adjusted by the teacher/instructor or the players themselves based on accessibility needs or preferences. Successful learning outcomes usually come from structured learning, meaning the curriculum must be followed while the game world can conceal any rigid structures by creating emotional engagement with the players, who then have their own motivation to proceed with the tasks. The most successful gamification design results are the ones where players may forget that learning goals are the main aim of the gamified experience and pursue the tasks with high personal motivations towards completion (Pavlas et al. 2010). To achieve these results in gamification, designers must balance learning methods, structured content, and the perceived experience aimed at the player. In practice, it is necessary to have a diverse team of experts creating gamification products, where subject matter experts work closely with game designers to achieve the most optimal and balanced solution for players/learners (Piispanen 2024a).

In the case of merging expertise between quantum physics and game development, the most prominent and effective results have been through community-driven events dedicated to making games with quantum theory and mechanics—the quantum game jams (Kultima et al. 2021, Piispanen et al. 2023c). The annual quantum game jam has been producing on average 10–20 games a year for the past decade, and results vary in the genre and platform of games (e.g., games made for mobile, PC, non-digital games), and by the ways of quantum physics theory or technology implemented (Piispanen et al. 2025). Quantum games have been defined as "games that reference the theory of quantum physics, quantum technologies, or quantum computing through perceivable means, connect to quantum physics through a scientific purpose or use quantum technologies" (Piispanen et al. 2023a). In general, some quantum games are simply inspired by the principles of quantum physics, some utilize simulations, and some work with actual quantum computers (in case of the games made with open access cloud services such as Qiskit (6) by IBM).

Key themes we wish to address are the narrative structure of VR experiences, the incorporation of numerical simulations of quantum physical systems to contextualize quantum physics, and the adaptability of interactive storytelling (Smed et al. 2021) to cater to varying levels of student learning practices. We will also explore feedback mechanisms and assessment tools employed in both case studies to measure the effectiveness of the VR setups in achieving educational goals. In the following two case studies, both VR gamified solutions feature educational content of quantum physics, but the design principles and interaction methods differ based on the specific interactive storytelling design principles of each application. In the next part of this chapter, we will explore each case study with specific interaction designs and technical requirements, focusing on design decisions and implementations.

CASE STUDY: "QWIZ–QUANTUM IS MAGIC" VR PUZZLE GAME

"QWiz", short for "Quantum Wizard", is a VR puzzle game made for the very first edition for the Oculus Quest headset by Meta(7). The game is set in a medieval wizard's den, where you play as an apprentice learning the secrets of forces governing nature, referring to quantum physical phenomena. The task is simple; move a liquid from one vial to another that is connected with a vent, and by doing so the player needs to find the most optimized solution to the puzzle. The player controls two levers which correspond to two specific parameters in a numerical simulation, which affect the way the liquid is being transferred between the vials. In particular, the game sources its parameters from a numerical simulation called "Quantum Black Box" (8) developed for citizen science game prototypes (Piispanen 2024a) in collaboration between researchers of University of Turku (UTU) and Aalto University (AU) under the Center for Quantum Engineering project "QPlay" (9). This tool numerically simulates a complex time-dependent optimal control problem which is one of the key ingredients for creating a quantum logic gate, which is a core element in quantum computation (Piispanen 2024a).

The levers can be moved from left to right independently and simultaneously. These actions are directly affecting the behavior of the liquid in the puzzle visualization by the use of the QBB. The player gets multiple additional visual cues during the process of solving the puzzle. These indicate how suitable their procedure is by color changes of the liquid, a gauge-device with indicating lights, and the shape of an electric arc behind the workbench (Figure 3.1).

The game is designed with two main goals, the first was to acquire data from the player solutions for scouring new optimizing procedures for the underlying problem through a citizen science approach, and the second was to expand it to a learning environment. The gameplay does not presume the player to have any previous knowledge of quantum physics or methodologies related to the system simulated by the QBB. The puzzle elements are designed to induce an intuitive and fast-paced gameplay, where players can adjust their tactics in puzzle solving according to the indicators of the puzzle completion success rate. The player is encouraged to explore the environment and interact with the surroundings, where all the items are interactable. This design approach allowed us to immerse the player to the given setting, thus allowing for possible intuition gain of the studied problem. The educational elements in the applications present themselves as some of the items that unlock 'hidden' knowledge of quantum physics, which will help in solving the given puzzle, for example, the scrolls on the table and the shelves.

However, the player is not required to use any of these to complete the puzzles. The game also has a leaderboard where players can compete for the best results of the puzzles. The results correspond to parameters such as the speed of solving the puzzle and how stable the result is based on the selected difficulty level.

THE DESIGN DECISIONS IN QWIZ

From the very beginning of the collaboration between the quantum physics researchers from UTU and the game development team at MiTale, it was important to establish the needs and expectations of the results that would benefit the research project goals. VR, as the platform of choice, was selected by the physicists wanting to integrate, at that time, the latest gaming technologies and make long lasting impact of the immersive experiences for the users. The project was initiated in 2019 when the Oculus Quest first generation of headsets by Meta became available on the market, before which the VR equipment required expensive gear and higher computing processing power. Based on the previous experience in working with such VR settings by the team (both physicists and game developers in this project), it was concluded that simpler and easier accessible gear would be better choice, not just for the project at the stage of development, but for the future iterations and expanding the content further as needed. The general public did not yet have much experience with VR. In addition, previous generation equipment still had quite many issues in regards to motion sickness and accessibility challenges. Unlike previous setups where a VR headset had been connected to the computer with multiple cables and needed a set of beacons to set the gameplay environment, Oculus Quest did not require any additional gear nor connection to the external devices, and the onboarding of the player with the use of the VR device became much easier and faster. To achieve the most impactful results for the commercial purposes and popularizing science, the selected platform was the best choice on the market since most of the common issues have been resolved by Meta in their Oculus Quest headset.

The design process started once methodologies related to the citizen science aspects were set by the researchers, and the game designers started iterating the possible game mechanics that would match the requirements for the numerical simulation, the challenges of the VR development and the user-centered design principles. There are many elements which may affect the game design processes towards completely new ways of understanding the role of the game designer and the role of the player, along with the variety of direction(s) in their 'dialogue(s)' through the gameplay experiences (Skult and Smed 2022).

In a VR setting, one of the most impactful aspects is the *interaction design*, in which unlike in more traditional aspects of interaction that require the screen which displays the content and input devices that relate to the set of actions the player can do in the game world. As already stated, in VR the player takes an active role in the game world, to which the UI/UX common best practices now do not apply from conventional 2D interfaces. The type of player movement in the VR setting along with the floating UI elements can cause confusion, possible motion sickness, and other inconveniences depending on very individualistic specifications of each and every player (Valmorisco et al. 2024). In the case of QWiz, we decided to limit the player movement to a minimal area for the player to reach, not requiring any long-distance transitions across the game world. This also allows them to comfortably sit in a chair while in the VR setting and interact with the close surroundings.

This static setup gave us more control over the puzzle design and the QBB integration, with an onboarding process for the players to get familiar with the controls, user interface, their role and task in such a setting. The vials and other devices important for solving the puzzles, are placed inside the game on a table as a dedicated 'workstation' where all interactable puzzle elements situate. Even though we call it a static setting, the player can freely move and make multiple steps from the real world that positively enhance the interactions with the virtual world, allowing the player to feel as the active part of the narrative. The game world allows multiple types of interaction with objects in the setting (Figure 3.1), such as dropping the items on the floor or rearranging the books on the shelves. None of these actions have a distractible features nor a failure condition, and their main aim is to enhance the natural interaction with the virtual elements. One of the main features was that no UI elements were separated from the game world, but instead each indicator within the game progression was visually placed as an intact part of the experience. In particular, the puzzle progression and success rate to reach the solution could be followed by three different visual cues within the surrounding:

1. The first and most prominent indicator was the color change of the liquid based on the player interaction (Figures 3.1 and 3.2).
2. The second indicator was the behavior of an electric arc, which was connecting two poles behind each vial and is a direct visualization of the probability distribution of the one-dimensional system simulated real time though the QBB.
3. The third indicator was the custom-designed gauge device indicating three sections: red (failing), yellow (working towards the right solution), and green (reaching the right solution) in which a needle moves between the sections that light up with the corresponding color.

The reason behind the use of the three indicators is based on the initial play sessions in the prototyping stage. The designers concluded rather fast that players tend to follow multiple different types of indicators and not necessarily only one when solving the puzzle. Furthermore, some of the indicators contextually were not clear enough for all the players that we have conducted the initial gameplay sessions with. By having three indicators, we were able to expand upon the accessibility features and make the VR experience more user-friendly regardless of if the user had previously used any of the VR platforms. As a result, in the following gameplay sessions and public displays, we have received positive oral feedback on having the variety of the indicators giving the same type of information (the tracking of the success rate towards puzzle completion). Some of these players expressed that often they would commute between following certain indicators if they felt they provide clearer understanding of what should be done. From the interactions with the players, we concluded that the chosen set of colors and shape designs were improving the experience towards a visually appealing gameplay.

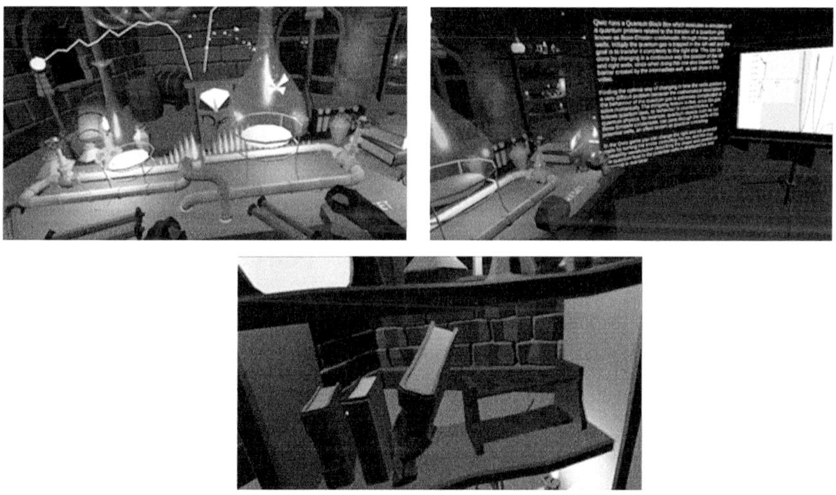

Figure 3.1 Scenes of QWiz VR environment showcasing the puzzle, the interaction and features of the learning content.

In the early stages of VR development and game design, designers addressed accessibility challenges by ensuring VR controllers used fewer inputs, making it easier for players to learn how to interact with the virtual world. The emphasis was on enabling intuitive gameplay that is based on self-motivation and discoveries within the environment itself, in comparison to more traditional design practices or teaching methods. Thus, player-centered design has been used throughout development, ensuring we accommodate technological, research-based, and game design requirements. In the initial stages of development, the numerical simulation seemed to provide random output and it was therefore challenging for the designers to understand what QBB could provide for the user experience. Once the purpose of the parameters and return values of QBB were set, it was important to find the fitting game mechanic that would clearly visualize these to the player. The final version of the game design did manage to provide a unique experience with each gameplay session.

For the game programmers, there were several challenges in working with the QBB. The biggest challenge in the prototyping stage was keeping the simulation steadily integrated with the game. The research team had observed challenges regarding the integration of QBB to games for some years through an annual game developing event "Quantum Game Jam" (Kultima et al. 2021, Piispanen 2024a). One of these challenges related to downloading and running of the games, as they required a separate downloading of QBB, also had further implications. In addition, the numerical simulation was hosted on the third-party servers to which any of the team members had direct access to. In cases where the servers performed slower, we would have to wait for the technical support from the third-party to assist. In particular, the location of the players would have different issues with delays, especially players outside of Finland. This issue was solved by changing the server host in the later stages of the development.

In addition, another challenge for designers and developers was creating an environment for the complex topic of quantum physics that would be intuitive and comprehensive for non-physicists. To achieve this, the designers decided to set the game in the medieval wizard-themed fantasy world, with stylized 3D aesthetics, that would also allow humorous elements in some of the interactions with the environment. The playfulness of the surrounding encourages players to discover the quantum phenomena on their own, governed by personal motivations and not by the requirements of the game. The puzzle can be solved in various ways, in which the fastest and most optimized results based on the selected difficulty level are being displayed to the leaderboard. This approach allows the players to challenge not just others but also their own results and keep improving their own rank, especially the players that are in the top three positions to keep their deserved titles.

One of the biggest tests of the game was conducted with a public audience at the annual event in "Science is Wonderful! -Marie Skłodowska-Curie Actions" (10) in Brussels, funded by the European Commission, at which the QWiz project was selected to be showcased at a dedicated booth. The visitors of the event were a wide range of different age groups and interests, including the school children and scientists from around the world. Based on observation, the younger users seemed to reach better scores compared to the older and more experienced players, which shows the importance of utilizing creative thinking alongside the traditional teaching methods. Since VR headsets were not yet available in the classroom setting, the project owners and researchers decided to port the game to a browser-based application (Figure 3.2) in which students can experience the lessons of quantum physics on their own devices through the eyes of the quantum wizard.

Figure 3.2 Screenshot of the WebGL version of QWiz.

CASE STUDY: "QPLAYGROUND", VR QUANTUM VISUALIZATION

The QPlayground project was conducted by the same physics research group and game developers behind the QWiz game. This time, the goal was to create a digital version for educational and outreach purposes of the famous art installation, Quantum Garden.

The Quantum Garden is an interactive art installation (Piispanen 2023b, Piispanen 2024b) that demonstrates key concepts of quantum physics, such as quantum superposition, interference, and the Schrödinger equation (Figure 3.3). The interface is based on the concept of Wobble Garden by the artist Robin Baumgarten, where the user interacts with springs mounted on a board of LED lights. Upon touching the springs, Quantum Garden numerically generates a particle in a quantum superposition in the network of springs. Each spring is connected to a set of LED-lights. The particle then moves through the network forming a wave-like visualization, which represents the probability distribution of the particle.

Figure 3.3 Quantum Garden installation, image source https://quantumgarden.net/.

Quantum Garden started as a citizen science project (Piispanen 2024b) where people could contribute to solving a quantum physics research problem. The simulation was later replaced with another that was found more suitable for educational and outreach purposes (Piispanen 2023b, 2024a). This newer simulation tool acted as the baseline for the numerical simulation in QPlayground.

In this project, the digital visualization of the analog installation was transformed into an interactive virtual reality experience for learning about quantum physical phenomena. Based on the specifications of the original project, the designers had to retain the initial way of interacting with the springs, and the way lights behaved.

The platform for the VR experience was once again the Oculus Quest headset by Meta, but with the updated feature of a hand-tracking system. The hand-tracking implementation was relatively straightforward, providing an immersive and closer interaction method that aligned with the initial design of the art installation. The main elements of the QPlayground virtual experience include:

1. *Interaction design* by utilizing hand-tracking and selecting appropriate hand gestures for the given tasks in the VR setting.
2. *Environment design* and establishing the rules of the game world.

3. *Visualization* in depicting the quantum physics phenomena through simulation, helping users to achieve the goal of the gamified experience.

Each element (Figure 3.4) was carefully designed to enhance both the entertainment and educational aspects of the project. The aim was to create a visually striking experience in the world of quantum physics while teaching the principles governing that experience. Furthermore, each design element depended on one another to create a meaningful user-centric response and enhance the player's journey.

Figure 3.4 Design of hand gestures and UI elements.

THE DESIGN DECISIONS IN QPLAYGROUND, VR QUANTUM VISUALIZATION

Interaction design was a critical aspect of this project, as we aimed to retain as much of the original concept from Quantum Garden as possible in the VR experience. This meant that the physical play of the springs and the following response implied with the colorful lights would be defined by the same principles in VR. In addition, it had become apparent that VR would allow adding the missing guidance for the player to interact with the springs, or in VR setting, a node-system. The two main actions for the player are activating the quantum phenomena by initiating the simulation, and by following the visual cues of the simulation selecting a node that they assume the particle would occupy.

The second important design action was the layout of the gameplay area in the virtual setting. Instead of keeping the shape of the node structure and number of nodes, we expanded the experience into an almost full 360-degree dome of nodes, allowing the simulation to run all around the player. This further enhanced the physical aspect of the player's presence in the simulation, making them fully immersed in the simulation. To enhance this presence, we encourage players to use hand gestures instead of controllers, though controllers remain available for accessibility purposes. The hand-tracking feature was implemented to respond to specific hand gestures that triggered the activities (e.g., initiating the visualization, selecting the nod, activating the simulation) within the environment and its activated elements.

We decided that all UI design would be part of the player representation and the environment itself. The virtual hands had user interface elements on them, particularly on the forearms and dorsal sides, providing for intuitive interaction. The numerical simulation in Quantum Garden was created with Python and required translating it to a C# environment. Additionally, this required the adjustment on the colors of the nodes from the original to better match the environment and interaction principles within the newly set QPlayground. In QPlayground, each node in the network is presented with a sphere that also changes its size according to the simulation. Once again, we have limited the play area towards a 'static' approach in which the environment would adjust by the player's position of standing or sitting. Just as in QWiz, the player is free to move within a specific area so that they can better observe the 360-degree surrounding and visual effects by the quantum simulation.

Onboarding to the interactive visual experience and learning content was facilitated by a pixie, a non-playable character (NPC), introduced as a being from the quantum world of very small particles and acting as a companion throughout the game. This character narrated the backstory, outlined the challenges ahead, and provided tips on how to solve them. Educational content was available by interacting with the pixie at any point during gameplay. We included both narrated and written content to enhance accessibility for players.

THE RESULTS OF TWO CASE STUDIES

Both projects were initially designed for VR environments, however due to COVID-19 pandemic in early 2020 and the need for online learning content, they were ported to web-based applications, allowing us to address unique game design and interaction design challenges from each project. While QWiz was designed to serve as a tool for citizen science purposes with real-time simulations (Figure 3.2), making the game design principles and environmental storytelling flexible to adjust based on test results and player feedback, the QPlayground project had a more artistic vision where direct interaction with the simulation was the guiding design mechanic. For the online browser-based prototype, the nodes were arranged in a pattern on a flat surface, resembling the original Quantum Garden installation (Figure 3.3). This allowed us to improve interactive storytelling features, resulting in a more cohesive player experience design.

The project results gave positive outcomes in both outreach and educational activities, including the additional insights to relevant fields of interests for physicists and game developers within the team members. For the physicists, the outcome of each play was to be recorded and analyzed further with machine learning methodologies in the study of quantum state-transfer processes within the framework of quantum optimal control (Brif et al. 2010, Koch 2016). The user data was also intended to be further analyzed for better understanding of the ways that players interact with the simulation, but due to discontinuation of the governing project, such plans were not carried out. Instead, the physicists were able to learn about the challenges, limitations, and advantages of numerical simulations for citizen science and outreach purposes and quantum game development (Piispanen 2024a). For game developers, it has been an eye-opening experience and the potential opportunities inspired towards using quantum computation and simulations in game design and development. The project resulted with multiple uses (Piispanen 2024a) of the QBB being utilized with the narrative, the mechanics and the world building, which could be explored further with different case studies and implementation methods. We thank the partners from IBM, University of Turku, Aalto University, MiTale, and above all—players, who made exceptional contributions in the results of this article. Laura Piispanen gratefully acknowledges that her research has been funded by the Väisälä Foundation and the Alfred Kordelin Foundation.

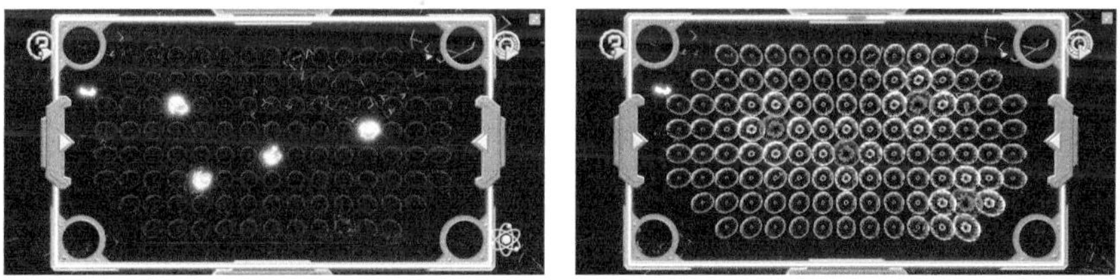

Figure 3.5 QPlayground, WebGL version available at https://qplaylearn.com/games/quantum-state/quantum-playground/index.html.

CONCLUSION AND FUTURE STEPS

With the emergence of XR (extended reality) solutions, VR technology is at the forefront of elevating interactive storytelling design principles. Additionally, market trends in the metaverse and rapid developments in generative AI (artificial intelligence) technology significantly influence software and hardware development. This growing demand requires more content, especially as VR devices become more affordable for common household use. Furthermore, emerging quantum technology and computation are profoundly shaping software and engineering trends (Wootton 2020), necessitating new expertise and skills from game and software developers, including quantum literacy. Quantum computing platforms, such as those provided by IBM, Google, and Microsoft among others, offer online access to quantum computers and simulations, allowing us to explore technical and design innovations in our own fields of interests and development (Seskir et al. 2022).

Conventional game design and interactive storytelling practices (Smed et al. 2021) help us adapt to these changes, benefiting developers, researchers, and consumers alike. By integrating and adopting the established best practices with new ways of introducing the design and technical capabilities of the emerging technologies, we can better understand their benefits and limitations while addressing user needs and interests. This approach is particularly important for education and lifelong learning, enabling the creation of tailored learning journeys for individuals more effectively than ever before (Pavlas et al. 2010, Ahmed 2021, Sugiarto et al. 2024). The two case studies presented in this chapter offer a glimpse into the vast possibilities arising from combining various scientific and entertainment fields with a common goal. Each team member contributed their expertise and learned from other industry practices, fostering innovation. In both projects, interactive storytelling served as the binding medium, helping team members communicate their visions and develop a cohesive platform for players to experience the learning content. Story-based content also demystifies complex terms, making quantum physics an ideal case study subject.

For future development of interactive storytelling in gamification and VR environments, we intend to continue both research and industry applications with the latest available technologies. We aim to involve players from the early stages of development to collaboratively find new approaches that meet the specifications and requirements of gamified solutions and their users. Regarding the use of quantum computation and simulation in game and gamification design, we are still in the early stages of potential transformation. Further research will provide more insights for implementing interactive storytelling design with emerging technologies.

ENDNOTES

[1] QWiz–Quantum is Magic. 2019. WebGL port: https://qplaylearn.it/game-qwiz.

[2] QPlayground WebGL port. 2020. https://qplaylearn.com/games/quantum-state/quantum-playground/index.html.

[3] Quantum Garden. 2018. Quantum Garden art installation: https://quantumgarden.net/.

[4] Minecraft: https://www.minecraft.net/en-us.

[5] MiTale, game development company from Turku, Finland: https://www.mitalegames.com/.

[6] Qiskit [kiss-kit] is an open-source SDK for working with quantum computers at the level of pulses, circuits and application modules, see https://qiskit.org/.

[7] Quest headsets by Meta: https://www.meta.com/fi/en/quest/.

[8] Quantum Black Box—open source by Dr. Matteo Rossi: https://gitlab.utu.fi/matros/quantum-black-box.

[9] QPlay (QPlayLearn): https://qplaylearn.com/.

[10] "Science is Wonderful! - Marie Skłodowska-Curie Actions": https://marie-sklodowska-curie-actions.ec.europa.eu/science-is-wonderful.

REFERENCES

Ahmed, S. 2021. Quantum games and simulations: Applications in education, outreach, and research. Århus Universitet. 216.

Brif, C., Chakrabarti, R. and Rabitz, H. 2010. Control of quantum phenomena: Past, present, and future. New Journal of Physics. 12(7): 075008.

Chiofalo, M., Foti, C., Lazzeroni, C., Maniscalco, S., Michelini, M., Seskir, Z., et al. 2021. A game for quantum physics education. *In*: Proceedings of the 3rd World Conference on Physics Education, (Hanoi, Vietnam). 13–16.

Koch, C. 2016. Controlling open quantum systems: Tools, achievements, and limitations. Journal of Physics. Condensed Matter: An Institute of Physics Journal. 28.

Kultima, A., Piispanen, L. and Junnila M. 2021. Quantum game jam: Making games with quantum physicists. Academic Mindtrek 2021 (New York, NY, USA). Association for Computing Machinery. 134–144.

Nita, L., Smith, L. and Cramman, H. 2023. The challenge and opportunities quantum literacy for future education and transdisciplinary problem-solving. Research in Science and Technological Education. 41: 564–580.

Pavlas, D., Heyne, K., Bedwell, W., Lazzara, E. and Salas, E. 2010. Game-based Learning: The impact of flow state and videogame self-efficacy. *In*: Proceedings of the Human Factors and Ergonomics Society Annual Meeting. 54(28): 2398–2402.

Piispanen, L., Morrell, E., Park, S., Pfaffhauser, M. and Kultima, A. 2023a. The history of quantum games. *In*: 2023 IEEE Conference on Games (CoG). 1–8.

Piispanen, L. 2023b. Designing quantum games and quantum art for exploring quantum physics. *In*: IEEE Conference on Games (CoG), Boston, MA, USA. 1–8.

Piispanen, L., Anttila, D. and Skult, N. 2023c. Online quantum game jam. Proceedings 7th International Conference on Game Jams, Hackathons, and Game Creation Events (ICGJ '23), (New York, NY, USA), Association for Computing Machinery. 18–27.

Piispanen, L. 2024a. Developing Quantum Games, Quantum Art, and Simulation Tools for Exploring Quantum Physics. Master's thesis, University of Turku.

Piispanen, L. 2024b. Quantum citizen science games on the timeline of quantum games. EPJ Plus Focus Point Issue: Citizen Science for Physics: From Education and Outreach to Crowdsourcing Fundamental Research. 1–8.

Piispanen, L., Pfaffhauser, M., Wootton, J., Togelius, J. and Kultima, A. 2025. Defining quantum games. EPJ Quantum Technol. 12: 7 https://doi.org/10.1140/epjqt/s40507-025-00308-7.

Seskir, Z.C., Migdał, P., Weidner, C., Anupam, A., Case, N., Davis, N., et al. 2022. Quantum games and interactive tools for quantum technologies outreach and education. Optical Engineering. 61.

Singh, C. 2007. Student difficulties with quantum mechanics formalism. *In*: Proceedings of the Physics Education Research Conference, Syracuse, NY, AIP Conf. Proc., Melville New York. 883: 185–188.

Singh, C., Belloni, M. and Christian, W. 2006. Improving students' understanding of quantum mechanics. Physics Today. 59(8): 43–49.

Skult, N., Smed, J. 2022. The Marriage of quantum computing and interactive storytelling. Games and Narrative: Theory and Practice. Springer Cham. 191–206.

Smed, J., Suovuo, T., Trygg, N., Skult, P. and Hakonen, H. 2019. The digital campfire: An ontology of interactive digital storytelling. *In*: J. Thakur (Ed.). Modern Perspectives on Virtual Communications and Social Networking. 82–92. IGI Global.

Smed, J., Suovuo, T., Skult, N. and Skult, P. 2021. Handbook on Interactive Storytelling. John Wiley & Sons. https://dx.doi.org/10.1002/9781119688167.

Sugiarto, R., Purwanto, S., Utama, A., Nopembri, S., Hartanto, A. and Mahardhika, N. 2024. Problem-based learning (PBL), teaching games for understanding (TGfU) learning models, on learning outcomes reviewed from, and students' learning motivation. Fizjoterapia Polska. 24(2): 250–258.

Valmorisco, S., Raya, L. and Sanchez, A. 2024. Enabling personalized VR experiences: A framework for real-time adaptation and recommendations in VR environments. Virtual Reality. 28: 128.

Wootton, J.R. 2020. Procedural generation using quantum computation. *In*: FDG '20: Proceedings of the 15th International Conference on the Foundations of Digital Games. Article No. 98. 1–8. https://doi.org/10.48550/arXiv.2007.11510.

WEB REFERENCES

Minecraft: https://www.minecraft.net/en-us.

MiTale, game development company from Turku, Finland: https://www.mitalegames.com/.

Qiskit [kiss-kit] is an open-source SDK for working with quantum computers at the level of pulses, circuits and application modules, see https://qiskit.org/.

QPlay (QPlayLearn): https://qplaylearn.com/.

QPlayground WebGL port. 2020. https://qplaylearn.com/games/quantum-state/quantum-playground/index.html.

Quantum Black Box—open source by Dr. Matteo Rossi: https://gitlab.utu.fi/matros/quantum-black-box.

Quantum Garden. 2018. Quantum Garden art installation: https://quantumgarden.net/.

Quest headsets by Meta: https://www.meta.com/fi/en/quest/.

QWiz –Quantum is Magic 2019. WebGL port: https://qplaylearn.it/game-qwiz.

"Science is Wonderful!—Marie Skłodowska-Curie Actions". https://marie-sklodowska-curie-actions.ec.europa.eu/science-is-wonderful.

Chapter **4**

Using VR Technology for Teaching Letterpress

Cetin Tüker*[1], Selen Başer Nejat[2] and Başak Ürkmez[3]
[1]Graphic Design Department, Mimar Sinan Fine Arts University (TR)
Emails: selen.baser@msgsu.edu.tr, basak.urkmez@msgsu.edu.tr

INTRODUCTION

Typographic design is one of the essential elements of graphic design. Many terms widely used in typography are rooted in old letterpress technology; for example, the term 'leading' refers to the spacing between lines of text, created by placing thin strips of lead between the lines to increase the vertical distance and improve readability in old letterpress technology. Today's graphic design practice is largely computerized, and students need help understanding typography terms as they are rooted in old technology, but still used in new technology. Hence, to enrich the learners' experience and conceptual knowledge of typography, we offer an elective course named "Letterpress Printing", in which learners can understand the etymology of technical terms and learn to use a real-world letterpress atelier to experience the behavior of paper, ink, and lead with on-site experience.

To enhance the practical aspects of the course through a blended learning strategy, we have developed an educational simulation

*For Correspondence: cetin.tuker@msgsu.edu.tr

DOI: 10.1201/9781003581642-4

environment—a virtual letter press atelier—utilizing immersive VR (IVR) technology specifically designed for graphic design students. The scope encompasses an in-depth exploration of various letterpress processes and tools, offering a comprehensive educational experience. By providing a cost-effective and practical alternative to traditional letterpress ateliers, the study aims to address financial constraints and enhance the accessibility of such learning opportunities for students anytime and anywhere they want.

The aim of this study is to create an IVR letterpress simulator: (i) to teach how letterpress process and tools works to graphic design students—which can be a cost-effective and practical alternative to real-world letterpress atelier—providing similar learning gains while reducing learners' cognitive load during instruction, and (ii) to evaluate the adoptability of the technology by students and instructors.

LITERATURE BACKGROUND

The rapid advancement of technology has brought significant changes to educational practices across various disciplines. Among these, the integration of VR has emerged as a transformative tool, offering immersive and interactive learning experiences that were previously unattainable. In this section, a broader look from the VR in education to narrowing down to design education to focusing on the VR in graphic design education has been selected. Also this section examines the enduring value of traditional methods such as letterpress printing.

A comprehensive bibliometric analysis by Rojas-Sánchez et al. (2023) revealed key trends and influential works in VR in education, highlighting the main topics, authors, sources, and countries contributing to the literature. From 2010 to 2021, a significant number of articles were published, with a marked surge in interest during the COVID-19 pandemic. This period saw a notable increase in VR usage, primarily driven by students, although institutions were initially hesitant to adopt this disruptive technology (Rojas-Sánchez et al. 2023). Rojas-Sánchez et al. (2023) also report on various simulation-based educational systems, such as those for vehicle driving (Hsu et al. 2016), pharmacology (Dubovi et al. 2017), a remote access VR laboratory for programmable logic controllers (Yerden and Akkuş 2020), and instructional systems for training workers on assembly tasks (Vélaz et al. 2014).

Further analysis of immersive technology research in education between 2001 and 2021 underscores the evolution and diversification of this field. By examining 2,665 articles, researchers identified two major clusters related to VR technology in education: augmented reality and virtual worlds (Mohsen and Alangari 2024). The study found that immersion research in education is deeply rooted in theoretical frameworks such as constructivism, experiential learning, and cognitive load theory (Mohsen and Alangari 2024). The fact that most studies adopt constructivism and experiential learning as their theoretical framework is a significant finding, underscoring the impact of the research on the field and indicating a gap in the educational VR literature concerning research that combines direct instruction with VR environments.

Despite the large number of articles highlighting the diverse nature of immersive technology in education, a systematic study by Jiawei and Mokmin (2023) covering publications from 2016–2022 identified only five articles related to IVR in visual communication design education. None of these studies focus on an instructional environment within a VR simulator. The study by Jiawei and Mokmin (2023) aims to explore the trends in the application of VR to art and visual communication design education between 2016 and 2022. It examines current research on using VR technology with visual communication design students in immersive environments, identifies the variables considered in such research, and investigates the types of VR used in visual communication design. Unfortunately, considering the number of articles published, it can be concluded that there is a noticeable gap in using VR technologies in graphic design and visual communication design education.

At this stage of the literature review, due to the close relationship between architecture and graphic design and the lack of sufficient studies on the use of VR in graphic design education, the focus has also been on studies that explore the use of VR in architectural education. The representation strength of VR technology in architecture has led educational research in this area to focus on architectural history. Learning from the major works in architectural history is an important method for architectural education. Considering that the representational capability of photographs is often insufficient, it is quite understandable that the field of architectural history has quickly embraced VR. Şahbaz's (2020) work focuses on the development of an interactive VR program (IHVR) for a historical Greek bathhouse. This study showed that students using VR experienced improvement in learning architectural details compared to traditional methods. The immersive nature of VR allowed students to virtually explore and interact with the building, leading to a deeper comprehension of its spatial and design elements. This suggests that VR can be an effective hypermedia tool in architectural education, offering a realistic and engaging way to study historical structures (Şahbaz 2020). The instructional success achieved in this study suggests that similar success could be attained in the field of letterpress as well.

Expanding on the use of VR in architectural history courses, another study explored its impact on students' learning abilities (Ibrahim et al. 2021). By creating virtual environments for modern architectural examples, researchers found that students in the VR condition performed better in terms of knowledge gain and analytical and critical thinking skills compared to those in traditional settings. The study also highlighted gender differences, with male students reporting higher satisfaction levels but also experiencing more issues with the VR equipment, such as its weight and associated nausea. These findings suggest that VR not only enhances educational outcomes but also requires careful consideration of user experience to maximize its benefits (Ibrahim et al. 2021).

In contrast to the technological advancements in VR, the culture of letterpress printing in art and design education presents a different yet equally valuable perspective. A study (Gridneff et al. 2021) on letterpress workshops in the UK and Ireland over the past four years examined the historical and contemporary significance of this traditional printing technique. The research involved a collaborative project among multiple colleges and a systematic survey of letterpress workshops since 1955. The findings highlight the evolving role of letterpress in education, emphasizing its enduring value and the shift towards more immersive and collaborative learning experiences. This exploration of letterpress culture underscores the importance of preserving traditional methods while integrating innovative approaches in educational practices (Gridneff et al. 2021).

Collectively, these studies illustrate the diverse applications and benefits of immersive technologies and traditional methods in education. While VR offers transformative opportunities in fields like architectural education, enhancing learning through interactive and immersive experiences, the enduring relevance of traditional techniques like letterpress printing provides a rich, historical context that continues to influence modern educational practices. Understanding the interplay between these approaches can inform the development of more holistic and effective educational strategies that cater to varied learning preferences and needs.

RESEARCH QUESTIONS

Examining traditional letterpress atelier and immersive VR simulator environments (where environment refers to the combination of physical space and training method);

- **RQ1:** What is the impact of real-world and VR workshops on cognitive load of students during training, and what are the potential explanations for this?
- **RQ2:** What differences are observed between the real-world and VR workshops in terms of usability?

- **RQ3:** What are the pros and cons of both learning environments according to students?

INSTRUCTIONAL FRAMEWORK

The educational simulation system we present here is a part of a broader definition called digital instructional media. According to Clark (1994), as supported with scientific evidence, media does not influence learning but is a vehicle to deliver instruction to learners. Therefore, learning gain comes from the instructional method. Here, we use the attributes of instructional media (e.g., capabilities of zoom in/out into details, capability to repeat the same process easily, etc.), in our case the simulation system, to enrich the learning environment.

The instructional methodology of this application is based on current scientific principles of instructional technology and is organized according to "elaboration theory" (Reigeluth et al. 1980). The content is structured with sequential learning episodes, each lasting two to three minutes, involving direct instruction followed by immediate practice, supported by a 'scaffolding' strategy. According to the Elaboration Theory, instruction begins with a broad overview, narrows to specific topics, and then returns to a broader scope, helping learners connect detailed information with the overall framework (Reigeluth et al. 1980).

Direct instruction is a teaching method characterized by explicit, structured, and teacher-centered strategies, where the teacher provides clear explanations of the content, models the desired skills or knowledge, and leads students through guided practice with feedback (Rosenshine 2012). Complementing this approach is the scaffolding technique (Ninio and Bruner 1978), in which an expert offers support to a novice as needed during the learning process. As the novice gains experience and confidence, the expert gradually reduces the level of assistance (a process known as the guidance fading effect), eventually allowing the learner to work independently.

The direct instruction portion of each learning episode lasts 2–3 minutes, aligning with cognitive load theory (Sweller 1988). This theory suggests that working memory, responsible for processing new information, is limited to handling 3–7 chunks at a time, and this capacity diminishes with mental fatigue. If learning episodes exceed this duration, learners may experience cognitive overload, and if too much information is presented, some may be lost from working memory to make room for new data (Paas and Van Merriënboer 1994, Sweller et al. 2019). Therefore, keeping learning episodes within this time frame helps prevent fatigue and optimizes information retention.

METHOD

Given the three proposed research questions, a within-subjects design was employed with students enrolled in the Letterpress Printing course ($n = 8$). This is because this team of students specialized in manual typesetting and hand-press printing was asked to test the newly developed printing simulator and provide feedback on its usability, its effects on instruction, and at which stage of the teaching process it could be used. Since this elective course was available to students from various semesters, participants ranged from the third to the seventh semester. The study was conducted at the 14th week of the course. Multiple sets of data were collected in alignment with the research questions. Overall research design flowchart is provided in Figure 4.1.

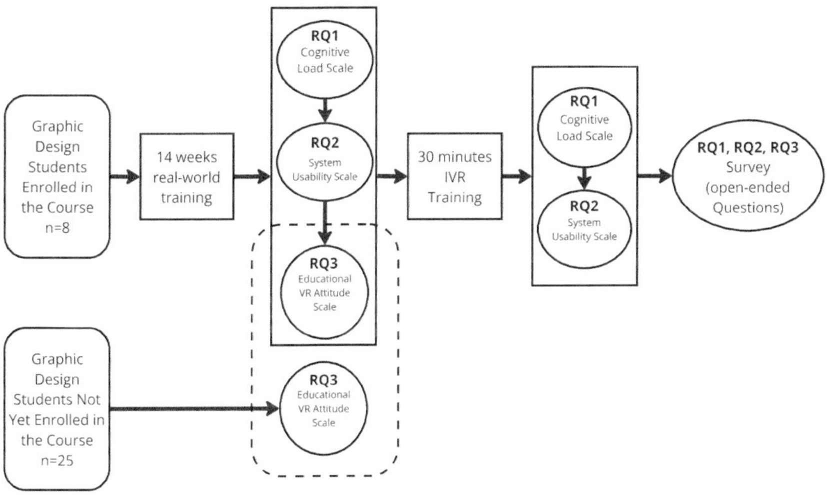

Figure 4.1 Flowchart of the research design for examining real-world and VR workshops.

The research design for RQ1 involves measuring the cognitive loads of students focusing on the training process after 14 weeks of real-world workshop training and measuring the cognitive loads of same students focusing on the training process just after training in IVR environment using the Cognitive Load Scale (Paas and Van Merriënboer 1994) adapted into Turkish (Kılıç and Karadeniz 2004). In addition to the cognitive load scale, students were also asked which training they found more challenging and the reasons for this with open-ended questions.

The research design for RQ2 involves measuring and comparing the perceived usability scores of real-world letterpress printing process and the same process in IVR simulator. System Usability Scale (SUS) (Brooke 1996)

Figure 4.4 Overall view of VR workshop.

LAYER 1: LEARNING HOW TO USE LETTERPRESS WORKSHOP

The first episode serves as a comprehensive introduction to the following four episodes. As explained by Reigeluth et al. (1980) in his elaboration theory of instruction, the goal at this stage is to form a basic level of knowledge network in the student's mind about what they will learn shortly. This foundational knowledge network also determines the relationships between the detailed information to be learned in subsequent episodes. The detailed information elaborated in later episodes will be integrated into the network initially formed in the first episode.

The second episode (Figure 4.5) is the verbal description of the basic components of a metal type (or sort, which is a metal or wooden block with a typographic character etched on: it) using a virtual type object scaled up tens of times. The aim of this episode is to teach learners: (i) the essential components of a metal type; (ii) the correct use of professional terminology; and (iii) how to closely observe a metal type, guiding learners to notice details that might otherwise be overlooked, given that a metal type is typically no larger than 1–2 cm in the real world. Additionally, this episode introduces two essential tools used in typesetting, the "composing stick" and 'tweezer', to the learners.

In the third episode (Figure 4.6), cabinets that house collections of font drawers, and the differences between a font and a typeface are explained verbally and demonstrated with examples. The aim of this episode involves the student learning the relationships between the letter case, cabinet, font, typeface, and font family. At the end of the episode, as the student will begin typesetting in the next episode, they pick up a 'tweezer' in their right hand and a "composing stick" in their left hand.

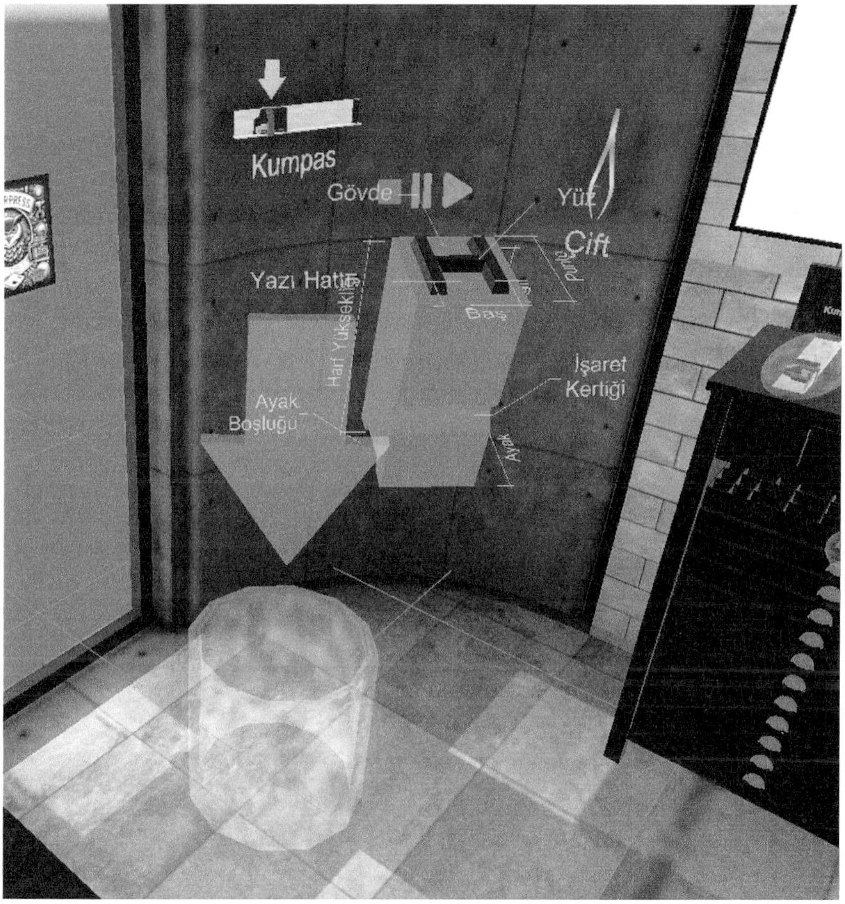

Figure 4.5 Metal type instruction station.

The fourth episode (Figure 4.7) consists of a verbal explanation followed by a practical section. The verbal explanation provides information about the letter case (one of the cabinet's drawers). It explains the origins of the terms UpperCase and LowerCase. The example case is organized according to the Turkish alphabet, with the placement of letters within the case determined by their frequency of use in Turkish. At the end of the verbal explanation, the student is asked to set the virtual types forming a given sentence using a tweezer, selecting letters from the virtual letter case before them, and placing them into the composing stick (see video in Appendix). The student chooses each

Figure 4.6 Left–Detail of the font cabinet. Right–Font cabinet in the simulator.

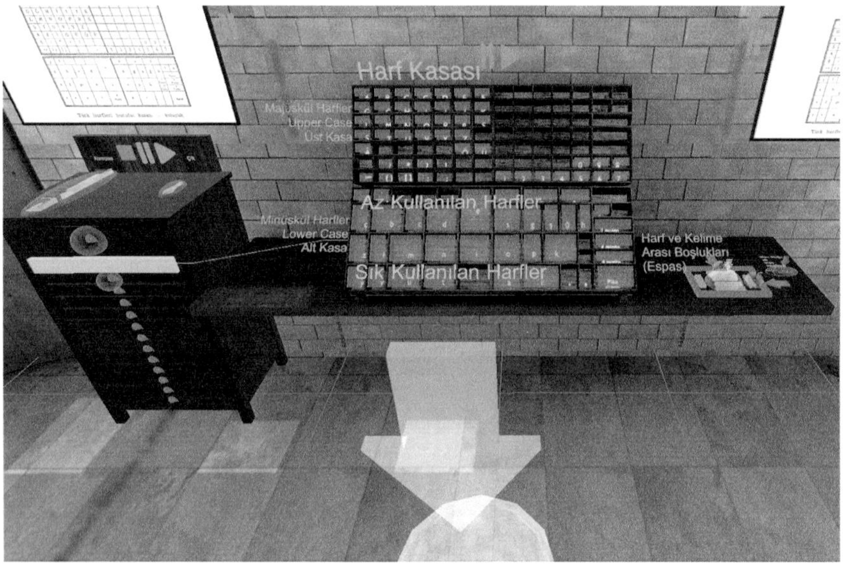

Figure 4.7 Type cases.

letter by touching the tip of the virtual tweezer to the interactive surface above each type in the case and pressing the trigger on the control stick. The selected type automatically arranges itself in the composing stick. Once the typesetting is complete, the student is verbally directed by the voice-over on what to do next. The student transfers the arranged types to the table by touching the composing stick to an empty chase object on the table and pressing the trigger of the hand controller. Each step is verbally instructed by the voice-over, including taking the quoin block and the quoin key from the table, fitting it into the chase, and locking the mold. This completes the typesetting process.

The fifth and final episode (Figure 4.8) is entirely interactive (see video in Appendix). It involves the student carrying out the steps from mounting the prepared chase from the previous episode onto the manual letterpress to the actual printing on virtual paper. In this episode, after each step is successfully completed, the voice-over guides the student on what to do next and why it is necessary to proceed in that manner. The steps include: (i) mounting the chase onto the manual letterpress; (ii) applying ink to the press's ink plate; (iii) evenly distributing the ink across the plate; (iv) loading paper into the letterpress; (v) completing the final printing. Completing this episode successfully allows the student to experience the entire printing process from start to finish.

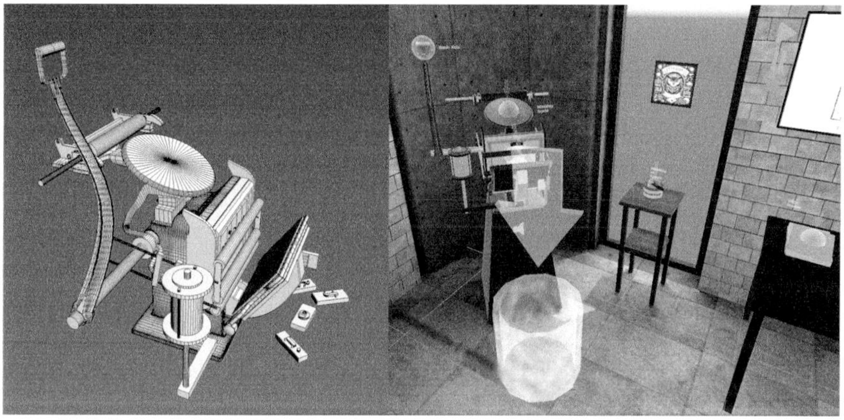

Figure 4.8 Left—Detail of the hand press. Right—Hand press in the simulator.

If a student is experiencing this training for the first time, the explanations are longer and more detailed. In subsequent repetitions, the explanations become shorter, consisting only of brief instructions about the sequence of tasks to be performed. As the student becomes more proficient, they can completely turn off the explanations and work independently, finding their own way. This gradual transition of responsibility fosters a sense of empowerment and independence in the students, enhancing their learning experience.

LAYER 2: AUDIO SUPPORTED EXHIBITION

The virtual workshop also displays images on its virtual walls representing significant individuals, technologies, and events in Turkish and world printing history. Each image has optional audio descriptions lasting 1–3 minutes. The texts in these audio descriptions are also available in written form on the website and in the PDF documents described in Layer 4.

LAYER 3: VIDEOS

In the virtual workshop, there are a total of 10 videos that play on surfaces resembling monitors mounted on the walls of the virtual workshop. One can access the same videos via the website and YouTube channel described in Layer 4, and even through QR codes in printable PDF booklets. According to Clark (1994), there is no difference in learning outcomes between a video playing on a real-world screen and playing on a virtual screen in a virtual environment. Furthermore, the virtual environment and headsets can create an extraneous load on students' working memory, hindering their ability to follow videos comfortably in the virtual environment. The purpose of making videos accessible in the virtual environment is to provide an additional opportunity for students to access this resource. Even if they may not choose to watch the entire video in the virtual environment, they can be aware that a knowledge source is available in the PDF document or website. This access to additional resources ensures that students feel supported and well-equipped in their learning journey, enhancing their learning experience.

LAYER 4: WEBSITE

The IVR environment naturally facilitates the easy repetition of the training sessions, making it a successful and effective training environment for procedural and hands-on tasks. The learning outcomes targeted by the audio-supported exhibition (Layer 2) and videos (Layer 3), which were secondary outputs aimed at enhancing the student's general knowledge about the subject, contain an overwhelming amount of information when all viewed together, exceeding the capacity of the student's working memory. Considering that the devices and interfaces inevitably used in the VR environment also impose an extraneous load on the working memory, it is not feasible to acquire enough time and repetition for this amount of information to be experienced in VR and transferred to long-term memory. In this context, a website and a YouTube channel (see Appendix) have been created to allow students access to the same information anytime in an environment that imposes less extraneous load. Thus, students can encounter all the information they experienced during the VR sessions again on both YouTube and the website, allowing them to study at their own pace for extended periods.

RESULTS AND DISCUSSION

The discussion of the results provides a detailed insight into the usability of both the real-world and VR environments, highlighting cognitive load and student attitudes toward VR technology. In light of the following findings, the first research question (RQ1) investigates whether there is a significant difference in cognitive load between the real-world workshop and the VR simulator.

A Wilcoxon signed-rank test was conducted to compare the cognitive loads of the real-world workshop group and the VR simulator group. There was no statistically significant difference between the median cognitive loads of the real-world workshop group (Mdn = 5) and the VR simulator group (Mdn = 3), $T = 6.0$, $p = .339$.

The lack of a significant difference in the cognitive loads experienced by the two groups can be explained in several ways. First, the study was conducted in the 14th and final week of the course. By that time, students had become accustomed to and automatized the letterpress printing process. It can be assumed that higher cognitive loads occurred during the earlier weeks of the course, when students were newly introduced to the printing system, but decreased as their knowledge and experience with the process increased. Previous research (Sweller et al. 2019) suggests that as learners engage with and become familiar with new knowledge, it becomes automatic, and the cognitive load it imposes on working memory decreases. Additionally, most students had no prior experience with an IVR system. It is expected that they would experience a high extraneous cognitive load while adapting to a system they encountered for the first time. Furthermore, the IVR simulator is a constrained environment, limited by the capabilities of the headset, controllers, and the application itself. Students may perceive the inability to perform familiar real-world tasks as easily as they would in reality as a cognitive load. This could be due to the structured and guided nature of virtual simulations, which can help users focus on specific tasks without the distractions or unpredictability often present in real-world environments. The responses students provided in the survey also support this result. Their limited prior experience with VR and their inability to perform everything they wanted in the VR environment were reported as disadvantages by the students (Table 4.2). All these factors can be considered confounding variables in the study and could be explored further in detail. However, at this stage, planning a controlled experiment to eliminate these confounds is beyond the scope of the current study.

Having explored the cognitive load differences in RQ1, the second research question (RQ2) shifts focus to the perceived usability differences between the real-world and VR workshops. It first examines students' attitudes toward VR, considering that these attitudes might influence usability outcomes and qualitative analyses in RQ3. This allows the research to assess any potential biases in the results.

The attitudes of the students taking the course towards VR could affect both their SUS (Demirkol and Şeneler 2018) responses and the results of other qualitative analyses, potentially introducing bias. To determine whether the students taking the course constitute a distinct group compared to the remaining students in the graphic design program, the VR Attitude Scale (Karaoğlan-Yılmaz et al. 2023) was administered to both the students enrolled in the course (experiment group n = 8) and those who had not yet taken the course but were expected to do so within the next 2–3 semesters (control group n = 25). A Mann-Whitney U test was conducted to determine whether there were differences in scores between the experimental group and the control group. The median score was not significantly different between the experimental group (Mdn = 3.444) and the control group (Mdn = 3.777), U = 97.5, z = –0.084, p = 0.932, using an exact sampling distribution for U. Therefore, it can be concluded that the students taking the course are not different than those who had not taken the course yet regarding to their attitude towards using VR in education. The VR Attitude Scale (Karaoğlan-Yılmaz et al. 2023) is a 5-point Likert-type scale, where values above 2.5 indicate a positive attitude of the students towards the subject. In this context, the values of 3.444 and 3.777 suggest that graphic design students have a slightly positive attitude towards the use of VR in education.

Since the students enrolled in the course do not differ from other graphic design students in terms of their attitudes toward VR, the usability of both the workshop and the VR simulator can now be evaluated and compared. The SUS (Demirkol and Şeneler 2018) was used to measure the perceived usability of the existing real-world letterpress process during the 14th and final week of the semester. Students were clearly informed that they were assessing the usability of the typesetting and hand-press process, not the course itself. After administering the SUS, the same group of students experienced the VR simulator. Immediately following their experience with the letterpress workshop in the IVR environment, the SUS was administered again, and the results were compared. Therefore, the data reflects the outcome of the students' 14-week experience with the traditional typesetting and hand-press process, as opposed to the scale applied immediately after the typesetting and hand-press process in IVR experience. Unlike the instruction period in the IVR environment, students typically do not experience the real-world letterpress workshop in a single workshop session.

A Wilcoxon signed-rank test was conducted to determine whether there were differences in scores of SUS values of real-world workshop and SUS values of IVR Simulator. The results indicated that the median scores for SUS real-world workshop (Mdn = 57.5) and SUS VR (M = 71.25) were significantly different, T = 1.5, p = .016. This significant difference suggests that users found the virtual reality simulator to be more usable compared to the real-world workshop.

The higher SUS scores for the VR simulator may be attributed to the immersive and interactive nature of virtual environments, which tend to offer more intuitive and user-friendly interactions. Additionally, the VR simulator provides a controlled and consistent environment, reducing variability and potentially improving usability scores. Specifically, the VR workshop contained fewer objects in terms of spatial complexity, and interactions with the environment and objects unrelated to the instructional goals were significantly limited. Furthermore, the real-world hand-press equipment requires much more time and effort to prepare for printing, as it involves numerous adjustments that directly affect the quality of the printed material. Since these details were not related to the intended learning outcomes, they were omitted in the virtual version. This minimized unnecessary distractions and reduced extraneous cognitive load caused by the environment and unrelated objects. The qualitative questionnaire results support the conclusion that the details mentioned as disadvantages of the real-world workshop contribute to extraneous cognitive load on students, leading to distractions and potentially negatively affecting learning (Table 4.1). Since these details were omitted in the IVR simulator, they were not referenced in Table 4.2.

To further understand the strengths and weaknesses of both learning environments, RQ3 investigates the pros and cons of the real-world and virtual workshops from the students' perspectives. This approach not only supports and validates the quantitative data but also collects experiential insights that cannot be captured through the scales used. A survey with open-ended questions was administered to the students via Google Forms regarding their real-world letterpress workshop experience prior to the IVR experience. Immediately after the IVR session, another survey was conducted to gather feedback on the VR letterpress workshop. Students were asked to compare both experiences and indicate the advantages and disadvantages of each relative to the other.

Students generally expressed satisfaction with their real-world letterpress workshop experiences and stated that the course was beneficial to them. Their negative experiences related to the workshop can be categorized into four main areas: (i) using the equipment; (ii) metal type; (iii) maintaining the proper sequence of tasks; (iv) organizing workshop equipment and maintaining workshop order. Among the most frequently mentioned negative aspects by the students were the challenges that do not serve the course objectives, such as the need for skill to keep the hand-press operational, clean it, and make fine adjustments to the machine, as well as the difficulty of inserting and removing the heavy type cases from the cabinets (Table 4.1).

Table 4.1 Disadvantages of the real-world letterpress workshop

Using the Equipment
The handpress Settings of the machine Cleaning the equipment Distributing the ink on the plate evenly Assembling and locking up the chase (type, quoin, furniture etc.) and transferring to hand press
Metal Type (Sort)
Difficulty in seeing small type sizes Large type sizes not fitting in the composing stick Adjusting the measurements of spacers and leading Locking the type in the chase Inserting and removing the galleys in cabinets (because of weight)
Maintaining Proper Sequence of Tasks
Organizing Workshop Equipment and Maintaining Workshop Order

In the students' experiences with the virtual workshop, it is observed that positive comments outweigh negative ones. Negative comments focus on the prior experience with the VR equipment and simplified interaction with the environment which limits the capabilities of the workshop in the IVR simulator compared to the real-world workshop. These limitations increase the usability of the simulator for beginners but for experienced learners this advantage can quickly diminish because they probably want to get rid of the limitation for better creativity (Table 4.2).

In the positive comments, the most frequently emphasized point is that the virtual workshop serves as a tool capable of teaching fundamental equipment, tasks, and sequences quickly and clearly. While the real-world workshop is preferred for hands-on experience, the virtual workshop is highlighted as an effective learning environment, particularly for introductory-level training. Other positive comments mainly focus on the logistical advantages of the simulator, such as accessibility from remote locations, avoiding the waste of expensive materials for instructional purposes, and the ability to quickly detect production errors before the printing stage (Table 4.2).

Clark's (1994) position, as noted in his famous article, emphasizes that media are merely vehicles for delivering instruction and do not directly influence learning outcomes. He argued that different media (such as textbooks, television, or computers) are used for economic and logistical reasons—like cost, accessibility, and convenience—rather than because they inherently improve learning outcomes. The students' experiences with the simulator likely highlight this point, as their reflections suggest that the IVR simulator's role in this learning environment is more logistical than pedagogical.

Table 4.2 Advantages and disadvantages of IVR simulator

Advantages
The experience can be accessed from any location with a computer (PCVR version) without the need to physically go to the workshop.
There is no crowded classroom environment or waiting in line.
Initial lessons include the identification of materials, explanations on how to use them, a step-by-step guide to the processes involved in letterpress printing, and supportive instructions and guidance.
Rapid training can be provided.
Materials that are costly, fragile, perishable, or consumable in a real workshop can be used in the virtual workshop without concern.
Errors in the process that might not be detected until the printing stage in a real workshop can be quickly identified in the virtual workshop, preventing loss of time and effort.
Terminology related to the letterpress printing process can be learned much more easily. Since the information is presented in the simplest form, visually and three-dimensionally, learning becomes significantly easier.
Materials that might be difficult to examine in real life due to their size and shape can be easily examined in the virtual environment.
Disadvantages
If the user has no prior experience with VR, they may need some time to adapt.
Not everything that can be done in the real-world workshop can be performed in the virtual workshop.

CONCLUSION

This study aims to identify and preserve the materials of letterpress workshops that are disappearing, incorporate the letterpress technique into graphic design education as an elective course, and develop a VR simulator for the fundamental and distance learning of this classic technique. At the final part of the study, the cognitive load and overall usability of traditional letterpress workshop and immersive VR simulator environments was compared in the context of graphic design education. The findings from the System Usability Scale (SUS) and Cognitive Load Scale suggest that although there is no significant difference between the cognitive loads of both environments, the VR simulator provides a more user-friendly learning environment than the traditional letterpress workshop. The immersive and controlled nature of the VR environment likely contributes to its higher usability scores, offering an intuitive interface and minimizing unnecessary distractions.

Students' feedback further highlights the effectiveness of the VR simulator, particularly for introductory level training. The ability to repeatedly engage with the material, receive immediate feedback, and access the training from any location with a computer makes the VR environment a valuable educational tool. Despite some initial adaptation required for users unfamiliar with VR, the benefits, such as rapid training and the safe use of virtual materials, outweigh the disadvantages. The real-world workshop, while offering essential hands-on experience, presented several challenges unrelated to the course's educational objectives. These included the difficulty of maintaining and cleaning equipment, the complexity of fine-tuning the machines, and the physical burden of handling heavy type cases.

At this stage, we, the authors, would like to add to the students' views. Developing such a VR application requires substantial programming knowledge, effort, and time. Additionally, it is advisable to seek the guidance of an experienced team in instructional design. The development process of the application presented here, including three-dimensional modeling, instructional design, collection of instructional materials, writing of texts within a scenario, testing on students, and making necessary corrections, took approximately 500 hours.

In conclusion, the immersive VR simulator is an effective and efficient tool for teaching the fundamentals of letterpress printing, providing a clear and structured learning experience that reduces cognitive load and enhances usability. While real-world workshops remain indispensable for practical experience, the VR environment offers a complementary approach that can significantly enrich the learning process, especially for beginners.

ACKNOWLEDGEMENTS

This project was supported by Mimar Sinan Fine Arts University, Scientific Research Projects unit. Project name: Identification and Acquisition of the Extant Materials of Letterpress Printing in Turkey, and Transferring them to the Distance Education Environment by Using Current Technologies. Project Number: 2021/31.

APPENDIX

Youtube Channel of the Virtual Workshop
https://www.youtube.com/@VRLetterpressWorkshop.
Website of the Virtual Workshop
https://vrletterpress.wixsite.com/vrletterpress.

REFERENCES

Brooke, J. 1996. SUS: A quick and dirty usability. Usability Evaluation in Industry. 189(3): 189–194.

Clark, R.E. 1994. Media will never influence learning. Educational Technology Research and Development. 42(2): 21–29.

Demirkol, D. and Şeneler, Ç. 2018. A Turkish translation of the system usability scale: The SUS-TR. Uşak Üniversitesi Sosyal Bilimler Dergisi. 11: 237–253. DOI: http://dx.doi.org/10.29217/uujss.495.

Dubovi, I., Levy, S.T. and Dagan, E. 2017. Now I know how! The learning process of medication administration among nursing students with non-immersive desktop virtual reality simulation. Computers and Education. 113: 16–27. https://doi.org/10.1016/j.compedu.2017.05.009.

Gridneff, R., Cooper, A. and Haslam, A. 2021. Letterpress: A survey of print culture or an immersive learning experience. *In*: Cumulus Conference Proceedings Roma. 1681–1694.

Hsu, K.S., Jiang, J.F., Wei, H.Y. and Lee, T.H. 2016. Application of the environmental sensation learning vehicle simulation platform in virtual reality. Eurasia Journal of Mathematics, Science and Technology Education. 12(5). https://doi.org/10.12973/eurasia.2016.1525a.

Ibrahim, A., Al-Rababah, A.I. and Bani Baker, Q. 2021. Integrating virtual reality technology into architecture education: The case of architectural history courses. Open House International. 46(4): 498–509.

Jiawei, W. and Mokmin, N.A.M. 2023. Virtual reality technology in art education with visual communication design in higher education: A systematic literature review. Education and Information Technologies. 28(11): 15125–15143.

Karaoglan-Yilmaz, F.G., Yilmaz, R., Zhang, K. and Ustun, A.B. 2023. Development of educational virtual reality attitude scale: A validity and reliability study. Virtual Reality. 27(3): 1875–1885.

Kılıç, A.G.E. and Karadeniz, Ö.G.Ş. 2004. Hiper ortamlarda öğrencilerin bilişsel yüklenme ve kaybolma düzeylerinin belirlenmesi. Kuram ve Uygulamada Eğitim Yönetimi. 40(40): 562–579.

Kortum, P.T. and Bangor, A. 2013. Usability ratings for everyday products measured with the system usability scale. International Journal of Human-Computer Interaction. 29(2): 67–76.

Kortum, P. and Peres, S.C. 2015. Evaluation of home health care devices: Remote usability assessment. Journal of Medical Internet Research Human Factors. 2(1): e4570.

Lewis, J. and Sauro, J. 2009. The factor structure of the system usability scale. Human Centered Design. 94–103.

Mohsen, M.A. and Alangari, T.S. 2024. Analyzing two decades of immersive technology research in education: Trends, clusters, and future directions. Education and Information Technologies. 29(3): 3571–3587.

Ninio, A. and Bruner, J. 1978. The achievement and antecedents of labelling. Journal of Child Language. 5: 1–15.

Paas, F.G. and Van Merriënboer, J.J. 1994. Instructional control of cognitive load in the training of complex cognitive tasks. Educational Psychology Review. 6: 351–371.

Peres, S.C., Pham, T. and Phillips, R. 2013. Validation of the system usability scale (SUS) SUS in the wild. *In*: Proceedings of the Human Factors and Ergonomics Society Annual Meeting. 57(1): 192–196. SAGE Publications.

Reigeluth, C.M., Merrill, M.D., Wilson, B.G. and Spiller, R.T. 1980. The elaboration theory of instruction: A model for sequencing and synthesizing instruction. Instructional Science. 9: 195–219.

Rojas-Sánchez, M.A., Palos-Sánchez, P.R. and Folgado-Fernández, J.A. 2023. Systematic literature review and bibliometric analysis on virtual reality and education. Education and Information Technologies. 28(1): 155–192.

Rosenshine, B. 2012. Principles of instruction: Research-based strategies that all teachers should know. American Educator. 36(1): 12.

Sweller, J. 1988. Cognitive load during problem solving: Effects on learning. Cognitive Science. 12(2): 257–285.

Sweller, J., van Merriënboer, J.J. and Paas, F. 2019. Cognitive architecture and instructional design: 20 years later. Educational Psychology Review. 31(2): 261–292.

Şahbaz, E. 2020. VR-based interactive learning in architectural education: A case on Safranbolu Historical Bathhouse. ICONARP International Journal of Architecture and Planning. 8(1): 342–356.

Tullis, T.S. and Stetson, J.N. 2004. A comparison of questionnaires for assessing website usability. *In*: Usability Professional Association Conference. 1: 1–12.

Vélaz, Y., Rodríguez Arce, J., Gutiérrez, T., Lozano-Rodero, A. and Suescun, A. 2014. The influence of interaction technology on the learning of assembly tasks using virtual reality. Journal of Computing and Information Science in Engineering. 14(4). https://doi.org/10.1115/1.4028588.

Yerden, A. and Akkus, N. 2020. Virtual reality remote access laboratory for teaching programmable logic controller topics. International Journal of Engineering Education. 36(5).

Chapter **5**

A Survey of the Use of Extended Reality and Spatial Computing in the Aviation Industry

Sercan Şengün*[1] and Melike Bezgin[2]
[1]Games and Interactive Media, Nicholson School of Communication and Media, University of Central Florida, Orlando, FL, USA
Email: sercan.sengun@ucf.edu
[2]Born Immersive, London, UK. Email: melike@born.net

INTRODUCTION

It is predicted that there will be a 20% increase in demand for personal aviation and air transport services over the next 20 years, exacerbating the current workforce and training shortage issues in the industry (Van Benthem and Herdman 2021), as well as the need for more secure and profitable operations. Accordingly, like many industries, the aviation industry is also looking into solutions involving emerging and developing technologies. The extended reality (XR)[1] market in aviation

1 In this chapter, we use the term XR (Extended Reality) as an umbrella term for the technologies related to Virtual Reality (VR), Augmented Reality (AR), Mixed Reality (MR), and spatial computing. While we recognize the nuance between such technologies and content created for them, we already see some of the terms being used together and/or interchangeably in the surveyed research.

*For Correspondence: sercan.sengun@ucf.edu

DOI: 10.1201/9781003581642-5

is projected to grow roughly 17.5 times, from $78 million in 2019 to $1.365 billion by 2025 (Globalnewswire 2019). Contrary to the belief that XR technologies reduce costs by 2–5% for aviation companies, they actually offer measurable savings ranging from 25–90% (Eschen et al. 2018). Moreover, aviation companies implementing XR training practices report reduced error rates and nearly a 50% improvement in security issues (Zamkovoi et al. 2019).

Accordingly, we perform a systematic meta-study of academic research that investigates the incorporation of XR technologies into the aviation industry. We provide summaries and statistics of highlighted research as well as distill and list key findings out of them. We also highlight the key reasons why using XR can become transformative for the aviation industry citing industry facts and figures, such as insights into maintenance factors, error rates, fast training times, etc. We prioritize research with participants from the industry; however, we also include theoretical, and proof-of-concept works when possible.

METHODOLOGY

The meta- study survey mobilized UCF Library's[2] Primo VE search access. The search was limited to studies from 2016 onward that are in English and available as peer-reviewed journal article, conference proceeding article, book, or book chapter. The year 2016 was selected as it marks the release of popular commercial tethered and untethered visual reality (VR) headsets. Despite Razer OSVR HDK and Samsung Gear VR being released in November 2015, the year 2016 marks the major releases such as Oculus Rift, HTC Vive, PlayStation VR, Pico VR, Microsoft Hololens, and more. The search string was:

("aviation") AND ("virtual reality" OR "augmented reality" OR "mixed reality" OR "spatial computing")

The search yielded 371 results.[3] After eliminating other meta studies and false positive results, we were left with 103 studies, all of which were manually analyzed, coded, and categorized based on their industry field, methodology, technology focus, and participant involvement.

SURVEY RESULTS

The survey results were manually analyzed and were first coded into five categories based on the specific aviation field they target, then into another five categories based on their methodologies (Table 5.1).

2 https://library.ucf.edu/.

3 As of June 2024.

Table 5.1 The results of the survey

Aviation Field	Methodology	Authors	Technology	Participants
MRO	System design, development, and testing	Jonaid et al. 2023	VR	N/A
		Gómez-Cambronero et al. 2023	VR	22 engineering students
		Li 2023	VR	N/A
		Wu and Vu 2022	VR	N/A
		Lee et al. 2022	VR	N/A
		Siyaev and Jo 2021	MR	N/A
		Bortsova and Panfilov 2021	XR	N/A
		Matos et al. 2019	VR	N/A
		Hong and Wenhua 2017	AR	N/A
	User study	Xue et al. 2024	AR	30 engineering students
		Key et al. 2022	AR	4 technicians
		Wu and Hung 2022	MR	25 engineering students
		Bernard et al. 2022	VR	112 students
		Bernard et al. 2020	VR/digital twins	6 maintenance operators
		Bernard et al. 2019	VR/digital twins	6 maintenance operators
	User study (comparative)	Wang et al. 2024	MR	120 technicians
	Theory/ overview	Macchiarella et al. 2023	AR	N/A
		Yang et al. 2023	XR	N/A
		Ainakulov et al. 2022	VR	N/A
		Van Vooren 2019	VR	N/A
		Gilbert 2016	AR	N/A
	Perceptions research	Wang et al. 2016	AR	41 aviation students
Pilot training	System design, development, and testing	Wang et al. 2023	AR	N/A
		Auer et al. 2023	VR	24 pilot students

(Table 5.1 *Contd.*)

(Table 5.1 *Contd.*)

Aviation Field	Methodology	Authors	Technology	Participants
		Sonnenfeld et al. 2023	VR	N/A
		Erickson et al. 2023	VR	6 pilots
		Reyes et al. 2023	VR	20 pilots
		Rostami et al. 2023	VR	N/A
		Thomas et al. 2023	VR	215 pilot students
		Reddy et al. 2022	VR	6 pilot students
		Reyes et al. 2022	VR	N/A
		Pradhan et al. 2022	VR	19 pilot students
		Livatino et al. 2022	VR	N/A
		Wu and Kuo 2022	VR	N/A
		Dymora et al. 2021	VR	17 pilot students
		Irvin et al. 2021	VR	N/A
		Alce et al. 2020	AR	N/A
		Peysakhovich et al. 2020	VR	10 pilot students
	User study	Ayala et al. 2024	AR/eye tracking	20 pilots
		Cross et al. 2023	VR	52 pilot students
		Fussell 2023	VR	10 pilot students
		Harris et al. 2023	VR	18 pilot students
		Pejemsky et al. 2021	VR	46 pilot students
		Labedan et al. 2023	VR	10 pilots
		Labedan et al. 2021	VR	4 pilots
		Hight et al. 2022	VR	17 pilots
		Moesl et al. 2021	AR	43 pilots
		Coleman and Thirtyacre 2021	AR	16 pilots

Aviation Field	Methodology	Authors	Technology	Participants
		Andrievskaia et al. 2020	XR	47 pilots
		Oberhauser et al. 2018	VR	28 pilots
		Thomas et al. 2021	VR	30 pilot students
	User study (comparative)	Ziccardi et al. 2024	XR	30 pilots
		Newton et al. 2023	XR	24 pilots
		Moesl et al. 2023a	AR	59 pilot students
		Guthridge and Clinton-Lisell 2023	VR	120 pilot students
		Zhang et al. 2023	VR	118 pilots
		Ke et al. 2023	VR/eye tracking	46 pilots
		Carr et al. 2023	VR	45 untrained participants
	Interview and focus groups	Kim et al. 2024	AR	17 instructors
		Blundell and Harris 2023	AR	11 pilots
		Oh et al. 2021	MR	6 pilots
	Perceptions research	Fussell and Truong 2023	VR	310 pilot students
		Moesl et al. 2022	AR	31 pilots, 22 instructors
		Schaffernak et al. 2020	AR	60 pilots and instructors
		Audu et al. 2021	VR	47 pilots
		Fussell and Truong 2020	VR	1636 pilot students
		Luisier et al. 2019	VR	3 pilot students
	Theory/ overview	Morrison et al. 2023	XR	N/A
		Valentin and Choi 2023	XR	N/A
		Akselrad 2023	AR	N/A
		Pechlivanis et al. 2023	XR	N/A
		Newton 2022	XR	N/A
		Biggs et al. 2018	AR	N/A

(Table 5.1 *Contd.*)

(Table 5.1 *Contd.*)

Aviation Field	Methodology	Authors	Technology	Participants
Design and manufacturing	System design, development, and testing	Tavares et al. 2024	XR/digital twin	N/A
		Zhang et al. 2024	XR/digital twin	N/A
		Guo et al. 2022	MR	10 pilots
		Guo et al. 2023	VR	N/A
		Yevtodyeva 2020	AR	N/A
		de Crescenzio et al. 2019	VR	N/A
		Fuchs et al. 2021	VR	N/A
		Walther et al. 2021	VR	N/A
Air traffic and emergency	System design, development, and testing	Tan et al. 2023	AR	N/A
		Moruzzi et al. 2023	XR	N/A
		Moesl et al. 2023b	AR	59 air control trainees
		Shah et al. 2019	AR	N/A
		Liu et al. 2023	AR	N/A
		Xue et al. 2023	XR	N/A
		Conde et al. 2022	XR/digital twins	N/A
		Han et al. 2019	MR/ hologram	N/A
		Zhuo 2023	VR	N/A
		Zou 2022	VR	N/A
	User study	Crutchfield et al. 2022	VR	15 air controllers
		Truschzinski et al. 2017	VR	25 untrained participants
	Interview and focus groups	Hagl et al. 2018	AR	7 air controllers
		Meister et al. 2022	AR	6 instructors
		Updegrove and Jafer 2017	VR	4 air controllers
Passenger services	System design, development, and testing	Mohd et al. 2022	AR	N/A

Aviation Field	Methodology	Authors	Technology	Participants
	User study	Buttussi and Chittaro 2017	VR	96 potential passengers
		Buttussi and Chittaro 2020	VR	72 potential passengers
		Chittaro et al. 2018	VR	68 potential passengers
	Perceptions research	Williamson et al. 2019	VR	80 potential passengers
	Theory/ overview	Jiang et al. 2023	MR	N/A
		Taneja 2019	XR	N/A

The research methodologies focused on system design, development, and testing (*n* = 44; 42.7%), user studies (*n* = 32; 31.1%), interviews and focus groups (*n* = 6; 5.8%), perceptions research (*n* = 8; 7.8%), and theory building and overviews (*n* = 13; 12.6%).

- **System design, development and testing:** This methodology category encapsulates the research based on design and development of applications, approaches, and curricula for using XR technologies in aviation. In some cases, the research was coupled with testing of the outcome with pilot groups.
- **User studies:** This methodology category involves testing existing software, hardware, and surveys with users, and the analyses of the results. We marked user studies that are comparative (between-subjects) versus within-subjects.
- **Interviews and focus groups:** The work in this methodology category held interviews or focus groups with small participant sizes to elicit insights on how XR technologies can be integrated into the aviation industry.
- **Perceptions research:** Like the previous interviews and focus group category, the work in this methodology mobilized surveys on large-scale populations to elicit perceptions of how XR technologies can be integrated into the aviation industry.
- **Theory/overview:** This methodology category collected research that engaged in building theory from or an overview of the existing practices and their potential enhancements with XR technologies.

We also noted if they mobilized a specific XR technology and the number and roles of their participants. The research focused on the following technologies: VR (*n* = 55; 53.4%), MR (*n* = 7; 6.8%), AR (*n* = 26; 25.2%), and XR (including spatial computing; *n* = 15; 14.6%). Additionally, we found two research studies including eye tracking, five including digital twins, and one including holograms.

The aggregated study participants from 57 out of 103 research totaled to 4049 participants outlined in Table 5.2.

Table 5.2 Aggregated numbers of study participants from our dataset

Participant Type	#
Pilots (licensed)	574
Pilot students	2732
Pilot instructors	59
MRO staff (technicians, operators, etc.)	136
MRO students	77
Air controllers	26
Air controller students	59
Potential passengers	316
Other (untrained participants)	70

The five fields that XR technologies were offered to be used in aviation were: (1) maintenance, repair, and overhaul (MRO) operations ($n = 22$; 21.4%); (2) passenger services ($n = 7$; 6.8%); (3) air traffic control and aviation emergency training ($n = 15$; 14.5%); (4) design and manufacturing in aviation ($n = 8$; 7.8%); and (5) pilot training ($n = 51$; 49.5%).

MAINTENANCE, REPAIR, AND OVERHAUL (MRO)

The aviation industry has noted that maintenance is a contributing factor in 14–21% of helicopter accidents and 12% of plane accidents (Bernard et al. 2022). Accordingly, the industry needs employees who perform tasks more accurately to increase safety, but also faster to decrease cost. Since employees trained with XR technologies in other fields are reported to demonstrate an increase in task completion speed (see Koutitas et al. 2021 who reports a 29% increase for EMS first responders), such efficiency cannot be ignored.

Our survey highlights several other key findings regarding the effectiveness and future potential of utilizing advanced training methods for high-cost, dangerous, and time- and effort-intensive tasks in aviation. These methods offer a practical alternative to traditional training approaches, providing disseminable and quantifiable training that are both accessible and measurable. Empirical evidence supports a verified increase in knowledge acquisition and retention among trainees, along with a significant improvement in problem-solving skills. The results underscore the undeniable importance of XR training methods, positioning them as essential components in the future of Maintenance, Repair, and Overhaul (MRO) operations in aviation.

For example, Eschen et al. (2018) suggest that the "time and effort for the interaction between the data basis and the worker" is the optimal measure for evaluating the general potential of MR support systems. Ainakulov et al. (2022) develop a risk analysis algorithm for virtual training of aircraft maintenance professionals, based on the International Standard ISO 31000 "Risk Management–Guidance". This algorithm, tested and verified on a VR version of Joint-Stock Company Aircraft Repair Plant No. 405 training, addresses scenarios that are too costly, dangerous, or time-consuming to practice in real life. Wu and Kuo (2022) created a VR application to train students in maintaining a Dornier 228-212 aircraft and are planning its integration into the curriculum of the Aviation Maintenance Training Center at National Formosa University. Wang, Anne, and Rope (2016) conducted a survey involving 41 participants with at least two years of theoretical and practical experience in aircraft system maintenance in an educational setting. They find that both ease of use and usefulness of augmented reality (AR) technology directly and indirectly influence the intention to use it in maintenance education. Lee, Woo, and Yu (2022) developed a multi-use aircraft maintenance virtual reality (VR) training module and conducted a comparative study with 40 participants. Half of the participants use the VR training module while the other half rely solely on video training. The study reveals that the VR group scores significantly higher in knowledge acquisition and retention in technical training than the video group. Bernard et al. (2019) developed a VR training tool for helicopter maintenance and tested its effectiveness with six operators chosen according to the standard NF EN ISO 15537. They suggested that incorporating haptics and physical parts can enhance VR training tools.

Van Vooren (2019) argues that the MRO sector, with around 50% of its workforce over 50 years old in certain European countries, must adopt VR training to attract younger aviation mechanics and ensure the sector's continuity. In a subsequent study, Bernard et al. (2022) observed 112 aviation maintenance students over two years as they used VR for learning and training. They concluded that prior VR experience enriches learning; simulations can be enhanced by adding physical elements to better synchronize virtual and real worlds; and that incorporating both VR and AR is essential in aviation maintenance training.

PASSENGER SERVICES

The survey identifies that engaging safety training methods, particularly immersive evacuation and emergency drills, have shown significant promise in enhancing participant engagement and effectiveness. The research points to the leadership role of smartphone-based AR applications in this domain, demonstrating their capacity to provide accessible and impactful training experiences. Furthermore, the social acceptability of VR as a training tool is projected to rise substantially in the coming years, indicating a broader acceptance and integration of these technologies into standard safety training protocols.

In our data, Chittora et al. (2018) created a mobile AR application to educate passengers about airline safety. In their between-group study, they observed a statistically significant increase in engagement, instructional simplicity, self-efficacy, real-world performance in time, and a reduction in errors for the group using the app. Buttussi and Chittora (2017) designed a serious game that simulates potential safety scenarios inside an aircraft that they expanded in 2020. In their user studies, they found that both the VR headset and AR smartphone apps had similar effects on knowledge gain, retention, and confidence. However, they noted that VR also enhanced trainees' engagement, satisfaction, and presence. Williamson, McGill, and Outram (2019) surveyed 80 participants about the social acceptability and usability of VR for in-flight entertainment. They suggested three design strategies to improve VR apps for in-flight entertainment: maintaining awareness of surroundings, minimizing extensive head or hand movements, and designing apps to support interruptions.

AIR TRAFFIC CONTROL AND AVIATION EMERGENCY TRAINING

Our data emphasizes collision avoidance, airport visual management, and accident investigation and prevention as the highlights of this field. These areas have demonstrated substantial benefits from advanced training techniques. Additionally, the research underscores the importance of high-fidelity design guidelines in developing these training programs. High-fidelity simulations ensure a realistic and immersive experience, which is crucial for effective learning and skill acquisition in these critical areas.

As examples, Updegrove and Jafer (2017) conducted extensive interviews with 13 air-control professionals and industry vendors from the Federal Aviation Administration (FAA) Academy's Air Traffic Control (ATC) training program to explore the potential expansion through new technologies. They highlighted the potential of VR, cloud-based trainers, and voice recognition and synthesizing in reducing training costs and time, while emphasizing the ongoing importance of desktop simulators. Additionally, there is an intention to transition from low- and medium-fidelity simulations to high-fidelity ones. Moesl et al. (2023) carried out a comparative study involving 59 participants divided into two groups for Collision Avoidance Training, using AR and a generic physical simulator. The results indicated that the AR training group demonstrated significantly better scanning patterns than the control group. Zhuo (2023) introduced a VR app designed for civil aviation airport visual management. The study concluded that this system offers a more vivid experience than traditional intelligent civil aviation airport management systems, eliminating dead ends. It provides superior visualization technology compared to traditional two-dimensional abstract research, enhancing the simulation research of efficiency, safety, and capacity in various airport areas.

DESIGN AND MANUFACTURING IN AVIATION

Previous research indicates that 70% of product lifecycle costs are determined during the design phase (Stapelberg 2009), and XR technologies can have evident impact at this phase. For example, in 1994, General Motors Company in Detroit established a virtual reality center costing $5 million, which has since saved $80 million in the design of new cars (Neretin et al. 2021). This technology has eliminated the need for creating preliminary clay models, wind tunnel testing of full-scale models, and several crash tests, as these are now conducted in a virtual space using electronic models. Similarly, in the operations and maintenance of industrial products, the use of XR digital twins has reduced the time required to author operations from 96 minutes to 51 minutes, a 53% decrease (Vincent et al. 2017).

The survey findings identify the most effective applications of cabin, cockpit, and flight deck design, as well as preliminary aircraft design processes. These areas benefit significantly from the integration of innovative design guidelines. Key among these guidelines are heads-up displays (HUDs) that enhance communication across design teams and optimize information processing. By improving real-time information sharing and processing, HUDs facilitate more efficient and cohesive design workflows, ultimately leading to superior design outcomes in both cabin and cockpit environments, as well as during the initial stages of aircraft development.

Particularly, Fuchs et al. (2021) presented a design methodology for testing conceptual cabin designs using VR. They found that VR technology allows for cost-effective iteration, evaluation, and optimization of various new cabin designs before validating the concepts with a physical prototype. Neretin et al. (2021) developed a VR application to evaluate the ergonomics of the MS-21 aircraft pilot cabin and concluded that integrating VR/AR technologies into the design processes is essential. Walther et al. (2021) developed an interface capable of deriving detailed 3D geometry of the fuselage and cabin, which aids in expediting the preliminary aircraft and cabin design processes.

PILOT TRAINING

In an XR-enabled military aviation training program, 13 out of 20 pilots graduated in half the time compared to traditional training methods (Lewis and Livingston 2018). This type of training speed is of high interest to commercial aviation, both for flight and ground staff. The aggregated results from our identified research pool highlight the most effective training subjects in aviation as pilot pre-flight inspections, pilot emergency procedures, and screening pilots for elevated risk. Key design guidelines for these training programs include eliminating extra effort to start the training, as well as mobilizing eye-tracking and other telemetry data. Perceptions about XR pilot training indicate that users typically do not have health concerns regarding VR, AR, and spatial computing technologies, a finding supported by observations of low symptoms.

Other significant highlights reveal that VR consistently provides elevated enjoyment and a sense of presence. Virtual trainings are shown to result in higher self-efficacy and knowledge retention, particularly valuable for introductory training sessions. Moreover, these virtual trainings do not hinder student mastery compared to real-life training, demonstrating their effectiveness and value in aviation training programs.

Here we particularly want to highlight the studies of Schaffernak et al. (2020), Moesl et al. (2021), Fussell (2023), and Fussell and Truong (2020) who surveyed a total of 636 pilot students and flight instructors based on their perception of effectiveness of XR technologies use in pilot training and reported positive results. As examples of development, Dymora et al. (2021), Van Benthem and Herdman (2021), Thomas et al. (2021), and Oberhauser and Dreyer (2017) all developed VR training applications for pilots and pilot trainees and tested them with commercial pilots and pilot students. Their results indicate high self-efficacy and low discomfort during XR enhanced training processes.

DISCUSSION AND RESULTS

We identify five main categories of incorporating XR technologies into the aviation industry: (1) maintenance, repair, and overhaul (MRO) operations; (2) passenger services; (3) air traffic control and aviation emergency training; (4) design and manufacturing in aviation; and (5) pilot training.

In MRO, XR technologies offer various ways to streamline tasks. Technicians can access real-time data, schematics, and step-by-step instructions through AR headsets, reducing error rates and increasing efficiency. VR can enable immersive training for complex MRO procedures, ultimately enhancing safety and productivity. For passengers, airlines can use immersive modules for safety briefings, making information more engaging and memorable. AR can enhance in-flight entertainment by providing interactive content and personalized experiences through passengers' own devices, enhancing their inflight journey. In air traffic control training, XR technologies offer trainees realistic, risk-free simulations of complex air traffic scenarios, enhancing their ability to manage busy skies efficiently and safely. These technologies can provide a dynamic, hands-on learning environment, improving decision-making and responsiveness for air traffic controllers. In design, engineers and designers can use these technologies to create and assess aircraft concepts in immersive environments, where they can fine-tune not only the technical aspects but also the ergonomic aspects of the aircraft, ensuring passenger and crew comfort and safety. This accelerates innovation, reduces design iterations, and leads to more efficient, ergonomic, and advanced aircraft, shaping the future of aviation. Finally, these technologies offer immersive, realistic flight simulations, enabling trainees to practice in various scenarios, weather conditions, and aircraft types. This enhances skill development, safety, and cost efficiency while reducing the need for physical flight hours for pilot trainees.

As we explore the vast horizons of the aviation industry, it becomes clear that XR technologies are not just technological novelties; but they will become essential components of a future where aviation reaches new heights, paving the way for innovation and excellence.

REFERENCES

Alce, G., Klang, K., Andersson, D., Nyström, S., Wallergård, M., Niehorster, D.C., et al. 2020. Using augmented reality to train flow patterns for pilot students-an explorative study. *In*: Proceedings of 7th International Conference on Augmented Reality, Virtual Reality, and Computer Graphics. 12242: 215–231.

Andrievskaia, P., van Benthem, K. and Herdman, C.M. 2020. Neural correlates of mental workload in virtual flight simulation. pp. 521–528. *In*: Stephanidis, C., Antona, M. and Ntoa, S. (eds). HCI International 2020 – Late Breaking Posters. HCII 2020. Communications in Computer and Information Science, vol 1294. Springer, Cham.

Ainakulov, Z., Pirmanov, I., Koshekov, K., Astapenko, N., Fedorov, I., Zuev, D., et al. 2022. Risk assessment of the operation of aviation maintenance personnel trained on virtual reality simulators. Transport and Telecommunication. 23(4): 320–333.

Akselrad, D. 2023. Visions of control: The head-up display, perceptual labor, and a lesson for augmented reality. Technology and Culture. 64(3): 761–784.

Audu, O., van Benthem, K. and Herdman, C.M. 2021. Validation of virtual reality cognitive assessment for pilots across the lifespan. Lecture Notes in Computer Science. 12767. Springer, Cham.

Auer, S., Anthes, C., Reiterer. H. and Jetter, H-C. 2023. Aircraft cockpit interaction in virtual reality with visual, auditive, and vibrotactile feedback. *In*: Proceedings of the ACM on Human-Computer Interaction. 10(7): 420–443.

Ayala, N., Mardanbegi, D., Zafar, A., Niechwiej-Szwedo, E., Cao, S., Kearns, S., et al. 2024. Does fiducial marker visibility impact task performance and information processing in novice and low-time pilots? Computers and Graphics. 119: 103889.

Bernard, F., Zare, M., Sagot, J.C. and Paquin, R. 2019. Virtual reality simulation and ergonomics assessment in aviation maintainability. *In*: Proceedings of the 20th Congress of the International Ergonomics Association (IEA 2018). 141–154. Springer: Cham.

Bernard, F., Zare, M., Sagot, J., Paquin, R., Toccafondi, G. and Parlangeli, O. 2020. Using digital and physical simulation to focus on human factors and ergonomics in aviation maintainability. Human Factors. 62(1): 37–54.

Bernard, F., Xavier B., Raphael P., Martial P., Killian M., Nicolas B., et al. 2022. Digital simulation tools in aviation maintainability training. Computer Applications in Engineering Education. 30(2): 384–395.

Biggs, A.T., Geyer, D.J., Schroeder, V.M., Robinson, F.E. and Bradley, J.L. 2018. Adapting virtual reality and augmented reality systems for naval aviation training. Naval Medical Research Unit, Dayton Wright-Patterson AFB United States.

Blundell, J. and Harris, D. 2023. Designing augmented reality for future commercial aviation: A user-requirement analysis with commercial aviation pilots. Virtual Reality. 27: 2167–2181.

Bortsova, P. and Panfilov, P. 2021. Smart maintenance framework based on spatio-visual computing: The case of aircraft MRO. *In*: Proceedings of 32nd DAAAM International Symposium on Intelligent Manufacturing and Automation. 0673–0684.

Buttussi, F. and Chittaro, L. 2017. Effects of different types of virtual reality display on presence and learning in a safety training scenario. IEEE Transactions on Visualization and Computer Graphics. 24(2): 1063–1076.

Buttussi, F. and Chittaro, L. 2020. A comparison of procedural safety training in three conditions: Virtual reality headset, smartphone, and printed materials. IEEE Transactions on Learning Technologies. 14(1): 1–15.

Carr, L., Wallis, G., Perry, N. and Riek, S. 2023. Spatial learning in a virtual reality Boeing 737NG flight deck. Lecture Notes in Computer Science. 14018. Springer, Cham.

Chittaro, L., Corbett, C.L., McLean, G.A. and Zangrando, N. 2018. Safety knowledge transfer through mobile virtual reality: A study of aviation life preserver donning. Safety Science. 102: 159–168.

Coleman, J. and Thirtyacre, D. 2021. Remote pilot situational awareness with augmented reality glasses: An observational field study. International Journal of Aviation, Aeronautics, and Aerospace. 8(1).

Conde, J., Munoz-Arcentales, A., Romero, M., Rojo, J., Salvachúa, J., Huecas, G., et al. 2022. Applying digital twins for the management of information in turnaround event operations in commercial airports. Advanced Engineering Informatics. 54: 101723.

Cross, J.I., Boag-Hodgson, C.C. and Mavin, T.J. 2023. Measuring presence and situational awareness in a virtual reality flight simulator. Aviation Psychology and Applied Human Factors. 13(2): 83–94.

Crutchfield, J., Kang, Z., Fraga, R.P. and Lee, J. 2022. Identification of expert tower controller visual scanning patterns in support of the development of automated training tools. Lecture Notes in Computer Science. 13318. Springer, Cham.

de Crescenzio, F., Bagassi, S., Asfaux, S. and Lawson, N. 2019. Human centred design and evaluation of cabin interiors for business jet aircraft in virtual reality. International Journal on Interactive Design and Manufacturing. 13(2): 761–772.

Dymora, P., Kowal, B., Mazurek, M. and Romana, S. 2021. The effects of virtual reality technology application in the aircraft pilot training process. *In*: IOP Conference Series: Materials Science and Engineering. 1024(1): 012099. IOP Publishing.

Erickson, I., Hidalgo, M., Reynolds, J., Ficke, C., Krumholtz, V., Drucker, J., et al. 2023. Proof of concept for a data-driven VR spatial disorientation training tool for navy pilots. *In*: Proceedings of the Human Factors and Ergonomics Society Annual Meeting. 67(1): 1350–1355.

Eschen, H., Kötter, T., Rodeck, R., Harnisch, M. and Schüppstuhl, T. 2018. Augmented and virtual reality for inspection and maintenance processes in the aviation industry. Procedia Manufacturing. 19: 156–163.

Fuchs, M.K., Beckert, F., Biedermann, J. and Nagel, B. 2021. Experience of conceptual designs and system interactions for the aircraft cabin in virtual reality. *In*: AIAA Aviation 2021 Forum. 2773.

Fussell, S.G. and Truong, D. 2020. Preliminary results of a study investigating aviation student's intentions to use virtual reality for flight training. International Journal of Aviation, Aeronautics, and Aerospace. 7(3): 2.

Fussell, S.G. 2023. A review of user experience requirements for a procedural training task in virtual reality. *In*: Proceedings of the Human Factors and Ergonomics Society Annual Meeting. 67(1): 1472–1477.

Fussell, S.G. and Truong, D. 2023. Accepting virtual reality for dynamic learning: An extension of the technology acceptance model. Interactive Learning Environments. 32(9): 5442–5459.

Gilbert, A. 2016. Augmented reality for the US air force. Lecture Notes in Computer Science. 9740. Springer, Cham.

Globalnewswire. 2019. Global AR and VR Market in Aviation (2019–2025). https://www.globenewswire.com/news-release/2019/12/17/1961393/0/en/Globa-AR-and-VR-Market-in-Aviation-2019-2025-Set-to-Register-a-CAGR-of-61-2-with-Massive-Opportunities-in-AI-and-ML-Integration.html.

Gómez-Cambronero, Á., Miralles, I., Tonda, A. and Remolar, I. 2023. Immersive virtual-reality system for aircraft maintenance education: A case study. Applied Sciences. 13(8): 5043.

Guo, W., Wang, X., Deng, Z. and Li, H. 2022. A civil aircraft cockpit control device design using a mixed reality device. Lecture Notes in Computer Science. 13318. Springer, Cham.

Guo, W., Wang, X., Li, Y. and Wang, L. 2023. Research on evaluation of cabin design based on virtual reality. pp. 586–593. *In*: Stephanidis, C., Antona, M., Ntoa, S. and Salvendy, G. (eds). HCI International 2023 Posters. HCII 2023. Communications in Computer and Information Science, vol 1832. Springer, Cham.

Guthridge, R. and Clinton-Lisell, V. 2023. Evaluating the efficacy of virtual reality (VR) training devices for pilot training. Journal of Aviation Technology and Engineering. 12(2): 1–14.

Hagl, M., Friedrich, M., Papenfuss, A., Scherer-Negenborn, N., Jakobi, J., Rambau, T., et al. 2019. Augmented reality in a remote tower environment based on VS/IR fusion and optical tracking. Lecture Notes in Computer Science. 10906. Springer, Cham.

Han, K., Shah, S.H.H. and Lee, J.W. 2019. Holographic mixed reality system for air traffic control and management. Applied Sciences. 9(3370).

Harris, D.J., Arthur, T., de Burgh, T., Duxbury, M., Lockett-Kirk, R., McBarnett, W., et al. 2023. Assessing expertise using eye tracking in a virtual reality flight simulation. The International Journal of Aerospace Psychology. 33(3): 153–173.

Hight, M.P., Fussell, S.G., Kurkchubasche, M.A. and Hummell, I.J. 2022. Effectiveness of virtual reality simulations for civilians, *ab initio* pilot training. The Journal of Aviation/Aerospace Education and Research. 31(1).

Hong, Z. and Wenhua, L. 2017. Architecture and key techniques of augmented reality maintenance guiding system for civil aircrafts. Journal of Physics. 787(1): 12022.

Irvin, W., Goldie, C., O'Brien, C., Aura, C., Temme, L. and Wilson, M. 2021. A virtual reality aviation emergency procedure (EP) testbed. *In*: Proceeding SPIE 11759, Virtual, Augmented, and Mixed Reality (XR) Technology for Multi-Domain Operations II, 1175909 (12 April 2021); https://doi.org/10.1117/12.2585952.

Jiang, Y., Tran, T.H. and Williams, L. 2023. Machine learning and mixed reality for smart aviation: Applications and challenges. Journal of Air Transport Management. 111: 102437.

Jonaid, S.M.H., Noh, H.M., Yusoff, M.R., Zuhudi, N.Z.M., Wahab, M.H.A., Daud, S.M., et al. 2023. Virtual reality for gas turbine engine training at part 147 and part 145 organization: Review on implementation factors and challenges. *In*: AIP Conference Proceedings. 2808(1).

Ke, L., Zhang, Z., Ma, Y., Xiao, Y., Wu, S., Wang, X., et al. 2023. Evaluating flight performance and eye movement patterns using virtual reality flight simulators. Journal of Visualized Experiments. 195.

Key, K., Ma, M., Towne, C., Choi, I., Hu, P.T., Franzman, S.C., et al. 2022. Preliminary findings: Application of maintenance instructions displayed in augmented reality. Lecture Notes in Computer Science. 13318. Springer, Cham.

Kim, J., Wang, K., Miller, J. and Dorneich, M.C. 2024. Creating augmented reality-based experiences for aviation weather training: Challenges, opportunities, and design implications for 3D authoring. Ergonomics. 1–17.

Koutitas, G., Smith, S. and Lawrence, G. 2021. Performance evaluation of AR/VR training technologies for EMS first responders. Virtual Reality. 25: 83–94.

Labedan, P., Darodes-de-Tailly, N., Dehais, F. and Peysakhovich, V. 2021. Virtual reality for pilot training: Study of cardiac activity. *In*: Proceedings of the 16th International Joint Conference on Computer Vision, Imaging and Computer Graphics Theory and Applications (VISIGRAPP 2021) - Volume 2: HUCAPP, 81-88.

Labedan, P., Dehais, F. and Peysakhovich, V. 2023. Comparison of cardiac activity and subjective measures during virtual reality and real aircraft flight. Communications in Computer and Information Science. 1691: 112–131.

Lee, H., Woo, D. and Yu, S. 2022. Virtual reality metaverse system supplementing remote education methods: Based on aircraft maintenance simulation. Applied Sciences. 12(5): 2667.

Lewis, J. and Livingston, J. 2018. Pilot training next: Breaking institutional paradigms using student-centered multimodal learning. *In*: Proceedings of Interservice/Industry Training, Simulation, and Education Conference (I/ITSEC) 2018. Orlando, FL.

Li, S. 2023. Design and development of aviation aircraft maintenance training platform based on VR technology. Procedia Computer Science. 228: 898–906.

Liu, S., Liu, H. and Tian, Y. 2023. Augmented reality framework and application for aviation emergency rescue based on multi-agent and service. pp. 237–248. *In*: Nakamatsu, K., Patnaik, S., Kountchev, R., Li, R. and Aharari, A. (eds). Advanced Intelligent Virtual Reality Technologies. Smart Innovation, Systems and Technologies, vol 330. Springer, Singapore.

Livatino, S., Mohamed, M., Morana, G., Gainley, P., Iqbal, Y., Nguyen, T.H., et al. 2022. Are we ready for take-off? Learning cockpit actions with VR headsets. pp. 147–153. *In*: De Paolis, L.T., Arpaia, P. and Sacco, M. (eds). Extended Reality. XR Salento 2022. Lecture Notes in Computer Science, vol 13445. Springer, Cham.

Luisier, J., Yooyen, S. and Deebhijarn, S. 2019. Perceptions of Thai aviation students on consumer grade VR flight experiences. Proceedings. 39(1): 8.

Macchiarella, D., Yu, J., Liu, D. and Vincenzi, D.A. 2023. Augmented reality as a means of job task training in aviation. pp. 65–86. *In*: Vincenzi, D.A., Molous, M., Hancock, P.A., Pharmer, J.A. and Ferraro, J.C. (eds). Human Factors in Simulation and Training. CRC Press.

Matos, N., Gamito, P., Pinto, M., Ferreira, J., Oliveira, L., Pantelakis, S., et al. 2019. Implementation of advanced technologies into Aeronautic integrated maintenance concept: Use of virtual reality in ground-floor training maintenance execution. *In*: MATEC Web of Conferences, 304, 6002.

Meister, P., Miller, J., Wang, K., Dorneich, M.C., Winer, E., Brown, L.J., et al. 2022. Designing three-dimensional augmented reality weather visualizations to enhance general aviation weather education. IEEE Transactions on Professional Communication. 65(2): 321–336.

Moesl, B., Schaffernak, H., Vorrager, W., Braunstingl, R., Herrele, T. and Koglbauer, I.V. 2021. A research agenda for implementing augmented reality in *ab initio* pilot training. Aviation Psychology and Applied Human Factors. 11(2): 118–126.

Moesl, B., Schaffernak, H., Vorrager, W., Holy, M., Herrele, T., Braunstingl, R., et al. 2022. Towards a more socially sustainable advanced pilot training by integrating wearable augmented reality devices. Sustainability. 14: 2220.

Moesl, B., Schaffernak, H., Vorraber, W., Braunstingl, R. and Koglbauer, I.V. 2023a. Performance, emotion, presence: Investigation of an augmented reality-supported concept for flight training. Applied Sciences. 13: 11346.

Moesl, B., Schaffernak, H., Vorraber, W., Braunstingl, R. and Koglbauer, I.V. 2023b. Multimodal augmented reality applications for training of traffic procedures in aviation. Multimodal Technologies and Interaction. 7(3).

Mohd, N.S., Aziz, M.A. and Ismail, H.N. 2022. Iskandar.my: Framework of mobile augmented reality travel app. pp 113–127. *In*: Hassan, A. and Rahman, N.A.A. (eds). Technology Application in Aviation, Tourism, and Hospitality. Springer, Singapore.

Morrison, K., Perkins, A. and Hanson, A. 2023. HUD training and extended reality solutions. pp. 549–559. *In*: Chen, J.Y.C. and Fragomeni, G. (eds). Virtual, Augmented and Mixed Reality, HCII 2023, Lecture Notes in Computer Science. Springer, Cham.

Moruzzi, M.C., Santhosh, S., Corsi, M., Bagassi, S. and de Crescenzio, F. 2023. Design and implementation of eye tracking application for generation of augmented reality content on spatial see through display of remote and virtual control tower (RVT). International Journal on Interactive Design and Manufacturing. 17: 1859–1867.

Neretin, E.S., Kolokolnikov, P.A. and Mitrofanov, S.Y. 2021. Prospect for the application of augmented and virtual reality technologies in the design, production, operation of aircraft, and training of aviation personnel. Journal of Physics. 1958(1): 012030.

Newton, D.C. 2022. Human factors considerations for head-worn displays in civil aviation. pp. 233-250. *In*: Chen, J.Y.C. and Fragomeni, G. (eds). Virtual, Augmented and Mixed Reality: Applications in Education, Aviation and Industry. Springer, Cham.

Newton, D.C., Hesselroth, J. and DiDomenica, R. 2023. Impacts of dual head-up display use on workload in the civil aviation flight deck: Implications for crew coordination. pp. 560–571. *In*: Chen, J.Y.C. and Fragomeni, G. (eds). Virtual, Augmented and Mixed Reality, HCII 2023, Lecture Notes in Computer Science. Springer, Cham.

Oberhauser, M., Dreyer, D., Braunstingl, R. and Koglbauer, I. 2018. What's real about virtual reality flight simulation? Comparing the fidelity of a virtual reality with a conventional flight simulation environment. Aviation Psychology and Applied Human Factors. 8(1): 22–34.

Oh, C., Lee, K. and Oh, M. 2021. Integrating the first person view and the third person view using a connected VR-MR system for pilot training. Journal of Aviation/Aerospace Education and Research. 30(1): 21.

Pechlivanis, K., Ziakkas, D. and Flores, A.D.C. 2023. Extended reality in aviation training: The commercial single pilot operations case. pp. 228–239. *In*: Zaphiris, P., Ioannou, A., Sottilare, R.A., Schwarz, J., Nah, F.F., Siau, K., Wei, J. and Salvendy, G. (eds). HCI International 2023 - Late Breaking Papers. Springer, Cham.

Pejemsky, A., van Benthem, K. and Herdman, C.M. 2021. Comparing the impact of state versus trait factors on memory performance in a virtual reality flight simulator. pp. 369–376. *In*: Stephanidis, C., Antona, M. and Ntoa, S. (eds). HCI International 2021 - Late Breaking Posters. HCII 2021. Communications in Computer and Information Science, vol 1498. Springer, Cham..

Peysakhovich, V., Monnier, L., Gornet, M. and Juaneda, S. 2020. Virtual reality vs. real-life training to learn checklists for light aircraft. *In*: Proceedings of the 1st International Workshop (ETAVI 2020). 47–53. ETH Zurich.

Pradhan, G.N., Galvan-Garza, R., Perez, A.M., Bogle, J. and Cevette, M.J. 2022. Generating flight illusions using galvanic vestibular stimulation in virtual reality flight simulations. Frontiers in Neuroergonomics. 3.

Reddy, G.S.R., Spencer, C.A., Durkee, K., Cox, B., Cotton, O.F., Galbreath, S., et al. 2022. Estimating cognitive load and cybersickness of pilots in VR simulations via unobtrusive physiological sensors. Lecture Notes in Computer Science. 13318. Springer, Cham.

Reyes, C.I.A., Wozniak, D., Ham, A. and Zahabi, M. 2022. An adaptive virtual reality-based training system for pilots. *In*: Proceedings of the Human Factors and Ergonomics Society Annual Meeting. 66(1): 1962–1966.

Reyes, C.I.A., Wozniak, D., Ham, A. and Zahabi, M. 2023. Design and evaluation of an adaptive virtual reality training system. Virtual Reality. 27: 2509–2528.

Rostami, M., Kamoonpuri, J., Pradhan, P. and Chung, J. 2023. Development and evaluation of an enhanced virtual reality flight simulation tool for airships. Aerospace. 10(5): 457.

Schaffernak, H., Moesl, B., Vorraber, W. and Koglbauer, I.V. 2020. Potential augmented reality application areas for pilot education: An exploratory study. Education Sciences. 10(4): 86.

Shah, S.H.H., Han, K. and Lee, J.W. 2019. Interaction paradigms for air traffic control and management in mixed reality. Lecture Notes in Computer Science. 11575. Springer, Cham.

Siyaev, A. and Jo, G. 2021. Towards aircraft maintenance metaverse using speech interactions with virtual objects in mixed reality. Sensors. 21: 2066.

Sonnenfeld, N.A., Nguyen, B., Duruaku, F., Alonso, A., Carney, M., Smith, E. and Jentsch, F. 2023. Flightcrew procedures experimental training: Simulation testbed design, development, and interactive demonstration. *In*: Proceedings of the Human Factors and Ergonomics Society Annual Meeting. 67(1): 253–258.

Stapelberg, R.F. 2009. Handbook of Reliability, Availability, Maintainability, and Safety in Engineering Design. United Kingdom: Springer.

Tan, J., Ye, H., Xu, C., He, H. and Liao, X. 2023. SkyroadAR: An augmented reality system for UAVs low-altitude public air route visualization. Drones (Basel). 7(9): 587.

Taneja, N.K. 2019. Re-platforming the Airline Business to Meet Travelers' Total Mobility Needs. London: Routledge.

Tavares, S.M.O., Ribeiro, J.A., Riberio, B.A. and de Castro, P.M.S.T. 2024. Aircraft structural design and life-cycle assessment through digital twins. Designs. 8(29).

Thomas, R.L., Dubena, R., Camacho, G., Nieves, N., Barcza, T., Green, S., et al. 2021. Usability of the virtual reality aviation trainer for runway-width illusions. The Collegiate Aviation Review International. 39(2).

Thomas, R.L., Albelo, J.L.D. and Wiggins, M. 2023. Enhancing pilot training through virtual reality: Recognizing and mitigating aviation visual and vestibular illusions. International Journal of Aviation, Aeronautics, and Aerospace. 10(3).

Truschzinski, M., Betella, A., Brunnett, G. and Verschure, P.F.M.J. 2017. Emotional and cognitive influences in air traffic controller tasks: An investigation using a virtual environment? Applied Ergonomics. 69: 1–9.

Updegrove, J.A. and Jafer, S. 2017. Optimization of air traffic control training at the Federal Aviation Administration Academy. Aerospace. 4(4): 50.

Valentin, Y. and Choi, H. 2023. Visual attention in extended reality and implications for aviation safety. pp. 572-584. *In*: Chen, J.Y.C. and Fragomeni, G. (eds). Virtual, Augmented and Mixed Reality, HCII 2023, Lecture Notes in Computer Science. Springer, Cham.

Van Benthem, K. and Herdman, C.M. 2021. A virtual reality cognitive health screening tool for aviation: Managing accident risk for older pilots. International Journal of Industrial Ergonomics. 85: 103169.

Van Vooren, J. 2019. Virtual reality training for aviation maintenance, repair and overhaul (Vi-Mro 1.0). *In*: European Distance and E-Learning Network (EDEN) Conference Proceedings. 1: 518–523.

Vincent, H., Benoit, J., Xavier, S. and David, B. 2017. Inoovas—Industrial ontology for operation in virtual and augmented scene: The architecture. *In*: Proceedings of 4th International Conference on Control, Decision, and Information Technologies (CoDIT). 0300–0305.

Walther, J.N., Hesse, C., Biedermann, J. and Nagel, B. 2021. High fidelity digital cabin mock-up based on preliminary aircraft design data for virtual reality applications and beyond. *In*: AIAA Aviation 2021 Forum. 2775.

Wang, Y., Anne, A. and Ropp, T. 2016. Applying the technology acceptance model to understand aviation students' perceptions toward augmented reality maintenance training instruction. International Journal of Aviation, Aeronautics, and Aerospace. 3(4): 3.

Wang, K., Miller, J., Meister, P., Dorneich, M.C., Brown, L., Whitehurst, G., et al. 2023. Development and implementation of an augmented reality thunderstorm simulation for general aviation weather theory training. Journal of Imaging Science and Technology. 1–14.

Wang, Z., Li, L., Liu, Y., Jiang, Y., Wang, Y. and Dai, Y. 2024. An experimental study on mixed reality-based user interface for collaborative operation of high-precision process equipment. The International Journal of Advanced Manufacturing Technology. 132: 2443–2459.

Williamson, J.R., McGill, M. and Outram, K. 2019. Planevr: Social acceptability of virtual reality for aeroplane passengers. *In*: Proceedings of the 2019 CHI Conference on Human Factors in Computing Systems. 1–14.

Wu, W.C. and Kuo, L.Y. 2022. Virtual reality: A new method for smart aviation maintenance training services. pp. 35–37. *In*: Vu, V.H., Wu, W.C. and Kuo, L.Y. (eds). System Innovation in a Post-Pandemic World. CRC Press.

Wu, W. and Vu, V. 2022. Application of virtual reality method in aircraft maintenance service: Taking Dornier 228 as an example. Applied Sciences. 12(14): 7283.

Wu, W. and Hung, C. 2022. Development of engine maintenance technology with mixed reality: Taking Pratt and Whitney JT9D as an example. Aerospace. 9(12).

Xue, Y., Liu, H., Tian, Y. and Li, X. 2023. Study on the visualization modeling of aviation emergency rescue system based on systems engineering. pp. 173–186. *In*: Nakamatsu, K., Patnaik, S., Kountchev, R., Li, R. and Aharari, A. (eds). Advanced Intelligent Virtual Reality Technologies. Smart Innovation, Systems and Technologies, vol 330. Springer, Singapore.

Xue, Z., Yang, J., Chen, R., He, Q., Li, Q. and Mei, X. 2024. AR-assisted guidance for assembly and maintenance of avionics equipment. Applied Sciences. 14: 1137.

Yang, Y., Keivanpour, S. and Imbeau, D. 2023. Integrating X-reality and lean into end-of-life aircraft parts disassembly sequence planning: A critical review and research agenda. The International Journal of Advanced Manufacturing Technology. 127: 2181–2210.

Yevtodyeva, M.G. 2020. Additive manufacturing and augmented reality as new production technologies in the aviation industry. Vestnik MGIMO-Universiteta. 13(5): 307–330.

Zamkovoi, A.A., Komarova, N.V. and Novikov, S.V. 2019. Rethinking the education of aviation specialists for a new era. Russian Engineering Research. 39(3): 268–271.

Zhang, M., Wang, M., Feng, H., Liu, X., Zhai, L., Xu, X., et al. 2023. Pilots' spatial visualization ability assessment based on virtual reality. Aerospace Medicine and Human Performance. 94(6): 422–428.

Zhang, H., Chen, S., Wang, H. and Qin, Y. 2024. Surface performance of titanium alloy brake shell polished by industrial robot based on digital twin. International Journal of Aerospace Engineering. 6130930.

Zhuo, P. 2023. Application research of virtual reality technology in intelligent civil aviation airport visual management. Academic Journal of Science and Technology. 5(2): 109–112.

Ziccardi, A., van Benthem, K., Liu, C.C., Herdman, C.M. and Hajra, S.G. 2024. Towards ubiquitous and nonintrusive measurements of brain function in the real world: Assessing blink-related oscillations during simulated flight using portable low-cost EEG. Frontiers in Neuroscience. 17: 1286854.

Zou, L. 2022. Application research of computer virtual reality technology in civil aviation safety management system. *In*: 2022 International Conference on Data Analytics, Computing and Artificial Intelligence (ICDACAI): 108–112. IEEE.

Chapter **6**

Non-Conventional Virtual Reality Mechanics

Taneli Nyyssönen*, Teijo Lehtonen and Jouni Smed
Department of Computing, Faculty of Technology,
University of Turku, Finland

INTRODUCTION

Virtual reality (VR) is an immersive medium that allows the body to take part in interactions (natural interaction), unlike standard digital applications which mainly use hands through an input device. Interaction in VR usually happens via controllers, but it also includes head-based camera motion (as the user's headset is the first-person camera) which always guarantees a perfect camera angle without any design effort, unlike in non-VR applications.

However, there are many other ways to interact in VR, such as hand-tracking, eye-tracking, or walking in space on physical treadmills, which can further enhance the experience. Drawbacks are discussed in this chapter with some practical use case scenarios for various non-conventional VR mechanics.

The interaction happens through *core mechanics*, which refers to a process where input from the user is transferred to the application as functionality (output) through the usage of some input device(s)

*For Correspondence: ttjnyy@utu.fi

DOI: 10.1201/9781003581642-6

which are accessed via a user interface (UI). Figure 6.1 showcases this relationship with some VR-specific examples added. Mindful design of mechanics is vital for the usability of applications.

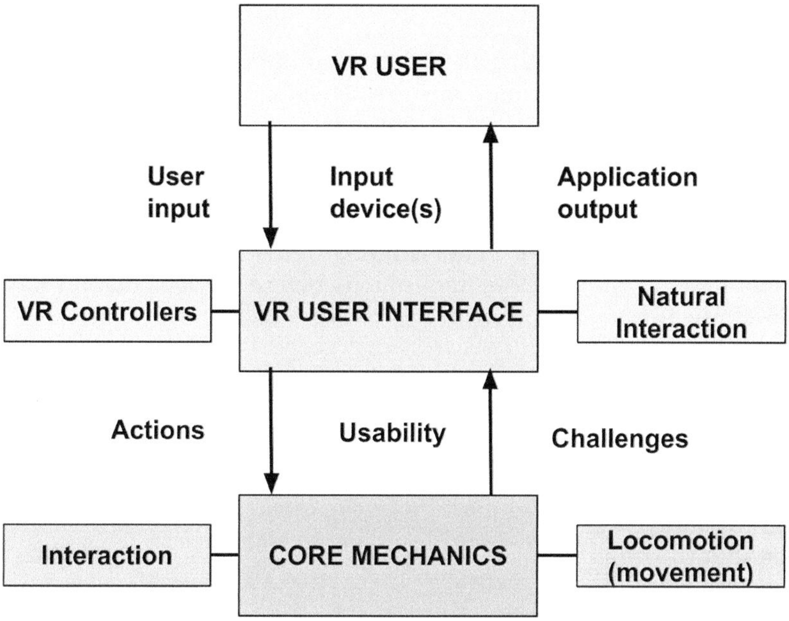

Figure 6.1 Relationships between core mechanics, user interface, and the user with examples for VR. Adapted from (Adams 2014, p. 38).

This chapter begins by discussing why realism is important in VR mechanic design and how it can be achieved in the section "Need for Realism in Virtual Reality Mechanics". In the following section, the reader will be familiarized with the concept of hand-tracking and what needs to be taken into account when utilizing gestures rather than controllers. Gestures are analyzed more profoundly showcasing, e.g., their cultural implications and design limitations in the next section. Furthermore, some less frequently utilized VR mechanics, such as eye-tracking and pulse sensor use are portrayed in section "Rarer Mechanics". Finally, the potential future applications of these interfaces as well as their limitations are presented in the Conclusion section.

NEED FOR REALISM IN VIRTUAL REALITY MECHANICS

Realism is an often-desired aspect of VR experiences as it enhances immersion, however, not as often are the implications and drawbacks of that realism considered. Utilizing, e.g., higher quality graphics will require more expensive hardware to run, limiting the target audience.

Moreover, designing realistic mechanics might require compromises in usability, increase development time, and require specific hardware with little cross-platform compatibility, which are large issues when utilizing natural interaction mechanisms. Although, when successfully implemented, the mechanics can greatly enhance the experience, but even in those cases the specific optimal scenario for each mechanic might include only a narrow field of topics.

In this section, some attempts at creating realistic VR interaction are described, and what type of compromises those attempts require. The idea is to get a better understanding of the mechanics design with an emphasis to think of the implications before implementation rather than afterwards.

Interaction Fidelity

When it comes to determining whether a virtual interaction is 'good' or 'bad', there are many metrics that can be utilized, namely at least:

- usability,
- immersion,
- strain,
- VR-sickness induced, and
- interaction fidelity.

Of these metrics, interaction fidelity is a less utilized and known concept. It is defined by McMahan et al. (2016) as "the objective degree of exactness with which real world actions are reproduced in an interactive system". The interaction fidelity can be analyzed using its evaluation tool *Framework for Interaction Fidelity Analysis* (FIFA) (McMahan et al. 2012) with three metrics:

- *biomechanical symmetry*, which means how well the used mechanics mirror the simulated real-world actions (e.g., haptic feedback),
- *input veracity*, which refers to the accuracy at which the interaction is captured by the input devices (e.g., latency, tracking radius), and
- *control symmetry*, which describes the degree of exactness with which a real-world theoretical transfer function is reproduced through interaction (e.g., handling an object with a hand-tracked hand is near identical to how one would handle a physical object, whereas using a ray going out from the user's hand/controller is not) (McMahan et al. 2016).

The interaction fidelity suffers from the *uncanny valley* effect (McMahan et al. 2016), meaning that medium fidelity interaction mechanisms are worse in terms of usability than the high (very realistic) and low (not realistic at all). Thus, by definition, hyper realistic VR mechanics need to also have a high interaction fidelity.

An overview of the main concerns when developing or utilizing natural UIs is displayed in Figure 6.2, which illustrates the many caveats and pitfalls of developing natural (or non-conventional) VR mechanics.

How could one then achieve high interaction fidelity in VR? A simple example is walking. In a room-scale VR which does not have any artificial locomotion mechanics, such as joystick-based movement, the user is able to freely walk around physically which also moves them within the VR application. This method has the highest interaction fidelity, as it directly corresponds to real-world action. However, it has limitations when used on its own, mainly that the real physical room space will define the maximum movement range, which usually is only up to three square meters or less. To mitigate this while keeping the interaction fidelity high, there are various treadmills, such as Omni One (Virtuix Inc. 2024), which allow the user to walk or run in place, preserving the interaction fidelity mostly. Drawbacks to these are the price, portability, and space requirements. Additionally, due to safety, the user needs to either be harnessed to the system or at least have physical barriers nearby, which can lessen the immersion.

Button Pressing versus Moving Controllers

One simple example about realism in VR is whether to have the user to just press buttons on the controllers while the location of the controllers does not matter, or to require the user to complete a certain motion that mimics the performed action via the controllers. As an example, this serves the previous research by Nyyssönen and Smed (2021) which compares the differences between realistic and 'game-like' interaction techniques in VR puzzle games.

The study tested mechanics for swimming, climbing, and crawling (as a joint puzzle), and seeking hidden objects. Each of the mechanics have two puzzle levels, realistic and game-like. The main idea is that the realistic mechanics attempt to emulate the real-world actions with high interaction fidelity, e.g., for swimming the user needs to move their hands in a swimming-like motion while 'climbing' in the water with lessened gravity, creating the sensation of water physics. The game-like mechanic functions with just pressing and holding buttons, which greatly decreases the interaction fidelity, but might be easier and cause less strain. An illustration for this can be seen in Figure 6.3. The findings in the study show that swimming felt a lot more immersive when utilizing the realistic mechanics, but it somewhat depended on the

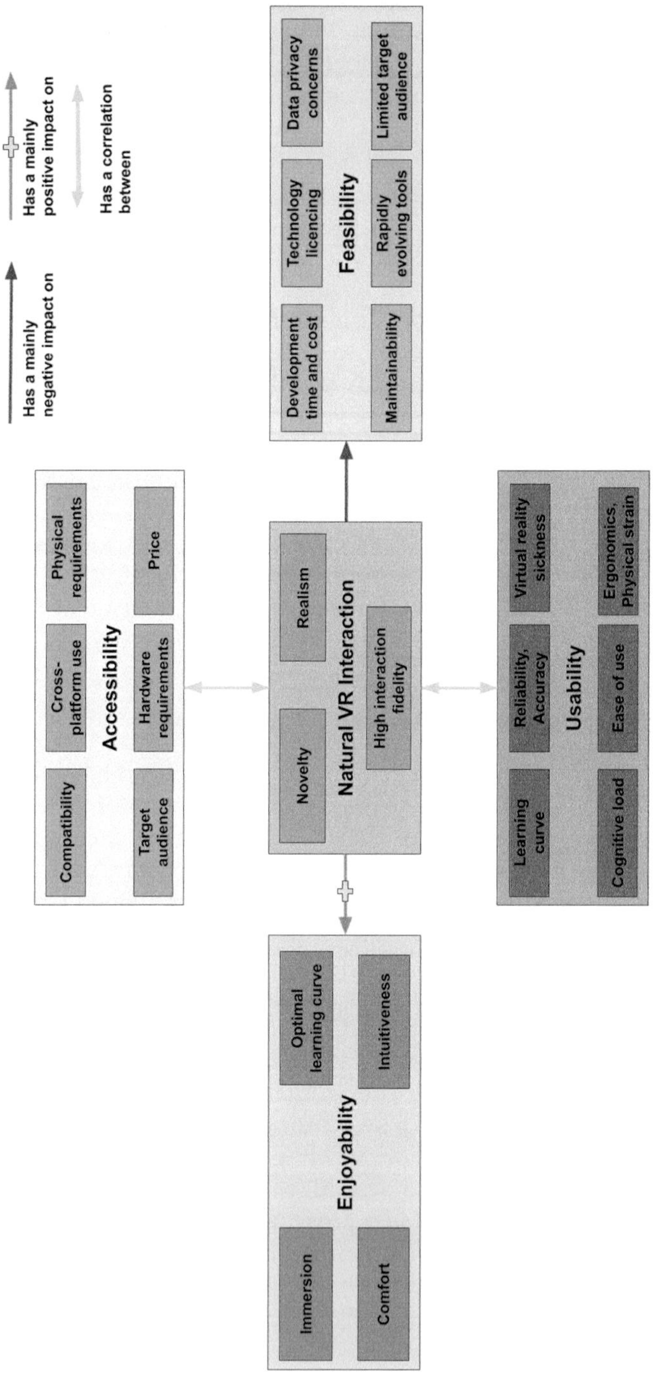

Figure 6.2 Relationships that need to be considered when developing natural interaction for VR.

user's previous experience with games and VR. More experienced users were prone to preferring the realistic mechanic, while less experienced users tended to enjoy the game-like mechanics more. However, overall, the realism was preferred over the potential ease of use that game-like mechanics can provide.

The main takeaway of this topic is that button pressing can be easier to grasp for novice VR users, while with experience more realism can be preferred even if it would require more effort. Furthermore, applications such as games prefer the added immersion of realism while others, e.g., work applications, often prefer usability at the cost of realism.

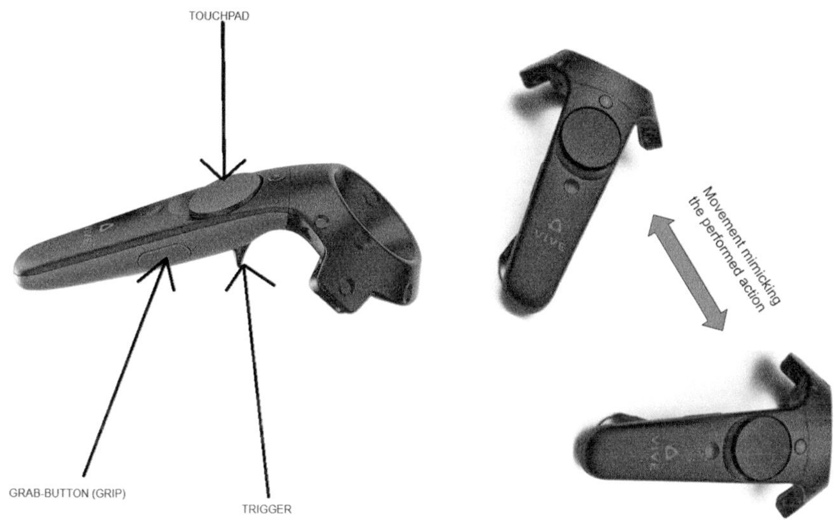

(a) The most common way to interact is via pressing buttons on controllers where the controller's position does not impact the interaction.

(b) A more immersive option is to move the controller in a way that mimics the performed (real-world) action (in combination with button presses or not).

Figure 6.3 Button pressing versus moving the controllers, showcasing a HTC Vive controller (HTC Corporation 2016).

Attempting to Force User Pose

Climbing and crawling were other mechanics explored in the study by Nyyssönen and Smed (2021). Crawling is difficult to create with high interaction fidelity as it is not possible to force the user to stay in a crawling position, or return the user to that if they, e.g., stand up into a virtual ceiling. The study's idea was to attempt to force the crawling by not allowing the user to move forward without being in the correct pose. This was achieved by having climbable panels on the floor, with which the user needed to drag themselves forward, thus 'crawling' , (see Figure 6.4 for reference). The user was prevented from cheating by requiring the headset position to be a certain distance from the climbable panels on the floor, so at least they needed to have their head near the floor. Additionally, the user could not throw themself forward, as a hand was only allowed to detach from a panel when grabbing hold of another one with the other hand. The users were dissuaded from standing up into the virtual ceiling because of a teleportation feature that would reroute them backwards in the course. This crawling mechanic worked well, and it preserved the interaction fidelity compared to real crawling at least in a mediocre way. The game-like mechanic was standard joystick-based locomotion with physical crouching when going through low tunnel environments.

Figure 6.4 Showcase of the panels on the floor and walls which were used to simulate realistic crawling and climbing in the article by Nyyssönen and Smed (2021).

In the realistic climbing, the user needed to hold the grab-button while climbing on panels laid out on the side of walls, releasing the button with one hand when reaching for the next panel, affording falling down due to user error. For the game-like mechanic, the panel attaching functioned as a toggle, so holding the button down was not required.

The test served as an interesting look into forcing user position and pose in VR, showing that it is somewhat possible to utilize mechanics design to limit user movements without physical intervention. This mechanic has a high interaction fidelity, but it is worth questioning how enjoyable it is to mimic the physical world completely, considering comfort and strain especially. Additionally, often the user is willing to suspend their disbelief and will obey the instructions of the application without explicitly forcing their hand.

Camera Model Benefits of VR for Realistic Puzzle Design

The third mechanic explored in the study Nyyssönen and Smed (2021) was finding objects that are hidden inside other objects. This relates to the usage of the user-directed camera in VR (camera follows the headset), which is one of the most distinct differences between VR and standard digital applications. Namely, the player no longer *plays as* a character, but they rather *are* the character inside the virtual world. This means that additional considerations must be included, such as player height and posture, but it also allows the developers to spend less time with camera control design.

The benefits apart from design ease include additional immersion and high level of interaction fidelity, but it also affords specific design paths to take place. The idea in the study was that unlike in standard applications with strictly planned camera control at all times, in VR the user can move the camera basically wherever their head fits, allowing the utilization of the full space of, e.g., a room for hiding items. The idea stipulates that if one was to hide items in a standard digital puzzle game, then the implemented camera controls would reveal the possible hiding locations, thus giving hints about where the items are hidden just based on the camera controls. For example, if the character could crouch in a standard game, then that would tell the player that there can be something hidden on the crouch level, and the depth of the crouch would indicate what the level is. Alternatively, not being able to crouch would instantly tell the player that a large part of the explorable space is off limits and cannot contain any items. An example of this indication for non-VR versus VR camera control is displayed in Figure 6.5.

The same does not work in VR due to the inherent camera control, which means that, e.g., seeing a set of holes in a wall could mean that any of them might hide something, whereas in a standard game the player could consider camera height and disregard some of them without exploration. This becomes more pronounced when adding small 'tunnels' inside holes that are in other objects, as tested in the study. This means that in VR it is possible to put one's head through a hole, then twist the head sideways and in an angle to locate a hidden item, an action which in a standard game would be indicated to the player to be either impossible or possible long before considering if an item is hidden there. Consequently, the implementation of a specific camera model will indicate that there is a reason for that camera model, meaning that at least *something* is hidden so that all of the camera model's features need to be utilized (at least in general). Due to this difference, the VR camera model is very interesting, and hide and seek -type puzzles can feel more rewarding to both design and take part in.

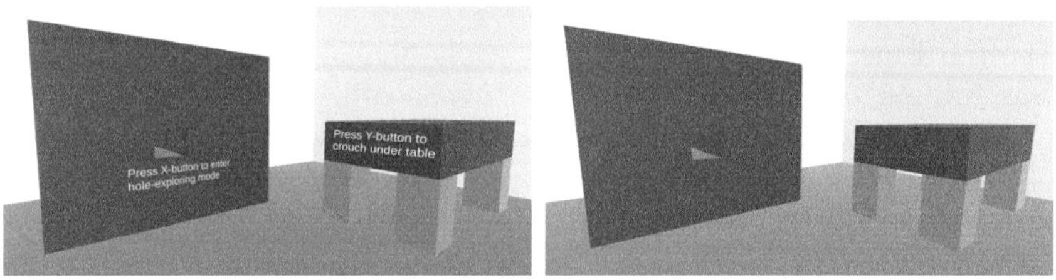

(a) In a non-VR application the user would be indicated whether it is possible to explore a hole in a wall or crouch under a table.

(b) In a VR application there is no need to give the user hints about possible camera movements due to the VR's inherent physical camera control.

Figure 6.5 Non-VR versus VR camera model example.

A specific disadvantage of the camera model relates to the users' differing height, as it means that the VR world is viewed at a different angle for different people, e.g., children and adults usually have considerable height differences that manifest in VR applications. This also means that users who choose to sit versus stand experience this height difference, which adds design considerations such as whether to have multiple versions of the application in different scales, which only really works in single-user environments.

HAND-TRACKING VERSUS CONTROLLER USE

VR features *3D UIs* and the terms *tangible* or *graspable* interface are mentioned frequently in related research, referring to digital interfaces which are interactable via the physical dimension in some way (Fitzmaurice et al. 1995, Fitzmaurice and Buxton 1997, Ha and Woo 2010, Kang et al. 2020), e.g., a computer mouse using a personal computer, or VR controllers selecting something. A prime example of graspable interfaces is the *hand-tracking* (HT) mechanic. HT means that the user's hands are tracked by some type of tracking apparatus, such as cameras or wearable tracking devices, such as gloves. HT affords much higher interaction fidelity than using standard VR controllers, but it comes with caveats and restrictions which make it unsuitable for all scenarios. This section will parse through a study comparing controllers and HT by Nyyssönen et al. (2022).

Usability Differences

In the case study (Nyyssönen et al. 2022) a controller-based UI is closely replicated via HT as a gesture-based UI and tested in the same virtual environment. The use case of the application is 3D design review, i.e., visualizing objects and manipulating them in VR. The study highlights many of the following aspects related to the usability of HT versus controllers:

Differences in experienced strain between controllers and hands are mainly that the controller can weigh on hands/arms, while performing gestures can cause strain in general and in repetition, although without the extra weight. For the controllability, controllers have a limited amount of buttons, whereas there are technically an infinite number of possible gestures, albeit they have to be distinct enough to not get mixed. Furthermore, controllers are an unnatural way of interacting compared to hands, but many people have a lot of experience using them to offset this, although there are many different controller types that need to be learned. Gestures are more sensitive to hand size and shape differences than controllers, and it is more difficult to check for gesture accuracy than a button press. It is also impossible for some users to perform various gestures due to inflexibility of fingers or previous injuries etc. Finally, gesture use can invoke the *Midas touch problem* similar to eye-tracking use (Jacob 1990), which means that all hand movements are detected as input, rather than just the ones which are intended, causing unintentional input. This basically cannot occur when using controllers due to the strong intent required to press a button.

Additionally, gesture usage can be less precise than controller usage, which can be seen the easiest when navigating in menus. Menus are often navigated via ray-based interaction in VR, which works to a certain extent with standard controllers. However, there is a chance for the *gorilla arm syndrome* (Boring et al. 2009), which refers to the unnatural position of people's arms/hands when interacting with arms extended without any arm support, that can cause discomfort and strain, often referred to as heaviness in arms. It is possible that hand-tracking use could reduce the unwanted gorilla arm syndrome by removing the controller weight. However, there is evidence to the contrary with mid-air gesture use (Hincapié-Ramos et al. 2014), albeit clever gesture design can overcome the issue at least partially (Hansberger et al. 2017). Furthermore, another issue for gesture-based pointing tasks is that it is easy to accidentally move the hand and thus the interaction ray when performing a select action (often the pinch-gesture) with gestures. This issue does not manifest in the same way with controllers, as pressing a button can be done more easily with a stationary hand. Due to this issue, menus in VR that rely on hand gestures need to be larger than traditional digital menus. Namely, the buttons need to be bigger so that the offset between the aimed location and the aimed location after the select gesture does not interfere with button selection. An example of a VR gesture-based menu with enlarged buttons is shown in Figure 6.6.

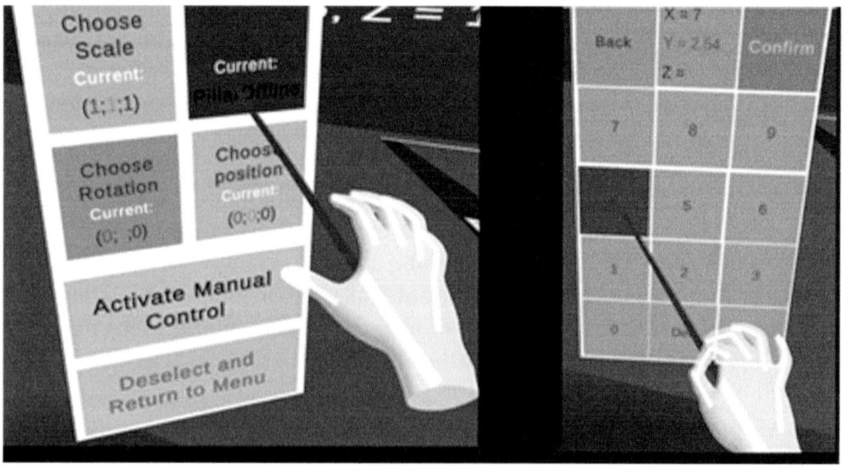

Figure 6.6 Gesture-based menu example showing how large the buttons need to be for accurate use (Nyyssönen et al. 2022).

Immersion Differences and Virtual Reality Sickness

The act of holding controllers is a clear immersion disruptor as it signals to the user that they are inside of a VR application, whereas using one's hands mimics the real world, allowing for easier suspension of disbelief. Another immersion impact comes from button pressing, as that is something humans have not evolved to do, unlike gestures which are utilized constantly accompanying speech.

Performing actions with gestures also involves the physical body to a greater extent than using controllers, which can lead to the higher connection between body movement and virtual movement inside VR. This higher connection potential could help to reduce VR sickness, which occurs due to the brain perceiving motion that is not felt by the body.

Compatibility and Cross-platform Use

Due to the hand-tracking mechanisms and algorithms being different from device to device, it is difficult to transfer gesture commands of one device to an application built for another. This issue is further exacerbated due to the lack of designated gesture libraries for actions.

For controllers however, it is rather simple to build cross-platform functionality, not only because most VR-controllers utilize similar inputs such as trigger, grip, and touchpad or joystick. The standards for registering a button press are also pretty similar across all VR controller types, and even if there are a few anomalies, such as the HTC Vive Cosmos (HTC Corporation 2019) having two trigger buttons, they will still mostly work, especially after the OpenXR standard (Khronos Group 2019) was adopted.

CHALLENGES AND ADVANTAGES OF GESTURE USER INTERFACES

Gesture UIs offer higher immersion than controller use, while having considerable usability challenges. However, there are other aspects to consider when utilizing them. These include at least:

- communication,
- cultural context,
- usage environment,
- handedness, and
- uni- and bimanuality.

Tracking Technology

Gestures can be detected in multiple ways, but the most common ones are using cameras which detect either visible light or infrared, or by using a tracking glove of some kind. The tracking also requires an algorithm to understand the data that is captured by the sensors, but the design of those is too deep a topic for this chapter, and there exists a plethora of research related to designing robust hand-tracking algorithms (Wang et al. 2020, Lemak et al. 2020). Instead, the focus relates to the tracking hardware, and why should any of them be used over others.

Hand-tracking gloves have existed for a long time with countless variations, each attempting to be more accurate than the one before it. Nowadays the accuracy is nearly one-to-one with the real hand movement, allowing for precise gesture-based interaction in VR, e.g., Hi5 VR glove (Noitom 2018). Gloves are also not very sensitive to lighting conditions. The drawbacks of gloves are their price, incompatibility with other hardware solutions or hand sizes/shapes, comfort issues, and additionally they can lessen immersion compared to pure HT without any wearables.

Another common approach is a camera either in the VR-headset (inside-out) or an external camera elsewhere in the play space (outside-in). The cameras can use either visible light, such as the Meta Quest 2 (Meta 2020), or combine it with infrared such as the Varjo VR-3 or XR-4 (Varjo 2018) with its Ultraleap Gemini sensor (Ultraleap 2024). Visible light only approach has the advantage of being cheaper and it can work well in good lighting conditions. However, utilizing it in darker areas can become problematic. Infrared sensors do not have such issues and work almost the same independent of the lighting conditions, but they cost more.

When comparing glove-based approaches to cameras, the main distinction is the freedom that cameras afford to the users' hands. Additionally, with gloves the users' immersion can suffer, but tracking often works better in all conditions when compared to the camera-based approach. Major weaknesses with most camera-based approaches are the limited tracking range of the cameras, occlusion issues when, e.g., overlapping hands, in addition to the sensitivity differences in lighting conditions. As a takeaway, the use of either gloves or camera-based tracking should be decided based on the project needs and budget.

Unimanual and Bimanual Gestures

Unimanual (single-handed) or *bimanual* (dual-handed) gesture use affects the gesture UI designers greatly. There can be many potential reasons for why a certain gesture should be performed with just one hand or why it requires both. Naturally, gestures often try to mimic the real-world actions that performing them in a VR system relates to, which means that actions which are in the real world performed with two hands require two hands also in VR. Nevertheless, this is not always possible or advised.

A study by Nyyssönen et al. (2024) compared unimanual and bimanual gesture UIs in VR, with the following benefits and disadvantages noted for both interface types:

Unimanual gestures afford *simplicity* in terms of action activation, resulting in more rapid functionality. However, they are more prone to user errors and the Midas touch problem. Additionally, when the gesture controls function with just one hand, the other hand can rest during actions or perform another function, affording multi-tasking. An example of multi-tasking would be using the left hand to move forward while simultaneously moving up with the right hand.

Bimanual gestures afford *control* over the interaction to a higher degree than unimanual gestures do. The main advantage is easier avoidance of the Midas touch problem due to actions only activating when both hands are in a specified pose. Naturally, this slows down action activation and removes the option for multitasking.

Bimanual gestures are useful when the required actions are precise and mistakes could cause serious issues, such as remote medical operations using VR. Unimanuality and easier action initiation is useful for situations where multi-tasking is necessary, and user errors cannot cause any real harm. Also, when needing to switch between different actions rapidly it is better to utilize unimanuality in most cases. The result of the study showed that unimanual gestures were preferred by the sample. Other works related to handedness in gestures include, e.g., Schäfer et al. (2021) who compared two one-handed and two-handed UIs in a teleportation-based locomotion system. Their study found that unimanual gestures were preferred due to ease of activation while bimanuality felt more reliable to those who preferred it, although the consensus was that there was no preference. In conclusion, bimanual and unimanual gestures are useful depending on the context, and neither is necessarily better.

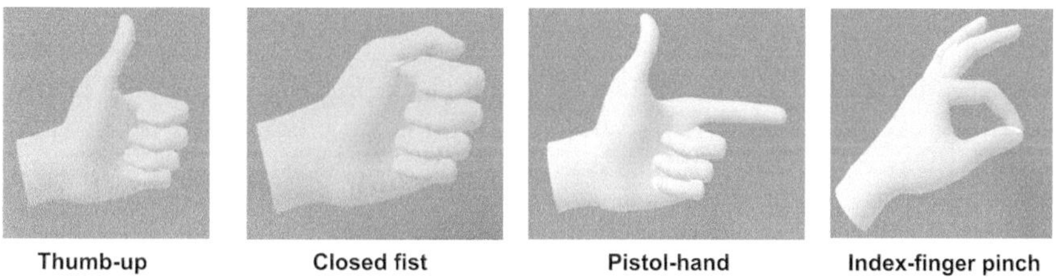

Figure 6.7 Gesture controls example by Nyyssönen et al. (2024) showing a few simple commands.

An overview of some possible gestures can be seen in Figure 6.7. The gestures can be performed either unimanually using one hand or bimanually by combining a gesture with another one on the other hand. A functionality exception is, e.g., the thumb- up gesture, which does nothing on its own, but can amplify the effect of the gestures it is combined with. It is important to remember that these are just examples, and there are no fixed rules for how gestures should be designed.

Gesture Interpretation and Detection

Gestures can be classified into three main categories: *Temporal*, *Contextual*, and *Instruction-based* (Vuletic et al. 2019).

Temporal refers to the gestures being *static* (Vinayak et al. 2013) (hand stays still) or *dynamic* (McNeill 1992) (hand moves from one gesture state to another). Opting for static gestures is often more feasible, as dynamic gestures can be hindered by potential tracking issues and could cause unnecessary physical strain for the user, in addition to being difficult to perform for users with low hand dexterity (Vuletic et al. 2019).

Contextual gestures are classified into *communicative* and *manipulative* types (Quek 1995). Communicative gestures attempt to communicate something to others, such as concepts, directions, locations, or shapes. They can also be part of application-specific language, where their meaning is context-locked. Manipulative gestures are employed to alter the spatial properties of objects, such as changing their position or orientation (Quek 2004). These gestures may also serve communicative functions in different contexts. For instance, Nyyssönen et al. (2024) describe a scenario where a thumb-up gesture, typically a positive signal in English-speaking cultures, is instead used to adjust speed within the application's language, thereby classifying it as both communicative and manipulative. (McNeill 1985, 2006, Quek 1995, 2004)

Instruction-based gestures consist of *prescribed* and *freeform* gestures. Prescribed gestures are part of a defined gesture language or library and cannot be altered by the user. They are designed to initiate a specific action without ambiguity or room for interpretation. Conversely, freeform gestures are composed of a series of smaller movements combined to form a more complex action that is subsequently recognized as a specific function. Examples of these could include drawing a shape in the air, which then leads to the creation of an object resembling the drawn shape. Alternatively, an object might be moved in space by tracing a path with one's finger. These gestures are not preset and rely on the user's discretion and creativity (Vuletic et al. 2019).

Gestures are strongly tied to the culture in which they are used. This means that designers need to be careful which gestures to include for which target audience. The aforementioned thumb-up gesture would be received rather poorly if it was used in a communicative purpose in Iran (where it is deemed an offensive gesture), while a diver would understand it as a sign that one is about to end their dive and head to the surface, likely due to some issue.

Additionally, whether the gestures are detected as correct or incorrect is important knowledge for the user performing them. The main way to achieve this is by adding functionality to a gesture and hoping that the user notices this, but this only works when the gesture is correctly recognized. There also needs to be a way to show when and why a gesture is not recognized currently and give the user an idea for how to remedy the situation. One solution is to implement color-codes denoting the stages of recognition (Figure 6.8). In it a recognized hand performing an action is indicated via a green color, a hand in a correct gesture but in an incorrect rotation or during a setting where that gesture functionality is disabled (such as in menus) is colored yellow, while hand in an unrecognized pose is white.

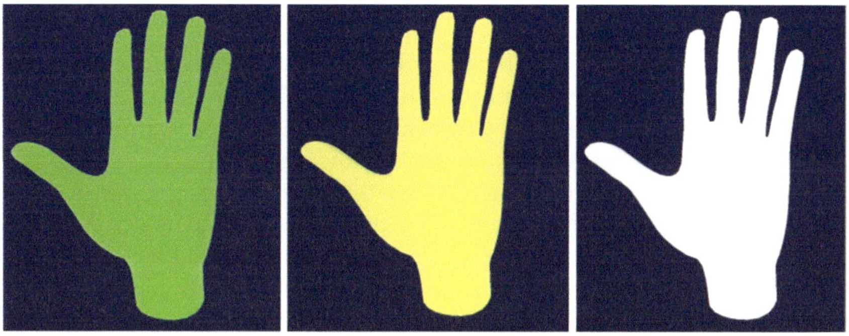

Figure 6.8 Gesture recognition color scheme by Nyyssönen et al. (2024).

RARER MECHANICS

HT is a well-known interaction technique, and it has been studied for a long time in various contexts. It also has many practical applications today. However, rarer natural VR mechanics also exist, which include at least eye- and face-tracking in addition to utilizing subconscious sensors, such as heart rate or galvanic skin response. The applications for these mechanics are, however, often either just case studies for research, or specialized devices aimed at aiding disabled users. Their impact on the issues of VR such as VR sickness is also largely unexplored, and they could potentially aid in solving them.

Eye-Tracking

Eye-tracking is widely recognized as a key objective measurement of usability in research, particularly when subjective measures may be misleading. In VR, eye-tracking proves especially effective by allowing simultaneous tracking of head and eye movements. This capability has been extensively utilized in virtual learning environments, establishing its value in VR usability studies (Rappa et al. 2019, Shadiev and Li 2023).

Eye movements typically measured by eye-tracking technology include *fixations*, where the eyes pause to focus on a particular area, and *saccades*, which are quick eye movements between points of interest. Together, fixations and saccades contribute to a person's overall perception, forming what are known as *scan paths*—sequences of eye movements indicative of shifts in attention and cognitive processes (Rayner 1998). Furthermore, *the eye-mind hypothesis* (Just and Carpenter 1980) suggests that the visual information the eyes focus on is precisely what the brain processes.

In VR, eye-tracking has been explored as a method for controlling locomotion, including techniques like wink-based and gaze-based teleportation, or combining eye-tracking with electroencephalography (EEG) for gesture-initiated teleportation. However, continuous use of eye movements for control is limited by the Midas touch problem meaning the unintentional actions triggered by natural eye movements, and the potential for visual fatigue from repetitive movements. Moreover, eye-tracking has shown promise in redirected walking strategies in VR, allowing users to move physically in a virtual space that appears larger than the actual physical space, with eye-tracking aiding in predicting user movement intentions with significant accuracy (Zank and Kunz 2016). (Prithul et al. 2022, Chen and Hou 2022, Kim et al. 2022, Linn 2017, Lu et al. 2020)

Additionally, research into *eye dominance* highlights the variations in individuals' ability to use one eye over another, affecting the feasibility of eye-dependent technologies. Eye dominance describes the phenomenon where one eye performs better than the other in certain visual tasks. This difference is typically evaluated in three main categories: *acuity* (sharpness), *binocular rivalry* (which eye sees more often), and *sighting* or *eyedness* (eye use preference). Among these, sighting is the most frequently used method to assess eye dominance (Porac and Coren 1976, Chaurasia and Mathur 1976, Mapp et al. 2003, Ooi and He 2020). Typically, the dominant eye, which is relied upon more, is harder or even impossible to close quickly or properly by itself, whereas the other eye closes easily. (Chan and Chang 1960, Palmer 1976, Porac and Coren 1976, Chaurasia and Mathur 1976, Mapp et al. 2003, Ooi and He 2020).

Eye dominance can be either weak or strong, and in extreme cases render one eye almost unusable if its signal processing capabilities are extremely weak. With a significant portion of the population (99%) exhibiting a dominant right or left eye (of some degree), any eye-based technology must accommodate the inability of some users to close just one eye (Chaurasia and Mathur 1976, Reiss and Reiss 1997, Eser et al. 2008).

An article by Nyyssönen et al. (in press) explored eye-openness as a locomotion directing mechanic and a speed adjuster using the Reverb G2 Omnicept Edition VR headset (Hewlett-Packard 2021). In the study, closing one eye would strafe the user either to the left or right, based on the currently active mechanic. The possibilities were either towards the open eye, i.e., closing the right eye would strafe left and vice versa, or towards the closed eye, meaning a synchronicity between the direction and the closed eye. Additionally, it was possible to perform a wink of correct length with either eye on its own to alternate between the mechanics, affording the use of the system with just one eye if desired (for strong eye-dominance). In another part of the study, eye-openness was utilized as either a brake or a throttle, i.e., closing one eye would either double or halve the speed. There was also a short waiting period for each wink to be detected to allow subconscious blinks with both eyes to occur without affecting the mechanics, thus avoiding the Midas touch problem.

The results showed that eye-dominance played a large role in the eye-preference of the users, meaning that users with a clearly dominant eye preferred to close the recessive eye more, as it was deemed easier. The system would be ideal for users with limited hand-using ability, as it is hands-free. However, users with no impairments preferred to use a more standardized way of directing their movement via turning their head, showing that it is difficult to introduce novel VR mechanics at least in short studies due to the adjustment phase required.

Subconscious Sensors and Context-Awareness

In the article of Nyyssönen et al. (in press) related to VR locomotion using eye-openness, another mechanic was utilized as well. This mechanic was the heart rate, which belongs to the subconscious reactions happening in the body. Subconscious reactions can be useful when the idea is to measure the experience in non-verbal ways, but performance is not an accurate enough measurement to determine usability. Heart rate which, while possible to be influenced in minor ways through, e.g., breathing speed, is a general indicator for stress in humans (although not in all situations). Higher stress, achieved by activities such as exercise, will increase the pulse, while lower stress, e.g., resting/sleeping, will decrease it. Pulse is however rarely used as a direct mechanic, but rather as an indicator.

This is why the study was keen on seeing whether pulse could be utilized in VR locomotion to adjust the movement speed. The pulse's impact was tested both with a direct relationship to the speed, i.e., increasing pulse increased the speed and vice versa, in addition to an inverted relationship. The study included an obstacle course for users to complete, and measured their pulse during it. The pulse was compared to an individual base heart rate that was prior measured in a VR setting, and the current pulse's difference to the prior rate was used to modify the speed. The main idea was that in case the user started having trouble with the obstacles, their stress would increase resulting in higher pulse, which would lower the speed and make the experience better. The opposite mechanic was tested for comparison. This is an example of *context-awareness* in VR applications, where the goal is to tailor each experience based on individual needs using non-verbal cues to automatically detect the optimal settings for any given time.

However, the results showed that there was no clear preference between a direct and inverse relationship of the pulse and the speed, leading to more questions about the use of pulse as a VR mechanic, although the sample was small. Additionally, the study showed that the usability of subconscious reactions is difficult to rate, due to the inherent difficulty of noticing them in the first place despite added visuals in the application. There was also contemplation about the accuracy of photoplethysmogram (PPG) sensors used in the study and the restrictions they create, such as requiring the user to stay still for the best tracking.

Other subconscious reactions than pulse have also been measured in VR applications, but their use as a mechanic is non-existent. An example for a mechanic-based purpose is *ManySense VR*, a Unity-based (Unity Technologies) software which attempts to synchronize user's avatar with their actions via the help of eye and face tracking, electroencephalogram, pulse, respiration, and galvanic skin response (Moon et al. 2022). The main difficulty is that the research surrounding the interpretation of the signals is lacking, thus making the utilization of them as mechanics difficult.

Furthermore, there are some devices which are capable of measuring many of the signals simultaneously, such as *Galea* (OpenBCI 2024), which is a brain-computer interface integrated into a VR HMD Varjo XR-3 (Varjo 2018), that includes EEG (brain activity), PPG (pulse), EMG (muscle motor sensor), EDA (sweat sensor), and eye-tracking. These types of devices can be used, e.g., for locomotion with face muscle movements or to detect the user's fatigue levels based on sweat output, offering a new world of interaction possibilities for VR.

CONCLUSION

The main results are that non-conventional VR mechanics have a high learning curve and drawing usability comparisons between one system and another can be difficult due to the lack of data about their optimal design. Additionally, the best use-case scenarios for them are likely to be specific, meaning that one form of interaction, e.g., hand-tracking, could be best suited for certain applications and certain demographics.

The major limitations are that the studies that are looked at in this chapter contain rather few participants, and the devices that are used lack precision and reliability.

In the future, the physical world might become more intertwined with the digital world, resulting in natural interfaces becoming more commonplace. There have been some indications through the devices that are being manufactured that controllers would disappear entirely and all UIs would utilize hand- or eye-tracking to function.

Another option is that natural UIs will fade away as they cannot be made intuitive or reliable enough. It could also be that the technology does not become comfortable enough to use, e.g., VR and AR headsets are still deemed too heavy for everyday use.

There is also a third option, which is that the technology can be made usable and safe enough for its adoption, but the cultural behavior norms prevent widespread adoption of the technology. For example, the technology might disturb those who do not use it, leading to it being abandoned. Alternatively, the technology might cause serious safety issues, such as mixed reality content displayed in the real world distracting traffic and causing accidents.

A final concern is that using natural interfaces is bound to give up more data on the user than before. Large companies that provide the devices or host the platforms could harvest user's data from hand and eye-movements and use it to diagnose or predict diseases for marketing purposes or it could be used to silence political opposition, e.g., via face-tracking disabling access to platforms. Furthermore, there are concerns with using digital rights management with eyes, such as preventing users from recording what they see when DRM-content is playing.

Some likely developments in the near future include the improvement of brain-computer UIs and eye-tracking, thus it is interesting to see how their role will change in VR applications. There is also potential for wearable technology to increase in adoption with trackers able to follow body parts precisely. Whatever the future will be, it is vital for designers to find ways to overcome the usability challenges that these new technologies bring.

REFERENCES

Adams, E. 2014. Fundamentals of Game Design, 3rd Ed. Pearson Education Inc.

Boring, S., Jurmu, M. and Butz, A. 2009. Scroll, tilt, or move it: Using mobile phones to continuously control pointers on large public displays. *In*: Proceedings of the 21st Annual Conference of the Australian Computer-Human Interaction Special Interest Group: Design: Open. 24(7): 161–168. ACM.

Chan, S.T. and Chang, K.S.F. 1960. Relation of eye dominance and eye closure. Nature. 185(4712): 539.

Chaurasia, B. and Mathur, B. 1976. Eyedness. Acta Anatomica. 96(2), 301–305.

Chen, X.-L. and Hou, W.-J. 2022. Gaze-based interaction intention recognition in virtual reality. Electronics. 11(10).

Eser, I., Durrie, D.S., Schwendeman, F. and Stahl, J.E. 2008. Association between ocular dominance and refraction. Journal of Refractive Surgery. 24(7): 685–689.

Fitzmaurice, G.W. and Buxton, W. 1997. An empirical evaluation of graspable user interfaces: Towards specialized, space-multiplexed input. *In*: Proceedings of the ACM SIGCHI Conference on Human Factors in Computing Systems (CHI '97). 43–50. ACM.

Fitzmaurice, G.W., Ishii, H. and Buxton, W.A.S. 1995. Bricks: Laying the foundations for graspable user interfaces. *In*: Proceedings of the SIGCHI Conference on Human Factors in Computing Systems (CHI '95). 442–449. ACM Press/Addison-Wesley.

Ha, T. and Woo, W. 2010. An empirical evaluation of virtual hand techniques for 3D object manipulation in a tangible augmented reality environment. *In*: 2010 IEEE Symposium on 3D User Interfaces (3DUI). 91–98. IEEE.

Hansberger, J.T., Peng, C., Mathis, S.L., Areyur Shanthakumar, V., Meacham, S.C., Cao, L., et al. 2017. Dispelling the gorilla arm syndrome: The viability of prolonged gesture interactions. pp. 505–520. *In*: S. Lackey and J. Chen (eds). Virtual, Augmented, and Mixed Reality. Springer International Publishing.

Hewlett-Packard. 2021, May. HP Reverb G2 Omnicept Edition VR Headset. https://www.hp.com/gb-en/vr/reverb-g2-vr-headset-omnicept-edition.html.

Hincapié-Ramos, J.D., Guo, X., Moghadasian, P. and Irani, P. 2014. Consumed endurance: A metric to quantify arm fatigue of mid-air interactions. *In*: Proceedings of the SIGCHI Conference on Human Factors in Computing Systems. 1063–1072. ACM.

HTC Corporation. 2016. HTC Vive Controller. https://www.vive.com/eu/accessory/controller/.

HTC Corporation. 2019. HTC Vive Cosmos VR Headset. https://www.vive.com/sea/product/vive-cosmos/features/. Accessed on April 23, 2024.

Jacob, R.J.K. 1990. What you look at is what you get: Eye movement-based interaction techniques *In*: Proceedings of the SIGCHI Conference on Human Factors in Computing Systems. 11–18.

Just, M.A. and Carpenter, P.A. 1980. A theory of reading: From eye fixations to comprehension. Psychological Review. 87(4): 329–354.

Kang, H.J., Shin, J.-H. and Ponto, K. 2020. A comparative analysis of 3D user interaction: How to move virtual objects in mixed reality. *In*: 2020 IEEE Conference on Virtual Reality and 3D User Interfaces (VR). 275–284. IEEE.

Kim, J., Jang, H., Kim, D. and Lee, J. 2022. Exploration of the virtual reality teleportation methods using hand-tracking, eye-tracking, and EEG. International Journal of Human–Computer Interaction. 39(20): 4112–4125. https://doi.org/10.1080/10447318.2022.2109248

Khronos Group. 2019. OpenXR Standard. https://www.khronos.org/openxr/. Accessed on April 23, 2024.

Lemak, S., Chertopolokhov, V., Uvarov, I., Kruchinina, A., Belousova, M., Borodkin, L., et al. 2020. Inertial sensor-based solution for finger motion tracking. Computers. 9(2).

Linn, A. 2017. Gaze Teleportation in Virtual Reality. Master's thesis, KTH, School of Computer Science and Communication (CSC).

Lu, X., Yu, D., Liang, H.-N., Xu, W., Chen, Y., Li, X., et al. 2020. Exploration of hands-free text entry techniques for virtual reality. ISMAR, Porto de Galinhas, Brazil. 344–349.

Mapp, A.P., Ono, H. and Barbeito, R. 2003. What does the dominant eye dominate? A brief and somewhat contentious review. Perception and Psychophysics. 65(2): 310–317.

McMahan, R., Bowman, D., Zielinski, D. and Brady, R. 2012. Evaluating display fidelity and interaction fidelity in a virtual reality game. IEEE Transactions on Visualization and Computer Graphics. 18: 626–633.

McMahan, R.P., Lai, C. and Pal, S.K. 2016. Interaction fidelity: The uncanny valley of virtual reality interactions. pp. 59–70. *In*: S. Lackey and R. Shumaker (eds). Virtual, Augmented, and Mixed Reality. Springer International Publishing.

McNeill, D. 1985. So you think gestures are nonverbal? Psychological Review. 92(3): 350–371.

McNeill, D. 1992. Hand and Mind: What Gestures Reveal about Thought. University of Chicago Press.

McNeill, D. 2006. Gesture and communication. pp. 58–66. *In*: K. Brown (ed.). Encyclopedia of Language and Linguistics, 2nd Ed. Elsevier.

Meta Platforms Inc. 2020. Meta Quest 2 VR Headset. https://www.meta.com/fi/en/quest/products/quest-2/.

Meta Platforms Inc. 2022. Meta Quest Pro VR Headset. https://www.meta.com/fi/en/quest/quest-pro/.

Moon, J., Jeong, M., Oh, S., Laine, T.H. and Seo, J. 2022. Data collection framework for context-aware virtual reality application development in Unity: Case of avatar embodiment. Sensors. 22(12).

Noitom. 2018. Hi5 VR Glove. https://hi5vrglove.com/. Accessed on April 8, 2024.

Nyyssönen, T. and Smed, J. 2021. Exploring virtual reality mechanics in puzzle design. The Computer Games Journal. 10(1): 65–87. https://doi.org/10.1007/s40869-020-00120-6.

Nyyssönen, T., Helle, S., Lehtonen, T. and Smed, J. 2022. A comparison of gesture and controller-based user interfaces for 3D design reviews in virtual reality. *In*: Proceedings of the 55th Annual Hawaii International Conference on System Sciences. http://hdl.handle.net/10125/79552.

Nyyssönen, T., Helle, S., Lehtonen, T. and Smed, J. 2024. A comparison of one- and two-handed gesture user interfaces in virtual reality: A task-based approach. Multimodal Technologies and Interaction. 8(2): 10. https://doi.org/10.3390/mti8020010.

Nyyssönen, T., Blackburn, J., Lehtonen, T. and Smed, J. (in press). Eye-openness and pulse-tracking in virtual reality as a navigation mechanic. Virtual Reality. Springer. In review.

Ooi, T.L. and He, Z.J. 2020. Sensory eye dominance: Relationship between eye and brain. Eye and Brain. 12: 25–31.

OpenBCI. 2024. Galea VR Headset. https://galea.co/#specs. Accessed on May 15, 2024.

Palmer, L.L. 1976. Inability to wink an eye and eye dominance. Perceptual and Motor Skills. 42(3): 825–826.

Porac, C. and Coren, S. 1976. The dominant eye. Psychological Bulletin. 83(5): 880–897.

Prithul, A., Bhandari, J., Spurgeon, W. and Folmer, E. 2022. Evaluation of hands-free teleportation in VR. *In*: Proceedings of the 2022 ACM Symposium on Spatial User Interaction (Article 5, 6 pages). ACM. https://doi.org/10.1145/3565970.3567683.

Quek, F. 2004. The catchment feature model: A device for multimodal fusion and a bridge between signal and sense. Eurasip Journal on Applied Signal Processing. 2004(11): 1619–1636.

Quek, F.K. 1995. Eyes in the interface. Image and Vision Computing. 13(6): 511–525.

Rappa, N., Ledger, S., Teo, T., Wong, K., Power, B. and Hilliard, B. 2019. The use of eye tracking technology to explore learning and performance within virtual reality and mixed reality settings: A scoping review. Interactive Learning Environments. 30(7): 1338–1350.

Rayner, K. 1998. Eye movements in reading and information processing: 20 years of research. Psychological Bulletin. 124(3): 372.

Reiss, M. and Reiss, G. 1997. Ocular dominance: Some family data. Laterality. 2(1): 7–16. https://doi.org/10.1080/713754254

Schäfer, A., Reis, G. and Stricker, D. 2021. Controlling teleportation-based locomotion in virtual reality with hand gestures: A comparative evaluation of two-handed and one-handed techniques. Electronics. 10(6): 715.

Shadiev, R. and Li, D. 2023. A review study on eye-tracking technology usage in immersive virtual reality learning environments. Computers and Education. 196.

Ultraleap. 2024. Ultraleap Gemini. https://www.ultraleap.com/tracking/gemini-hand-tracking-platform/. Accessed on April 15, 2024.

Unity Technologies. 2024. Unity3D Game Engine. Available online: https://unity.com/.

Varjo. 2018. Varjo XR Headsets. https://varjo.com/xr-headsets/. Accessed on April 15, 2024.

Vinayak, Murugappan, S., Liu, H. and Ramani, K. 2013. Shape-it-up: Hand gesture-based creative expression of 3D shapes using intelligent generalized cylinders. Computer-Aided Design. 45(2): 277–287.

Virtuix Inc. 2024. Virtuix Omni One. https://omni.virtuix.com/. Accessed on April 10, 2024.

Vuletic, T., Duffy, A., Hay, L., McTeague, C., Campbell, G. and Grealy, M. 2019. Systematic literature review of hand gestures used in human-computer interaction interfaces. International Journal of Human-Computer Studies. 129: 74–94.

Wang, J., Mueller, F., Bernard, F., Sorli, S., Sotnychenko, O., Qian, N., et al. 2020. RGB2Hands: Real-time tracking of 3D hand interactions from monocular RGB video. ACM Transactions on Graphics. 39(6).

Zank, M. and Kunz, A. 2016. Eye tracking for locomotion prediction in redirected walking. *In*: 2016 IEEE Symposium on 3D User Interfaces (3DUI). 49–58. IEEE.

Chapter **7**

Knowledge through Virtual Art Systems of Didactic Communication

Frederico Fialho Teixeira*[1] and Müge Belek Fialho Teixeira[2]
[1]School of Architecture, Design and Planning, The University of Queensland, Brisbane, Australia
[2]School of Architecture and Built Environment, Queensland University of Technology (QUT), Australia. Email: muge.teixeira@qut.edu.au

INTRODUCTION

Our ongoing immersion in various spaces leads to the continuous generation of new cognitive pathways, whether through conscious effort or unconscious assimilation. This project explores how virtual art, specifically through the framework of "Systems of Didactic Communication," can enhance this interplay and foster a more holistic approach to learning. This dynamic nature of knowledge construction is mirrored in the way we interact and understand space around us; to truly experience any space, presence is essential. The artwork titled "The One and the Multiple," underscores the importance of unanswered questions and the creative aspects of human existence, advocating for a learning philosophy that values intuition as much as rational thought.

*For Correspondence: f.frederico@uq.edu.au

DOI: 10.1201/9781003581642-7

It presents a model of inquiry not only for designers and artists but also for educators seeking to integrate creativity into their pedagogical strategies.

The interaction connecting the construction of knowledge and spatial experience is pivotal to understanding how one learns and creates environments. Knowledge is not a static entity but a dynamic construct that evolves within our minds through both intellectual contemplation and empirical experience (Shields 2023). Intellectual contemplation allows us to process and integrate new information, forming connections with our existing knowledge, while empirical experience provides the sensory input and practical engagement necessary for deeper understanding and retention. This dynamic multimodal nature of knowledge construction is mirrored in the way we interact with space; to truly experience any space, presence is essential. Our ongoing immersion in various spaces leads to the continuous generation of new cognitive pathways, whether through conscious effort or unconscious assimilation.

Knowledge construction involves both cognitive and sensory processes, requiring us to engage with our surroundings actively. Additionally, intellectual contemplation enables the integration of abstract concepts, facilitating critical thinking and problem-solving. Empirical experience, on the other hand, anchors these abstract concepts in tangible reality, ensuring that learning is not only theoretical but also applicable in real-world contexts. The synergy between contemplation and experience fosters a robust learning environment where knowledge is continually reshaped and refined.

Spatial experience plays a crucial role in this process. Our interaction with physical and virtual spaces influences how we perceive and understand the world around us. Architectural spaces can evoke emotions, stimulate creativity, and foster a sense of belonging. Similarly, virtual environments can provide immersive experiences that enhance learning and cognitive development. By navigating and interacting with these spaces, we create new cognitive pathways, enhancing our ability to learn and innovate (Kim and Lee 2022). Axiomatic to both knowledge construction and spatial experience, the concept of presence is vital. In this context, presence refers to the feeling of being immersed in a space, whether physical or virtual. This sense of immersion allows for a more profound and impactful learning experience. When we feel present in a space, we are more likely to engage fully with our surroundings, absorb information more effectively, and retain knowledge longer. This is particularly important in educational settings, where the goal is to create meaningful and lasting learning experiences.

Virtual reality (VR) significantly expands on this dynamic interplay by providing immersive environments that can simulate real-world scenarios and abstract concepts alike. VR allows learners to interact with and manipulate their surroundings in ways that are not possible in traditional educational settings (Chan et al. 2022). In architectural education, VR can simulate complex design projects, enabling users to experience and refine their creations in a virtual space before implementing them in the real world. VR also enhances experiential learning by providing immediate feedback and the ability to revisit and revise virtual experiences. This iterative process reinforces learning and helps solidify knowledge. Moreover, VR can cater to diverse learning styles by integrating visual, auditory, and kinesthetic elements, ensuring that a multimodal dimension allows all users to engage and understand a spatial experience (Philippe et al. 2020).

This study explores how virtual art, specifically through the framework of "Systems of Didactic Communication", can enhance the interplay between knowledge construction and spatial experience. Inspired by the artwork titled "The One and the Multiple", this framework challenges traditional notions of learning and creativity. It suggests that genuine knowledge acquisition extends beyond mere information transfer to embrace the full potential of creative thought. By utilizing multimodal spatial experiences and virtual reality, "Systems of Didactic Communication" offers a new paradigm for education, where creativity and spatial understanding are central to the learning process (Figure 7.1).

Figure 7.1 Exhibition of "The Multiple and the One" sculpture and its VR experience.

Virtual art environments, designed with principles of interactivity and immersion, provide unique opportunities for experiential learning.

These environments allow learners to engage with content in novel ways, fostering creativity and intuitive exploration. By integrating digital platforms and virtual reality, educational experiences can transcend theoretical confines and impact real-world understanding. This approach advocates for a holistic learning philosophy that values intuition and rational thought equally, promoting a more inclusive and creative didactic paradigm.

Fundamentally, this project argues for a didactic system that is inherently dynamic, one that fosters the synthesis of creative expression and spatial knowledge. It challenges the traditional dialectic of knowledge as merely an accumulation of facts, proposing instead that true learning emerges from the creative exploration of space and the integration of multidisciplinary perspectives. By blending humanity's creative impulses with technological mastery in VR, this framework aims to create a holistic approach to knowledge that considers spatial understanding as a critical component of intellectual and creative development.

FOUNDATIONS

In traditional architecture, spaces are designed with fixed forms and functions. However, Novak's "Liquid Architecture" challenges this notion by introducing environments that can change shape, function, and form in real-time (Novak 1991). These virtual environments are constructed using advanced computational techniques and algorithms that allow for a high degree of flexibility and responsiveness. For example, walls can shift, lighting can alter, and entire spatial configurations can reorient themselves based on how users move through and interact with the space.

This responsiveness makes Liquid Architecture particularly suited for didactic purposes. In a learning environment, the ability to adapt to the needs of individual users can significantly enhance the educational experience. For instance, a virtual classroom designed with Liquid Architecture principles can modify its layout to facilitate different teaching methods, such as transitioning from a lecture-based format to small group discussions or hands-on activities seamlessly. This adaptability ensures that the learning environment is always optimal for the didactic activities taking place.

LIQUID ARCHITECTURE THROUGH TRANSVERGENCE

Marcos Novak's concept of "Liquid Architecture" represents a transformative approach to space design, where virtual environments are not static but rather dynamic and responsive to user interactions. This idea draws from the principles of transvergence, which involves blending multiple disciplines and perspectives to create novel and adaptive solutions. Liquid Architecture embodies this by crafting spaces that are in a continuous state of flux, evolving based on the needs, actions, and interactions of their users (Figure 7.2).

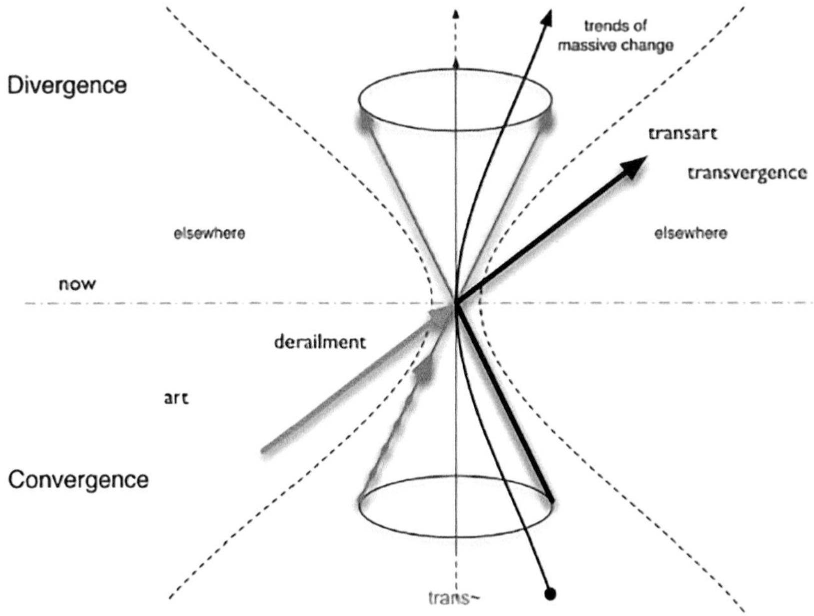

Figure 7.2 The diagram represents the definition of Transvergence by Marcos Novak, as the derailment of knowledge to elsewhere.

According to Marcos Novak, transvergence recognizes true statements to be islands in an alien archipelago, sometimes only accessible by leaps, flights, and voyages on vessels of artifice that advances translinearity by tactics of derailment. During prototyping possible scenarios that incrementally or significantly improve the originally inherited situation, letting knowledge outside of art to transverge will result in creating a new understanding (problem space) toward unprecedented designs. In this respect, an artist is an individual who is trying hard to take a step forward for the world. Transvergence shapes up by applying critical thinking simultaneously or hybridly through qualitative influences through perception and quantitative aspects, in this case the digital and computational methods. In order to transverge and become transmodal, the artist should be able to deterritorialize by releasing from the rigid disciplinary rules aligned with the discipline. One should be able to think laterally by reaching to a state of immanence through trying hard to understand unconceivable obscure issues that are outside of the comfort zone. Nevertheless, only through such a path, one can have a body without organs, where one can reach to the level of transcendental empiricism and ask the right question to finally initiate the process of creative thinking (Novak 2002).

The dynamic nature of "Liquid Architecture" offers several benefits as a didactic process. Firstly, it allows for personalized learning experiences. Virtual environments can be tailored to meet the specific needs and preferences of each learner. The dynamism of virtual environments allows users to adjust the environment to provide additional resources, such as interactive simulations or detailed visualizations, thereby fostering a deeper understanding of the material. Additionally, these environments encourage active learning. Instead of passively receiving information, users can engage with the content in interactive ways. In a virtual environment, users can manipulate 3D models, observing how changes in one part affect its overall space (Kretzer 2017). This kind of hands-on learning is made possible by the fluid and responsive nature of "Liquid Architecture". Marcos Novak's concept of "Liquid Architecture" redefines how we think about and interact with spaces, making it a powerful tool for didactics. By creating environments that are dynamic, responsive, and adaptable, Liquid Architecture enhances the learning experience, promoting active engagement and personalized didactic. These virtual environments, designed to be in a state of constant flux, not only respond to user interactions but also evolve to meet the changing needs of learners, making them ideal for educational purposes. This innovative approach holds significant promise for the future of education, offering new ways to engage and inspire users.

TOTAL WORK OF ART AND VIRTUAL REALITY INTEGRATION

While the focus on dynamic environments is a crucial trait, the multimodal aspect allows different users to experience and understand a space in different manners. The idea of multimodal design derives from the concept of "Total Work of Art" (Gesamtkunstwerk), originally proposed by Richard Wagner, which emphasizes the integration of various art forms—such as music, drama, and visual arts—into a single, immersive experience. Wagner envisioned this as a way to create a more profound and holistic artistic expression, where the synergy of different media could evoke deeper emotional and intellectual responses from the audience. This concept is foundational in understanding how different forms of art can combine to enhance the overall impact of an experience (Raz 2019).

Wagner's vision of the Total Work of Art was to unify disparate artistic elements into a cohesive whole, where each component—be it musical score, stage design, or narrative—contributes to the overall effect. This integration was intended to transcend the limitations of individual art forms, creating a more powerful and encompassing experience for the audience. Wagner's operas, such as "The Ring of the Nibelung", are prime examples of this approach, where the music, libretto, staging, and visual elements are meticulously crafted to work in concert, offering a fully immersive experience.

The concept of the Total Work of Art has been significantly expanded in the field of VR, where visual, auditory, and spatial elements can be seamlessly combined to create comprehensive learning environments. In VR, the integration of multimedia elements is not just additive but synergistic, enabling the creation of experiences that are far more engaging and effective than the sum of their parts. VR environments can simulate real-world scenarios and abstract concepts alike, providing a rich, interactive canvas for didactic content. In a VR setting, the principles of the Total Work of Art are applied by blending various sensory inputs to create an immersive educational experience. Visual elements, such as 3D models and animations, can be combined with auditory cues like spoken instructions and background music to enhance engagement and retention. Spatial elements, including the layout and interactivity of the virtual environment, add another layer of depth, allowing learners to navigate and manipulate the space in ways that facilitate active learning.

Figure 7.3 UQ VisLab immersive environment navigating through a 3D scanned point cloud environment.

This is now applicable across visualization facilities worldwide, this can also be experienced in the UQ VisLab, where users can see and hear space as they navigate through, with the spatial configuration of the lab adapting to their actions (Figure 7.3). This not only makes the learning process more engaging but also helps in better understanding and retention of complex concepts by providing immediate, multisensory feedback (Gibson 1979). By leveraging immersive multimedia integration, virtual art can provide a richer and more engaging didactic experience. The immersive nature of VR allows learners to experience concepts in a way that traditional educational methods cannot match. For instance, historical events can be recreated in VR, allowing users to 'witness' and interact with these events, providing a deeper understanding of the context and significance. Moreover, the interactivity of VR enables a more personalized learning experience. Each user can explore the virtual environment at their own pace, focusing on areas they find challenging or interesting. This adaptability ensures that the educational content is tailored to individual learning styles and needs, making the learning process more effective and enticing.

The idea of the Total Work of Art, as envisioned by Richard Wagner, finds a powerful contemporary application in the field of VR. By integrating visual, auditory, and spatial elements, VR can create comprehensive and immersive learning environments that provide richer and more engaging didactic experiences. This multimedia integration not only enhances the effectiveness of educational content but also transforms the learning process into an interactive and personalized journey, aligning perfectly with modern educational goals. Through VR, the Total Work of Art achieves its full potential, offering an innovative approach to education that leverages the synergy of multiple art forms to foster deeper understanding and engagement.

EXPERIENTIAL LEARNING AND DIDACTIC TRANSDISCIPLINARY

Experiential learning, as highlighted in the document on Global Transdisciplinary Education, involves engaging users in real-world, cross-cultural experiences that foster a deeper understanding and appreciation of diverse perspectives (Scharoun et al. 2023). This approach is crucial for developing systems of didactic communication that leverage virtual art to create immersive, interactive learning environments. Transdisciplinary education leverages the Total Work of Art by integrating diverse cultural, intellectual, and sensory experiences into the learning process. By engaging users in real-world projects that span different cultures and disciplines, this educational approach promotes a deeper appreciation of global perspectives and the interconnectedness of various fields of knowledge. For instance, this transdisciplinary project might involve users from architecture, information technology, and interaction design working together on the understanding of the urban environment. Based on the definition of the prefix trans-, being beyond one's cultural contexts and their original discipline environments, in this manner users gain a richer understanding of the complexities involved in global issues and develop skills in cross-cultural communication and collaboration (Feldman and Shapiro 1992).

The integration of Wagner's Total Work of Art into VR environments is particularly effective in developing systems of didactic communication. These systems use virtual art to create immersive, interactive learning environments that engage users in a multisensory experience. This approach enhances the learning process by making abstract concepts tangible and relatable through the use of visual, auditory, and spatial elements. Based on these premises, VR y can simulate diverse cultural and disciplinary settings, allowing users to experience different environments and perspectives firsthand. Often VR experiences provide users with an immersive experience that includes not only the visual reconstruction of the site but also ambient sounds and interactive elements that convey the cultural and spatial context. This multisensory approach helps users to better understand and appreciate the nuances of different cultures and spatial understanding (Fox and Kemp 2009).

The notion of the Total Work of Art, as envisioned by Richard Wagner, finds a powerful contemporary application in the field of virtual reality. By integrating visual, auditory, and spatial elements, VR can create comprehensive and immersive learning environments that provide richer and more engaging didactic experiences. This multimedia integration not only enhances the effectiveness of educational content but also transforms the learning process into an interactive and personalized journey, aligning perfectly with contemporary educational goals. In the context of transdisciplinary education, Wagner's approach is crucial for developing systems of didactic communication that leverage virtual art to create immersive, interactive learning environments. These environments engage users in real-world, cross-cultural experiences that foster a deeper understanding and appreciation of diverse perspectives. By blending the principles of the Total Work of Art with the capabilities of VR, educators can create innovative and impactful educational experiences that prepare users to navigate and address the complexities of our interconnected world.

METHODOLOGY

"The One and the Multiple", an artwork exhibited at the Home: Suburban Utopia event at the State Library of Queensland (Corley 2018), serves as a pivotal case study for exploring the integration of virtual art in educational contexts (Figure 7.4). The artwork utilizes multimodal spatial experiences combining a sculpture generated from an existing space and VR to examine the relationship between digital knowledge, creativity, and spatial understanding (Kiesler 1939). The conceptual framework of this artwork is based on the integration of transvergence, a principle that blends multiple disciplines and perspectives to create novel and where the necessary element is space (Bergson 2012).

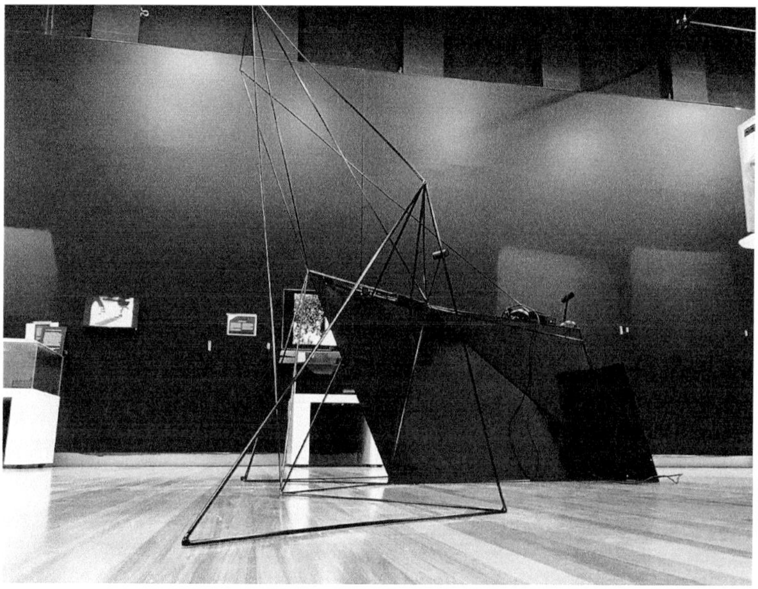

Figure 7.4 Exhibition of "The One and the Multiple" sculpture and its VR experience.

TRANSVERGENCE: BLENDING DISCIPLINES AND SPATIAL EXPERIENCES

Transvergence is at the heart of "The One and the Multiple", representing a synthesis of various artistic, scientific, and technological disciplines. This approach transcends traditional disciplinary boundaries, creating a holistic and multifaceted learning experience. By integrating elements from art, architecture, digital media, and education, the artwork offers a comprehensive perspective that enriches the learning process. Transvergence allows for the combination of diverse methodologies and ideas, fostering innovation and creativity. In "The One and the Multiple", this is achieved through the collaborative efforts of artists, technologists, and educators, each bringing their unique expertise to the project.

This multidisciplinary collaboration ensures that the virtual environment is not only visually and interactively compelling but also educationally effective. This transdisciplinary approach integrates insights and methodologies from various disciplines—such as art, architecture, education, and technology—to create a holistic learning experience. By drawing on diverse fields, the artwork addresses complex educational challenges from multiple angles, providing a richer and more nuanced understanding of the subject matter. This transdisciplinary integration is evident in the way the artwork combines artistic expression with didactic objectives, creating an environment where learning and creativity are seamlessly intertwined. By engaging with different disciplines, users can develop a broader perspective and a deeper understanding of the interconnectedness of knowledge. The One and the Multiple offered a multimodal, immersive experience, where space functions in parallel tectonic and virtual conditions (Foucault 1984).

INTEGRATION OF DIGITAL KNOWLEDGE AND CREATIVITY

"The One and the Multiple" challenges traditional notions of knowledge acquisition by emphasizing the integration of digital knowledge and creativity. The artwork uses digital media—such as 3D models, animations, and interactive simulations—to physically and virtually present complex spatial concepts in a tangible manner. This integration encourages users to think creatively and intuitively, exploring abstract ideas through direct simultaneous interaction between a physical representation and a virtual environment. Creativity is fostered through the design of the virtual space, which is both aesthetically pleasing and functionally educational. The virtual environment is designed to stimulate curiosity and inspire creative thinking, making learning a stimulating and impactful experience (Oosterhuis et al. 2006).

Virtual reality (VR) provides the technological foundation for "The One and the Multiple", enabling the creation of immersive and interactive environments. VR allows users to navigate and interact with the digital space in real-time, offering a sense of presence and immersion that is critical for experiential learning. In this artwork, VR is used to create a dynamic and engaging environment where users can explore, manipulate objects, and experience the content in a hands-on manner. By adding navigation possibility, interactivity became a crucial aspect of the VR experience as it allows users to engage directly with the educational material in a spatial manner. This engagement promotes active learning, where users are participants rather than passive recipients of information. By interacting with the virtual environment, users can experiment with different scenarios, test their understanding, and receive immediate feedback, enhancing the learning process. The application of transdisciplinary processes in the artwork is a multilayered microcosm that has its own rules, structures, natives, and living organisms. It is in constant evolution and becoming. The fragments that form this microcosm have an effect far greater than the sum of its all fragments and they are connected to each other with portals. The artwork presents images of the same space in a different time. These portals are embodiments that hold the function of bridging different levels of realities in transdisciplinary artworks. These portals connect actual and virtual mediums, allowing simultaneous embodiments within spaces with different scales, fictions, and dimensions. Transdisciplinary microcosm has affordances. Gibson's (1979) concept of 'affordances', defines all "action possibilities" latent in the environment, objectively measurable and independent of the individual's ability to recognize them, but always in relation to the person who experiences and therefore dependent on their capabilities. In order to realize affordances of a transdisciplinary art space, one should 'understand' the microcosms and the activities that take place within it, through experience. The personal experience gained from a transdisciplinary art space, can emerge through a lived journey with space and an obtained feeling of déjà vu. During this journey with space, the happenings in the microcosms are understood, transacted, and by only then one could become a fragment of space.

There is a need for a new type of understanding beyond analytical thinking, in order to experience and understand a transdisciplinary art space. This new type of understanding emerges as a result of a balance between comprehension of the sculpture and the perception of the virtual space. In order to reach such an understanding, there is a need to question what is new and to take it to a plane of immanence. People who experience the "The One and the Multiple" transdisciplinary virtual space through immersive environments, require time to learn how to move, orientate, stroll, and only then will they obtain a new awareness on how to experience with their body and mind. The feelings and senses that disappear in a daily life's routine will emerge with a shocking effect through transdisciplinary spatial experience and create a new awareness (*erlebnis*) and the experience gained with spending time within a transdisciplinary art space will lead to an understanding of a new world and to evolve into a becoming with it (*erfahrung*). While producing, researching, and creating the architecture of the information age that allow becomings in virtual and actual with a simultaneous apprehension, transvergence aims to create (*poiesis*) poetically by using digital design methods as techne. While achieving this, it produces its own epistemology, hence becoming a creative paradigm.

"THE ONE AND THE MULTIPLE" EXHIBIT

"The One and the Multiple" exhibit, showcased at the Home: Suburban Utopia event at the State Library of Queensland, serves as an illustrative example of how virtual art can be leveraged to create immersive and interactive educational environments. This case study delves into the conceptualization, development, and impact of the exhibit, highlighting its significance in advancing systems of didactic communication. The exhibit was conceived as a response to traditional educational paradigms that often rely on passive information transfer. Inspired by the concept of "Systems of Didactic Communication", the exhibit aims to transcend these limitations by integrating digital knowledge, creativity, and spatial understanding. "The One and the Multiple" utilizes VR to create a multimodal, interactive environment where users can explore complex concepts through direct engagement with the digital space (Jay 2005).

The primary objective of the exhibit is to challenge conventional notions of learning and creativity. By employing physical and VR elements, the exhibit seeks to provide a holistic learning experience that embraces the full potential of spatial understanding and creative thought. It posits that genuine knowledge acquisition extends beyond mere information transfer to involve immersive, intuitive exploration of spatial environments. This approach aligns with the principles of the Total Work of Art, integrating various media to create a cohesive and impactful educational experience (Figure 7.5).

Figure 7.5 Visualization of the point-cloud within the immersive Virtual Reality content of the "The One and the Multiple".

DESIGN AND IMPLEMENTATION

The design and implementation of the virtual art environments will involve the use of advanced VR technologies. These environments will be created using a combination of 3D modeling software, interactive design tools, and multimedia integration platforms. The goal is to create spaces that are not only visually engaging but also interactive and responsive to user inputs. "The One and the Multiple" artwork exemplifies the integration of advanced VR technologies to create an immersive and interactive educational environment. The design and implementation of these virtual art environments are structured to leverage cutting-edge VR technology, combining artistic vision with educational objectives. This section outlines the detailed methodology employed in the creation of "The One and the Multiple."

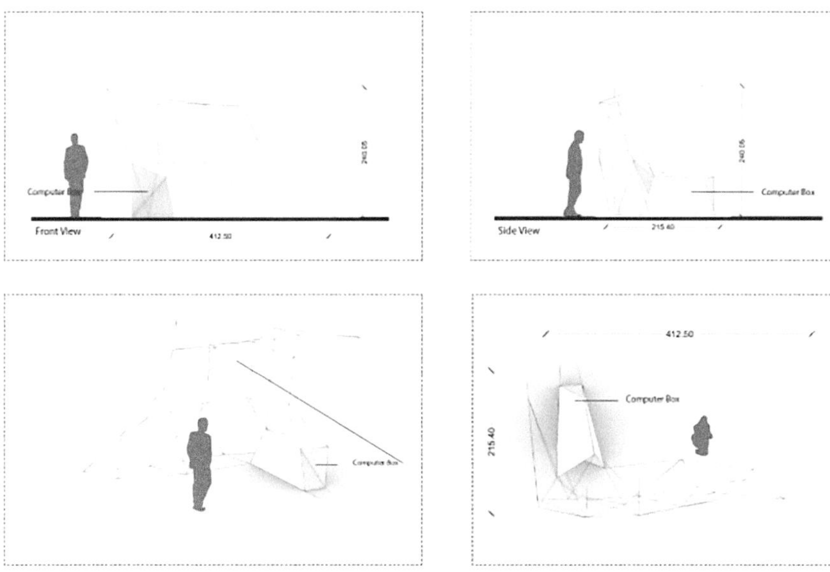

Figure 7.6 Integration from the physical sculpture with virtual reality requirements of the artwork.

The conceptual design phase constitutes the foundational step in developing "The One and the Multiple". This phase involves multiple disciplines ranging from architecture, art and computer science to define the educational goals and artistic vision of the project. The aim is to ensure that the final experience is both pedagogically effective and artistically compelling. Initial ideas and sketches are generated to visualize the proposed virtual environment, serving as a blueprint for subsequent stages of development. A narrative is then crafted to guide the user through the virtual experience, designed to be engaging and educational, providing a coherent structure for the immersive environment (Figure 7.6).

In the technological development phase, the technical creation of the virtual environment is undertaken using advanced VR tools and Computer Aided Design (CAD) software. This includes the use of software that included Rhino and Grasshopper for the physical sculpture, Cyclone 3D for processing 3D scans of the area through point clouds, and Unity to represent and create various elements of the virtual environment, from architectural structures to interactive elements. The virtual space is designed to ensure it is both visually appealing and functionally effective for educational purposes, which includes layout design, lighting, and texture application. Interactivity is implemented using game development platforms like Unity, involving the writing of scripts to enable user navigation and real-time feedback. Various media elements—audio and visual—are integrated into the VR environment, based on 3D scanned and recorded sounds to enhance immersion (Figure 7.7).

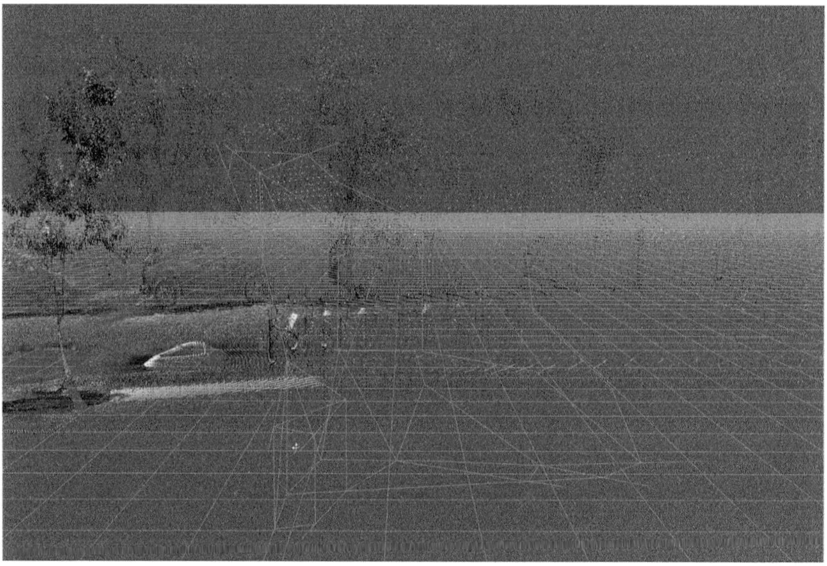

Figure 7.7 PointCloud context and topological generation of physical structure.

The final phase involves setting up the VR experience for public interaction and ensuring that it meets the highest standards of educational and artistic excellence. This includes configuring the VR hardware (Oculus Rift) and calibrating the system to ensure accurate tracking and seamless user experience. Clear instructions are provided for users on how to interact with the virtual environment, along with on-site support to assist users with any technical difficulties they may encounter. User interactions are observed and feedback collected through surveys and interviews to assess the overall impact and effectiveness of the VR experience.

The design and implementation of "The One and the Multiple" artwork involve a comprehensive methodology that integrates advanced virtual reality technologies with a robust conceptual framework. By leveraging VR's capabilities, the project creates an immersive, interactive, and educational environment that embodies the principles of transvergence and the Total Work of Art. Through meticulous planning, development, testing, and refinement, "The One and the Multiple" demonstrates the potential of virtual art to transform didactic practices and enhance knowledge construction.

SPATIAL EXPERIENCE

The exhibit was designed to immerse users in a virtual environment that encourages exploration and interaction. Through the use of advanced VR technologies, users were able to navigate and interact with various elements of the exhibit, facilitating a deeper understanding of the concepts being presented. The environment was designed to be dynamic and responsive, incorporating elements such as changing light, interactive objects, and adaptive spatial configurations. Interactivity was a key focus, achieved through programming scripts in Unity. These scripts enabled user interactions like object manipulation, navigation, and real-time feedback, enhancing the immersive experience. Multimedia elements, including sound scape, and navigation, were integrated to engage multiple senses and deepen user engagement (Kahl and Burckert 2012).

"The One and the Multiple" exhibit provided users with a rich, interactive experience. Upon donning the VR headset, users were transported into a meticulously crafted virtual environment. The exhibit's design allowed users to explore various digital spaces, interact with objects, and engage with the narrative in a personalized manner. The exhibit featured multiple interactive elements. For instance, users could manipulate virtual objects to see how their changes affected the environment. This hands-on interaction facilitated a deeper understanding of the exhibited concepts. The VR environment was also adaptive, responding to user actions by altering spatial configurations or triggering specific visual and auditory effects. This dynamic response kept users engaged and encouraged exploration. "The One and the Multiple" exhibit exemplifies the potential of virtual art to transform didactic practices. By leveraging advanced VR technologies, the exhibit creates an immersive and interactive environment that challenges traditional learning paradigms. Through its innovative use of digital media, interactivity, and spatial design, "The One and the Multiple" provides a compelling case for the integration of virtual art in educational settings. The exhibit not only enhances knowledge construction but also fosters creativity and intuitive exploration, offering a pathway toward more inclusive and dynamic didactic paradigms.

IMPACT ON KNOWLEDGE CONSTRUCTION

"The One and the Multiple" exhibit significantly impacts knowledge construction by leveraging the immersive and interactive capabilities of VR. This exhibit exemplifies how virtual art can transform abstract concepts into tangible experiences, thus enhancing the cognitive processes involved in learning. One of the primary impacts on knowledge construction is the enhancement of user engagement. By immersing users in a visually rich and interactive environment, the exhibit fosters a higher level of attention and interest. This heightened engagement facilitates deeper cognitive processing, making it easier for users to grasp complex concepts. The interactive elements, such as manipulating virtual objects and exploring dynamic spaces, promote active learning. Users are not passive recipients of information; instead, they actively engage with the content, which enhances their understanding and retention of knowledge. The exhibit also promotes experiential learning, a critical component in effective knowledge construction. Experiential learning theory posits that knowledge is created through the transformation of experience. By allowing users to interact directly with the virtual environment, "The One and the Multiple" provides experiential learning opportunities that traditional educational methods often lack. Users can experiment, make decisions, and observe the consequences of their actions in real-time, leading to a more profound and lasting understanding of the material.

Furthermore, the multimodal approach of the exhibit, which integrates visual, auditory, and tactile elements, caters to different learning styles. This inclusive approach ensures that a broader range of users can benefit from the educational content, regardless of their preferred learning modality. The combination of these sensory inputs helps to create a more holistic learning experience, reinforcing the material through multiple channels and aiding in memory retention. By integrating creative and intuitive exploration into the learning process, "The One and the Multiple" also encourages critical thinking and problem-solving skills. The dynamic nature of the virtual environment, which adapts to user interactions, challenges users to think creatively and make connections between different pieces of information. This process of exploration and discovery is crucial for developing higher-order cognitive skills, which are essential for deep learning and application of knowledge in real-world contexts.

CHALLENGES AND LIMITATIONS

Despite its numerous benefits, "The One and the Multiple" exhibit also faces several challenges and limitations that need to be addressed to fully realize the potential of VR in educational contexts. One significant challenge is the technical complexity involved in creating high-quality virtual environments. Developing detailed 3D models, programming interactivity, and integrating multimedia elements require specialized skills and advanced software tools. This complexity can make the development process time-consuming and costly, potentially limiting the scalability of such projects. Moreover, maintaining and updating the VR content to keep it relevant and functional adds to the ongoing resource requirements.

User discomfort and disorientation, commonly known as VR sickness, present another challenge. Some users may experience symptoms such as nausea, dizziness, or headaches when using VR, which can hinder their ability to engage with the content. This issue is particularly pertinent in educational settings, where prolonged use of VR may be required. Developers need to consider ergonomic and design factors that minimize these adverse effects to ensure a comfortable user experience. The exhibit's reliance on VR also raises concerns about the digital divide. Access to high-quality VR experiences may be limited to users in well-resourced environments, potentially exacerbating educational inequalities. Ensuring that VR-based didactic tools are accessible to a diverse audience, including those in underprivileged or remote areas, is crucial for promoting equitable learning opportunities.

Finally, there is the challenge of integrating VR experiences with traditional didactic systems that may not be fully equipped to incorporate the interactive and experiential nature of VR learning. Developing appropriate pedagogical strategies and assessment tools that align with VR-based education requires substantial effort and innovation from educators and policymakers. In conclusion, while "The One and the Multiple" exhibit demonstrates the transformative potential of VR in enhancing knowledge construction, it also highlights several challenges and limitations. Addressing these issues is essential for the broader adoption and effective implementation of VR in educational contexts. By overcoming these barriers, virtual art and VR technologies can provide innovative and impactful educational experiences that enhance learning outcomes and foster creativity and critical thinking skills.

CONCLUSION

The integration of virtual art into educational systems offers a transformative approach to knowledge construction and spatial experience. "The One and the Multiple" exhibit exemplifies how advanced VR technologies can be harnessed to create immersive, interactive learning environments that profoundly enhance the educational process. This integration is not merely about adding a new tool to the educator's arsenal; it represents a fundamental shift in how knowledge can be conveyed and comprehended. By leveraging concepts such as transvergence, liquid architecture, and experiential learning, virtual art creates dynamic and engaging educational experiences.

While transvergence, which blends multiple disciplines and perspectives and allows for a holistic and multifaceted approach to learning, this approach requires one to transcend traditional disciplinary boundaries, enabling users to draw connections across various fields of knowledge, fostering a more integrated and comprehensive understanding. Additionally, Liquid architecture, a concept that envisions spaces as fluid and adaptable, is particularly suited to VR environments. These virtual spaces can evolve in real-time based on user interactions, creating a responsive and personalized learning experience. This adaptability ensures that the educational content remains relevant and engaging, accommodating the diverse needs and learning styles of users. In "The One and the Multiple," this principle is applied to create an environment where users can explore and interact with the space in ways that traditional physical environments cannot offer. Experiential learning, which emphasizes learning through experience, is significantly enhanced by VR. In virtual environments, learners can engage directly with educational content, manipulating and experimenting with it in real-time. This hands-on approach not only aids in the retention of information but also encourages active participation and critical thinking. "The One and the Multiple" utilizes experiential learning to allow users to navigate and interact with complex concepts in a tangible and intuitive manner, making abstract ideas more accessible and understandable.

"Knowledge Through Virtual Art: Systems of Didactic Communication" fosters creativity by providing a platform where users can explore and experiment freely. In a VR environment, the constraints of the physical world are removed, allowing for limitless possibilities in design and interaction. This freedom encourages users to think outside the box, to experiment with new ideas, and to engage in creative problem-solving. The dynamic nature of virtual art ensures that learning is not a passive activity but an active, creative process. The integration of virtual art into educational systems thus transforms knowledge construction from a static transfer of information into a dynamic, interactive process. It enables users to engage with content on a deeper level, fostering not only comprehension but also innovation and creativity. By providing immersive, responsive, and engaging learning environments, virtual art supports the development of critical thinking skills and encourages lifelong learning through revisiting the experiences.

In conclusion, the incorporation of virtual art into education represents a significant advancement in how we approach teaching and learning. Concepts such as transvergence, liquid architecture, and experiential learning provide the foundation for creating rich, immersive educational experiences that enhance knowledge construction and foster creativity. "The One and the Multiple" exhibit demonstrates the potential of these technologies to revolutionize education, offering a model for how virtual environments can be used to create dynamic and effective systems of didactic communication. As we continue to explore and refine these approaches, the future of education holds the promise of becoming more engaging, inclusive, and innovative, fully realizing the potential of each learner through the transformative power of virtual art. By blending humanity's creative impulses with technological mastery in virtual reality, "The One and the Multiple" artwork advocates for a holistic approach to knowledge that considers spatial understanding as a critical component of intellectual and creative development. Fundamentally, "The One and the Multiple" argues for a didactic system that is inherently dynamic, one that fosters the synthesis of creative expression and spatial knowledge. It challenges the traditional dialectic of knowledge as merely an accumulation of facts, proposing instead that true learning emerges from the creative exploration of space and the integration of multidisciplinary perspectives. This approach to knowledge construction and dissemination offers a pathway toward a more inclusive and creative educational paradigm, where the potential of each learner can be fully realized in the confluence of art, technology, and spatial intuition.

ACKNOWLEDGEMENTS

This research uses a number of open-source plugins and tools, particularly, LunchBox for Rhino and Grasshopper and Unity Point Cloud Viewer. We would like to thank the community for providing these tools. Additionally, we acknowledge the commitment and support of UQ Engineering, Architecture and Information Technology, Information Technology Department, in particular Ben Ziegenfusz and Architect Shuwei Zhang. Their collaboration has been instrumental in advancing our research and enhancing the outcomes of this project.

REFERENCES

Bergson, H. 2012. Time and Free Will: An Essay on the Immediate Data of Consciousness. Dover Publications.

Chan, C.S., Bogdanovic, J. and Kalivarapu, V. 2022. Applying immersive virtual reality for remote teaching architectural history. Education and Information Technologies. 27(4): 4365–4397. https://doi.org/10.1007/s10639-021-10786-8.

Corley, F. 2018. Home: Suburban Obsession Exhibition. State Library of Queensland, Brisbane.

Feldman, Y. and Shapiro, E. 1992. Spatial machines: A more realistic approach to parallel computation. Communications of the ACM. 35(10): 60–73.

Foucault, M. 1984. Des espaces autres. Architecture, Mouvement, Continuité. 5: 46–49.

Fox, M. and Kemp, M. 2009. Interactive Architecture. Princeton Architectural Press.

Gibson, J.J. 1979. The Ecological Approach to Visual Perception. Houghton Mifflin.

Jay, M. 2005. Songs of Experience: Modern American and European Variations on a Universal Theme. University of California Press.

Kahl, G. and Burckert, C. 2012. Architecture to enable dual reality for smart environments. *In*: IE'12 Proceedings of the 2012 Eighth International Conference on Intelligent Environment. 42–49.

Kiesler, F. 1939. On correalism and biotechnique. Architectural Record. 86(3): 60–75.

Kim, N. and Lee, H. 2022. Exploring spatial design cognition using VR and eye-tracking. pp. 593–603. *In*: Gero, J.S. (ed.). Design Computing and Cognition'20. Springer, Cham. https://doi.org/10.1007/978-3-030-90625-2_35.

Kretzer, M. 2017. Towards a new softness. pp. 167–179. *In*: Kretzer, M. (ed.). Information

Materials. Springer. Cham. https://doi.org/10.1007/978-3-319-35150-6_5.

Novak, M. 1991. Liquid architectures in cyberspace. pp. 225–254. *In*: Benedikt, M. (ed.). Cyberspace: First Steps. MIT Press.

Novak, M. 2002. From speciation, transvergence, allogenesis: Notes on the production of the alien. Architectural Design. 72(3): 64–71. John Wiley & Son.

Oosterhuis, K., Feireiss, L. and Themans, M. 2006. Game Set and Match II: The Architecture Co-laboratory on Computer Games, Advanced Geometries, and Digital Technologies. Episode Publishers.

Philippe, S., Souchet, A.D., Lameras, P., Petridis, P., Caporal, J., Coldeboeuf, G., et al. 2020. Multimodal teaching, learning, and training in virtual reality: A review and case study. Virtual Reality and Intelligent Hardware. 2(5): 421–442. https://doi.org/10.1016/j.vrih.2020.07.008.

Raz, G. 2019. Virtual reality as an emerging art medium and its immersive affordances. pp. 995–1014. *In*: Carroll, N., Di Summa, L.T. and Loht, S. (eds).

The Palgrave Handbook of the Philosophy of Film and Motion Pictures. Springer.

Scharoun, L., Teixeira, M.B.F., Hills, D., Teixeira, F.F., Flynn, D. and Gudur, R. 2023. Understanding design culture from east to west: A transdisciplinary approach to teaching. pp. 225–248. *In*: Scharoun, L., Crowther, P., Meth, D., Brough, D., Teixeira, M.F.L.A. and Osborne Burton, L. (eds). Contemporary Design Education in Australia: Creating Transdisciplinary Futures. Intellect.

Shields, J.A.E. 2023. Phenomenology and architecture: Examining embodied experience and graphic representations of the built environment. pp. 315–336. *In*: Yoshimi, J., Walsh, P. and Londen, P. (eds). Horizons of Phenomenology. Springer, Cham. https://doi.org/10.1007/978-3-031-26074-2_15.

Chapter **8**

Development of a Systems Modeling Language Framework in Virtual Reality and Mixed Reality Environments: A Comparative Analysis

Kaan Karatas and Elif Surer*
Department of Modeling and Simulation, Graduate School of Informatics, Middle East Technical University
Emails: karatas.kaan@metu.edu.tr, elifs@metu.edu.tr

INTRODUCTION

Model-Based Systems Engineering (MBSE) is becoming increasingly popular and may become the prominent methodology in the field of Systems Engineering. Campo et al. (2022) has found that in academics, the positive view against MBSE is overwhelming against the negative view and application of MBSE in many industries is increasing while having skepticism that the view might be biased by the industries commercial pressures. With the increase in popularity of MBSE, many commercial products such as Enterprise Architect of Sparx Systems or Engineering Systems Design Rhapsody by IBM have started to keep up with the most

*For Correspondence: elifs@metu.edu.tr

DOI: 10.1201/9781003581642-8

current modeling language standards such as Architecture Analysis and Design Language (AADL) or Systems Modeling Language (SysML). However, there are no commercially available software that utilize Extended Reality, an umbrella term including Virtual Reality (VR), Augmented Reality (AR), and Mixed Reality (MR). This study aims to find the advantages and/or disadvantages of designing SysML models in VR and MR by defining a new framework for System Design.

A prototype of the framework is developed and evaluated via user feedback collected through user test sessions from 30 people who are working in industry with engineering background or graduate students who study in related fields. The participants of the user tests are divided into two groups based on their background, systems engineering (SE) group who understand what systems engineering is and have worked as or with systems engineers and interactive design and game development (IDGD) group who are experienced with either extended reality tools or worked with game or physics engines. The user tests were conducted with an equal number of participants from each group.

The prototype is developed as a VR and MR application as well as a desktop application so that the test participants run a set scenario in each environment. The participants are then asked to fill out Immersive Tendencies Questionnaire (ITQ) (UQO Cyberpsychology Lab 2004, Witmer and Singer 1998) to evaluate the participants' reactions against similar experiences, System Usability Scale (SUS) Questionnaire (Brooke 1996) to determine the usability of the system based on the participants' perspectives and thoughts, User Experience Questionnaire (UEQ) (Laugwitz et al. 2008, Schrepp et al. 2017) to examine if the prototype has unfavored features that could affect the participants, and finally Presence Questionnaire (PQ) (Witmer and Singer 1998) to measure if the VR and MR applications feel immersed in the environment.

This chapter starts with an introduction to the scope of the study in the first section. The second section presents the state-of-the-art through related work. The third section describes the development and architecture of the framework's prototype. The fourth section expresses the evaluation procedure from participant selection to data collection. The fifth and sixth sections demonstrate the acquired data and analysis of its importance. Finally, the seventh section summarizes the study and what can be built upon the findings.

LITERATURE REVIEW

MBSE has been an evolving field started with the definition of the term by Wymore (1993) with their book titled as the term. Industrial companies have been switching from DBSE to MBSE and many researchers have been exploring its potential and disadvantages. Adedjouma et al. (2020) explored the advantages of MBSE and found that MBSE can reduce redundancy, which happens due to separate documents describing the same functionality through different perspectives and increase productivity since the models are easier to understand due to their visual aspects.

Cameron and Adsit (2020) reached out to hundreds of participants through online courses to estimate how established MBSE is in the industry. They conducted a poll that revealed that while half of the participants took these courses to advance their knowledge in the field, only one third were able to practice MBSE in their work. Papke et al. (2020) studied how enterprises should switch to MBSE and what mistakes should be avoided if such a switch is chosen. They identified seven perspectives that need to be considered and explained that switching to MBSE is not just a switch in systems engineering method but a switch in the enterprise's architecture as well. Such revelations signified how difficult it is to adapt to the new systems of engineering methodology for long-running companies.

MBSE has been more than just a method to describe one system. DeLaurentis et al. (2022) expanded the definition of MBSE for a system of interest perspective to system of system perspective. They split the process of System of Systems Engineering (SoSE) into four phases and described how MBSE should be utilized in each phase. Furthermore Yang et al. (2023) created a model and simulated the interaction of complex weapon equipment using MBSE. Their study showed that the ever-increasing complexity of weapon systems can be simplified using MBSE and systems can be simulated in pre-developmental stages to find potential problems reducing the risks of facing snowball effects caused by design mistakes.

Integrating VR with MBSE has been another topic of study with increasing popularity and accessibility of the devices. However, Lutfi and Valerdi (2020) identified that while there had been several works about the potential of VR being used in MBSE, each research in integrating VR with MBSE had their individual applications and there was a lack of common framework in the literature. They designed their own framework combining the exported designed systems models from Cameo System Modeler (CMS)—a commercially available modeling software—and their own developed software in Unity Engine. They created an API that allows CMS to directly load the models onto VR devices. Their framework also aimed to simulate the product behavior in the VR environment to evaluate the model in its pre-development state (Lutfi and Valerdi 2021). They made a prototype example of a ground-based telescope system and integrated VR with MBSE through their framework (Lutfi and Valerdi 2023).

Oberhauser (2021) defined another framework using a stacked diagram approach to visualize the inter-diagram relationships. Their framework design started as a way of showing relationships for any modeling language and used UML models as an example. Oberhauser (2022) advanced their design to incorporate SysML with additional features. Their framework uses the 3D space provided by the virtual environment to stack different 2D diagrams on top of one another and uses the third dimension to link these dimensions' relations. These relations can provide other stakeholders a clearer and simpler view. Finally, they expanded the capabilities of the stacked view to display traceability between requirements and developed code as well as traceability between requirements and test descriptions (Oberhauser 2024). Their implementation can also report test coverage with their results. They managed to export software level requirements and test results by labeling their code and importing these requirements into their virtual environment. They defined customized connectors for the traceability and test coverages. Each test also had a display showing the success rate to show the overall status of a live software system.

METHODOLOGY

The proposed framework is monolithic software that can run independent of any commercially available modeling application. The framework consists of two main components—SysML library and visualization adapters. An illustration of the framework's architecture in UML model view including the external dependencies and target hardware is shown in Figure 8.1.

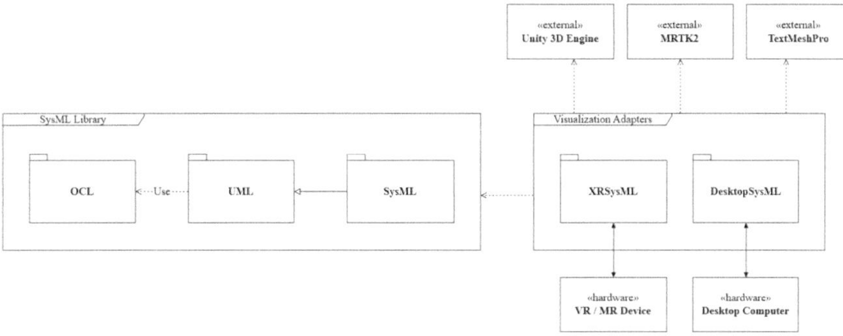

Figure 8.1 UML model view of the SysML framework architecture.

SysML library contains three packages that follow the Object Management Group's (OMG) Systems Modeling Language (OMG 2019) design. OMG SysML extends OMG Unified Modeling Language

(OMG 2017) which uses definitions from OMG Object Constraints Language (OMG 2011) for the class descriptions. SysML library also has a manager class SysMLProject that serves the purpose of an API through method calls and an event class SysMLEvents that contains certain events that are invoked by SysMLProject when any changes such as addition or removal of new elements in the SysML structure occurs. SysML library is a standalone C# application that uses only C# built-in functionalities.

The visualization adapters contain all necessary UI elements' scripts, prefabricated objects and configurations required to export the application to the target hardware. The visualization adapters are developed using Unity Engine. All prefabricated objects use custom developed scripts extending the MonoBehavior class of Unity Engine. Visualization for desktop computers and Virtual Reality or Mixed Reality devices are developed as separate applications named DesktopSysML and MRSysML, respectively. These packages share mostly common behavior scripts, but the prefabricated objects differ due to one environment being 2D and the other being 3D. The visual adapters utilize the materials defined in the Mixed Reality Toolkit (MRTK)—a toolkit originally developed by Microsoft and is now developed by a group of independent contributors to provide a common look and feel. The MRSysML package also uses MRTK as an integration tool for different VR and MR devices.

DESIGN PATTERNS

Singleton Design Pattern (McDonough 2017) allows for all objects in one process to access the same instance of the object regardless of which class it is called from. The initialization function of singleton classes is generally kept private and generally has a public instance object instead. When another class accesses the public instance object, if it is not initialized, the Singleton class initializes it and returns the object. For multi-threaded operations, there are generally different lock mechanisms to create a thread safe implementation. For the framework, singletons are used to create public events through singular classes and store a common library of objects.

Event Listener Design Pattern (Richards 2015) allows objects to interact with one another without having to use functional pointers or lambda functions. Event Listener Design Pattern simplifies expandability by having set events call certain functions of specific objects. Combined with Singleton Design Pattern, a set of globally accessible events can easily be maintained. For the framework, events are commonly used to refresh or update the user interface in accordance with user actions.

SYSML LIBRARY

For the SysML library, implementation of UML and SysML follow the OMG specifications almost exactly with little deviation. On the other hand, OCL does not follow the OMG specification and is only emulated. OCL required usage of multiple inheritance which is not supported by C# programming language. C# allows for multiple inheritance only for interfaces. Therefore, an exact implementation of OCL is not possible without using any external system such as a database or redundant implementation of hundreds of common interfaces for each non-abstract class.

OCL is emulated using two kinds of objects, namely, OCLObject and OCLManager. The OCLManager class uses the singleton design pattern. The OCL Manager has a two-dimensional hashed map, where the first key is an identifier integer, second key is object type and third as OCLObject. Each OCLObject requires an identification number (ID) to initialize and adds itself to the OCLManager's hashed map. Objects of the same ID are expected to be the same objects generalizations or specializations. Therefore, each OCLObject can access other types of itself through the OCLManager's hashed map using their ID. For UML and SysML, an interpretation of the OCLIsKindOf and OCLAsKind methods are implemented. OCLIsKindOf returns a boolean if the given object is of another type. The OCLAsKind method returns the object as the other type. For example, Comment is a generalization of Element, so if a Comment object's OCLIsKindOf method is called with Element type as argument, it would return true and if OCLIsKindOf method is called with Named Element type as argument, it would return false. The Element kind of Comment can be accessed by calling the OCLAsKind method with Element type as argument.

Each class in UML or SysML is defined by inheriting an OCLObject of its kind. All classes initialize their generalizations if they do not exist in the OCLManager. Recursively this would allow for initializing all direct and indirect generalizations of an object just by initializing the child type. Each object defines its direct and indirect generalizations as properties that can be obtained through the OCLManager and can access their operations, properties, and variables through the property. For example, the Comment object can access the Element object's properties and has its own GetOwnedElements property defined to call for the element and use its property. No UML or SysML object holds other objects as variable but just keeps their IDs to make sure that in case of removal of an object from OCLManager, no unused pointers remain, and the C# garbage collector can correctly free the memory when an object is removed.

The implementation of OCLManager acts as a transient database in the RAM and the two-dimensional hashed map reduces the access time of each object to the minimal delay. Since each object in UML and SysML consists of few primitive typed data, the OCLManager can keep thousands of objects in the memory.

Finally, SysML has an accessor class named SysMLProject. The SysMLProject initializes the model and acts as a medium between the visualization and library. All addition and removal operations are done through the SysMLProject, and it uses an event listener design pattern to invoke events in case of addition, update, or removal. The events are stored in a SysMLEvents singleton so that all classes can access these events easily.

VISUALIZATION ADAPTERS

DesktopSysML and MRSysML are separate applications developed as separate projects in Unity Engine, displayed in Figure 8.2 and 8.3, respectively. DesktopSysML is compiled to be run on Windows x64 systems and MRSysML is compiled to be run on Meta Quest 2. MRSysML has two separate scenes, one with Passthrough enabled for mixed reality and other without Passthrough for virtual reality. MRSysML supports usage of Meta Quest 2 Controllers as well as Meta Quest 2 Hand Interaction. MRSysML uses the MRTK for simplified integration of Meta Quest 2 and the aforementioned features.

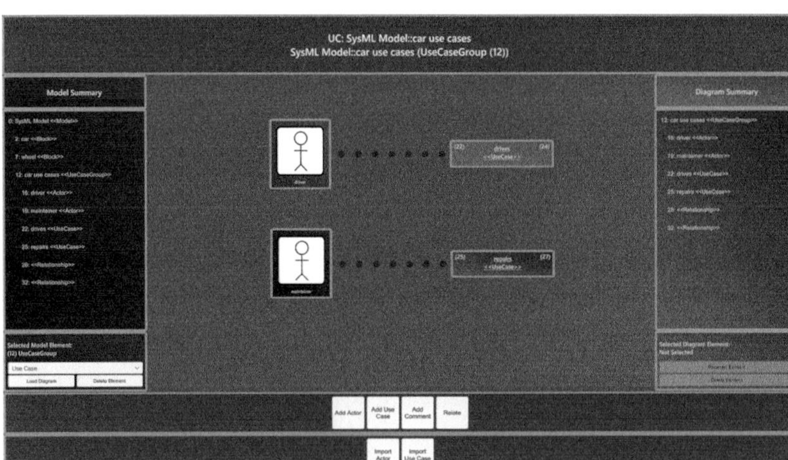

Figure 8.2 User viewing a use case diagram in DesktopSysML.

Both DesktopSysML and MRSysML use Unity Engine UI for GUI elements. MRTK allows using raycasters from the controllers or hand interaction on Unity GUI elements and the defined pre-fabricated objects can be switched between the mouse and keyboard, and MRTK GUI, by simply adding or removing two components on the UI game objects.

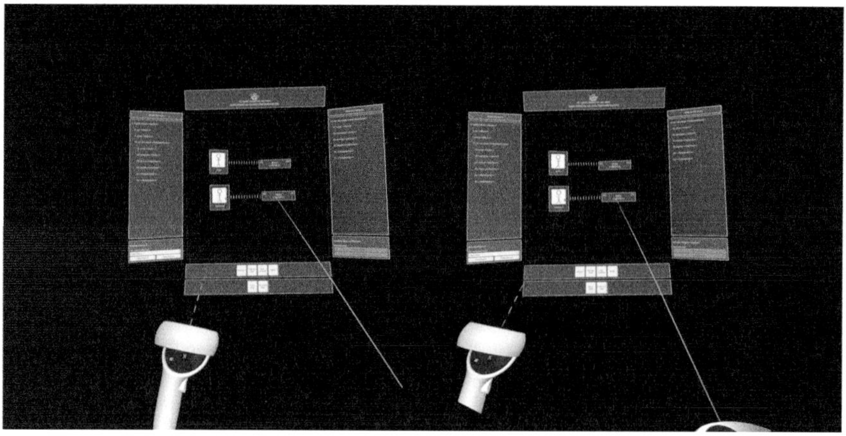

Figure 8.3 User viewing a use case diagram in MRSysML from including the view from both eye cameras.

For visual display, MRTK's holographic materials are used on both DesktopSysML and MRSysML to keep a similar look and feel. Both adapters consist of one static display and one dynamic display. The static display contains the main elements that would show the SysML model. It consists of five sections. The diagram visualization box shows the visual display of the active displayed diagram. The title bar section shows the actively loaded diagram, and for MRSysML it also acts as an anchor that the user can use to move it around. The model summary section allows for a holistic view of what the model contains. It allows for the user to navigate in-between diagrams. The diagram summary bar shows the contents of the active displayed diagram. The two action bars that contain the add and import buttons for the user can be used to interact with the project. The dynamic display contains the windows that pop-up when the user attempts to create content. For MRSysML, the static display does not move unless the user attempts to move it but always faces the user while the dynamic display follows the headset with a fixed height difference, distance, and angular difference.

For the user input, MRSysML uses a customized version non-native virtual keyboard implementation of MRTK for text input while DesktopSysML relies on the keyboard of the computer. MRSysML allows for the user to select through raycast from controllers or hands while DesktopSysML allows for the user to select via the mouse's left button.

For window and button management, all button actions invoke events and windows listen to these events and all windows act accordingly to these events. All events are stored in a WindowEvents singleton class so that all windows and buttons can access it easily. Each window is initialized with its window type and has to implement a response to three events, Apply, Close and Activate Buttons, which can invoke these three events. Upon initialization, each window sends a query through events to check if another window of the same type exists. If so, the window destroys itself to make sure to not overlap with any other windows. The Activate function expects window type as an argument. When the Activate function is called through event invocation, if the window type matches the initialization window type, the window is activated. If the window type does not match and the window is currently active, it deactivates itself automatically. Apply and Close events do not expect any arguments. When the Apply event is called, the window applies the function it is assigned. For example, a SysML Comment Creation Window initializes a SysML Comment and adds it to the SysML project. After the Apply function is called through invocation, the windows are automatically deactivated. After the Close function is called through invocation, the windows are automatically deactivated.

EVALUATION

The process of evaluation covers participant selection to data collection, and it is thoroughly explained in this section.

PARTICIPANT SELECTION

People who work in defense, information technology and game development industries as well as university students who study in similar fields are invited to participate in the user tests. The attendance was on a voluntary basis. The participants were asked a few questions to be categorized as being familiar with MBSE or being familiar with extended reality or software engineering technologies. Since the goal is to evaluate the framework from different perspectives, people with industrial experience in the field are compared with people who have experience developing similar frameworks and software. A group of 30 participants volunteered to attend the user tests.

USER TESTS

A user test scenario was prepared to be performed using both DesktopSysML and MRSysML. The scenario was almost identical for both applications with the only difference being, while using MRSysML, the static display can be moved around through user interaction and the scenario expects the users to move the display around therefore having experienced the whole application. The scenario was to design the concept of a calculator using systems engineering approaches. While the scenario did not include any ambiguity and was completely definite, the users were allowed to freely explore any additional functionalities of the prototype.

The scenario consists of five parts. The first part is the basics which introduces the participant to the application's GUI and user interaction. The second part expects the user to define the main elements of the project into the root package diagram. The third part expects the user to define the subcomponents of a calculator block's block definition diagram. The fourth part expects the user to define the calculator block's calculation activity diagram to define how calculation is processed. The fifth and final part expects the user to model a use case diagram by defining the actors of the calculator system, its use cases, and their relationships.

SysML has nine diagram types categorized as behavior diagrams, structure diagrams and requirement diagrams. The scenario consists of two of the four Structure Diagrams, Block Definitions Diagram and Package Diagram, and two of the Behavior Diagrams, Activity Diagram and Use Case Diagram. Since the goal of the research is to compare the two environments through different perspectives, the other kinds of diagrams were not included in the scenario to keep it understandable and simple.

STANDARD QUESTIONNAIRES

Four different standard questionnaires—Immersive Tendencies Questionnaire (ITQ), Presence Questionnaire (PQ), System Usability Scale (SUS) and User Experience Questionnaire (UEQ)—are used to evaluate the participants profiles and the benefits of the framework. Each provides a unique perspective and allows the framework to be evaluated by each questionnaire and the cross correlations that can be identified.

Immersive Tendencies Questionnaire is originally designed by Witmer and Singer (1998) as a 29-question questionnaire and was later revised and simplified by UQO Cyberpsychology Lab (2024) to include 18 questions. It is used to identify the behavior of the participant against instruments that are designed to keep their attention such as books, television shows, or computer games. The questionnaire measures the participants with regard to their tendency to focus, tendency to be involved, tendency to be emotional and tendency to play games. The revision by UQO Cyberpsychology Lab has introduced emotions as a factor. The scoring of each factor is done as follows:

- Focus = Q1 + Q2 + Q3 + Q8 + Q13
- Involvement = Q4 + Q5 + Q10 + Q12 + Q18
- Emotions = Q11 + Q15 + Q16 + Q17
- Games = Q6 + Q9 + Q14

The immersive tendencies questionnaire is used as an enabler to determine if either group has different tendencies and to determine if these tendencies may correlate with the results of another questionnaire.

The Presence Questionnaire is a 32-question questionnaire designed by Witmer and Singer (1998) which provides an analytical measurement of the participants' subjective sense of presence in a virtual environment. The questionnaire defines the sense through four factors and seven subscales. According to Witmer et al. (2005), instead of the initially proposed factors, using four new factors yield more consistent and meaningful results. These factors are, how involved the environment made the user feel (involvement), how accurate the user's senses are (sensory fidelity), how realistic and immersive the environment felt (Adaptation and Immersion), and how understandable the user interface is (Interface Quality). The scoring formulas are explained as follows:

- Involvement = Q1 + Q2 + Q3 + Q4 + Q6 + Q7 + Q8 + Q10 + Q14 + Q17 + Q18 + Q29
- Sensory Fidelity = Q5 + Q11 + Q12 + Q13 + Q15 + Q16
- Adaptation and Immersion = Q9 + Q20 + Q21 + Q24 + Q25 + Q30 + Q31 + Q32
- Interface Quality = 21 – Q19 – Q22 – Q23

A comparative analysis comparing both groups is conducted to see if either group has a stronger sense of presence in the virtual environment.

System Usability Scale is a 10-question scale designed by Brooke (1996) which intends to objectively assess usability through the feedback of the users regarding the product in question. The users evaluate each question from one to five and the usability score of the system is calculated as follows:

- O = Sum of all odd numbered question – 5
- E = 25 – Sum of all even numbered question
- SUS Score = (O + E) × 2.5

Each participant of the user test completes the questionnaire twice, once for DesktopSysML and again for MRSysML. To differentiate the usability of the framework in both environments, a comparative analysis is performed.

User Experience Questionnaire designed by Laugwitz et al. (2008) is a questionnaire with 26 unique attributes where the user is asked to relate their experience for each attribute. Each attribute consists of two opposite ends such as annoying and enjoyable or fast and dull. Each attribute can be scored one to seven ranging from one end to the other with a score of four meaning the experience did not feel either way.

Schrepp et al. (2017) has created a benchmark for the UEQ that is generated by averaging the results of 21,175 people from 468 unique studies. Their benchmark measures the product's user experience quality with respect to the results from other studies. The 26 scales in the questionnaire are weighted to six unique scales. Attractiveness measures if the overall impression is likable. Perspicuity measures if the system is easy to understand. Efficiency measures if the system is free of redundant actions. Dependability measures if the overall impression is under user control. Stimulation measures if the system is exciting to use or not. Novelty measures if the system is unique and creative.

The weighted sum of all attributes determines the rating for each scale which is put through the benchmark. Based on the rating of each scale, it is deemed one of six ranks. Excellent rank is for the top 10% of all studies. Good rank is for the top 25 to 10% of all studies. Above average rank is for the top 50 to 25% of all studies. Below average rank is for the bottom 50 to 25% of all studies. Bad rank is for the bottom 25% of all studies.

Each participant is requested to answer the questionnaire twice, once for DesktopSysML and again for MRSysML. A comparative analysis comparing the result for each application is applied to each group to discover the strengths and weaknesses of each application.

OPEN-ENDED QUESTIONS

After each user test session, the users were asked four open-ended questions to understand the reasons behind their responses. The first question is what their perceived strengths and weaknesses of using an MR or VR environment for such a framework are, the participants were allowed to provide any amount of strength or weakness as they wanted. The second question is which environment they prefer to work in and the reason for their preference. The third question is which controlling device (keyboard and mouse, controller, or hand interaction) they prefer to work with and the reason for their preference. The fourth and final question is what suggestion they would have to improve the framework and the prototype.

RESULTS

Immersive Tendencies Questionnaire

The box plot for the results of the Immersive Tendencies Questionnaires for SE group and IDGD group are shown in Figure 8.4.

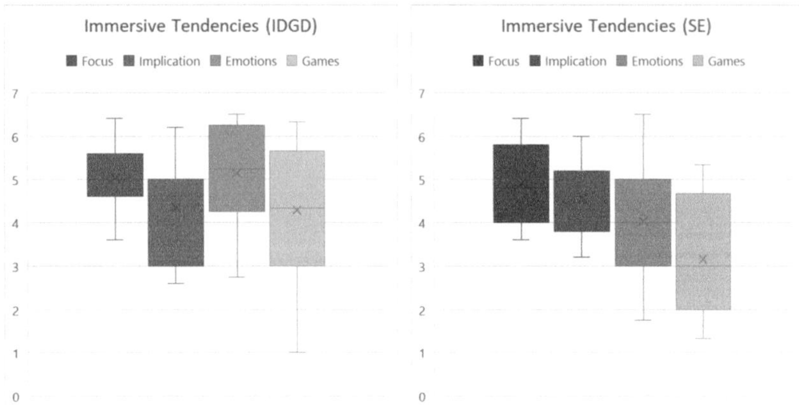

Figure 8.4 Box plot of the ITQ scores of participants aggregated by groups.

Since the ITQ scores are not normally distributed and the two groups are independent, the Mann-Whitney U Test is used to see if the two groups have a statistically significant difference on any of the attributes. The results are listed in Table 8.1.

Table 8.1 Mann-Whitney U Test results of ITQ scores for comparing the SE group with the IDGD group

Attribute	SE Group U-Value	IDGD Group U-Value	Minimum U-Value	Z-Value	P-Value
Focus	123.5	101.5	101.5	– 0.436	0.659
Implication	101.0	124.0	101.0	0.456	0.645
Emotion	164.0	61.0	61.0	– 2.115	0.034
Games	162.0	63.0	63.0	– 2.032	– 0.042

Since the significance level threshold is 0.05, the scores of the SE and IDGD group regards to Focus and Implication are statistically significant.

Presence Questionnaire

The box plot graph SE and IDGD groups' Presence Questionnaire scores for are as depicted in Figure 8.5.

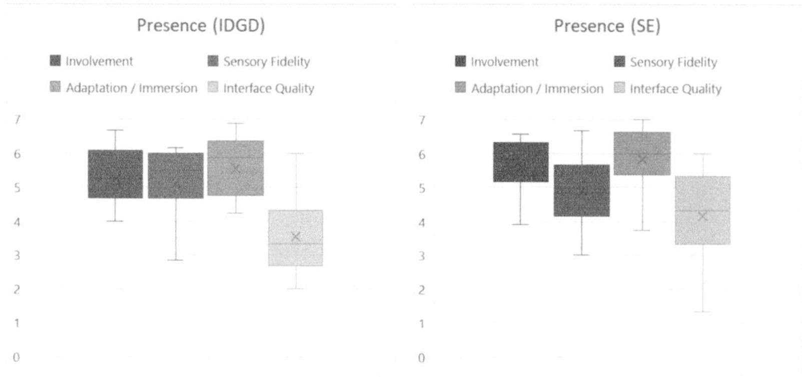

Figure 8.5 Box plot of the PQ scores of participants aggregated by groups.

Since the PQ scores are not normally distributed and the two groups are independent, the Mann-Whitney U Test is used to see if the two groups have a statistically significant difference regarding any of the attributes. The results are listed in Table 8.2.

Table 8.2 Mann-Whitney U Test results of PQ score for comparing the SE group with IDGD group

Attribute	SE Group U-Value	IDGD Group U-Value	Minimum U-Value	Z-Value	P-Value
Involvement	81.5	143.5	81.5	1.265	0.204
Sensory Fidelity	135.5	89.5	89.5	−0.933	0.352
Adaptation/ Immersion	93.0	132.0	93.0	0.788	0.430
Interface Quality	78.0	147.0	78.0	1.410	0.159

Since the significance level threshold is 0.05, the scores of the SE and IDGD group regards on all attributes are statistically insignificant.

SYSTEM USABILITY SCALE

The box plot of the System Usability Scale scores for SE group and IDGD group are as depicted in Figure 8.6.

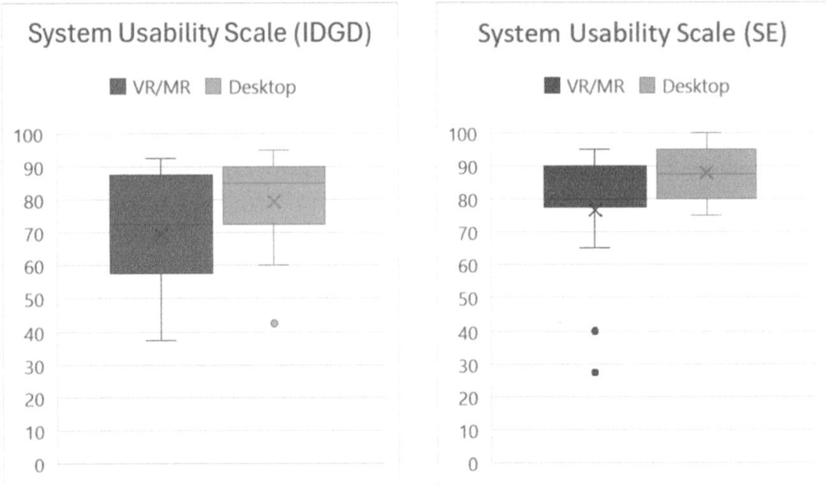

Figure 8.6 Box plot of the distribution of the SUS score for SE group and IDGD group.

Since the SUS scores were not normally distributed, but the results for MRSysML and DesktopSysML are dependent, the statistical significance is investigated by applying the Wilcoxon Signed-Rank Test. The results are listed in Table 8.3.

Table 8.3 Wilcoxon Signed-Rank Test results of SUS score for comparing the MRSysML with DesktopSysML

Group	MR/VR W-Value	Desktop W-Value	Minimum W-Value	Z-Value	P-Value
SE	14.0	106.0	14	–2.612	0.009
IDGD	20.5	99.5	20.5	–2.243	0.025
Joint	67.5	397.5	67.5	–3.3938	0.007

Since the significance level threshold is 0.05, the DesktopSysML is statistically significantly found to be more usable.

USER EXPERIENCE QUESTIONNAIRE

The user experience questionnaire is evaluated using its own benchmarks designed by the user experience group (Schrepp et al. 2017), who designed the user experience questionnaire as well. The benchmark ranks and mean values for each attribute are listed in Table 8.4.

Table 8.4 Benchmark attribute ranks and scores for each group and application

	SE Group		**IDGD Group**	
Attribute	MRSysML	DesktopSysML	MRSysML	DesktopSysML
Attractiveness	1.99 (Excellent)	1.14 (Below Avg)	1.21 (Above Avg)	0.76 (Below Avg)
Perspicuity	1.73 (Good)	2.23 (Excellent)	1.07 (Below Avg)	1.73 (Good)
Efficiency	1.27 (Above Avg)	1.98 (Excellent)	0.27 (Bad)	1.28 (Above Avg)
Dependability	1.58 (Good)	1.72 (Excellent)	0.78 (Below Avg)	1.53 (Good)
Stimulation	2.05 (Excellent)	0.78 (Below Avg)	1.72 (Excellent)	0.43 (Bad)
Novelty	1.70 (Excellent)	−0.48 (Bad)	1.32 (Good)	−0.43 (Bad)

For both groups, MRSysML excels at Attractiveness, Stimulation and Novelty while DesktopSysML excels at Perspicuity, Efficiency and Dependability.

OPEN-ENDED ANSWERS

When asked about the strengths and weaknesses of the VR and MR framework, participants provided 80 answers, 41 strengths that can be categorized into four groups and 39 weaknesses that can be categorized into six groups. The categories are enjoyable, text input difficulty, cumbersome, immersive, 3D viewing, intuitiveness, unfamiliarity, health concerns, imprecise and device availability. Enjoyable means the overall work felt pleasurable. Textual input difficulty means the participant had trouble with the virtual keyboard. Cumbersome means that the participant felt limited, and the prototype felt slow to operate. 3D viewing means that the participant found the 3D environment allowed for them to grasp the model better with depth as a dimension. Intuitiveness means the participant could easily adapt to the usage of the prototype's controls. Unfamiliarity means the participant had trouble adapting to VR and MR due to lack of past experiences. Health concerns means that the participant was afraid of using VR and MR for a long duration due to visual problems or carrying the weight of the headset could cause neck problems. Imprecise means the controls of the VR and MR device felt less precise compared to desktop applications. Device availability means that the participant finds VR and MR devices to be too expensive or limited due to similar reasons. The categories and the number of responses for each category is shown in Figure 8.7.

but similar experiences. Regarding the User Experience and Usability questionnaires, while both groups had different mean values, the distributions are similar. Both groups found the desktop prototype to be more usable, efficient, and easier to adapt to. On the other hand, VR and MR prototypes are found to be more enjoyable and engaging.

Most participants found controllers to be superior for object manipulation compared to using a mouse. However, using virtual keyboards with controllers felt cumbersome to many. Being able to use all ten fingers to type on a physical keyboard had an overwhelming preference. While the initial goal was to compare keyboard and mouse against controllers or hand interaction, a subgroup of the participants has claimed that being able to use a physical keyboard for textual input and controllers for other tasks would be the optimal solution. While the capabilities of Meta Quest 2 are limited on this front, the more advanced MR devices have capabilities to identify the real-world environment as a mesh grid and combining it with hand interaction, virtual keyboards can be used to type with ten fingers. Alternatively, MR devices allow for usage of physical keyboards as well, however most are limited to desktop applications mirrored onto the VR and MR devices views.

Even though the participants' system usability scale scores were statistically significantly worse for MR and VR prototype, the number of participants that prefer VR and MR environments were similar to the number of participants preferring the desktop environment. Participants that prefer VR and MR have commented that while they had trouble with the current state due to unfamiliarity and textual input, they found VR and MR to be more enjoyable and interactive and specifically for VR environment immersion helped them focus more. Usability of the VR and MR prototype may also be reduced due to lack of familiarity with such devices.

A third of the participants have highlighted that one of the main strength points for VR and MR environments is the 3D environment. Having multiple relationships in a 2D environment can cause confusion due to overlapping relationship lines. Having the third dimension allows the users to identify the ports where each line is connected to. One of the main strength points of MBSE being having the holistic view in a singular place, the third dimension allows better differentiation of diagram elements and their relationships from one another.

One sixth of the participants found the device to be tiresome and shared that they felt it would be unhealthy to use in longer sessions. However, the same argument can be used with desktop applications as well. The ergonomics of the devices is getting better as the technology is developed just as it is with office environments.

Overall, the VR and MR framework compared to the desktop application is neither better nor worse but has advantages and disadvantages. The participants' feedback shows that the VR and MR framework is a user-friendly and fun environment to work in which can be advanced through improvements to increase its usability.

CONCLUSION

In large scale projects with requirements becoming ever more convoluted, systems engineering is a critical discipline to simplify complicated problems. MBSE is becoming a well-known methodology through its advantages such as a simpler holistic view of a design. Usage of VR and MR for MBSE can enhance the performance of the systems engineer by providing a more immersive experience or enabling the third dimension for visualization and is an increasingly common topic of research.

In this study a framework of a monolithic application to perform model-based systems engineering in virtual or mixed reality is proposed as an alternative to using commercially available desktop applications and visualizing the designs in virtual environments. The framework is evaluated by user testing sessions conducted with 30 participants with an equal number of people with system engineering background or interactive design and game design background. The data gathered from these sessions were investigated through the lens of usability, user experience and participant perceptions. The results have shown that the framework is an enjoyable and engaging tool which can be further improved by additional features to support input systems and productivity.

Since SysML and similar modeling languages use syntactic diagram elements, textual input is vital and virtual reality tools' input systems can be cumbersome. Similar research with alternative input systems such as speech to text or combining keyboards with hand interaction may provide significant improvement. While the results have shown a positive perspective from the participants' standpoint, for a larger scale adaptation by a company or group of workers may be investigated to see the efficiency increase or drop. Finally, an improved collaborative framework can be designed to see if having multiple users interacting with the same model concurrently may or may not be beneficial for MBSE.

REFERENCES

Adedjouma, M., Thomas, T., Mraidha, C., Gerard, S. and Zeller, G. 2020. From document-based to model-based system and software engineering. *In*: Open Source Software for Model-Driven Engineering (OSS4MDE'16). 27–36. Saint Malo.

Brooke, J. 1996. SUS: A quick and dirty usability scale. Usability Evaluation in Industry. 207–212.

Cameron, B. and Adsit, D.M. 2020. Model-based systems engineering uptake in engineering practice. IEEE Transactions on Engineering Management. 67(1): 152–162.

Campo, K.X., Teper, T., Eaton, C.E., Shipman, A.M., Bhatia, G. and Mesmer, B. 2022. Model-based systems engineering: Evaluating perceived value, metrics, and evidence through literature. Systems Engineering. 26(1): 104–129.

DeLaurentis, D., Raz, A. and Guariniello, C. 2022. MBSE for system-of-systems. Handbook of Model-Based Systems Engineering. 1–29.

Laugwitz, B., Held, T. and Schrepp, M. 2008. Construction and evaluation of a user experience questionnaire. pp. 63–76. *In*: Holzinger, A. (ed.). HCI and Usability for Education and Work. USAB 2008. Lecture Notes in Computer Science, vol 5298. Springer, Berlin, Heidelberg. https://doi.org/10.1007/978-3-540-89350-9_6 .

Lutfi, M. and Valerdi, R. 2020. Virtual reality in model based systems engineering: A review paper. Communications in Computer and Information Science. 197–205.

Lutfi, M. and Valerdi, R. 2021. Framework for integration of virtual reality into model based systems engineering approach. Lecture Notes in Networks and Systems. 131–139.

Lutfi, M. and Valerdi, R. 2023. Integration of SysML and virtual reality environment: A ground-based telescope system example. Systems. 11(4): 189.

McDonough, J.E. 2017. Singleton design pattern. Object-Oriented Design with ABAP. 137–145.

Oberhauser, R. 2021. VR-UML: The Unified Modeling Language in virtual reality: An immersive modeling experience. Lecture Notes in Business Information Processing. 40–58.

Oberhauser, R. 2022. VR-SysML: SysML Model Visualization and Immersion in Virtual Reality. *In*: MODERN SYSTEMS 2022, International Conference of Modern Systems Engineering Solutions. 61–66.

Oberhauser, R. 2024. VR-SysML+Traceability: Immersive requirements traceability and test traceability with SysML to support verification and validation in virtual reality. International Journal on Advances in Software. 16(2): 23–35.

Object Management Group® Standards Development Organization. 2011. Object Constraint Language. https://www.omg.org/spec/OCL/2.3.1.

Object Management Group® Standards Development Organization. 2017. Unified Modeling Language. https://www.omg.org/spec/UML/2.5.1

Object Management Group® Standards Development Organization. 2019. OMG Systems Modeling Language. https://www.omg.org/spec/SysML/1.6.

Papke, B.L., Wang, G., Kratzke, R. and Schreiber, C. 2020. Implementing MBSE: An enterprise approach to an enterprise problem. INCOSE International Symposium. 30(1): 1550–1567.

Richards, M. 2015. Software Architecture Patterns. O'Reilly Media.

Schrepp, M., Hinderks, A. and Thomaschewski, J. 2017. Construction of a benchmark for the user experience questionnaire (UEQ). International Journal of Interactive Multimedia and Artificial Intelligence. 4(4): 40.

UQO Cyberpsychology Lab. 2004. Immersive Tendencies Questionnaire.

Witmer, B.G. and Singer, M.J. 1998. Measuring presence in virtual environments: A presence questionnaire. Presence: Teleoperators and Virtual Environments. 7(3): 225–240.

Witmer, B.G., Jerome, C.J. and Singer, M.J. 2005. The factor structure of the presence questionnaire. Presence: Teleoperators and Virtual Environments. 14(3): 298–312.

Wymore, A.W. 1993. Model-Based Systems Engineering, 1st Ed. Chapman and Hall/CRC.

Yang, H., Xia, Z., Chen, Y., Zhu, L., Dai, L., Xu, R., et al. 2023. Research on visual simulation for complex weapon equipment interoperability based on MBSE. Multimedia Tools and Applications. 83(5): 13463–13482.

Chapter **9**

Custom Manufacturing 4.0: Identifying Emerging Augmented Fabrication Workflows to Support SME Advancement in the AEC Industry

Anthony P. Franzè*[1], Glenda A. Caldwell[2], Müge Belek Fialho Teixeira[3] and Markus Rittenbruch[4]

[1,2,3]School of Architecture and Built Environment, Queensland University of Technology (QUT)
Emails: g.caldwell@qut.edu.au; muge.teixeira@qut.edu.au

[4]School of Design, Queensland University of Technology (QUT)
Email: m.rittenbruch@qut.edu.au

INTRODUCTION

Driven by rapid technological progress over the past decade, Industry 4.0 (I4.0) has been established as a dominant paradigm and continues

*For Correspondence: a.franze@qut.edu.au

DOI: 10.1201/9781003581642-9

to transform industries, nations, and society (Schwab and Davis 2018). I4.0, characterised by advancements in computational power, artificial intelligence, robotics, additive manufacturing, and immersive technologies, including augmented reality (AR), is reshaping the global manufacturing sector (Kelly 2016). This shift is also socio-economic, influenced by sustainability concerns, labour shortages, shifting consumer preferences and dynamic global supply chains, significantly altering industries, nations, and society (Nahavandi 2019).

I4.0 transformation profoundly impacts the custom manufacturing companies servicing the architecture, construction, and engineering (AEC) industry, which manufacture increasingly sophisticated bespoke products such as parametric building facades and large-scale artworks. Custom manufacturers are typically small-to-medium enterprises (SMEs) with limited research and development (R&D) resources (ABS 2023) and are increasingly challenged in adapting to new economies of I4.0 AEC production (Dean et al. 2021). Within these production systems, increased quantities of complex analytical information and knowledge relating to materialisation have come to permeate a project's life cycle (Bernstein 2012). This complexity especially challenges the fabrication and assembly workflows of custom manufacturers operating in the AEC industry, which requires new approaches to translating design intent into construction execution efficiently.

In this chapter, we focus on supporting custom manufacturers to meet existing I4.0 challenges by revealing workforce productivity enhancements made possible through AR technology (Lammers et al. 2023) and, additionally, how the technology can support SMEs in preparing for a more human-centric Industry 5.0 (I5.0) paradigm on the horizon. Proponents of I5.0 contend that as technological advancement continues unabated, humans are at risk of being left behind as advanced manufacturing systems move toward completely autonomous and robotic approaches (Commission et al. 2021). In anticipation, proponents call for an I5.0 paradigm that extends I4.0's positive aspects by combining human ingenuity with machine efficiencies (Maddikunta et al. 2022). I5.0 emphasizes respecting workers' needs and leveraging their full capabilities. We believe that AR has an essential role in ensuring continued human involvement within future manufacturing systems (Commission et al. 2021).

Within present production approaches, architectural designers are creating increasingly sophisticated parametric designs and building information models (BIM). However, frontline fabrication workers still rely on limited 2D drawings and manual machines to help materialise design intent. Furthermore, the consideration for the nuances of fabrication and assembly is often not present in the traditional 2D documentation provided by larger AEC firms' 3D BIM models, with issues often arising for these fabricators in translating design intent through 2D drawings (Garcia et al. 2018, Reza Hosseini et al. 2016). This approach increases inefficiencies, leading to waste and lower productivity (Bernstein 2012), with responsibility and costs solely on the custom fabricator.

It is the primary authors' experience that large AEC firms are reluctant to supply 3D CAD (computer aided design) models with their 2D documentation to custom fabrication companies for several reasons: (1) open for interpretation, (2) IP (intellectual property) concerns, and (3) standardisation. Whilst 3D geometry is more descriptive than 2D information, 3D CAD models from larger AEC firms do not describe designed objects in a manner feasible for manufacture. Instead, there is an expectation that custom manufacturers interpret larger firms' design intent and utilise their manufacturing expertise to realise outcomes (Bernstein 2012). AEC firms may also have IP concerns sharing 3D models and, within the industry, 2D drawings constitute the only legal design document (Côté et al. 2013). As certified for construction, they offer standardised approaches across AEC to reduce error, risk, and liability (Côté et al. 2013).

As a result, a subset of SMEs, primarily custom metal fabricators servicing the AEC sector, have turned to relatively low-cost and versatile AR technology to extend 2D drawing and manual machine potentials for more efficient and productive workflows (Caldwell et al. 2019, Jahn 2022). However, despite growing attention among researchers and practitioners across architecture (Cheng et al. 2020, Song et al. 2021, Teixeira et al. 2021), design (Liu et al. 2021), and manufacturing (Bottani and Vignali 2019, Wang et al. 2020) significant gaps exist in theoretical and practice-based knowledge regarding AR's application in custom production processes (Mason et al. 2022).

BACKGROUND AND CONTEXT

Although the AEC industry has embraced I4.0 technologies such as robotics and additive manufacturing, AR technology, whilst having shown promise, has yet to develop its full potential in the industry. AR is an essential technology to consider, as human problem-solving skills are still inimitable when responding to real-world construction site challenges. AR has the unique quality of being able to help capitalise on this human capability and ingenuity (Jahn et al. 2018), providing a relatively cost-effective alternative and complement to other advanced manufacturing technologies, such as robotics.

It is also vital to note that although AR has lower upfront costs than other I4.0 technologies, such as robotics, specialist skill sets are still required, making it challenging for SMEs to invest the necessary resources to integrate the technology successfully (Chasin et al. 2022, Evans and Bosua 2017, Lammers et al. 2023). Companies typically require specific computer programming and CAD expertise to develop adequate AR responses for specific manufacturing workflows. Moreover, challenges around on-site use, registration accuracy, and multi-user synchronisation have historically limited the technology's application (Cheng et al. 2020).

Given its emergent nature, AR technology continues to undergo rapid transformations with new hardware devices, software applications and ecosystems. This section gives an overview of these technologies, including hardware devices and software applications. Some types of hardware include Spatial (projection-based) AR, mobile tangible user interfaces (TUIs), along with the Microsoft HoloLens head-mounted device (HMD). Spatial AR can provide large-scale shared experiences by projecting digital content directly onto the workpiece or site without users wearing devices, but it can be cost-prohibitive and less flexible than other approaches. TUIs are often mobile phone and tablet-based, which are both highly accessible but challenging to use in fabrication given the lack of depth perception and the need to hold them. The HoloLens 2 is particularly suited to industrial settings, given the removal of physical constraints through ergonomic hands-free operation, compute power, and natural interaction capabilities (Pose-Díez-de-la-Lastra et al. 2022).

As the device ecosystem has rapidly developed, so has AR software development, with applications suited towards AEC fabrication and precision-manufactured parts. Users can now obtain mobile 3D CAD development tools such as Xcode and Adobe Aero through iOS and Android stores to create introductory AR experiences and advanced applications using game engines such as Unity 3D and Unreal. Moreover, most CAD packages, such as SolidWorks, Keyshot 3D, Autodesk and Tekla, now provide integrated mobile AR applications, allowing users to visualise 3D CAD content overlayed in their physical environment. Additional commercial solutions provide high-end product visualisations, frontline worker training and instructions for manufacturing firms on mobile devices and HMDs, including HoloLens. For example, Microsoft Dynamics 365 Guides and PTC Vuforia Studio can help users create contextualised virtual work instructions and assembly guides for higher-precision parts (*On-the-job guidance* 2022). Furthermore, Trimble Connect mixed reality (MR) allows users to contextualise virtual BIM models and technical information on construction sites.

Regarding fabrication and assembly, three software applications, Fologram, Twin Build, and FabStation, present a significant step forward in AR integration and can be utilised across AR devices, such as HMDs and tablets. Fologram, developed by a software company of the same name, creates a live link between the CAD modelling software

Rhinoceros 3D's visual programming environment, Grasshopper 3D, and the HoloLens. Fologram moves beyond virtual work instructions, allowing users to intuitively overlay descriptive geometry, such as lines, curves and points, onto the physical workpiece, eliminating most of the need for 2D drawings and physical templates in highly complex production tasks (*Fologram* 2024). Fologram also develops Twinbuild, a cloud-based platform for large-scale, high-precision construction work, including site set-out, installation, assembly and prefabrication (*Twinbuild* 2024). Fabstation caters to steel fabricators, helping them visualise and assemble complex steel structures and integrates with CAD packages such as SolidWorks 3D, Tekla and Autodesk Inventor 3D (*FabStation* 2024). All three software applications provide practical, industry-tailored AR applications that improve production efficiency and worker productivity.

In this chapter, we define the utilisation of AR in custom manufacturing as *augmented fabrication*; this term, first introduced by Franze et al. (2022), encapsulates how fabricators employ interactive, contextually overlaid AR content to supersede traditional analogue approaches. Moreover, AR provides additional visual feedback to fabricators using manual machinery, enabling the production of higher-quality products. As such, augmented fabrication extends traditional practices, fostering entirely new ways of making and doing. In using AR, 2D drawings, physical templates and analogue tools are either enhanced or replaced by virtual descriptive geometry.

Figure 9.1 Augmented fabrication of a curved brick bench (*Fologram* 2020).

Augmenting fabrication is exemplified by the AllBrick and UTAS project by Fologram, shown in Figure 9.1, where teams of bricklayers rapidly assemble a complex curved wall in several hours. Given each brick's unique position and orientation, this task would typically be highly laborious and inefficient, relying on 2D documentation and physical templates. With AR, individual bricks are cut following virtual templates and placed following virtual outlines, reducing cumulative error. Further, utilising multiple teams in the bricklaying process significantly improves build speed, helping consistent brick bonding (Fologram 2024).

Augmented fabrication sees virtual points, lines, and arcs overlayed directly onto a workpiece, acting as a procedural and persistent visual reference guide. For example, a virtual fold line can be used as opposed to a physically scribed line on a piece of sheet metal to guide folding or an arc overlaid on a tube bending machine indicating to the user where the bend position and radius are required. This interactive and responsive reference geometry overlay, including 3D solids, surfaces and text, reduces the ambiguity fabricators face with a more holistic understanding and informed perspective throughout their fabrication journey.

In line with I5.0 values, AR can play an essential role in keeping humans in the loop as manufacturing systems continue to advance. As we will explore in further detail in the following section, augmented fabrication approaches bring the human touch back to the centre of manufacturing processes. The technology can also improve fabricators' well-being by improving task cognition and markedly lessening error, rework, and waste (Jahn et al. 2018) while synergising human and human-machine collaboration (Hahm et al. 2019)—all essential factors to consider in moving to a more human-centric I5.0.

DEVELOPMENT OF THE TAXONOMY

In the following section, we contextually analyse ten distinct augmented fabrication use cases from the literature to broaden understanding and inform the establishment of a taxonomy of emergent augmented fabrication workflows. This review considers ten cases from AEC research projects employing AR technologies to address the question: "What are the emerging patterns of AR usage in AEC-related custom manufacture?" to understand and highlight the challenges and possibilities of its adoption. Cases are limited to the past eight years since the advent of the HoloLens 1 in 2016, which, along with its successor, the HoloLens 2 in 2019, are both critical commercial AR developments given their processing power, utility, and accessibility (Goepel and Crolla 2020).

The use cases explore augmented fabrication approaches for materialising sophisticated custom products (Lu et al. 2021). By identifying and evaluating emergent trends, we aimed to inspire industry and academic communities and to elucidate an understanding of innovative applications of AR for fabrication and assembly. The use cases highlight AR's transformative ability to convert traditional AEC technical design workflows into more sustainable, efficient, human-centred processes through versatile expression of descriptive geometry. We believe these use cases provide relatable insights into approaches for custom manufacturers of differing technological capabilities.

Managing digital information flows profoundly impacts fabricators' traditional technical design workflows, where fabricators interpret design intent and translate it into construction execution (Bernstein 2012). The Royal Institute of British Architects (RIBA) classifies "technical design" as stage four in their Plan of Work (Davys 2019), which sees the completion of all design information required to manufacture and construct projects. Comparative designations of this technical design process internationally include "Detailed Design" and "Construction Documentation" (Davys 2019). Because different terms are used globally, all referring to similar parts of the process, it can be confusing as to what is required or intended for the different stages of the design-to-construction process. Figure 9.2 visually conveys the technical design workflow situated between the design and construction stages. The technical design workflow operates in a circular manner whereby manufacturers liaise

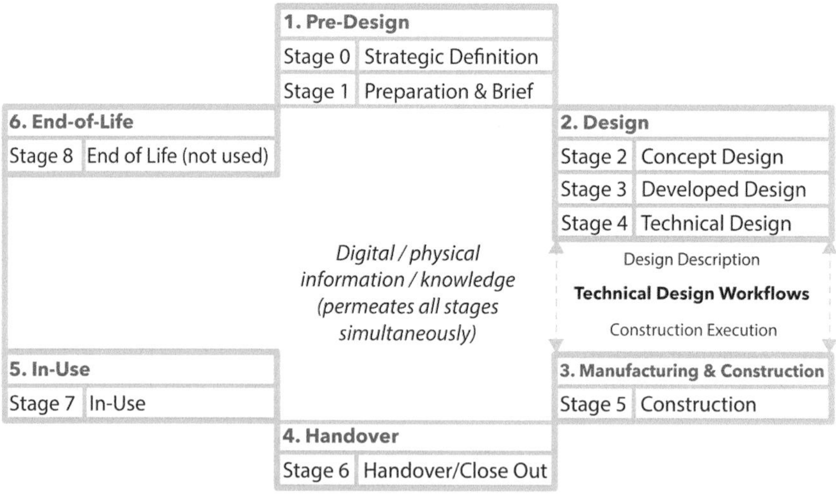

Figure 9.2 The authors' adaptation of the RIBA Plan of Work indicates the location of technical design workflows and how fabrication concerns increasingly impact early design stages.

with designers to ensure the outcomes meet the objectives set out in their design descriptions. Conversely, design descriptions may require adjusting to address manufacturing concerns as they occur. Within this system, architects and engineers are primarily responsible for design intent; however, fabrication and assembly considerations are often overlooked or unachievable through construction documentation sets (Bernstein 2012). Therefore, SMEs are limited to interpreting insufficient 2D drawings, considered the only form of legal design document certified for construction processes (Côté et al. 2013).

We evaluated ten cases and identified five workflow materialisation types in response to recurrent themes across the instances of AR use, grouped by process similarity, characteristics and task objectives, summarised in Figure 9.3. Categorising each workflow into a materialisation type aims to assist custom manufacturers in relating these prototypical studies to their existing workflows and foster insights into how they can integrate AR and add additional value across their business (Franze et al. 2022). Each workflow's characteristics are discussed, along with associated use cases. The types of materialisation are adaptive, intuitive, interactive, synchronised and revitalised materialisation, representing cases grouped by similarities in their characteristics and utilisation of AR technologies. Adaptive materialisation sees AR assisting designers in adapting parametrically

	Materialisation Type					Workflow Features									
	Adaptive	Intuitive	Interactive	Synchronised	Revitalised	MOCAP	Wearables	Spatial AR	Mobile TUI	HoloLens	Custom AR Device	Param. Optimisation	Custom Programming	Human-to-Human	Human-to-Machine
Making in Mixed Reality	■									■		■		■	
Augmented Construction	■								■	■		■	■	■	
ARgan		■							■	■		■		■	
Flowmorph		■								■			■	■	
RoMA			■								■	■	■		■
Reality is interface			■			■		■				■	■		■
Pop-up Factory				■						■		■	■		■
Crowdsourced Fabrication				■			■						■	■	■
Rawbot					■				■				■	■	■
Projectables					■			■					■		

Figure 9.3 A comparison chart of use case workflow materialisation types and features.

optimised structures to as-built site challenges in processes typically reserved for robots. The intuitive category sees AR acting as a conduit between responsive procedural software and human intuition to foster new morphological potentials. The interactive category explores AR's ability to enhance novel human-machine interaction potentials. Further, synchronised materialisation refers to AR supporting teams of novice workers to fabricate artefacts efficiently, while the revitalised category builds on this and identifies AR's role in sustainable production.

The cases 'ten workflow features provide introductory knowledge of parametric optimisation, required programming expertise, and hardware and software approaches. The next section begins by examining adaptive materialisation, allowing readers further to relate these prototypical studies to a company's technological readiness.

CASE STUDY ANALYSIS

Workflow: Adaptive Materialisation

This workflow allows designers to materialise pre-defined representations of complex free-form structures. Complex free-form structures target processes often requiring robotics due to their bespoke materiality and challenges in traditional manufacturing and even some advanced manufacturing like 3-axis CNCs or laser cutters. However, robots lack the human ability to respond to contextual site challenges and remain cost-prohibitive for many smaller custom manufacturers (Mitterberger et al. 2020). Given the design complexity involved, utilising 2D documentation methods would be infeasible within cost targets. In response, this construction system highlights a flexible AR approach, allowing designers to adapt parametrically optimised structures to as-built site challenges. In both cases, democratised workforces efficiently construct non-standard, free-form structures assisted by intuitive interfaces that provide workers with procedural and contextual virtual guidance during fabrication and construction tasks. The following two cases fit into this category.

Case 1: Making in Mixed Reality

In Making in Mixed Reality, Jahn et al. (2018) reflect on outcomes from a workshop at the 2018 Association for Computer-Aided Architectural Design Research in Asia (CAADRIA) conference in Beijing, China—employing a democratised workforce to fabricate and assemble a non-standard interwoven pipe structure.

Virtual model development utilises industry-standard, parametric CAD applications Grasshopper 3D, and Fologram. The virtual model informs procedural virtual overlays, which assist in guiding fabricators through pipe fabrication and assembly processes. Once completed, fabricators assess part suitability against the virtual assembly, markedly reducing errors and improving assembly efficiency (Jahn et al. 2018) Wearing Microsoft HoloLens HMDs, fabricators view virtual representations in context. They also adjust representations within the virtual environment to take on real-world tolerances. For example, fabricators verify physical bends against virtual counterparts during pipe bending operations to identify potential tool collisions.

As shown in Figure 9.4 (left), virtual overlays indicate each bending step, allowing the fabricator to account for the pipe twisting during bending operations, whilst in Figure 9.4 (right), on part completion, an assembler guided by virtual instruction interweaves the newly formed part into the structure. As a result, the assembler can determine immediate placement locations on upstream sequences. The authors of the study noted minor discrepancies between the virtual model and the constructed artefact during construction, resulting from bend inaccuracies caused by fabricators misinterpreting AR instructions.

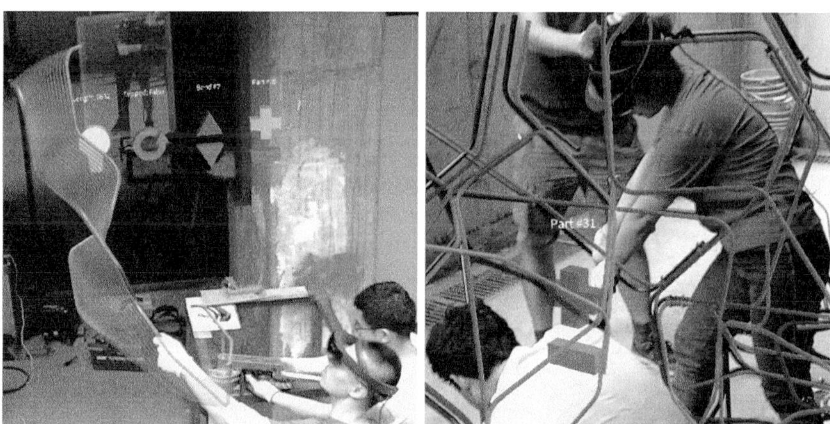

Figure 9.4 A fabricator evaluates a bent tube part (left), and (rights) a user weaves a newly formed component into the assembly (Jahn et al. 2018).

The Fologram software application allows designers to explore AR prototypes without needing extensive programming experience. In this case, AR approaches offer an alternative to 2D documentation and provide advantages over robotic processes, as humans can assist in producing context-adapted parts (Jahn et al. 2018).

Case 2: Augmented Construction

In Augmented Construction, Goepel (2019) introduces a project conducted in 2018 at the die Angewandte Institute of Architecture, Vienna—seeking to support a team of non-professionals to construct a scaled approximation of Corbusier's Ronchamp Chapel, Notre Dame du Haut's iconic south wall.

In this case, the design strategy is not replication but assembling an optimised parametric structure consisting of multiple discrete parts. A rationalised version of the south wall helps the study authors evaluate how AR headsets and TUIs, in this case, a mobile phone, could allow for as-built considerations in near real-time through physical-virtual feedback loops.

The virtualisation of each newly formed structural part helps achieve high adaptability in the construction system. Virtualised parts are continually evaluated against the existing virtual assembly, allowing designers to update the cladding system to suit dynamic geometric conditions. Finally, the cladding is assembled to the structure using cable binders at pre-drilled locations through virtual contextual overlays. Although hole alignment issues appeared during assembly, the system proved flexible enough to incorporate these without detriment to the overall assembly.

As seen in Figure 9.5, the team leader wearing a HoloLens HMD (head-mounted display) conveys assembly instructions on part placement to their co-worker. Using multiple HMDs in a teamwork scenario is helpful but challenging to implement as mobile users continually await instruction from headset users (Goepel 2019). Although this project is the only case study realised outdoors, the authors noted significant lighting interference with the HMDs. Therefore, a paravent shading solution is required to help view virtual content.

Figure 9.5 The assembly of Case 2 as seen through a TUI (Goepel 2019).

Workflow: Intuitive Materialisation

This workflow embraces human intuition and craftsmanship to realise complex, non-standard architecture. It relaxes the hyper-precision of contemporary production processes in search of greater possibilities (Goepel 2019). Computational design processes are utilised in design conception to synergise human-machine collaboration, allowing for an alternative approach exclusive to human or robotic workflows in exploring new-found morphologies (Hahm et al. 2019). AR provides the conduit between responsive procedural software and human decision-making. Simplified virtual representations convey suggested construction strategies but are not overly prescriptive, as human judgement influences project outcomes. Both use cases collapse the boundaries between design and making seen in contemporary architectural construction by relying on unknowable user–material interactions to realise novel outcomes.

Case 3: The ARgan Project

The ARgan project (Goepel and Crolla 2020) reflects on a workshop conducted at the Chinese University of Hong Kong in 2019, which called on a local group of sculptors to fabricate a complex bamboo structure (Figure 9.6). Within this context, the study authors implement a strategy relying upon user intuition to respond to material unexpectedness to realise an amorphous, double-curved shell surface, while procedural design software suggests construction approaches.

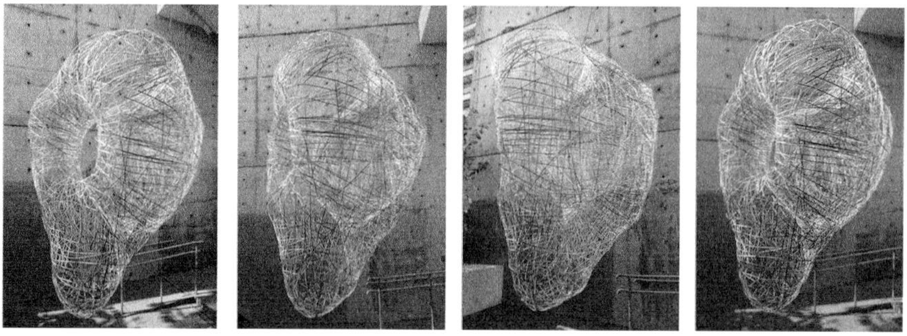

Figure 9.6 Completed ARgan bamboo structure (Goepel and Crolla 2020).

The software generates bi-directional flow patterns for suggested densification across the base structure. These flow patterns are expressed through the AR user interface (UI) by colourful visual overlays to guide assembly. Users weave bamboo splits highly intuitively, as the visual overlays are a suggestion and rely on their judgement to determine suitability. The construction sequence runs simultaneously between four teams of fabricators using HoloLens HMDs and hand-held smartphones.

AR provides significant improvements through virtual instruction of pre-drilling, sorting, densification and assembly processes. This use case rethinks current workflows to enable diverse material usage, extend morphological possibilities, and enhance workforce creative potential (Goepel and Crolla 2020).

Case 4: Flowmorph

Flowmorph by Hahm et al. (2019) reflects on a 12-month research project at the Bartlett School of Architecture, UCL, London, utilising the malleability of polymorphic plastic materials to inform a complex skeletal structure. A computational fluid dynamics (CFD) solver generates iterative fabrication strategies presented to users through the HoloLens UI, assisting them in determining suitable construction strategies. Figure 9.7 shows that the construction sequence was rationalised to its underpinning pyramidal structure of lines and points, forming simplified virtual guides. Users fabricate parts by heating and stretching plastic material through virtual intersection points, intuitively reacting to unexpected incidents and amending the virtual representation.

Figure 9.7 The user, assisted by rationalised virtual guides (left), produces the desired form (right) (Project title: FlowMorph: Institute\Bartlett BPro Research Cluster 9 2017/18, Project designers: Eri Sumitomo, Jie Sun, Yu-Hsin Huang Instructors: Soomeen Hahm and Alvaro Lopez Rodriguez).

This technique is made possible by registering hand gestures to alter virtual geometries. Two users wear HoloLens devices, while a third relies on explicit direction throughout fabrication. Due to the system's configuration, there are some limitations to the overall workpiece size, proximity, and HMD syncing issues. Users integrate material unexpectedness into a successful outcome by relaxing notions of precision and embracing human agency. The authors note that virtual misalignment and syncing issues with simultaneous HMD use require further research (Hahm et al. 2019).

Workflow: Interactive Materialisation

This workflow exemplifies human-machine interaction potentials extended through AR technologies by exploring novel approaches and rejuvenating historical processes through collaborative robotics, providing value-added approaches. The following case studies provide insights into prospective novel approaches and the renewal of historical processes through collaborative robotic approaches. The use of augmented reality merges human creative potential with the precision and kinematic opportunities afforded by robotic approaches (Mitterberger et al. 2020).

Case 5: RoMA

RoMA, developed by Peng et al. (2018), evaluates a novel robotic modelling assistant-exploring reflective practice potentials in human-machine collaboration. As the designer expresses form through the custom-built AR HMD, a robotic arm materialises the newly described geometry, facilitated by a proxemics-inspired handshake mechanism for safe and continuous human-machine interaction (Peng et al. 2018). This workflow allows the operator to interrupt prints or return complete control to the robot swiftly. In addition, the robot detects workpiece modifications, allowing designers to alter digital and physical objects on the fly. Currently, limited to smaller objects, this approach can provide designers with manufacturing insights earlier in the design workflow. Thus, the system informs desktop-based CAD modelling but offers a glimpse into future workflow possibilities.

Case 6: Reality is Interface

Reality is Interface (Running Moulds) by Bard et al. (2016) explores human-robot collaboration in high-skill domains—extending the potential of historical running mould-forming techniques through robotic and spatial AR technologies. Historically, this process required fabricators with a high degree of tacit knowledge to guide a rigid profile over a rapidly curing plaster. A physical guide driven through a sled system encapsulates the rigid profile. The dexterity required and sophistication of the guide design restricted running moulds to linear, circular or elliptical profiles. This study employs collaborative robots and motion capture (MOCAP) methods to realise previously unattainable running mould designs. Custom profile tools created for a six-axis robotic arm are pre-programmed offline to test kinematic feasibility. The workspace has a six-camera motion array to digitise hand-drawn geometry, which is displayed on a dashboard. Exploration of adapting the project for on-site construction can provide practical contextual interaction possibilities.

Workflow: Synchronised Materialisation

These processes explore collaborative, human-human and human-machine workflow strategies in the construction of non-standard architecture. Both processes rely upon pre-defined and controlled work sequences to increase build speed and minimise user error and resultant material wastage. Augmented technologies provide contextualised visual, audio and tactile feedback aimed at increasing users' task cognition. The studies depend on highly coordinated intelligent workspaces to allow unskilled workers to concentrate on applying human expression and dexterity.

Case 7: Pop-up Factory

In the Pop-up Factory, Betti et al. (2019) report on an interactive installation at the makeCity Festival in Berlin in 2018, exploring a novel design-build-assemble workflow to assess human-machine collaboration potentials, as shown in Figure 9.8.

Figure 9.8 The Pop-up factory, as seen through the HoloLens HMD UI (Betti et al. 2019).

The study authors invite the public to design and construct a custom foam brick tower. Wearing HoloLens HMDs, users access a custom multi-modal interface to control the process. Gesturally controlled modelling tools allow users to manipulate control points, influencing the overall tower design while the façade is formed by translating participants' audio signals. A bespoke software pipeline converts audio captured from a microphone atop the ABB 1200 robotic arm into machine code.

The code informs the fabrication of five uniquely textured foam bricks by the robotic arm, for then users to manually place through interactive visual guides assist placement atop the structure. Users express content with the user experience; however, the authors note that the users preferred to participate only once in the workshop, potentially due to time limitations. The study relies upon pre-defined definitions to increase production speed and improve material efficiency. However, according to the study's authors, pre-defined definitions may have limited structural outcomes and contribute to decreased user engagement. The theme of "active participation" (Betti et al. 2019) sees projects delivered by novice workers in aggregation. This approach can foster avenues for localised construction-site workflows of democratised workforces constructing pre-defined representations.

Case 8: Crowdsourced Fabrication

Crowdsourced Fabrication, developed by Lafreniere et al. (2016), reflects on an interactive exhibit conducted at the Autodesk University Conference in Las Vegas in 2015, aiming to address the main logistical challenges of fabrication and assembly processes. The study employs a large workforce of varying skill levels to collaboratively construct a non-standard tensegrity structure, which embraces advances in connectivity and wearables technologies to augment the construction process—constructed during a three-day workshop by conference attendees invited to spend 20 minutes of their time contributing to the aggregated build.

Volunteers supplied with smartwatches are provided unobtrusive guidance through production processes. These smartwatches provide users with visual instruction and additionally tactile and audio feedback if a process is completed or if users accidentally encroach into a safety zone. Worker spatial locations are continually tracked to optimise process efficiency, and collaborative robotics enable the fabrication of 222 unique tensegrity modules comprising three bamboo sticks and thread.

Each module connects with an adjacent module through a connector node fitted with a wireless RGB LED. A custom "foreman engine" application coordinates communications between the robot station, smartwatches and wireless LED nodes. The "foreman engine" is instrumental in coordinating the entire process and building status updates in real-time via monitor display. The project has potential for the construction site because each worker better understands their colleague's task progress and goal. Tactile and audio feedback provides workers operating noisy tools an indication of urgent developments on the worksite. Furthermore, there is typically confusion when relying on 2D drawings due to varying degrees of cognitive spatial ability. Workers with greater project awareness could use their initiative to prepare for the following tasks, resulting in reduced management pressure, increased worker agency and better workforce relationships.

Workflow: Revitalised Materialisation

This workflow shares similarities with Intuitavite Materialisation as it leverages human craftsmanship; however, it focuses more on facilitating approaches that extend local resource usage, waste streams and democratised workforce potentials in AEC processes. These case studies highlight the approaches being explored that aim to incorporate local and found materials into the construction of new objects. They offer innovative approaches for increasing sustainability within AEC processes, extending material usage.

Case 9: Rawbot

Rawbot, developed by Wu et al. (2019), is a "digital system for AR fabrication of bamboo structures through discrete digitisation of bamboo". This workflow facilitates the use of locally sourced bamboo to assemble structurally sound aggregated structures. A custom smartphone application employs an AI algorithm to learn the geometrical properties of bamboo to aid construction strategies. Users begin assembly by placing bamboo poles within the smartphone scanning zone. Then, the software overlays visual descriptors based on previous feature mapping operations, guiding users for optimal placement in the aggregate structure. This system offers AEC methods for incorporating local materials and democratised workforces (Wu et al. 2019).

Case 10: ProjecTables

In ProjecTables, Rasmussen and Merritt (2018) reflect on a study conducted at the Aarhus School of Architecture, Denmark. This is an innovative workflow utilising spatial AR to reduce computer numerical control (CNC) fabrication waste streams by extending material off-cut potentials as shown in Figure 9.9.

Figure 9.9: Projected part profiles being CNC cut out of scrap material (Rasmussen and Merritt 2018).

The system addresses resource waste by reusing discarded sheet material to produce new parts within an educational facility lab study. The system can be deployed directly on the CNC bed or an adjacent flat surface. Users place a selected off-cut material on the chosen workspace, where an overhead projector superimposes two-dimensional outlines of the artefact to be cut. Users can move and position parts to suitable solid regions of the material free of blemishes or scratches through mouse input. An advantage of this process is that users can prepare workpieces concurrently on a separate workspace during machine operation. In addition, they can place material arbitrarily on the CNC machine as the system employs computer vision to swiftly recognise pre-configured sheets through a cloud server. Qualitative user studies foster user insights into students using this system, with users generally content with the approach and suggesting enhancements, including displaying safe cutting margins between parts, creating shared tool paths and automating nesting.

This project stimulates a broader discussion for the research community to employ this as part of a related material-sharing practice. As captured and itemised scrap material can be fed into an online repository, could the AEC industry adopt a more comprehensive circular economy approach with scrap material shared amongst the industry?

DISCUSSION

Similar conclusions can be drawn across use cases, highlighting the potential for AR to improve AEC technical design workflows. In exploring the ten use cases, we identified six emerging trends: (1) *adaptation to as-built worksite conditions through near-real-time procedures*, (2) *improved user cognition and task comprehension enabled by gestural interfaces and virtual overlays*, (3) *enabling democratised workforce potentials*, (4) *synergising human-machine collaboration*, (5) *prospective team-based task enhancements*, and (6) *maximisation of local resource usage and material efficiency*.

1. *Adaptation to as-built worksite conditions through near-real-time procedures* is demonstrated in Case 1 as AR's versatility helps novice workers efficiently disseminate large quantities of complex digital information (such as BIM), reducing reliance on complex and incomplete construction documentation sets (Jahn et al. 2018). Case 2 illustrates fabricators' concerns being resolved by integrating physical part inconsistencies during construction while preserving design intent. Both cases illustrate how AR can provide a cost-effective alternative to automated robotics, utilising human capabilities to identify, interpret and resolve contextual site challenges. Additionally, AR HMDs may sometimes be impractical for specific construction tasks. Cases 2 and 9 show that TUIs provide cost-effective solutions that are less susceptible to light interference. However, they limit worker dexterity due to being hand-held. Within the *Synchronised Materialisation* workflow, Case 8's use of unobtrusive smartwatches provides an alternative means of task guidance and timely notifications via tactile feedback in noisy environments (Lafreniere et al. 2016).
2. *Improved user cognition and task comprehension enabled by gestural interfaces and virtual overlays* are apparent, given AR's ability to support fabrication workers with vast amounts of interactive virtual information. However, UI designers must consider how to provide virtual information in a spatial context efficiently. Moreover, AR interfaces are sensitive to light interference, as shown in Case 2, where custom shading solutions were needed to filter out sunlight, whilst Case 7 experienced UI issues due to glare from adjacent light sources. As most cases occur in controlled indoor environments, further research on AR use in outdoor construction sites would be beneficial. Both *Intuitive* workflow use cases illustrate AR's ability to improve user cognition. Case 3 allows users to cycle through complex procedural information flows using intuitive hand gestures. In Case 4, Flowmorph simplifies complex procedural information

through colour-coded lines and intersection points to improve user comprehension. The author of Case 2 expresses the need for future UI refinements, which consider significant filtering of information and means to identify individual components within assemblies (Goepel 2019). Finally, in Case 7, users experienced gestural recognition issues with "action buttons" located at the extremities of the AR interface (Betti et al. 2019).

3. *Enabling democratised workforce potentials*, as in Case 7, where novice workers receive induction training with AR HMDs, supporting their progression through a user-friendly workflow. Case 8 demonstrates how unobtrusive augmentation technologies and data analytics improve worker agency. Both use cases demonstrate that AEC is moving toward developing democratised workforce potentials and building existing local workforce capabilities. However, Lafreniere et al. (2016) note that expert oversight is still required, indicating the need for further quality control measures.
4. *Synergising human-machine collaboration* is a distinct advantage of utilising AR, which allows for an alternative to exclusively human or robotic workflows (Hahm et al. 2019). For example, the use cases within the *Intuitive Materialisation* workflow exemplify how AR interfaces provide a conduit between machine processing and human decision-making regarding complex human–material interactions. Further, Case 7 extends the potential for new design possibilities through audio capture, while Case 6 embraces human creative expression through gestural recognition. Further, robotic kinematics rejuvenate historical processes that rely upon unavailable tacit knowledge.
5. *Prospective team-based task enhancements* could be highly beneficial. However, most use cases do not explicitly evaluate AR team-based approaches, demonstrating a need for further research to support team-based construction tasks, as highlighted in Case 2, where a hierarchy of information saw users lose productivity awaiting instruction from the HMD user. In Case 4, syncing and virtual alignment issues occurred between users. However, with AR HMDs continually improving and becoming more accessible, custom fabricators and researchers have increased possibilities for exploring team-based scenarios in AEC workflows.
6. *Maximising local resource usage and material efficiency* is demonstrated in Case 9 as combining AI and AR fosters localised material usage and workforce utilisation (Wu et al. 2019). Further, Case 10, ProjecTables, demonstrates a sustainable solution that maximises resource usage and fosters communities of sustainable practice.

> Both cases within the *Adaptive Materialisation* workflow increase resource efficiencies and reduce error. Equally, the *Intuitive Materialisation* workflow highlights how relaxed notions of precision improve resource usage efficiencies and encourage new morphological potentials (Goepel and Crolla 2020).

Discussion of findings from the cases reflects strengths, challenges and insights into future research avenues to support the identification of AR implementation within custom production workflows. For example, innovative UI design should disseminate digital information (such as BIM) more intuitively to enhance user comprehension and extend human tacit knowledge for increased workforce competitiveness. Further research on AR teamwork in construction tasks that address syncing and alignment issues is also needed to support labour resourcing and team-based communication. Democratised workforce capabilities would benefit from innovative quality control measures and worker hierarchies best matched to worker capability (Lafreniere et al. 2016).

CONCLUSION

In this chapter, we highlighted AR's transformative effect on traditional custom manufacturing approaches, such as ambiguous 2D drawings and non-intuitive manual machinery processes in AEC-related domains, and the hurdles impeding the broader uptake of augmented fabrication practices across the sector. We contextually analysed ten international cases in AEC-related fabrication projects, providing SMEs initial insights into AR's practical benefits to support their advancement and adaptation to new economies of I4.0 production (Dean et al. 2021) and help prepare them for I5.0 on the horizon. Further, our development of a novel taxonomy that defines and categorises augmented fabrication provides a framework for SMEs to understand how AR can assist them by identifying potential applications and strategies for integrating the technology.

Despite augmented fabrication's potential, its use by custom manufacturers remains limited due to several contextual hurdles. These include SMEs' limited awareness of its benefits, a lack of resources for exploring AR adoption and knowledge of how to integrate the technology into their practice successfully (Franze et al. 2023). Therefore, stakeholders across policy, academia and industry are encouraged to provide a supportive environment, knowledge and resources for companies to leverage the technology's benefits (Mason et al. 2022).

Given the substantial advancements in I4.0 and promises of a more human-centred I5.0 future, our research endeavours will focus on exploring applied, user-centred approaches tailored to the custom fabricators' context. In doing so we will seek to better understand the socio-economic aspects of SMEs and consider the human aspect of the technology by working closely with fabrication end-users to ensure future AR development relevance. Further, given the relatively small sample size of this study, the prototypical nature of the use cases, and the rapidly evolving nature of AR, additional research is pertinent as it can assist custom fabricators in reevaluating existing processes and adopting AR to help them meet increased sustainability demands, uncertain supply chains and shifts in consumer expectations (Dean et al. 2021).

To conclude, while augmented fabrication is transformative, a directed strategy is required to achieve broader adoption of AR in the AEC industry. There is a need to build on our chapter's findings and continue to expand the emerging augmented fabrication taxonomy through ongoing collaboration between academia and industry. These collective insights are essential in developing a comprehensive I4.0 AR framework for SMEs to harness the technology's full potential whilst advancing the global manufacturing and AEC industry toward a more human-centric I5.0.

REFERENCES

ABS. 2023. Selected ICTs Used by Business (a)(b)(c), Year Ended 30 June 2022. Australian Bureau of Statistics. https://www.abs.gov.au/statistics/industry/technology-and-innovation/characteristics-australian-business/latest-release.

Bernstein, P. 2012. Intention to Artefact. pp. 64–71. *In*: S. Marble (ed.). Digital Workflows in Architecture: Design-Assembly-Industry. Birkhäuser.

Betti, G., Aziz, S. and Ron, G. 2019. Pop up factory: Collaborative design in mixed reality—interactive live installation for the makecity festival 2018 Berlin. *In*: Proceedings of the 37th International Conference on Education and Research in Computer Aided Architectural Design in Europe (ECAADe) & 23rd Conference of the Iberoamerican Society Digital Graphics. 3(7): 115–124. https://doi.org/10.52842/conf.ecaade.2019.3.115.

Bottani, E. and Vignali, G. 2019. Augmented reality technology in the manufacturing industry: A review of the last decade. IISE Transactions. 51(3): 284–310. https://doi.org/10.1080/24725854.2018.1493244.

Caldwell, G., Donovan, J., Teixeira, M. and Brogden, L. 2019. From open innovation to design-led manufacturing: Cases of Australian art and architecture. *In*: Annual Design Research Conference, Australia.

Chasin, F., Kowalkiewicz, M. and Gollhardt, T. 2022. How SME watkins steel transformed from traditional steel fabrication to digital service provision. MIS Quarterly Executive. 21(3): 205–225. https://aisel.aisnet.org/misqe/vol21/iss3/4.

Cheng J.C.P., Chen Keyu and Chen Weiwei. 2020. State-of-the-art review on mixed reality applications in the AECO industry. Journal of Construction Engineering and Management. 146(2): 03119009. https://doi.org/10.1061/(ASCE)CO.1943-7862.0001749.

Commission, E., for Research, D.-G., Innovation, Breque, M., De Nul, L. and Petridis, A. 2021. Industry 5.0: Towards a Sustainable, Human-centric and Resilient European Industry. Publications Office. https://doi.org/doi/10.2777/308407.

Côté, S., Trudel, P., Snyder, R. and Gervais, R. 2013. An augmented reality tool for facilitating on-site interpretation of 2D construction drawings. *In*: Proceedings of the 13th International Conference on Construction Applications of Virtual Reality (CONVR). London, UK. 316: 323.

Davys, M. 2019. RIBA plan of work. pp. 131–208. *In*: Small Practice and the Sole Practitioner. RIBA Publishing. https://doi.org/10.4324/9780429346118-6.

Dean, M., Rainnie, A., Stanford, J. and Nahum, D. 2021. Industrial policy-making after COVID-19: Manufacturing, innovation and sustainability. The Economic and Labour Relations Review. 32(2): 283–303. https://doi.org/10.1177/10353046211014755.

Evans, N. and Bosua, R. 2017. Exploring innovation in regional manufacturing SMEs. Small Enterprise Research. 24(2): 149–166. https://doi.org/10.1080/13215906.2017.1334226.

FabStation. 2024. Augmented reality steel software. Building Augmented Reality Steel Software for Industry 4.0; Eterio Realities Inc. https://fabstn.com/.

Fologram. 2024. Mixed Reality for the Workshop. https://fologram.com/.

Franze, A., Caldwell, G., Belek Fialho Teixeira, M. and Rittenbruch, M. 2023. Informing user-centred approaches to augmented custom manufacturing practices. 353–363. https://eprints.qut.edu.au/238911/.

Franze, A.P., Caldwell, G.A. and Teixeira, M. 2022. Employing AR/MR mockups to imagine future custom manufacturing practices. *In*: Proceedings of the OzCHI '22 34th Australian Conference on Human-Computer Interaction. https://dl.acm.org/doi/abs/10.1145/3572921.3576201.

Garcia, J.A., Mollaoglu, S. and Syal, M. 2018. Implementation of BIM in small home-building businesses. Practice Periodical on Structural Design and Construction. 23(2): 04018007. https://doi.org/10.1061/(ASCE)SC.1943-5576.0000362.

Goepel, G. 2019. Augmented construction. *In*: Proceedings of the 39th Annual Conference of the Association for Computer Aided Design in Architecture (ACADIA), 430–437. https://doi.org/10.52842/conf.acadia.2019.430.

Goepel, Garvin and Crolla, K. 2020. Augmented reality based collaboration: ARgan, a bamboo art installation case study. *In*: Proceedings of the 25th International Conference of the Association for Computer-Aided Architectural Design Research in Asia (CAADRIA). 313–322.

Hahm, S., Maciel, A., Sumitiomo, E. and Rodriguez, A.L. 2019. Exploring the Human-material Interaction in Digitally Augmented Craftsmanship.

Jahn, G. 2022. Mixed Reality Fabrication. School of Architecture and Urban Design.

Jahn, G., Newnham, C. and Beanland, M. 2018. Making in mixed reality. ACADIA // 2018: Recalibration. On Imprecision and Infidelity. 88–97.

Kelly, K. 2016. The Inevitable: Understanding the 12 Technological Forces That Will Shape Our Future. Penguin. https://play.google.com/store/books/details?id=SMe3CgAAQBAJ.

Lafreniere, B., Grossman, T., Anderson, F., Matejka, J., Kerrick, H., Nagy, D., et al. 2016. Crowdsourced fabrication. *In*: Proceedings of the 29th Annual Symposium on User Interface Software and Technology. 15–28. https://doi.org/10.1145/2984511.2984553.

Lammers, T., Guertler, M., Sick, N. and Deuse, J. 2023. It's coming home down under: The potential of digital work to overcome Australia's challenges in reshoring manufacturing. pp. 161–170. *In*: A. Shajek and E.A. Hartmann (eds). New Digital Work. Springer International Publishing. https://doi.org/10.1007/978-3-031-26490-0.

Liu, R., Peng, C., Zhang, Y., Husarek, H. and Yu, Q. 2021. A survey of immersive technologies and applications for industrial product development. Computers and Graphics. 100: 137–151. https://doi.org/10.1016/j.cag.2021.07.023.

Lu, W., Tan, T., Xu, J., Wang, J., Chen, K., Gao, S., et al. 2021. Design for manufacture and assembly (DfMA) in construction: The old and the new. Architectural Engineering and Design Management. 17(1–2): 77–91. https://doi.org/10.1080/17452007.2020.1768505.

Maddikunta, P.K.R., Pham, Q.-V., Prabadevi, B., Deepa, N., Dev, K., Gadekallu, T.R., et al. 2022. Industry 5.0: A survey on enabling technologies and potential applications. Journal of Industrial Information Integration. 26: 100257. https://doi.org/10.1016/j.jii.2021.100257.

Mason, C.M., Ayre, M. and Burns, S.M. 2022. Implementing industry 4.0 in Australia: Insights from advanced Australian manufacturers. Journal of Open Innovation: Technology, Market, and Complexity. 8(1): 53. https://doi.org/10.3390/joitmc8010053.

Mitterberger, D., Dörfler, K., Sandy, T., Salveridou, F., Hutter, M., Gramazio, F., et al. 2020. Augmented bricklaying. Construction Robotics. 4(3): 151–161. https://doi.org/10.1007/s41693-020-00035-8.

Nahavandi, S. 2019. Industry 5.0—A human-centric solution. Sustainability: Science Practice and Policy. 11(16): 4371. https://doi.org/10.3390/su11164371 On-the-job Guidance. 2022. Microsoft.com. https://dynamics.microsoft.com/en-us/mixed-reality/guides/.

Peng, H., Briggs, J., Wang, C.-Y., Guo, K., Kider, J., Mueller, S., et al. 2018. RoMA: Interactive fabrication with augmented reality and a robotic 3D printer. *In*: Proceedings of the 2018 CHI Conference on Human Factors in Computing Systems. 1–12. https://doi.org/10.1145/3173574.3174153.

Pose-Díez-de-la-Lastra, A., Moreta-Martinez, R., García-Sevilla, M., García-Mato, D., Calvo-Haro, J.A., Mediavilla-Santos, L., et al. 2022. HoloLens 1 vs. HoloLens 2: Improvements in the new model for orthopedic oncological interventions. Sensors. 22(13): 4915. https://doi.org/10.3390/s22134915.

Rasmussen, T.A. and Merritt, T. 2018. ProjecTables: Augmented CNC tools for sustainable creative practices. International Journal of Architectural Computing. 16(3): 227–242. https://doi.org/10.1177/1478077118792356.

Reza Hosseini, M., Banihashemi, S., Chileshe, N., Namzadi, M.O., Udaeja, C., Rameezdeen, R., et al. 2016. BIM adoption within Australian Small and Medium-sized Enterprises (SMEs): An innovation diffusion model. Construction Economics and Building. 16(3): 71–86. https://doi.org/10.5130/AJCEB.v16i3.5159.

Schwab, K. and Davis, N. 2018. Shaping the Future of the Fourth Industrial Revolution: A Guide to Building a Better World. Currency.

Song, Y., Koeck, R. and Luo, S. 2021. Review and analysis of Augmented Reality (AR) literature for digital fabrication in architecture. Automation in Construction. 128: 103762. https://doi.org/10.1016/j.autcon.2021.103762.

Teixeira, M.B.F., Pham, K., Caldwell, G., Seevinck, J., Swann, L., Rittenbruch, M., et al. 2021. A user-centred focus on augmented reality and virtual reality in AEC: Opportunities and barriers Identified by industry professionals. *In*: Proceedings of the 26th International Conference of the Association for Computer-Aided Architectural Design Research in Asia (CAADRIA) 2021. 273–283.

Twinbuild. 2024. Augmented reality for the construction site. https://twinbuild.com/

Wang, P., Zhang, S., Billinghurst, M., Bai, X., He, W., Wang, S., et al. 2020. A comprehensive survey of AR/MR-based co-design in manufacturing. Engineering with Computers. 36(4): 1715–1738. https://doi.org/10.1007/s00366-019-00792-3.

Wu, N.H., Dimopoulou, M., Hsieh, H.H. and Chatzakis, C. 2019. A digital system for AR fabrication of bamboo structures through the discrete digitization of bamboo. *In*: Souza, J.P., Henriques, G.C. and Xavier, J.P. (eds). Proceedings of 37 eCAADe and XXIII SIGraDi Joint Conference on Architecture in the Age of the 4th Industrial Revolution. 161–170. Blucher, 2019. https://doi.org/DOI 10.5151/proceedings-ecaadesigradi2019_538.

Chapter 10

Workflow for Augmented Reality Aided Design to Advanced Manufacturing: From Sketch to Robotic Assembly of Parametric Prototypes

Maryam Shafiei[1], Frederico Fialho Teixeira*[2], Islam Mashaly[3] and Jurij Karlovsek[4]

[1]Department of Architecture, American University in Dubai, Dubai, UAE

[2]School of Architecture, Design and Planning, The University of Queensland, Brisbane, Australia

[3]School of Sciences & Engineering, American University in Cairo, Cairo, Egypt

[4]School of Civil Engineering, The University of Queensland, Brisbane, Australia

INTRODUCTION

With rapid development of knowledge and skills in the computational and generative design fields, numerous tools have been developed

*For Correspondence: f.frederico@uq.edu.au

DOI: 10.1201/9781003581642-10

for designing and optimizing complex architectural forms. These innovative tools, techniques, plugins, and workflows have allowed for producing innovative architectural forms and structures, mostly relying on the skills of code developers. However, within the majority of such experiments the final design outcome is informed by certain parameters in predefined scripts, disregarding aesthetic desires of the end-users. Also, most such scripts can only be reproduced and employed by highly skilled technicians, designers, and researchers in computational design, and thus, less-computational skilled designers and educators are mostly removed from the benefits of these tools. The same phenomenon is visible in the field of advanced robotic manufacturing. Over the past decade, enormous efforts have been put to include robots and Cobots in architectural education, research, and practice. In particular, there's an emphasis in robotic arms which have been employed in the architecture field through milling, assembly, porosity, and hybridity methods (Mostafavi 2021).

For additive robotic manufacturing in architecture, a large number of studies have used different block types either standard (like brick or Jenga blocks) or non-standard blocks in unified or varied sizes. These projects have managed to instigate and implement complex workflows for novel structural systems, spatial qualities, and construction methods (Craney and Adel 2021, Hughes et al. 2021, Varela et al. 2021, Song et al. 2021a, Atanasova et al. 2020, Xian et al. 2020, Thoma et al. 2019, Adel et al. 2018, Willmann et al. 2016, Johns 2012). Although making substantial contributions to the field, most such studies and projects can only be used and performed by experts in computational design and robotics. Over the past decade, development of concepts and tools for User Interface (UI) as well as Augmented Reality (AR) have provided this opportunity to bridge this application gap by offering a setting to extend the use of complex design and fabrication scripts by non-experts.

Several studies have addressed the potentials of employing AR systems in architectural design and advanced manufacturing in the 2010s. The use of AR dates back to around the 1990s (Rosenberg 1992). In architecture discipline, it was initially more popular for visualization of architectural projects (Song et al. 2021b), then it was used for design and construction of complex forms or assembly of irregular forms, particularly by unskilled laborers (Jahn et al. 2018, 2019, Larsson et al. 2019, 2020, Yoshida et al. 2019). In more recent years, AR has also been used for on-site robotic fabrication as well as robotic block assembly (for example, see Akbari 2018, Hughes et al. 2021, Song et al. 2021a, Mitterberger et al. 2022). As highlighted by Song et al. (2021b), there have yet been limited studies on AR-immersive design and human-computer interactions, commonly performed by skilled users. Some notable recent studies have managed to fill part of this gap by simplifying robotic assembly workflow and integrating design and fabrication processes (Hughes et al. 2021, Varela et al. 2021, Song et al. 2021a).

Extending recent studies and through bridging AR immersive design and Human-robot collaboration in architecture, this research aims to propose an affordable workflow for robotic assembly and mass-customisation of parametric prototypes that can readily be used not just by skilled technicians and computational design experts but also by less-skilled construction workers, early-stage architectural students, and even residents of remote communities. It is particularly important as accessibility to skilled laborers and technicians is currently a serious challenge in many places around the world, even in developed countries. The paper probes the potentials of AR to comprehend normative computational design and robotic assembly approaches by actively including end-users, skilled or less skilled, in the design and robotic assembly process.

LITERATURE REVIEW

The integration of AR in architectural design and advanced manufacturing has significantly evolved over the past few decades, offering new potentials for design visualization, construction, and fabrication. Initially, AR was predominantly utilized for the visualization of architectural projects, allowing stakeholders to experience and assess designs in a more immersive manner (Bard et al. 2014). This immersive experience enabled designers and clients to interact with the architectural spaces virtually before any physical construction commenced, leading to better-informed decisions and reduced errors during the actual building phase. However, the application of AR has expanded far beyond mere visualization to encompass the design and construction of complex forms, particularly through robotic assembly processes involving both skilled and unskilled users (Hans et al. 2019).

The use of AR in architecture dates back to the early 1990s, primarily for visual representation (Wang 2009). During this period, AR served as a groundbreaking tool that allowed architects to overlay virtual objects onto the physical environment, providing a new dimension to the design process. The evolution of AR technology has been marked by significant milestones in enhancing human-computer interactions and immersive design experiences. For instance, the development of head-mounted displays and portable AR devices has revolutionized how architects and builders interact with digital models on-site (Kensek et al. 2012). These advancements have made it possible to visualize complex design elements directly within the physical context where they will be constructed, thereby improving accuracy and reducing the likelihood of costly mistakes. As the technology progressed, researchers demonstrated how AR could simplify robotic assembly workflows (Agati et al. 2020). Their studies showed that AR could make complex design and fabrication processes more accessible to non-experts, thus democratizing advanced manufacturing technologies. This development is particularly important given the growing challenge of skilled labor shortages (Song et al. 2021a). By enabling less experienced workers to engage with sophisticated design and assembly tasks through intuitive AR interfaces, the construction industry can address skill gaps and enhance productivity.

AR and Human-Robot Collaboration in Robotic Fabrication

Recent studies have shown the potential of AR to bridge the gap between design and fabrication, integrating immersive design experiences with robotic assembly. This integration not only enhances the accuracy and efficiency of the construction process but also democratises the use of advanced fabrication technologies (Luo et al. 2023). AR-assisted workflows enable real-time design modifications and collaborative efforts between designers and robots, facilitating a more interactive and user-centric approach to architectural fabrication. The collaboration between humans and robots in AR environments allows for the seamless translation of digital designs into physical structures, ensuring precision and adherence to the intended design specifications. The role of AR in human-robot collaboration extends to various aspects of the construction process, including site preparation, material handling, and component assembly. For example, AR can guide robotic arms in placing materials accurately, while also providing visual feedback to human operators to monitor and adjust the process as needed. This synergy between human intuition and robotic precision enhances the overall efficiency and quality of construction projects (Schubert et al. 2023).

Robotic fabrication has benefited immensely from the incorporation of AR, particularly in the assembly of parametric prototypes and complex spatial structures. Studies have highlighted the use of AR for on-site robotic fabrication and the assembly of intricate designs. These approaches have shown that AR can significantly improve the assembly process's precision and speed, making it feasible for use by less-skilled workers and in remote or under-resourced areas. By overlaying digital models onto physical construction sites, AR ensures that each component is placed with millimeter accuracy, reducing the need for rework and minimizing material waste. Moreover, AR technology facilitates the real-time monitoring and adjustment of robotic fabrication processes. By providing a visual interface that integrates design data with on-site conditions, AR allows for immediate feedback and corrections during construction. This capability is particularly beneficial in projects involving complex geometries and customized components, where traditional construction methods might struggle to achieve the required precision (Schubert et al. 2023).

Case Studies and Frameworks Models

Several case studies illustrate the successful application of AR in robotic assembly and digital fabrication. For instance, on automating Building Information Modelling (BIM) processes, provides valuable insights into the scalability and adaptability of AR in various contexts. study demonstrated how AR could enhance the efficiency showcased the potential of AR to streamline BIM workflows, reducing the time and effort required to update and manage digital building models. Additionally, AR demonstrated the efficacy of the technology in creating construction overlay instructions, further underscoring the potential in enhancing performance of an augmented reality application for built environment (Chalhoub and Ayer 2019). AR frameworks are overlay replicas of physical assets, and enable continuous monitoring and optimization of building performance through real-time data integration. AR enhances the utility of fabrication by providing an interactive interface for users to explore and manipulate virtual models within the physical space. This capability is particularly valuable for facility management, where AR can assist in identifying maintenance issues, planning renovations, and optimizing space utilization.

Importance of AR Data Visualization in Architectural Design and Fabrication

Despite the promising advancements, the integration of AR in architectural design and fabrication faces several challenges. These include issues related to data management, interoperability, legal and ethical considerations, and the need for comprehensive frameworks that can be universally applied across different scales and industries (Hajirasouli et al. 2022). Data management is a critical concern, as AR applications generate vast amounts of information that must be stored, processed, and accessed efficiently. Interoperability challenges arise from the need to integrate AR systems with existing design and construction tools, ensuring seamless data exchange and compatibility. Along with upskilling, legal and ethical considerations also pose significant hurdles, particularly concerning data privacy and security. As AR applications often involve the collection and processing of sensitive information, robust measures are required to protect user data and ensure compliance with regulations. Our research focuses on addressing these challenges by developing more robust and adaptable frameworks, enhancing real-time data visualization techniques, and exploring individual and personalized modes of using AR in human-robot collaboration and digital fabrication. This is crucial as advances in machine learning and artificial intelligence could play a crucial role in improving AR systems' capabilities, enabling more sophisticated interactions and autonomous decision-making processes. Furthermore, interdisciplinary collaboration between architects, engineers, computer scientists, and ethicists is essential to create holistic solutions that address the technical, social, and ethical dimensions of AR integration in architecture (Neely 2019).

The literature highlights the transformative impact of AR on architectural design and advanced manufacturing. By bridging the gap between design and fabrication, AR not only enhances the construction process's efficiency and accuracy but also makes advanced technologies more accessible to a broader range of users. Continued research and development in this field are essential to fully realize the potential of AR in creating more sustainable, efficient, and user-centric built environments. The ongoing evolution of AR technology promises to reshape the architectural landscape, fostering innovation and collaboration across disciplines and industries. By addressing current challenges and leveraging emerging opportunities, AR can contribute to the creation of resilient and adaptive built environments that meet the needs of contemporary society.

METHODOLOGY

Since a decade ago, several studies have developed complex design scripts and workflows to employ computational design strategies and robots for advanced manufacturing. Commonly in such experiments, the design process is linear while the intuitive and spontaneous design of the end-user is missed. Additionally, the workflow in the majority of these experiments can only be reproduced and employed by researchers or technicians with high expertise in computational design and robotic manufacturing fields. This study presents an affordable workflow for materialising design to robotic assembly of parametric prototypes that puts the end-users at the center of the design process. The process can easily be employed by students, designers or technicians with limited computing and robotic skills within educational, research, and industry settings. This proposed and tested workflow involves generating the form of the parametric prototype based on freehand drawings, controlling design parameters, and real-time optimization of the models. These particularly evaluate structural stability, solar radiation, and visibility rate, by employing AR to control design parameters and enhancing human-robot collaboration, and assembly of the prototype using a collaborative robot (Cobot). This mixed approach brings together the simplicity of the freehand drawings with the complexities of digital algorithms for digital manufacturing and AR-assisted design and assembly, closing the circle of design to robotic fabrication. This workflow expands the existing research in at least two directions. Firstly, it showcases a holistic and unified sketching to robotic assembly process that includes the user at the center of the process, and can be used for a variety of building blocks and complex spatial forms not just for brick laying as is common in the literature. Lastly, it makes the advanced technology available for expert or non-expert users, proposing a simplified but comprehensive workflow that can easily be used by less skilled users even in remote settlements with limited access to expert society.

Workflow Framework

The proposed workflow includes four main parts: free-hand drawing or sketching, form-finding through parametric design script, design optimization, and robotic assembly (Figure 10.1). AR has been employed at all these stages to simplify different tasks, generate an immersive design, optimization and assembly process, facilitate the accuracy and speed up the assembly, and for a synchronous visual communication with the robot. The proposed holistic workflow brings together the simplicity of the freehand drawings with complexities of digital algorithms for assembly and AR-assisted design and manufacturing, creating a shortcut between design concept and materialization of the final product. It facilitates real-time dynamic data transfer between different stages of design to manufacturing and illustrates a user-friendly setting for parametric design and robotic assembly particularly for less-skilled users.

The workflow puts the user at the heart of the design, optimization, and fabrication process, and actively includes the user's input in the final outcome. In this way, it goes beyond theories of shape grammar by making the grammar (Knight and Stiny 2015) that includes the bottom-up user's intervention along with the grammar informed by computational script. To put it differently, it offers a non-linear design, optimization, and assembly in service of skilled and unskilled users.

The workflow is capable of handling a variety of forms and could be used as indoor or outdoor walls, artwork, furniture, or even a shelter. This expands the use of such technology beyond high-tech architecture into artistic prototypes and everyday architecture. Also, this workflow

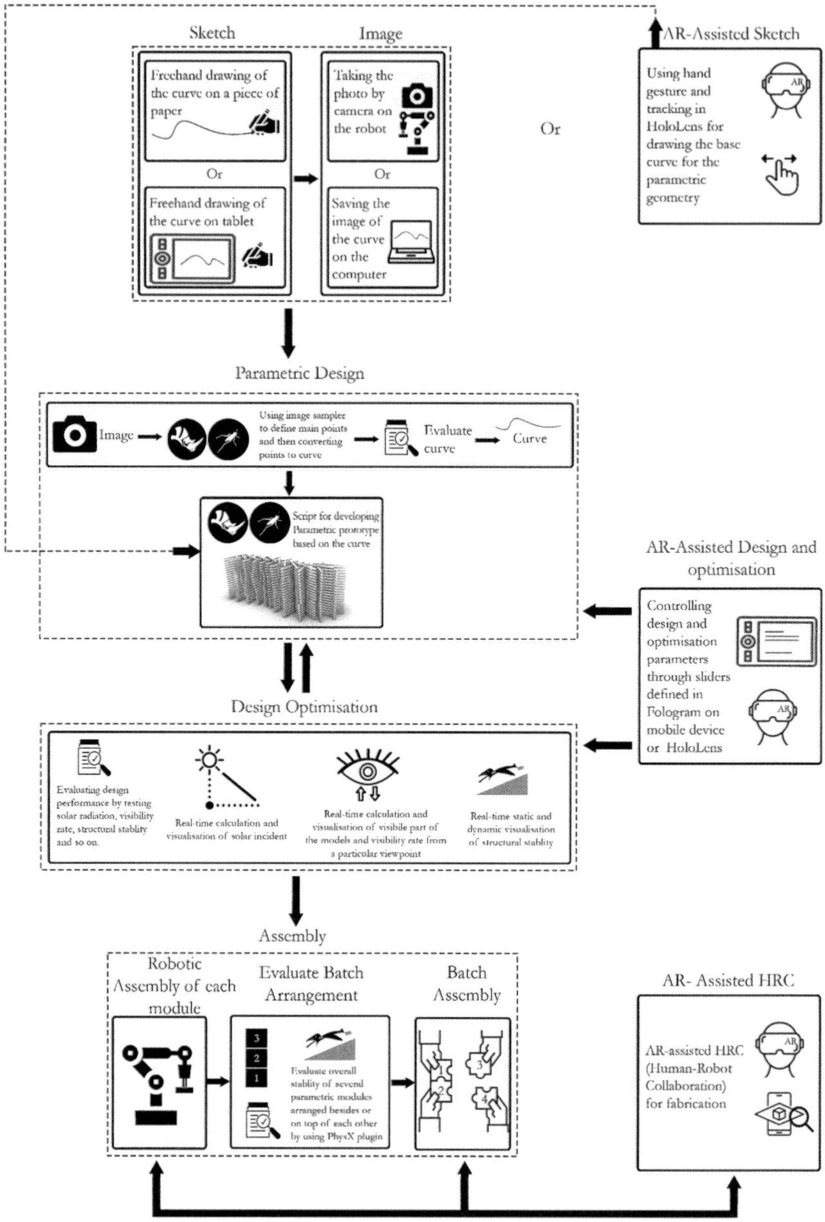

Figure 10.1 Proposed SkoboFab workflow for the sketch to robotic assembly of parametric prototypes.

should not be confused by a process for robotic block layering but rather as an attempt to simplify a comprehensive and complex design to robotic assembly of various parametric forms and sequential structures based on unified block materials that can be employed by less-skilled users. Last, but not least, the end product fabricated through this workflow could also be dismantled if needed, moving one more step toward a more sustainable construction industry. Acknowledging the broad application of the workflow and its replicability for a variety of forms and functions, this paper discusses the workflow for design to the assembly of a wall as the most common architectural component.

Phased Workflow

Due to the focus on non-expert use the workflow has three phases for ease of use. The first step of the workflow includes freehand drawing of a curve, representing the base for the parametric component. This paper tested three variations to the described workflow for sketching. In the first option, the lines were drawn on paper with a thick pen in front of the robot and then the user took photos from the lines through a camera mounted on the robot arm. The images were automatically saved in the predefined folder on the computer. In the second option, the lines were drawn by using a pen on a tablet and then automatically saved to the same folder on the computer. In both cases, the images were processed through a predefined script in the Grasshopper interface of the Rhino software to generate the main points and then the lines. By using the Image Sampler component in this script, the images were imported into Grasshopper and then each was overlaid by a grid of points to define the coordinates of the ink or thick lines. The images then were analyzed by the Brightness value of the Image Sampler component and the points with particular brightness were filtered and extracted by using the Dispatch component. The points were then converted to polyline and were thereafter smoothed multiple times to form a smooth polyline as the base of parametric geometry. In the third variation of this stage, AR assisted in generating real-time drawing of the main curve (Figure 10.2).

To do so, HoloLens 1 was connected to Rhino and Grasshopper through the Fologram platform. Employing hand tracking of HoloLens and recording the movements of the hand, a series of points were generated that were then connected to form the main curve. Additionally, mobile devices could also be used instead of HoloLens to draw the line. In doing so, the command "Track Device" within the Fologram should be used instead of hand tracking for recording the movement of the device and generating points.

Figure 10.2 Three alternatives for drawing initial curves including freehand drawing on paper (left), on tablet (middle), and via HoloLens (right).

According to our experiments, between these three variations for drawing the base polyline, it seems drawing on the tablet is quicker and the most reliable, requiring less adjustment to the script. It can be justified by considering that the saturation and brightness of images from freehand drawings on the paper can be different from time to time depending on the workshop light (particularly change to the natural light) and this could affect the image processing in the script. Also, using HoloLens 1 for hand tracking although tailors several steps for generating the curve, it is limited considering the need for steady movement of the hand and then manipulating the locations of the points in Rhino to generate the appropriate curves.

The polylines generated through mentioned options then formed the curves for a loft surface as the base shape for generating the parametric wall at the second stage. The surface was then divided into contours based on the height of the blocks where the blocks with defined size would lay on them and oriented according to the form of the original freehand drawings (Figure 10.3). The script allows adding the height of grout, glue, or any other type of adhesive to calculate contours' height. To create more freedom on design of the parametric component, several elements, particularly the curvature of the main polyline, number of its division, height of the prototype, and orientation of upper row blocks in relation to the initial row could also be controlled through sliders in the script.

At the third phase, design optimization, three main parameters, including solar radiation, visibility rate, and structural stability were employed to optimize the designed prototype. The aim of this stage is to employ AR to develop an open-ended and intuitive architectural design workflow that expands the application of computational design to less-computational skilled users, allows manipulation and unique input from the end-user, and enables immersive and real-time simulation for design optimization.

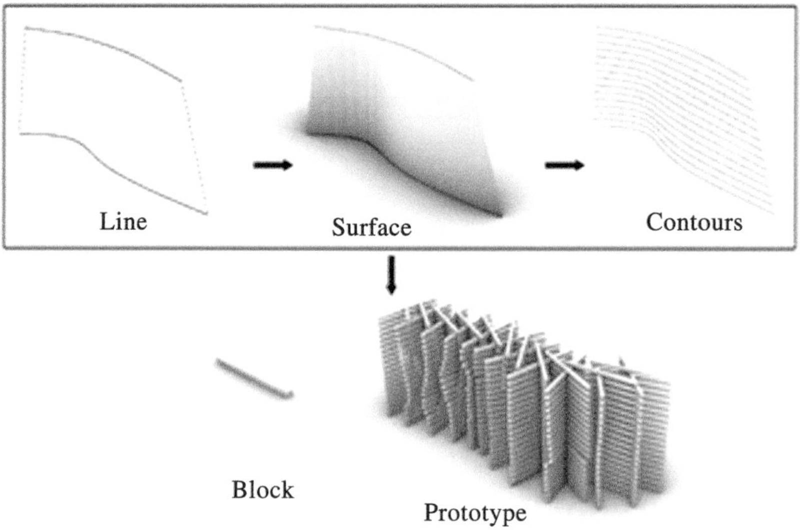

Figure 10.3 Steps from image processing to developing the parametric prototypes.

Solar Analysis Model

The analysis of solar radiation of the designed prototype was done by calculating the solar incident component in the environmental plugin Ladybug (Sadeguipour and Pak 2013). Solar incident takes into account the impacts of the orientation of the wall and blocks on energy usage which was an important parameter in this research with sustainability considerations. The calculation is informed by the EPW file of the selected location (Brisbane, Australia in this study), and the analysis time was set for day hours in the warmer months (1st Dec to 28th Feb, 8:00 am to 3:00 pm). As a necessary step to calculate solar incident, the sky matrix component of Ladybug was used to generate radiation for each patch of the sky. Direct and diffused radiation was exported from the EPW file, and the north direction was defined separately (aligned with -X axis in this study). Solar incident was calculated for a surface with the same size of the overall body of the wall located behind the wall (100 ml in this study to avoid clashing with the wall) while the designed parametric wall was defined as the context for analysis. The outcome of the analysis was exported as a mesh for visualization purposes and the total incident can be seen beside the analyzed model in KWh/m^2 (Figure 10.4). This real-time visualization provides an opportunity for end-users to monitor the impacts of changes in design parameters like block features, sizes, openings, and orientation on the solar incident of the model and adjust the model accordingly.

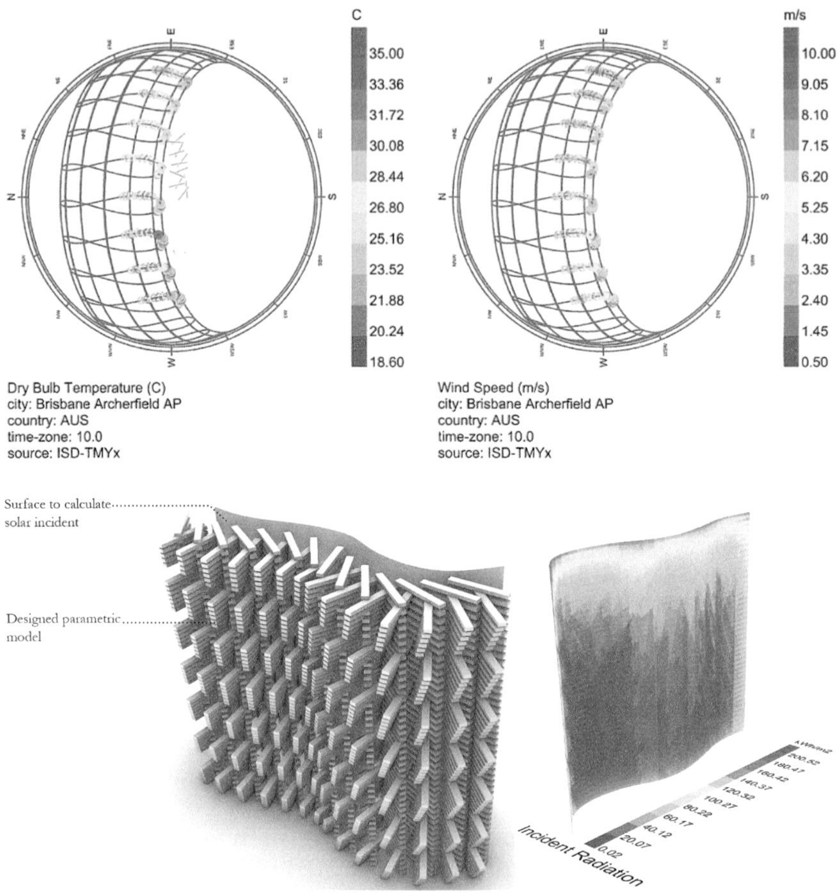

Figure 10.4 Solar incident analysis to optimize the designed prototype.

Visibility Analysis

As another design and optimization component, visibility of the prototype was also calculated in this research. This calculation demonstrates the portion and amount from the geometry of the prototype that can be seen from a particular point. This analysis was performed using the visibility percent component of Ladybug in Grasshopper. A sight curve was defined in the context of the design and then was divided into the desired number of viewpoints. These were then introduced to the program as viewpoints into the prototype. The calculation results in a color scheme gradient (from pink as zero visibility to blue as 100% visibility) demonstrating the invisible and visible parts of the geometry from the defined viewpoint (Figure 10.5).

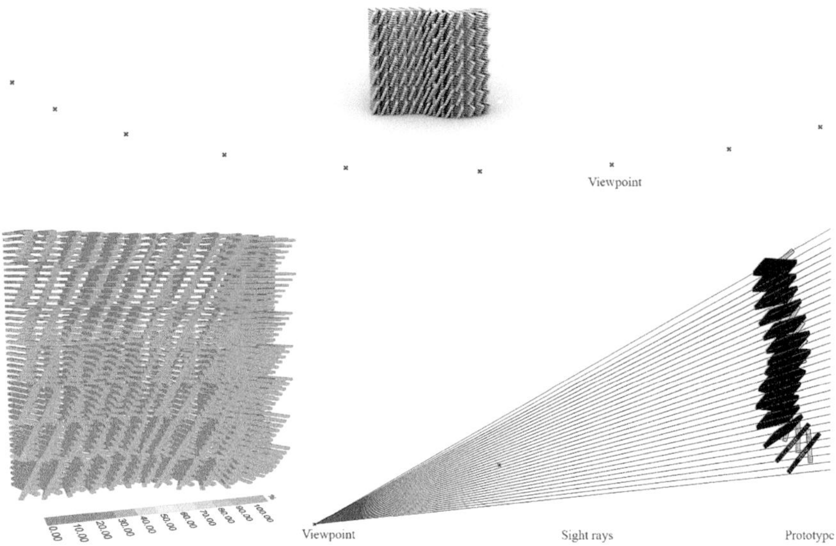

Figure 10.5 Visibility analysis of the designed prototype to define visible and invisible portions of the model from a particular viewpoint.

To complement this calculation, we developed the script for calculating the view percent, indicating the amount of sight and light rays passing through the openings of the model. For this calculation, a surface was defined right at the back of the geometry (inside part) to visualize the points where the sightlines pass through the wall. The surface then was subdivided in U and V directions by the number of rows and blocks in each row. This subdivision creates a network of endpoints of sightlines. The starting point for the sightline is the defined viewpoint as mentioned earlier. The command, Collision One/Many in Grasshopper, was used for this calculation, using view sightlines as a collider and the model as the obstacle. The dispatch command was then used to filter the blocked and unblocked sightlines. The number of unblocked sightlines then was divided by the number of total sightlines to calculate the approximate view percent of the object. Also, a circle was drawn around the center of these unblocked collision points on the view surface to visualize the visible points (Figure 10.6). This calculation allows the user to change generic design parameters like the number and orientation of the blocks to reach the desired view percent and visibility rate.

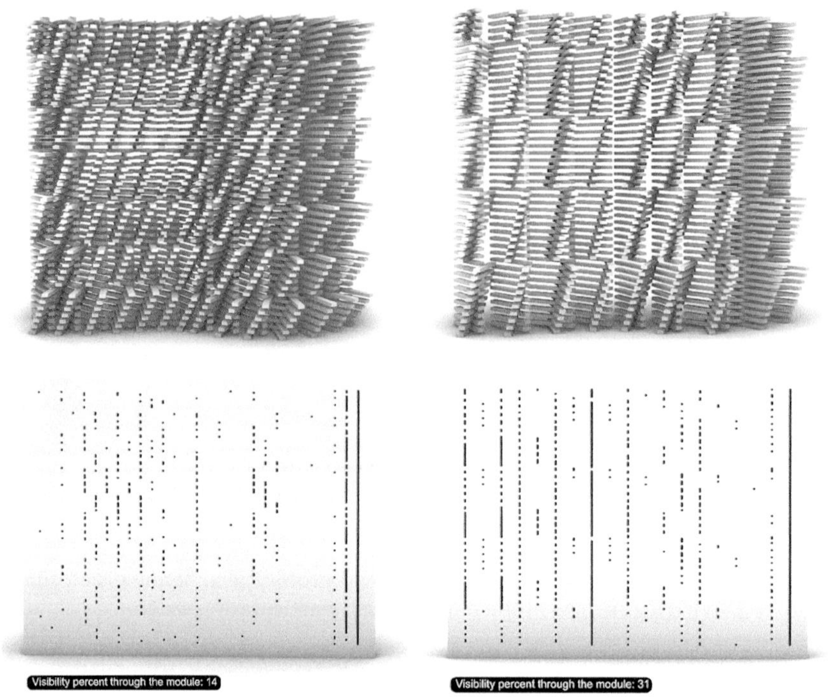

Figure 10.6 Calculating and visualizing visibility percent of sight rays through the model and changing the design to reach desired visibility rate.

Structural Stability Analysis

The overall stability of the form was then tested by employing the PhysX plugin for Grasshopper. This simulation allows for identifying the parts and exact blocks that may not be stable. It is worth mentioning this plugin may not accurately take into account the effect of adhesives between the blocks. This feature can also be controlled, to some extent, by changing the kinetic friction of the material in PhysX calculations. However, based on our experiment with several different forms, it remains substantially reliable for the structural stability of models with unified block shapes. In this step, it is important to define gravity on the same scale as the unit of Rhino. Also, the appropriate size of the table (larger than the prototype and in proper height position) would avoid unnecessary collisions in PhysX calculation. The calculations result in dynamic and static simulations. The dynamic simulation clearly indicates overall stability of the model through an animated simulation in which unstable elements would fall on the ground. The static simulation in this study is exported as a color scheme from blue to red as the most and least stable elements (Figure 10.7).

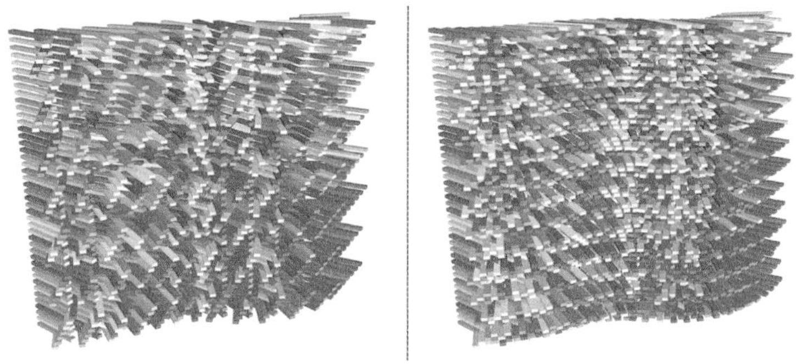

Figure 10.7 Real-time stability simulation of the designed prototype to define unstable blocks. The color range from blue to yellow to red indicates stable to unstable blocks. In this example, the module became fully unstable by increasing the number of blocks in each row from 14 to 27.

Following this optimization analysis, several design parameters could be adjusted to reach the desired form particularly polyline curvature, number of blocks in the rows, height of the module, and orientation of blocks. These elements could be adjusted in Grasshopper through changing a few sliders.

User Interface (UI) for Non-linear Design and Assembly

Except for initial creative input by the user through freehand drawings, the above-mentioned process of design and optimization follows normative linear computational design processes and heavily relies on the skills of technicians and researchers on computational design and Grasshopper. To meet the aim of the research in making technology available to less skilled computational designers, the study developed an open-ended, non-linear and intuitive design, and assembly workflow with an active involvement of the end-user. This phase of the study has developed and tested two main UIs as follows.

In the first approach, we employed the Human UI plugin for Grasshopper for visualizing and controlling design elements in Rhino (Figure 10.8). In this way, there is no need for the user to deal with the complex Grasshopper interface as all the important design and optimization parameters could be easily controlled through sliders and buttons on the Human UI. As Figure 10.8 demonstrates, this interface includes four main tabs of Design (3D model of block and module, slider to control the height of the module, information about number of blocks in each row, and the module), Optimization (including three sub-groups of solar, visibility, and stability analysis, and buttons to run these simulations), Cost Analysis (information about the number of blocks, their cost of per each module, and sliders to change the module based on available budget), and finally, Fabrication (3D model of final prototype, robot movements for assembly and virtual position of each block in the final prototype to control robotic fabrication). These groups and sub-groups were set as the proof of concept in this research and could be expanded and modified depending on the needs of final users.

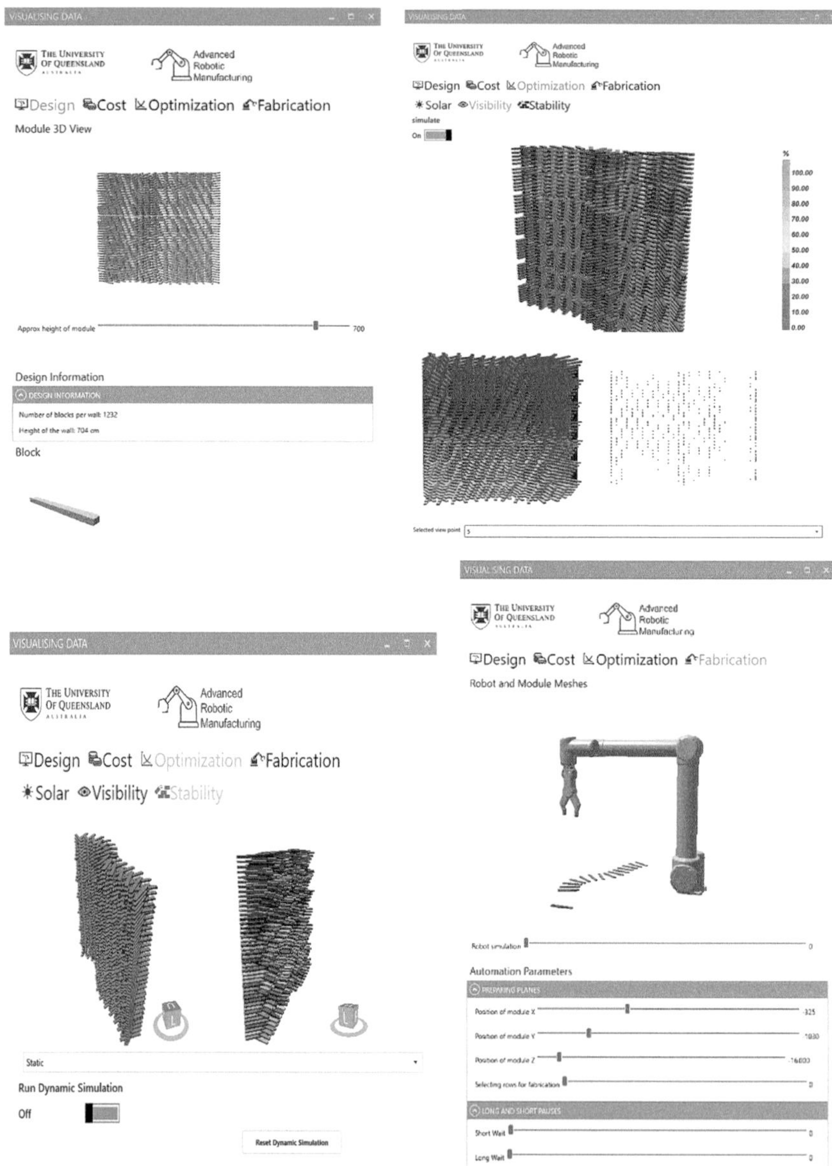

Figure 10.8 Contd.

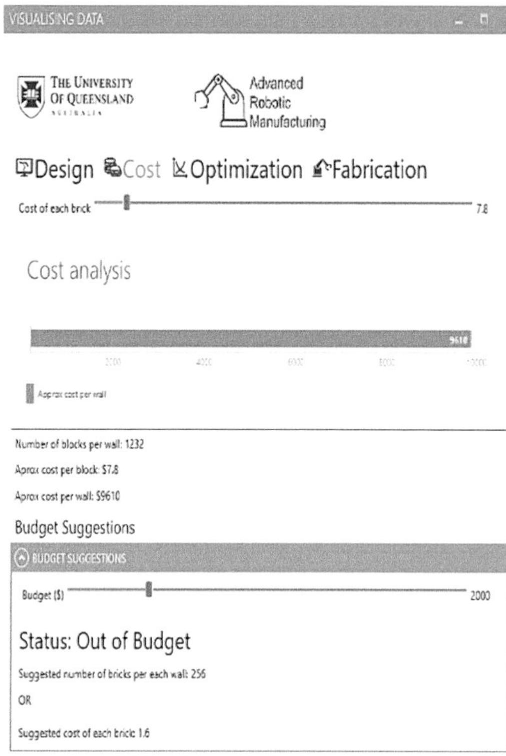

Figure 10.8 Developing a user-friendly interface by employing Human UI plugin for visualization and controlling design and fabrication parameters through sliders and buttons.

As the second approach we employed AR throughout the design and assembly process, putting user experience and simplicity of the workflow at the center of the process. To this end, we connected HoloLens 1 and a tablet (that could also be used for drawing the initial curve as mentioned earlier) to Rhino and Grasshopper using the Fologram platform. We developed five clusters of parameters to control and optimize the final design and assembly outcome including general design parameters, solar radiation parameters, visibility parameters, stability check, and fabrication (Figure 10.9). Each cluster included several key parameters affecting design and optimization. For each parameter, we defined one slider or boolean toggle button in Grasshopper that would be instantly translated into the same component in the Fologram platform (Figure 10.9). General design cluster included parameters like the height of the module, the distance between the blocks in each row, grout height, rotation of blocks and their movements in X and Y directions. For solar radiation analysis, the selected parameters included the north direction, timeframe of the analysis (starting and ending month, day, and hour) and simulation button. The visibility cluster included numbers and location of the viewpoints and simulation button. Stability check cluster included sliders and buttons to control kinetic friction value of the material, and dynamic and static simulations. And finally, the robotic fabrication cluster includes parameters such as the X, Y, and Z dimensions for the position of blocks as well as the module, slider to control pauses between each pick and place round, and simulation slider that allows for visualizing every step of the fabrication in advance of robot movements.

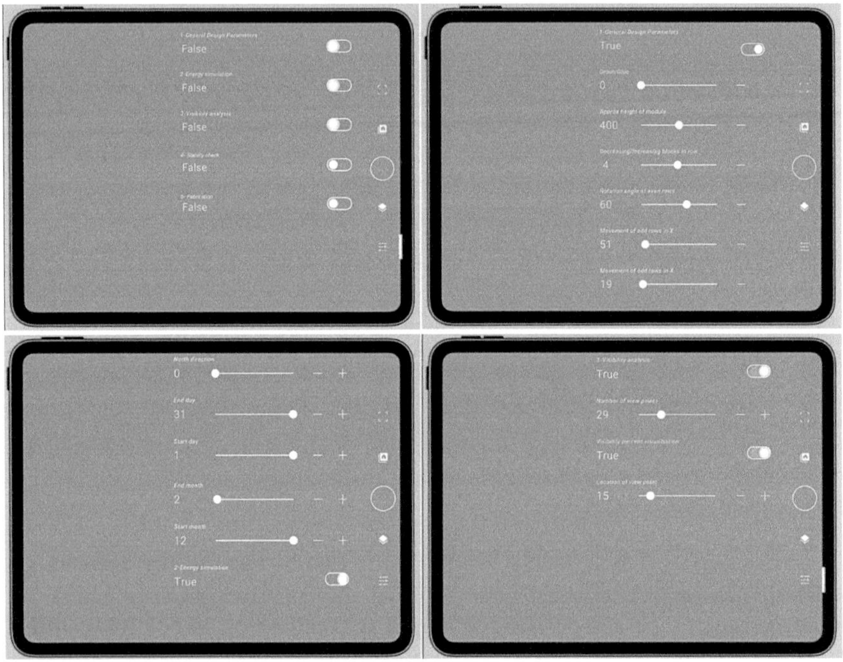

Figure 10.9 User interface of designed tabs and parameters for AR-assisted design and fabrication employing Fologram in tablet. Principle menu (top left) includes main design and simulation tabs, each including several clusters of parameters as the figure showcases for general design (top right), solar analysis (bottom left), and visibility (bottom right) parameters.

Upon scanning a QR code through Fologram, either on a tablet or on the HoloLens, to set up the location of the prototype in the real world, the module will appear on the devices with its background in real place. The user then can adjust the design, optimization, and assembly elements simply by moving the sliders and buttons (Figures 10.10 and 10.11). It is worth mentioning that this process is immersive and intuitive. As such, the user can manipulate design parameters to meet the aesthetic needs

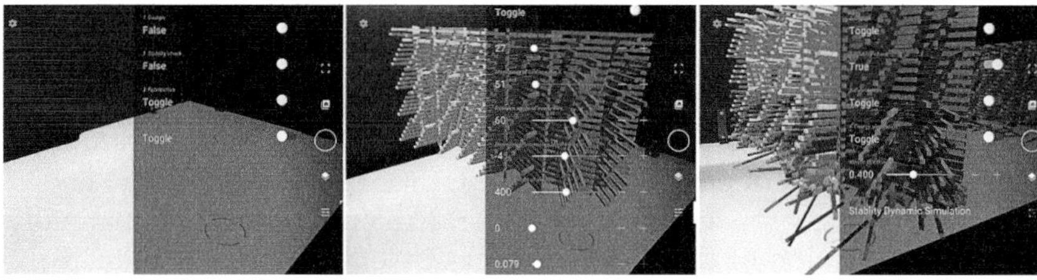

Figure 10.10 An example of structural stability simulation through AR on tablet.

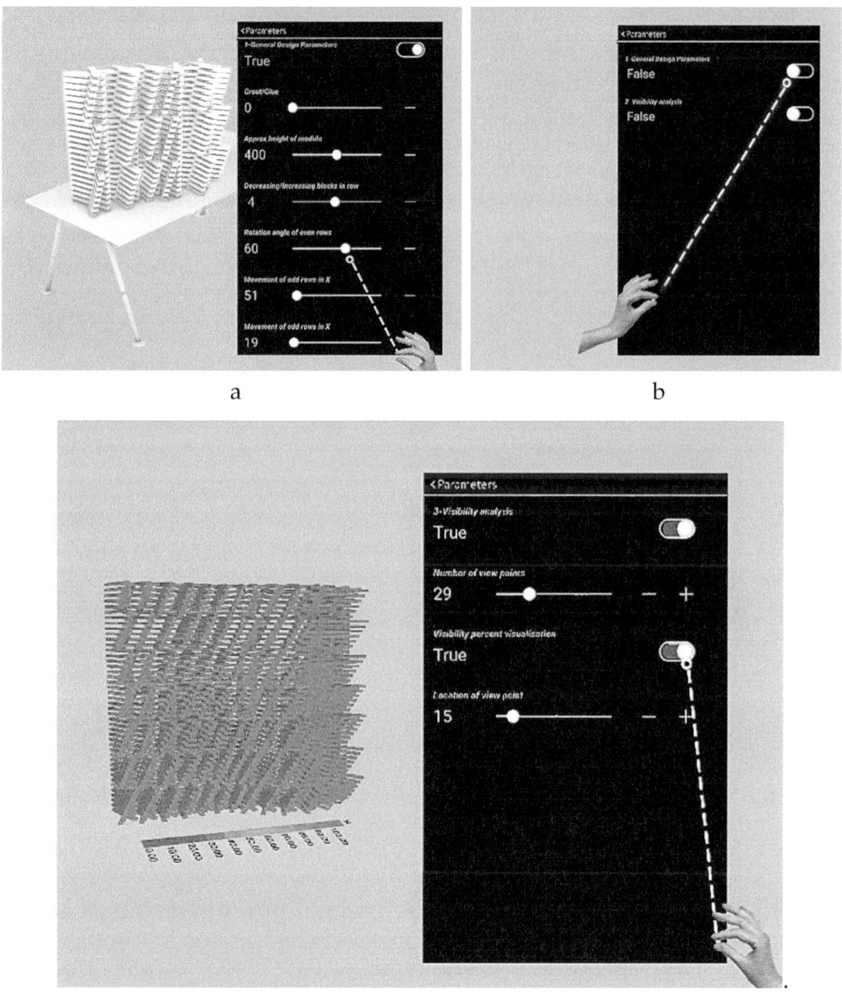

Figure 10.11 Fologram interface on HoloLens 1 showing defined sliders (a) and Boolean buttons, (b) to control design and optimization parameters (c) through AR.

as well. The end-user could define the blocks as 'moveable' in Fologram to intuitively move them in the desired directions. Accordingly, the user moves back and forth between predefined parameters in the Grasshopper script (controlled by sliders and buttons in Fologram) and their manipulation of design through AR, thus following an open-ended non-linear design strategy. For example, the end- user may manually change the location of some of the blocks by employing AR to increase or decrease visibility in a particular part rather than across the module or change the orientation or location of part of the model and then test the stability of the manipulated model. In this way, although the final product follows the main algorithm, it can be easily manipulated by the final user. This manipulation is not limited to the adjustment of normative design parameters as devised in the script and controlled in Fologram. But also, the end-user can intuitively change the location, orientation, and pattern of the blocks.

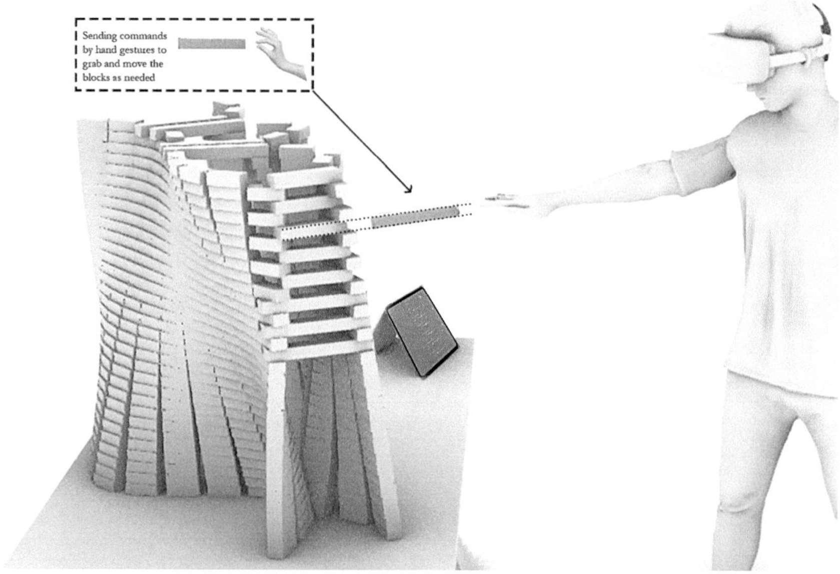

Figure 10.12 Example of manipulating location and patterns of blocks through AR.

Following the set-up of all the design and optimization parameters, AR was employed for robotic assembly of the final prototype (Figure 10.12). Application of robots in the architecture industry has become a necessity considering the opportunity it offers for fabricating non-standard forms, promoting creativity, higher precision, decreasing fabrication risk for humans by leaving dexterous tasks for robots, and reducing fabrication cost. In many cases, active collaboration of human and robot would allow development of a more effective fabrication workflow. In fact, human-robot collaboration (HRC) aims "to combine the best features of both human and robot. HRC can occur at different levels, whenever a robot and human are in close cooperation and possibly in contact with each other. The idea is to enhance the flexibility of the human and the speed, accuracy, and tirelessness of the robot in repetitive work. Some work phases are very difficult to automate; an attractive alternative is to keep them manual" (Salmi, et al. 2018, pp. 27–28). In this project, a human and a robot collaborate over a pick and place workflow in which the robot picks and moves the blocks to their destination positions and then keeps them for a certain amount of pause time (defined in the script and can be controlled by the end-user through AR), while the human connects the blocks using screws. The concept and workflow were successfully tested and validated for several case studies during this research (Figure 10.13).

Figure 10.13 Testing the workflow for employing AR in design and fabrication.

Necessity and Benefits of Employing AR in Design and Robotic Assembly

The proposed workflow in this paper concerns customization and adaptability of the process for the end-user and not just employing the advanced technologies in design and assembly. This workflow promotes participatory design by offering a hands-on approach to design and manufacturing, outlining the technologies and approaches that move beyond abstract technical strategies to include individuals in the design and manufacturing process. Accordingly, this methodological shift could enable local populations to have their voice in the design and even further, to be actively involved in constructing their living environment.

From a design perspective, the application of AR through the workflow discussed in this paper allows for simultaneously benefiting from the mathematical logic of the computational design script and the creativity of the user. While the overarching form follows the grammar from the Grasshopper script, the user can intervene in design by manually moving and rotating the blocks that by themselves are informed by immersive calculation of design performance. As the design and optimization parameters can be controlled by sending hand-gesture commands through HoloLens or sliders in mobile devices supporting Fologram, designers with limited skills in computational design can also benefit from using complex scripts developed by high-skilled researchers and technicians, and thus, the technology would be available for broader users in educational, research, and industry settings.

From the fabrication point of view, the proposed workflow allows quality control of the fabrication through an immersive overlay of digital and real models while improving the performance by actively involving a human in collaboration with the robot. AR is employed ensure parity between design and fabricated model, speeding up the fabrication and controlling the precision of fabrication through constant checking digital against real fabricated elements, adding marks on the timber elements to define direction of fabrication, informing the user of the intersection of the blocks which defines the position for connecting blocks, and batch assembly of modules. Through AR, the end- user can also control the exact location for picking-up and placing the blocks and filter the digital model to demonstrate the exact row or block that is under construction for quality control purposes through a series of sliders defined in Fologram. This workflow is developed for robotic assembly of modules that then can be combined through batch assembly for 1:1 scale fabrication of larger architectural elements.

CONCLUSION

This research presented a workflow for non-linear design and optimization as well as collaborative robotic assembly of timber prototypes by employing AR. The workflow involves affordable and accessible technology that can be used by less-computationally skilled educators, scholars, industry workers, and even for development of remote settlements where accessibility to experts and skills is a serious challenge. Employing AR allows putting the end-user at the center of the design and optimization process, including the user's intuitive and creative input in design along with the input from commonly complex calculations from computational design scripts. It also facilitates active HRC in fabrication, while could ensure the user of the precision and speed of fabrication. The study lays the foundation for future scenarios to use AR for design and fabrication in different directions. Firstly, the same workflow can be used for developing scripts for other design parameters like transparency ratio, energy usage and fabrication cost, and make all required calculations readily available for less-computational skilled designers, educators and laborers. Second, future research can employ machine learning and AI technologies along with the proposed workflow for drawing the initial sketch that would lead to design prototypes as they are designed by famous architects (for instance, how Zaha Hadid would design a parametric wall and how efficient it would be in terms of solar incident and visibility rate?). Third, future research can develop the HRC strategy to develop a non-linear fabrication process by including end-user's feedback and intervention in fabrication as well. It can be materialized through sending hand and figure gestures to the robot to execute the work when the human signals. Forthcoming and future research can also elaborate on how the proposed tool and framework contribute to improving teaching and learning experiences in architecture and civil engineering settings.

ACKNOWLEDGEMENTS

This research uses a number of open-source plugins and tools, particularly, PhysX, Ladybug, FUROBOT, and Human UI for Rhino and Grasshopper. We would like to thank the community for providing these tools. Additionally, we acknowledge the commitment and support of UQ Innovate, in particular John Stafford. Their collaboration has been instrumental in advancing our research and enhancing the outcomes of this project.

REFERENCES

Adel, A., Thoma, A., Helmreich, M., Gramazio, F. and Kohler, M. 2018. Design of robotically fabricated timber frame structures. ACADIA 2018 (Recalibration on Imprecision and Infidelity). 394–403.

Agati, S.S., Bauer, R.D., Hounsell, M.D.S. and Paterno, A.S. 2020. Augmented reality for manual assembly in industry 4.0: Gathering guidelines. *In*: 2020 22nd Symposium on Virtual and Augmented Reality (SVR). 179–188. IEEE.

Akbari. 2018. Cyber-Physical Construction: Negotiating Design and Making through Augmented Reality. Institute for Advanced Architecture of Catalonia (IAAC). http://www.iaacblog.com/programs/cyber-physical-construction.

Atanasova, L., Mitterberger, D., Sandy, T., Gramazio, F., Kohler, M. and Dörfler, K. 2020. Prototype as artefact design tool for open-ended collaborative assembly processes. ACADIA 2020 (Distributed Proximities). 350–359.

Bard, J., Gannon, M., Jacobson-Weaver, Z., Contreras, M., Jeffers, M. and Smith, B. 2014. Seeing is doing: Synthetic tools for robotically augmented fabrication in high-skill domains, ACADIA 14: Design agency. *In*: Proceedings of the 34th Annual Conference of the Association for Computer Aided Design in Architecture (ACADIA). Los Angeles 23–25. 409–416. ISBN 9781926724478.

Chalhoub, J. and Ayer, S.K. 2019. Exploring the performance of an augmented reality application for construction layout tasks. Multimedia Tools and Applications. 78(24): 35075–35098.

Craney, R. and Adel, A. 2021. Engrained performance: Performance-driven computational design of a robotically assembled shingle facade system. *In*: B. Slocum., V. Ago., S. Doyle., A. Marcus., M. Yablonina. and M.D. Campo (eds). Distributed Proximities. 604–613. *In*: Proceedings of the 40th Annual Conference of The Association for Computer Aided Design in Architecture (ACADIA 2020).

Hajirasouli, A., Banihashemi, S., Drogemuller, R., Fazeli, A. and Mohandes, S.R. 2022. Augmented reality in design and construction: Thematic analysis and conceptual frameworks. Construction Innovation. 22(3): 412–443.

Hughes, R., Osterlund, T. and Larsen, N.M. 2021. Integrated design-for-manufacturing and AR-aided-assembly workflows for lightweight reciprocal frame timber structures. Construction Robotics. 5: 147–157. https://doi.org/https://doi.org/10.1007/s41693-020-00048-3.

Jahn, G., Newnham, C. and Beanland, M. 2018. Making in mixed reality: Holographic design, fabrication, assembly and analysis of woven steel structures. *In*: Proceeding of 2018 ACADIA, Mexico City. 88–97.

Jahn, G., Newnham, C., Van Den Berg, N., Iraheta, M. and Wells, J. 2019. Holographic Construction, Design Modelling Symposium. Springer, Berlin. 314–324.

Johns, R.L. 2012. Augmented reality and the fabrication of gestural form. pp. 248–255. *In*: Brell-Çokcan, S. and Braumann, J. (eds). Robotic Fabrication in Architecture, Art, and Design. Wien New York: Springer.

Kensek, K., Noble, D., Schiler, M. and Tripathi, A. 2012. Augmented reality: An application for architecture. pp. 294–301. *In*: Proceedings: Computing in Civil and Building Engineering. https://doi.org/10.1061/40513(279)38

Knight, T. and George S. 2015. Making grammars: From computing with shapes to computing with things. Design Studies. 41: 8–28.

Larsson, M., Yoshida, H. and Igarashi, T. 2019. Human-in-the-loop fabrication of 3D surfaces with natural tree branches. *In*: SCF '19: Proceedings of the 3rd Annual ACM Symposium on Computational Fabrication. Association for Computing Machinery. New YorkNYUnited States https://doi.org/10.1145/3328939.3329000.

Larsson, M., Yoshida, H., Umetani, N. and Igarashi, T. 2020. Tsugite: Interactive design and fabrication of wood joints. *In*: Proceedings of the 33rd Annual ACM Symposium on User Interface Software and Technology. 317–327. https://doi.org/10.1145/3379337.3415899.

Luo, J., Mastrokalou, E., Aldabous, R., Aldaboos, S. and Lopez Rodriguez, A. 2023. Fabrication of complex clay structures through an augmented reality assisted platform. *In*: CAADRIA Proceedings. 413–422. Association for Computer-Aided Architectural Design Research in Asia (CAADRIA).

Mitterberger, D., Ercan Jenny, S., Vasey, L., Lloret-Fritschi, E., Aejmelaeus-Lindström, P., Gramazio, F., et al. 2022. Interactive robotic plastering: Augmented interactive design and fabrication for on-site robotic plastering.

In: CHI Conference on Human Factors in Computing Systems. Article No.: 174, Pages 1–18. https://doi.org/10.1145/3491102.3501842.

Mostafavi, S. 2021. Hybrid Intelligence in Architectural Robotic Materialization (HI-ARM): Computational, Fabrication and Material Intelligence for Multi-Mode Robotic Production of Multi-Scale and Multi-Material Systems. A+BE: Architecture and the Built Environment. https://doi.org/10.7480/ABE.2021.12.5799.

Neely, E.L. 2019. Augmented reality, augmented ethics: Who has the right to augment a particular physical space? Ethics and Information Technology. 21(1): 11–18.

Rosenberg, L. 1992. The Use of Virtual Fixtures as Perceptual Overlays to Enhance Operator Performance in Remote Environments. Stanford Univiversity CA Center for Design Research (AL/CF-TR-1994-0089).

Sadeguipour, M.R. and Pak, M. 2013. Ladybug: A parametric environmental plugin for grasshopper to help designers create an environmentally-conscious design. *In*: Proceedings of the 13th International IBPSA, Lyon.

Salmi, T., Ahola, Jari M., Heikkilä, T., Kilpeläinen, P. and Malm, T. 2018. Human-robot collaboration and sensor-based robots in industrial applications and construction. pp. 25–52. *In*: Henriette Bier (ed.). Robotic Building. Cham, Switzerland: Springer. https://doi.org/10.1007/978-3-319-70866-9_2.

Schubert, R., Bruder, G. and Welch, G. 2023. Intuitive user interfaces for real-time magnification in augmented reality. *In*: Proceedings of the 29th ACM Symposium on Virtual Reality Software and Technology. 1–10.

Song, Y., Koeck, R. and Luo, S. 2021a. AR Digi-Component; AR-assisted, real-time, immersive design and robotic fabrication workflow for parametric architectural structures. *In*: Projections, Proceedings of the 26th International Conference of the Association for Computer-Aided Architectural Design Research in Asia (CAADRIA) 2021. 2: 253–262. © 2021 and published by the Association for Computer-Aided Architectural Design Research in Asia (CAADRIA), Hong Kong.

Song, Y., Koeck, R. and Luo, S. 2021b. Review and analysis of augmented reality (AR) literature for digital fabrication in architecture. Automation in Construction. 128: 103762. https://doi.org/10.1016/j.autcon.2021.103762.

Thoma, A., Jenny, D., Helmreich, M., Gandia, A., Gramazio, F. and Kohler, M. 2019. Cooperative robotic fabrication of timber dowel assemblies. pp. 77–88. *In*: Leopold, C., Robeller, C. and Weber, U. (eds). Research Culture in Architecture. Berlin, Boston: De Gruyter.

Varela, P., Sousa, J. and Dias, J. 2021. Drawing-to-factory process using freehand drawing to drive robotic assembly of brick walls. *In*: Collaborative, Participative or Responsive design. Vol. 1. *In*: Proceedings of the eCAADe. 39: 189–194.

Wang, X. 2009. Augmented reality in architecture and design: potentials and challenges for application. International Journal of Architectural Computing. 7(2): 309–326.

Willmann, J., Knauss, M., Bonwetsch, T., Apolinarska, A.A., Gramazio, F. and Kohler, M. 2016. Robotic timber construction: Expanding additive fabrication to new dimensions. Automation in Construction. 61: 16–23.

Xian, Z., Hoban, N. and Peters, B. 2020. Spatial timber assembly: Robotically fabricated reciprocal frame wall. pp. 403–412. *In*: Werner, L. and Koering, D. (eds). Anthropologic: Architecture and Fabrication in the cognitive age - Proceedings of the 38th eCAADe Conference - Volume 2, TU Berlin, Berlin, Germany. 16-18 September 2020.

Yoshida, H., Larsson, M. and Igarashi, T. 2019. Upcycling Tree Branches as Architectural Elements through Collaborative Design and Fabrication. *In*: Proceedings of the Thirteenth International Conference on Tangible, Embedded, and Embodied Interaction. 589–593. Tempe, AZ, USA.

Chapter **11**

Extended Reality in Human-Robot Collaboration: Present and Future

Yuan Liu[1,2], Glenda Caldwell*[1,2], Müge Belek Fialho Teixeira[1,2], Markus Rittenbruch[1,3], Alan Burden[1,2] and Matthias Guertler[1,4]

[1]Australian Cobotics Centre, QLD 4000, Brisbane, Australia

[2]School of Architecture and Built Environment, Faculty of Engineering, Queensland University of Technology (QUT)

[3]School of Design, Faculty of Creative Industries, Education and Social Justice, Queensland University of Technology (QUT)

[4]School of Mechanical and Mechatronic Engineering, Faculty of Engineering and Information Technology, University of Technology Sydney (UTS)

INTRODUCTION

Extended Reality (XR) has been adopted across various fields, including education, tourism, museums, and medicine. In manufacturing, current systems focus on flexibility, reconfigurability (Prasad and Jayswal 2019), and the concept of 'human-in-the-loop' (Bhattacharya et al. 2023, Kusiak 2018), where human roles and decision-making are integrated with

*For Correspondence: g.caldwell@qut.edu.au

DOI: 10.1201/9781003581642-11

robotic systems. To further enhance collaboration between humans and robots, XR has emerged as a pivotal technology in Human-Robot Collaboration (HRC).

HUMAN-ROBOT COLLABORATION

To demystify HRC, the interaction between human and robot is categorised into four levels: full automation, coexistence, cooperation, and collaboration (Burden et al. 2022) (Figure 11.1). These levels range from no human-robot interaction (full automation) to simultaneous, task-based collaboration, reflecting varying degrees of physical contact, speed regulation, and safety requirements.

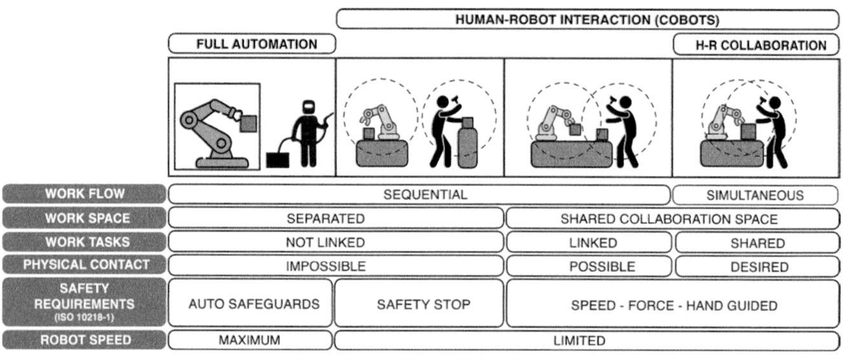

Figure 11.1 Types of human-robot relationships (Burden et al. 2022). Adapted from (Kopp et al. 2021).

HRC has seen widespread adoption across various fields. It has revolutionised agriculture through enhanced efficiency and precision (Polic et al. 2021), transformed medical and healthcare practices with improved surgical and diagnostic procedures (Baumkircher et al. 2022), provided support in social assistance roles (Babel et al. 2022), optimised logistics operations with advanced robotic systems logistics (Jost et al. 2018), and increased productivity in manufacturing (Siegele et al. 2021). In essence, HRC has become integral to the advancement and innovation within these diverse fields, fundamentally changing the landscape of workforce dynamics and operational methodologies.

EXTENDED REALITY IN HUMAN-ROBOT COLLABORATION

In HRC, emerging technologies such as Extended Reality (XR) show a pivotal trend across multifarious applications. To clearly illustrate these technologies, in this chapter, XR is defined as an umbrella term of immersive technology, which includes Virtual Reality (VR), Mixed Reality (MR), Augmented Reality (AR), and future realities (Kwok and Koh 2021, Milgram and Kishino 1994, Speicher et al. 2019). MR refers to all formats between reality and VR (Figure 11.2).

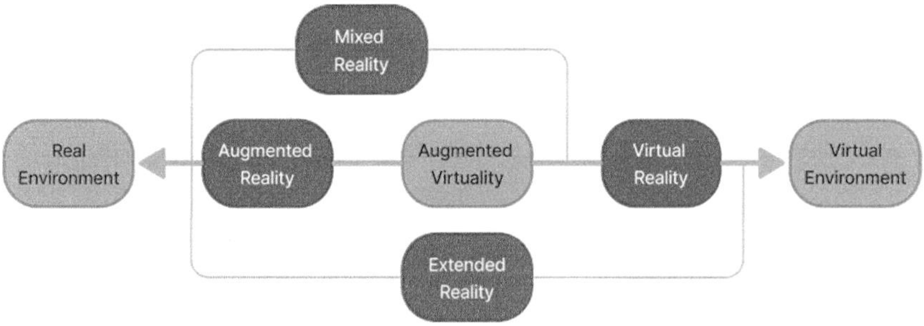

Figure 11.2 Reality-Virtuality definition. Adapted from (Milgram and Kishino 1994).

VR, for example, serves as an innovative development environment for robotic programming (Maragkos et al. 2019) and a simulation tool that enables researchers to dissect the intricacies of human interaction within HRC (Fratczak et al. 2019). It further acts as an instrument for augmenting quality assurance (Ratava et al. 2019) and evaluating system performance (Etzi et al. 2019).

AR provides a means for system evaluation (Havard et al. 2019), workspace design simulation (Cao et al. 2019), and aids in visualising robot behaviour (Bolano et al. 2019) and identifying faults (Avalle et al. 2019). MR, as an environment which blends the physical and the digital world, is increasingly employed as a pedagogical space for training purposes (Sievers et al. 2020) and as a development platform for programming (Rivera-Pinto and Kildal 2020). Furthermore, AR and MR are frequently used as user interfaces, enhancing the intuitiveness and efficacy of user interactions with robotic systems (Chacko and Kapila 2019, Zhang et al. 2020).

XR technologies enhance safety, optimise workspace design, improve data visualisation, train operators, and create intuitive interfaces. By reducing cognitive load and improving understanding, XR supports efficient human-robot collaboration, crucial for effective decision-making in complex and dynamic environments.

METHODOLOGY

This chapter is guided by a systematic literature review method Preferred Reporting Items for Systematic Reviews and Meta-Analysis (PRISMA) (Page et al. 2021) and Horizon Scan. Horizon Scan is not a conventional method for literature review, but an approach to explore potential trends and issues (Cuhls et al. 2015). Papers selected for this chapter focused on XR applied in HRC. Published peer-reviewed journal articles, conference papers and book chapters, written in English, were included. Quantitative, qualitative, and mixed-method studies were included in order to consider different aspects of XR applied in HRC. Papers that were reviews and irrelevant to the theme were excluded.

Given the multidisciplinary and cutting-edge nature of the topic, the search was conducted in the following databases from 2019 to April 2024: Scopus, IEEE Xplore, and ACM digital library. As listed in Table 11.1, keywords were identified in two sets. The first set of keywords was related to XR, and the second set of keywords was related to HRC. The Boolean operator "AND" is used between the two sets, and the "OR" operator is used within each set. Searches covered titles, abstracts, and full texts in the databases. The search strategy was drafted by Yuan Liu and further refined through team discussions. The final search strategy is ("Extended Reality" OR "Augmented Reality" OR "Virtual Reality" OR "Mixed Reality" OR AR OR VR OR MR OR XR) AND ("Human-Robot Collaboration" OR "Human-Robot Interaction" OR Cobot*). The final search was conducted on April 9, 2024, and search results were exported into Paperpile, and duplicates were removed by the Paperpile filter.

Table 11.1 Sets of keywords used in the search

XR	HRC
"Extended Reality" OR "Augmented Reality" OR "Virtual Reality" OR "Mixed Reality" OR AR OR VR OR MR OR XR	"Human-Robot Collaboration" OR "Human-Robot Interaction" OR Cobot*

From Figure 11.3, it is evident that there has been a significant increase in publications starting from 2023. Since the purpose of this chapter is to focus on the current and future of XR applied in HRC, the scope of the studies reviewed will be limited to the most recent research. Therefore, this chapter analyses studies from 2023 to the present. Figure 11.3 shows that before 2020, VR received more attention than other types of immersive technologies. From 2021 to 2022, AR gained the most attention. All types of XR technologies saw a significant increase in attention starting from 2023.

After the removal of duplicates, two reviewers screened the same 472 publications according to the title and abstract. After that, the full text of the selected records was scanned to remove the publications inconsistent with the research questions. Each exclusive criterion was discussed among all authors. PRISMA chart was adopted to illustrate the steps of paper identification and selection (Figure 11.4).

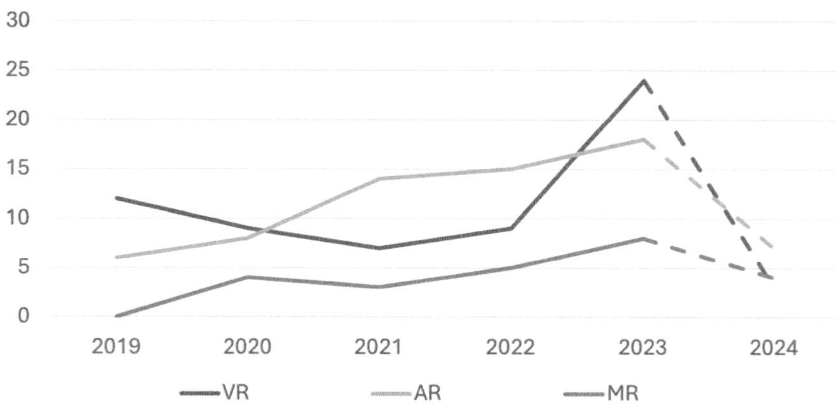

Figure 11.3 Number of papers per year (until April 9, 2024).

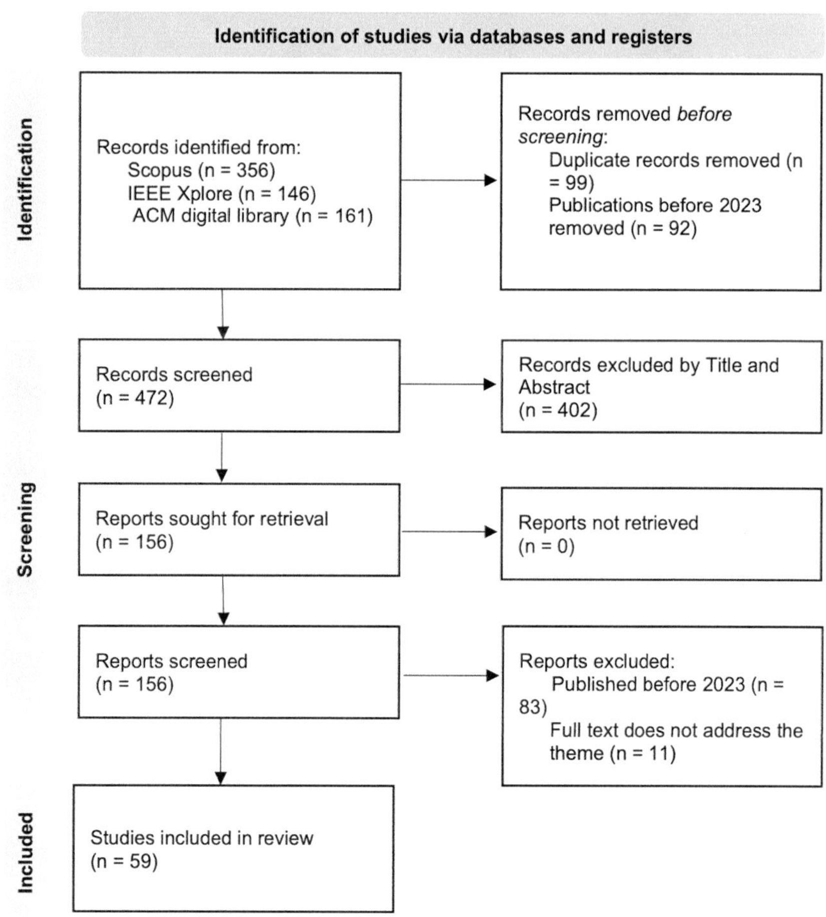

Figure 11.4 PRISMA flow chart.

RESEARCH FINDINGS

Types of XR in HRC

Figure 11.5 illustrates the various types of XR technologies applied in HRC from 2023 to the present, including VR (n = 21), AR ((n = 24), and MR (n = 11). One study utilises multiple types, such as VR and MR, and it is categorised under the broader term XR. As shown in Figure 11.5, AR received the most attention during 2023–2024, while XR, which includes multiple technologies in a single case, received the least attention.

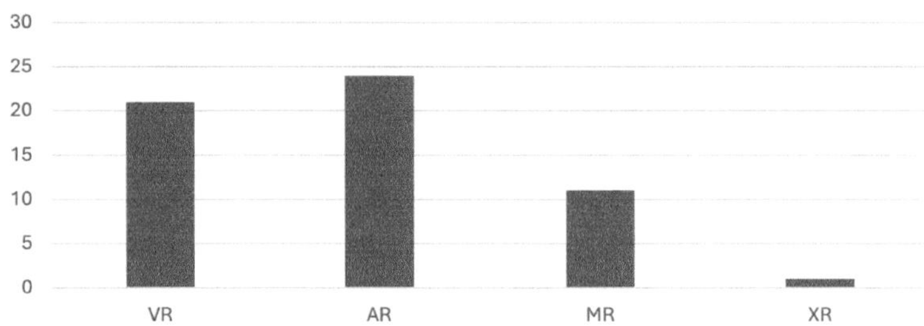

Figure 11.5 Types of XR in HRC.

Roles of XR in HRC

Figure 11.6 illustrates the various roles that XR technologies play in HRC. Generally, XR is primarily used as an interface. Other roles of XR include development environments, learning environments, platforms for design, visualisation, simulation, instruction and guidance, task and motion planning, and more.

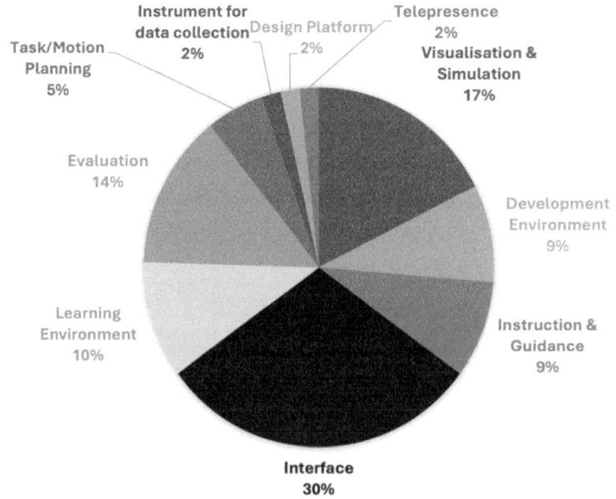

Figure 11.6 Roles of XR in HRC.

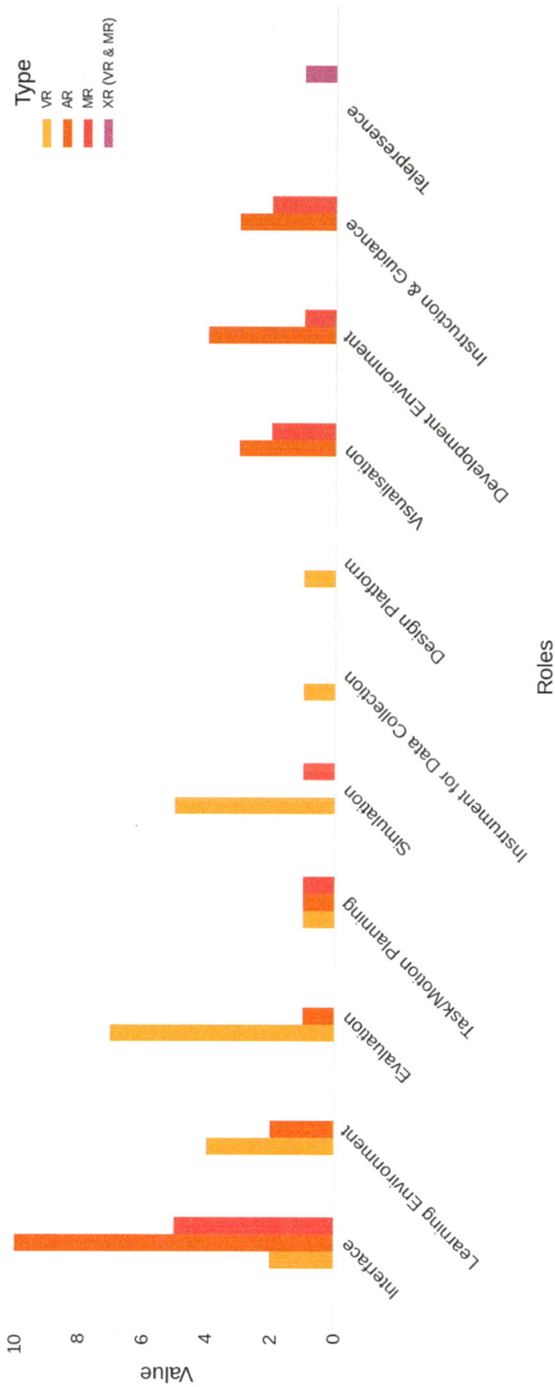

Figure 11.7 Roles of different XR in HRC.

Figure 11.7 shows that different types of XR play different roles in HRC. These roles are categorised by the types of XR technologies: VR, AR, MR, and a combination of these technologies labelled as XR (VR and MR). The vertical axis illustrates how often the roles are utilized in the analyzed literature. Each role of XR in HRC, based on existing studies, is described below.

Interface

Interface is the most prominent role that XR plays in HRC (n = 17), with AR leading significantly (n = 10), followed by MR (n = 5) and VR (n = 2). XR technologies enhance human-robot interaction by providing immersive and intuitive interfaces, real-time feedback, safe training environments, and improved collaboration and communication. These benefits make XR a powerful tool for enhancing the effectiveness and efficiency of human-robot interaction.

The VR-based interface allows humans to teleoperate with robots by reducing workload (Si et al. 2023). VR-based interfaces are used to correct perception errors and they got more preference than screen interfaces due to providing users with more immersive and enjoyable experiences (Wozniak et al. 2023). In manufacturing, an AR interface enables humans to interact with cobots performing various tasks. For instance, operators can carry out auxiliary maintenance tasks using AR-assisted visible guidance, free from spatial and human constraints (Liu et al. 2023).

AR-based interfaces perform well in improving the comprehension of cobots' actions, enhancing situation awareness, reducing ambiguity, and increasing efficiency in quality inspection (Kötter et al. 2023). Additionally, AR is applied in collaborative sorting systems to balance efficiency with occupational safety and health (Chen et al. 2023). Other benefits of an AR-based interface include supporting workspace awareness, confidence, and perceived control (Lunding et al. 2023), enhancing productivity, safety and trust (Chu and Liu 2023), enabling intuitive and safer communication between humans and robots (Matour and Winkler 2023a), facilitating intuitive path planning for a robot (Matour and Winkler 2023b), and combining with other technologies such as Brian-Computer Interface (BCI) to achieve interactive robotic path planning (Ji et al. 2023).

However, some researchers have investigated the impact of AR user interfaces on task performance, cognitive load, and situational awareness. The findings indicate that, in certain cases, AR-based interfaces negatively affect these factors compared to traditional graphical user interfaces (GUIs) (Kalatzis et al. 2023). These negative impacts highlight the need for further research and optimisation of AR technologies to enhance their effectiveness and usability.

MR-based interfaces facilitate quick implementation of variable impedance parameters in new environments or for different goals (Tran et al. 2024), enhance human-robot communication (Calzone et al. 2023), support HRC in fabrication (Shen and Hsu 2023), enable real-time and dynamic communication between human and robot in assembly process (David et al. 2023), and effectively convey robots' intentions to human (Macciò et al. 2023).

Task and Motion Planning

All types of XR have been applied in HRC for task and motion planning (n = 3). For example, VR has been used for the cloth folding task planning (Moletta et al. 2023), AR has been employed for planning the layout reconfiguration configuration for assembly tasks (Eswaran et al. 2024), MR has been used for intuitive motion planning (Nakamura and Sekiyama 2023). This widespread application of XR in the planning stage is due to its intuitive nature and cost-effectiveness, making it an ideal tool for visualising and optimising complex tasks and workflows.

Learning Environment

VR and AR are used as learning environments for training (n = 6). VR-based safety training has been shown to be more effective than traditional methods such as paper-based, video instruction, and instructor-based training (Dianatfar et al. 2023, 2024). In HRC welding tasks, VR-based training proved resilient to external disturbances and provided accurate feedback and guidance (Ye et al. 2023). VR is also implemented as a teaching and learning environment for HRC design (Ariansyah et al. 2023). Besides, AR has been used for training for energy optimisation in HRC (Heredia et al. 2023), and training operators for seamless collaboration between humans and high-payload robots (Andronas et al. 2023).

Tool for Evaluation

VR and AR are both used as tools for evaluation in HRC (n = 8). In this aspect, VR is the main type of XR technology used in existing studies (n = 7). For instance, VR-based tools can be used to test the interaction modalities (Puthenkalam et al. 2023), assess real-time ergonomics (Lanzoni et al. 2023), assess efficacy and safety (Sonntag et al. 2023), evaluate the collaboration between humans and robots (Gustavsson et al. 2023). They also validate the proposed method to optimize human posture during HRC tasks (Omidi et al. 2023), evaluate the trust and task performance between the robot with eyes and without eyes (Pilacinski et al. 2023), and measure human physiological and psychological response during HRC tasks (Jang et al. 2024). Except for VR, AR-based tools evaluate different visualisation formats in the HRC system (Cogurcu et al. 2023).

Simulation

VR shows the highest use in simulation (n = 5), with MR also contributing (n = 1). VR-based simulation is used for human behaviour data training (Dallel et al. 2023), and as a research tool to explore new concepts and validate existing approaches in the domain of HRC involving autonomous robots (Arntz et al. 2024). They are also used for robot integration (Tram et al. 2023), and used as an environment to study the effects of safety-restricted features like close distance during movements and events of robotic malfunctions (Legler et al. 2023). MR-based simulation is also used to ensure the safety distance between the human and the robot (Duan et al. 2023).

Visualisation

In this chapter, visualisation refers to XR technologies that can provide the experience of visualising the information of the HRC system in an immersive way. In HRC, some studies (n = 5) used AR and MR as approaches for visualisation. For example, AR presents different visualisations on demand and makes them context-aware to avoid visual clutter (Lunding et al. 2024), AR is used for learned visualisation for efficiency (Chandan et al. 2023) and visualisation of safety zones (Cogurcu and Maddock 2023). MR-based approaches are used to display and ensure the safety distance between the human and the robot (Duan et al. 2023) and provide feedback for safe and reliable construction (González-Böhme and Valenzuela-Astudillo 2023).

Development Environment

Traditionally, robot programming could only be performed by experts. While in some existing studies (n = 5), AR and MR are used for non-expert programming. As a development environment, AR is used the most (n = 4), which enables non-expert users to program reactive robot behaviours (Ikeda and Szafir 2024), teaches the robot new objects in its environment (Weber et al. 2023), sets virtual obstacles for developing an algorithm to improve prediction of human motion (Tung et al. 2024), and awareness of cognitive workload (Yang et al. 2023). Besides, MR has the ability to accelerate the process of programming the complex manoeuvres of a cobot (Calderón-Sesmero et al. 2024).

Instruction and Guidance

The benefit of AR and MR is that they blend digital components with the physical environment. This integration allows for effective instruction and guidance without compromising human awareness of the real world. In some cases (n = 5), AR and MR have been adopted for instruction and guidance during HRC.

For example, AR is used as an instruction to reduce workload, improve efficiency during assembly tasks (Moya et al. 2023), and enhance task performance (Fu et al. 2024). It is also used as real-time instruction for HRC on road maintenance (Bavelos et al. 2024). In addition, MR has been used to guide operators for mutual-cognition (Li et al. 2024), guidance and instruction for HRC fabrication (Htet Kyaw et al. 2024).

Other Roles of XR-Instruments for Data Collection, Design Platform, and Telepresence Platform

Other roles of XR in HRC include an instrument for data collection (n = 1), a design platform (n = 1) and telepresence (n = 1). VR can be utilised to collect eye-tracking data, which can be used for intent prediction. This application is highlighted in research demonstrating how VR technology can enhance data collection processes by providing precise and detailed insights into user intentions (Pettersson and Falkman 2023). Besides, VR technology is particularly useful in designing collaboration scenarios between humans and robots (Gustavsson et al. 2023). In another case, VR and MR are combined as a telepresence platform that allows a local user and a remote user to work together in robotics training scenarios (Calandra et al. 2023).

GUIDELINE AND FRAMEWORK

Apart from studies focusing on the application of XR with different roles in HRC, there are some studies proposing guidelines and frameworks for XR design in HRC (n = 2). Building on the design guidelines for Human-Robot Interaction (HRI) with assistive robots—which emphasize understandability, reliability, and accessibility (Wilkinson et al. 2021)—another study proposed additional AR guidelines for understanding robot intentions during HRC, i.e., anticipating a robot's behaviour (Eze and Crick 2023). The two studies incorporated principles such as low cognitive overhead, learnability and consistency, and responsiveness. Thus, their guidelines encompass a total of six principles:

- Understandable
- Reliable

- Accessible
- Low cognitive overhead
- Learnable and Consistent
- Responsive

In addition to guidelines and principles, there is an MR framework for Human-Robot Interaction (HRI) (Sopon et al. 2023). In this framework, Unity is used to generate a virtual environment that is displayed through Microsoft HoloLens. The Robotic Operating System (ROS) is employed to connect the digital twin with the physical robotics system, facilitating seamless integration and interaction between the virtual and physical worlds.

XR DEVICES USED IN HRC

Nowadays, various devices can be used to deliver immersive experiences for users. These generally include PCs, mobile devices, projectors, head-mounted displays (HMDs) and AR goggles. As shown in Figure 11.8, in HRC, the devices used are HMDs and mobile devices such as tablets and projectors. HMDs are used in most studies.

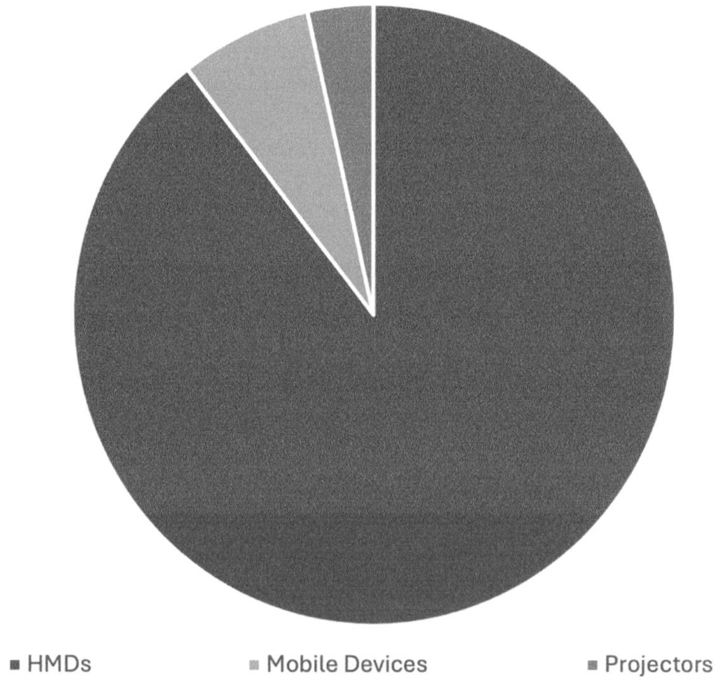

Figure 11.8 XR devices used in HRC.

As shown in Figure 11.9, among all the HMDs used in HRC, the Microsoft HoloLens series is the most frequently used in recent studies. The HTC Vive series is the second most commonly used. Other HMDs include the Oculus Rift, Meta Quest 2, Varjo XR-3, and Steam Valve Index.

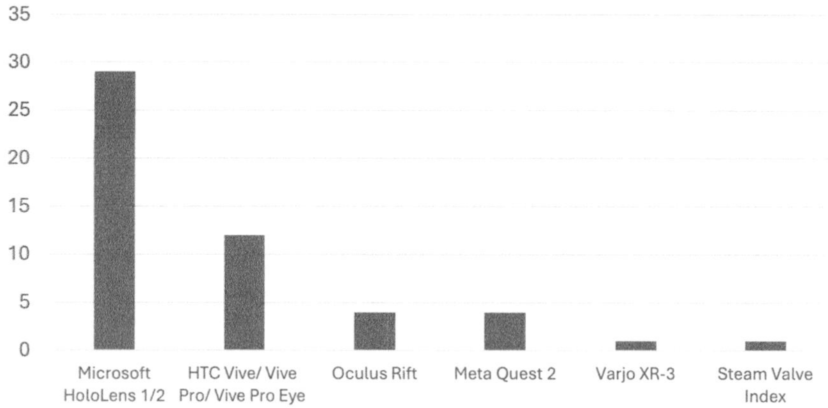

Figure 11.9 HMDs used in HRC.

TOOLS AND SOFTWARE USED FOR XR IN HRC

Aside from hardware, a variety of software is used for XR in HRC. Some software tools are more popular than others. For instance, Unity (https://unity.com/), a game engine, is the most widely used software for creating immersive environments in HRC. Other popular tools include Software Development Kits (SDKs) such as Vuforia (https://developer.vuforia.com/), another game engine like Unreal Engine 4 (https://www.unrealengine.com/), and APIs such as WebGL (https://www.khronos.org/webgl/). Additionally, AR authoring tools, simulation tools such as Solid Edge (https://solidedge.siemens.com/) and Webots (https://www.cyberbotics.com/), BIM-based platforms including Rhino 3D (https://www.rhino3d.com/) and Grasshopper (https://www.grasshopper3d.com/), and programming and development environments such as JADE (https://jade.tilab.com/) and Python are also utilised. In one case, authors use their own video datasets for specific scenarios (Figure 11.10).

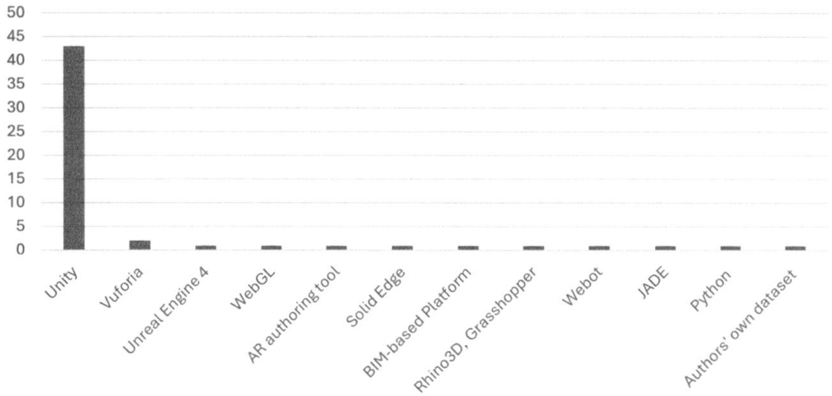

Figure 11.10 Tools and software used for XR in HRC.

DISCUSSION

The Present of XR in HRC

The result of this horizon scan provides significant insights into the applications and benefits of XR technologies based on the roles XR played in HRC. Currently, VR is used as an interface, a tool for evaluation, simulation, task and motion planning, a learning environment, a design platform, and an instrument for data collection. However, it is not typically used for visualisation, instruction and guidance. This is because conventional VR generates an entirely computer-generated (CG) immersive environment, which isolates users from the real world, making it less suitable for applications that require real-time interaction with and awareness of the physical environment.

AR overlays digital information onto the real world, which makes it ideal for enhancing and augmenting real-world interactions but less suitable for applications that require a fully immersive or controlled environment, such as simulations, data collection and design. Therefore, in current studies, AR is normally used for visualisation, development environments, interfaces, evaluation, learning environments, task and motion planning, as well as instruction and guidance.

MR focuses on blending the physical and digital worlds, providing immersive experiences that enhance real-time interactions and task execution. The boundaries between AR and MR are often blurry. As immersive environments, AR is considered a subset of MR (Figure 11.2). However, the term 'MR' is frequently used as a marketing term, as seen with devices like the Microsoft HoloLens and Apple Vision Pro. In this chapter, we use the terms based on the context of the environment and the references provided. From existing studies, MR is used for simulation, visualisation, programming, tasks and motion planning, interaction, instruction and guidance. However, this option is not ideal for design, given that design tasks often demand digital platforms that allow for easy manipulation and modification.

Telepresence can be achieved by combining VR and MR, enabling multi-human-robot teams to work together from different locations. However, this technology currently faces limitations due to the bandwidth constraints of existing 4G and 5G networks (Calandra et al. 2023). Nonetheless, the potential for overcoming these challenges lies in the development and deployment of next-generation networks, which promise higher speeds and greater bandwidth, thereby enhancing the effectiveness of telepresence solutions.

The availability of current guidelines and frameworks guiding the use of XR in HRC is limited. Current guidelines (Eze and Crick 2023) have been adapted from the design guidelines for HRI with assistive robots (Wilkinson et al. 2021). The framework for XR in HRC proposed in the existing study is case-focused. In another study, a framework consisting of a digital twin in MR, the ROS, and a robot in a physical environment for eye-in-hand perception was designed (Sopon et al. 2023). However, this framework is technology-focused. To meet human requirements, it is necessary to include human factors in the future development of frameworks.

In current research on XR in HRC, XR devices including HMDs, mobile devices, and projectors are used. However, PCs' and AR goggles are not mentioned in selected studies. That is because PCs' lack flexibility and AR goggles have a limited field of view (FoV). In addition to HMDs employed in most cases, projectors are employed in some cases for AR-based interface in HRC (Kötter et al. 2023, Deniša et al. 2023), tablets are used for AR-based visualisation (Chandan et al. 2023), and AR-based instruction and guidance (Moya et al. 2023), AR-based interface (Lunding et al. 2023), and AR for training (Heredia et al. 2023). There is potential to explore the use scenarios of AR goggles. Despite their limited FoV, AR goggles are flexible and lightweight compared to HMDs (Table 11.3), making them suitable for various applications where mobility and comfort are prioritised.

While for software and tools for developing XR in HRC, the game engine Unity is the most popular one. In some cases, Unity is combined with other tools for specific scenarios. For instance, Unity and WebGL combined for online AR-based visualisation (Chandan et al. 2023), Unity and Vuforia for AR-based interface (Liu et al. 2023), and Unity combined with Solid Edge for real-time ergonomic assessment in VR (Lanzoni et al. 2023). In specific areas such as HRC fabrication, BIM-based platforms, and CAD platforms such as Rhino 3D and Grasshopper are used (Htet Kyaw et al. 2024, Shen and Hsu 2023). In general, Unity is used commonly because it is powerful enough to support different platforms and users (Coronado et al. 2023). However, Unreal Engine and WebGL have the potential to be further explored. Unreal Engine offers photorealistic visuals that provide the most immersive visualisations. Additionally, tools like WebGL enable users to interact through web-based applications from different locations and devices, enhancing accessibility and flexibility.

The Future of XR in HRC

The Role of XR in HRC

Based on the current studies, Table 11.2 maps out the roles of XR in HRC for future studies to guide format selection. For different purposes, specific formats are suggested to optimise HRC through the integration of XR. This table serves as a reference for researchers and practitioners to choose the appropriate XR format that best fits their specific needs and objectives, ensuring that the chosen technology aligns with the desired outcomes and operational requirements.

Table 11.2 Guide for the role of XR in HRC

	VR	AR	MR	XR (VR and MR)
Visualisation		•	•	
Development Environment		•	•	
Instruction and Guidance		•	•	
Interface	•	•	•	
Learning Environment	•	•		
Evaluation	•	•		
Task/Motion Planning	•	•	•	
Simulation	•		•	
Instrument for Data Collection	•			
Design Platform	•			
Telepresence				•

XR Devices in HRC

As shown in Table 11.3, recently released HMDs and AR goggles demonstrate significant potential for future use in HRC. The latest HMDs offer improved display resolution, refresh rates, and reduced latency, making them increasingly powerful. AR goggles, on the other hand, are lightweight while still providing high resolution and refresh rates. Additionally, mobile devices such as tablets and smartphones

Table 11.3 Recently released XR devices (https://vr-compare.com/)

Device	Type	Resolution	Field of View	Refresh Rate	Latency	Weight	Battery	Released Date
Varjo XR-4	HMD	3,840 × 3,744 per-eye	120° × 105°	90 Hz	22 ms	665 g	Unknown	Nov-23
Apple Vision Pro		3,660 × 3,200 per-eye	unknown	90 Hz, 96 Hz, 100 Hz	12 ms	600–650 g	2 hours	Feb-24
Xreal Air 2 Pro	AR Goggle	1,920 × 1,080 per-eye	unknown	120 Hz	Unknown	75 g	Unknown	Nov-23
Viture Pro		1,920 × 1,080 per-eye	46° diagonal	120 Hz	Unknown	77 g	Unknown	Jun-24

remain highly accessible and user-friendly for mobile AR applications, and they continue to be a viable option for future use.

XR Software and Tools for HRC

Game Engines, such as Unity and Unreal Engine, are popular for content creation in XR development. Unity and Unreal Engine support real-time rendering and cross-platforms and devices through their XR plug-ins. Some researchers indicate a factor that affects researchers' preference for platforms is the learning curve (Coronado et al. 2023).

Web-based XR demonstrates trends in participatory design (Bhatia et al. 2021), and multi-medium systems (Schroepfer et al. 2024). This is because users can remotely interact with immersive systems through a web browser. Since the XR view is rendered in a web browser, it can be easily adapted to multiple devices, providing flexibility and accessibility for diverse user needs.

Design and User Experience

Existing design guidelines or recommendations are not specific to XR in HRC. For instance, the concept of scalable XR was introduced to enhance memorability and enable users to switch more easily between various degrees of XR (Memmesheimer and Ebert 2022). Five initial recommendations were developed for XR design in collaborative systems using a thematic approach focused on UX experts (Garcia and Andujar 2023). These recommendations are visual consistency, evaluating form-factor capabilities, establishing a consistent user flow of events, working with form-factor norms and expectations, and determining the context of use.

Including user experience and human factors in the design process is crucial. Current research focuses on the user experience of XR and the user experience of HRC (Prati et al. 2021). However, less attention is given to the user experience of XR in HRC (Khamaisi et al. 2021). Besides, our previous study identified that the integration of human factors and human-centred design into the design process will significantly reduce cognitive workload thus improving human decision-making quality during HRC tasks (Liu et al. 2024).

CONCLUSION

This chapter adopted PRISMA and Horizon Scanning methods to explore the multifaceted roles of XR in HRC, examining recent studies that utilize a range of XR devices, software, and tools, as well as ongoing studies related to the design of XR in HRC. The results indicate that different types of XR play different roles in HRC. Based on these findings, a guide for the role of XR in HRC has been developed for future reference. HMDs are the most widely used XR devices, but AR goggles and mobile devices also show potential as viable options. Game engines are powerful tools for XR content generation, with Unity being the most popular. However, Unreal Engine, with its capability to generate more realistic immersive environments, warrants further exploration. Web-based XR is emerging as a trend that facilitates cross-platform and cross-location interaction. Current designs often focus either on XR or HRC and with insufficient attention to user experience and human factors. Thus, future research should incorporate human factors and user-centric approaches to enhance the effectiveness and usability of XR in HRC. This comprehensive analysis underscores the importance of integrating advanced XR technologies with human-centric design to optimise human-robot collaboration.

REFERENCES

Andronas, D., Kampourakis, E., Papadopoulos, G., Bakopoulou, K., Kotsaris, P.S., Michalos, G., et al. 2023. Towards seamless collaboration of humans and high-payload robots: An automotive case study. Robotics and Computer-Integrated Manufacturing. 83: 102544. https://doi.org/10.1016/j.rcim.2023.102544.

Ariansyah, D., Colombo, G. and Pardamean, B. 2023. Toward Learning Factory for Industry 4.0: Virtual Reality (VR) for Learning Human–Robot Collaboration: Vol. 1029 LNEE. https://doi.org/10.1007/978-3-031-29078-7_10.

Arntz, A., Di Dia, A., Riebner, T., Straßmann, C. and Eimler, S.C. 2024. Teamwork makes the dream work: A virtual reality-based human-robot collaboration sandbox simulating multiple teams. *In*: Proceedings—2024 IEEE International Conference on Artificial Intelligence and eXtended and Virtual Reality, AIxVR 2024. https://doi.org/10.1109/AIxVR59861.2024.00057.

Avalle, G., De Pace, F., Fornaro, C., Manuri, F. and Sanna, A. 2019. An augmented reality system to support fault visualization in industrial robotic tasks. IEEE Access. 7: 132343–132359. https://doi.org/10.1109/ACCESS.2019.2940887.

Babel, F., Vogt, A., Hock, P., Kraus, J., Angerer, F., Seufert, T., et al. 2022. Step Aside! VR-based evaluation of adaptive robot conflict resolution strategies for domestic service robots. International Journal of Social Robotics. 14(5): 1239–1260. https://doi.org/10.1007/s12369-021-00858-7.

Baumkircher, A., Seme, K., Munih, M. and Mihelj, M. 2022. Collaborative robot precision task in medical microbiology laboratory. Sensors. 22(8). https://doi.org/10.3390/s22082862.

Bavelos, A.C., Anastasiou, E., Dimitropoulos, N., Oikonomou, G. and Makris, S. 2024. Augmented reality-based method for road maintenance operators in human–robot collaborative interventions. Computer-Aided Civil and

Infrastructure Engineering. 39(7): 1077–1095. https://doi.org/10.1111/mice.13185.

Bhatia, S., Björling, E.A. and Budhiraja, T. 2021. Exploring web-based VR for participatory robot design. *In*: Companion of the 2021 ACM/IEEE International Conference on Human-Robot Interaction. 109–112. https://doi.org/10.1145/3434074.3447139.

Bhattacharya, M., Penica, M., O'Connell, E., Southern, M. and Hayes, M. 2023. Human-in-loop: A review of smart manufacturing deployments. Systems. 11(1): 35. https://doi.org/10.3390/systems11010035.

Bolano, G., Juelg, C., Roennau, A. and Dillmann, R. 2019. Transparent robot behavior using augmented reality in close human-robot interaction. *In:* 2019 28th IEEE International Conference on Robot and Human Interactive Communication (RO-MAN). 1–7. https://doi.org/10.1109/RO-MAN46459.2019.8956296.

Burden, A.G., Caldwell, G.A. and Guertler, M.R. 2022. Towards human–robot collaboration in construction: Current Cobot trends and forecasts. Construction Robotics. 6(3): 209–220. https://doi.org/10.1007/s41693-022-00085-0.

Calandra, D., Pratticò, F.G., Fiorenza, J. and Lamberti, F. 2023. Exploring the Suitability of a Digital Twin- and eXtended Reality-based Telepresence Platform for a Collaborative Robotics |Training |Scenario over Next-generation Mobile Networks. https://doi.org/10.1109/EUROCON56442.2023.10198883.

Calderón-Sesmero, R., Duque-Domingo, J., Gómez-García-Bermejo, J. and Zalama, E. 2024. Development of a human–robot interface for cobot trajectory planning using mixed reality. Electronics. 13(3): 571. https://doi.org/10.3390/electronics13030571.

Calzone, N., Sileo, M., Mozzillo, R., Pierri, F. and Caccavale, F. 2023. Mixed reality platform supporting human-robot interaction. Lecture Notes in Mechanical Engineering. https://doi.org/10.1007/978-3-031-15928-2_102.

Cao, Y., Wang, T., Qian, X., Rao, P.S., Wadhawan, M., Huo, K., et al. 2019. GhostAR: A time-space editor for embodied authoring of human-robot collaborative task with augmented reality. *In*: Proceedings of the 32nd Annual ACM Symposium on User Interface Software and Technology. 521–534. https://doi.org/10.1145/3332165.3347902.

Chacko, S.M. and Kapila, V. 2019. Augmented Reality as a Medium for Human-Robot Collaborative Tasks. https://doi.org/10.1109/RO-MAN46459.2019.8956466.

Chandan, K., Albertson, J. and Zhang, S. 2023. Learning visualization policies of augmented reality for human-robot collaboration (Vol. 205). https://www.scopus.com/inward/record.uri?eid=2-s2.0-85164973754&partnerID=40&md5=15a2a29584987b318c42301daed97b6f.

Chen, J., Fu, Y., Lu, W. and Pan, Y. 2023. Augmented reality-enabled human-robot collaboration to balance construction waste sorting efficiency and occupational safety and health. Journal of Environmental Management. 348: 119341. https://doi.org/10.1016/j.jenvman.2023.119341.

Chu, C.-H. and Liu, Y.-L. 2023. Augmented reality user interface design and experimental evaluation for human-robot collaborative assembly. Journal of Manufacturing Systems. 68: 313–324. https://doi.org/10.1016/j.jmsy.2023.04.007.

Cogurcu, Y.E. and Maddock, S. 2023. Augmented Reality Safety Zone Configurations in Human-Robot Collaboration: A User Study. *In*: ACM/IEEE International Conference on Human-Robot Interaction. https://doi.org/10.1145/3568294.3580106.

Cogurcu, Y.E., Douthwaite, J.A. and Maddock, S. 2023. A Comparative study of safety zone visualisations for virtual and physical robot arms using augmented reality. Computers. 12(4): 75. https://doi.org/10.3390/computers12040075.

Coronado, E., Itadera, S. and Ramirez-Alpizar, I.G. 2023. Integrating virtual, mixed, and augmented reality to human–robot interaction applications using game engines: A brief review of accessible software tools and frameworks. NATO Advanced Science Institutes Series E: Applied Sciences. 13(3): 1292. https://doi.org/10.3390/app13031292.

Cuhls, K., Erdmann, L., Warnke, P., Toivanen, H., Toivanen, M., Giessen, A.V.D., et al. 2015. Models of Horizon Scanning: How to Integrate Horizon | Scanning into European Research and Innovation Policies.

Dallel, M., Havard, V., Dupuis, Y. and Baudry, D. 2023. Digital twin of an industrial workstation: A novel method of an auto-labeled data generator using virtual reality for human action recognition in the context of human–robot collaboration. Engineering Applications of Artificial Intelligence. 118: 105655. https://doi.org/10.1016/j.engappai.2022.105655.

David, J., Coatanéa, E. and Lobov, A. 2023. Deploying OWL ontologies for semantic mediation of mixed-reality interactions for human–robot collaborative assembly. Journal of Manufacturing Systems. 70: 359–381. https://doi.org/10.1016/j.jmsy.2023.07.013.

Deniša, M., Ude, A., Simonič, M., Kaarlela, T., Pitkäaho, T., Pieskä, S., et al. 2023. Technology modules providing solutions for agile manufacturing. Machines. 11(9): 877. https://doi.org/10.3390/machines11090877.

Dianatfar, M., Heshmatisafa, S., Latokartano, J. and Lanz, M. 2023. Feasibility analysis of safety training in human-robot collaboration scenario: Virtual reality use case. Lecture Notes in Mechanical Engineering. https://doi.org/10.1007/978-3-031-18326-3_25.

Dianatfar, M., Pöysäri, S., Latokartano, J., Siltala, N. and Lanz, M. 2024. Virtual Reality-based Safety Training in Human-robot Collaboration Scenario: User Experiences Testing. AIP Conference Proceedings. 2989: 020002. https://doi.org/10.1063/5.0189614.

Duan, L., Li, J., Bao, J., Lv, J. and Zheng, H. 2023. A MR-assisted and scene perception system for human-robot collaborative disassembly of power batteries. *In*: 2023 IEEE 19th International Conference on Automation Science and Engineering (CASE), Auckland, New Zealand, 2023. pp. 1-8. doi: 10.1109/CASE56687.2023.10260664.

Eswaran, M., Inkulu, A.K., Tamilarasan, K., Bahubalendruni, M.V.A.R., Jaideep, R., Faris, M.S., et al. 2024. Optimal layout planning for human robot collaborative assembly systems and visualization through immersive technologies. Expert Systems with Applications. 241: 122465. https://doi.org/10.1016/j.eswa.2023.122465.

Etzi, R., Huang, S., Scurati, G.W., Lyu, S., Ferrise, F., Gallace, A., et al. 2019. Using Virtual Reality to Test Human-robot Interaction during a Collaborative Task (Vol. 1). https://doi.org/10.1115/DETC2019-97415.

Eze, C. and Crick, C. 2023. Enhancing human-robot collaboration by exploring intuitive augmented reality design representations. *In*: Companion of the 2023 ACM/IEEE International Conference on Human-Robot Interaction. 282–286. https://doi.org/10.1145/3568294.3580089.

Fratczak, P., Goh, Y.M., Kinnell, P., Soltoggio, A. and Justham, L. 2019. Understanding human behaviour in industrial human-robot interaction by means of virtual reality. Article 19. https://doi.org/10.1145/3363384.3363403.

Fu, J., Pecorella, M., Iovene, E., Palumbo, M.C., Rota, A., Redaelli, A., et al. 2024. Augmented reality and human–robot collaboration framework for percutaneous nephrolithotomy: System design, implementation, and performance metrics. IEEE Robotics and Automation Magazine/ IEEE Robotics and Automation Society. 2–14. https://doi.org/10.1109/mra.2024.3358721.

Garcia, S. and Andujar, M. 2023. UI design recommendations for multimodal XR interfaces using a collaborative system. Virtual, Augmented, and Mixed Reality. 3–14. https://doi.org/10.1007/978-3-031-35634-6_1.

González-Böhme, L.F. and Valenzuela-Astudillo, E. 2023. Mixed reality for safe and reliable human-robot collaboration in timber frame construction. Buildings. 13(8): 1965. https://doi.org/10.3390/buildings13081965.

Gustavsson, P., Syberfeldt, A. and Holm, M. 2023. Virtual reality platform for design and evaluation of human-robot collaboration in assembly manufacturing. International Journal of Manufacturing Research. 18(1): 28. https://doi.org/10.1504/ijmr.2023.129303.

Havard, V., Jeanne, B., Lacomblez, M. and Baudry, D. 2019. Digital twin and virtual reality: A co-simulation environment for design and assessment of industrial workstations. Production and Manufacturing Research. 7(1): 472–489. https://doi.org/10.1080/21693277.2019.1660283.

Heredia, J., Zielinski, K., Schlette, C. and Kjærgaard, M.B. 2023. Empowering cobots with energy models: Real augmented digital twin cobot with accurate energy consumption model. *In*: IEEE International Workshop on Robot and Human Communication, RO-MAN. https://doi.org/10.1109/RO-MAN57019.2023.10309614.

Htet Kyaw, A., Spencer, L., Zivkovic, S. and Lok, L. 2024. Gesture recognition for feedback based mixed reality and robotic fabrication: A case study of the UnLog Tower. *In*: Computational Design and Robotic Fabrication: Vol. Part F2072 (pp. 331–345). Springer Nature Singapore. https://doi.org/10.1007/978-981-99-8405-3_28.

Ikeda, B. and Szafir, D. 2024. PRogramAR: Augmented reality end-user robot programming. ACM Transactions on Human-Robot Interaction. 13(1): 1–20. https://doi.org/10.1145/3640008.

Jang, Y., Jeong, I., Chauhan, H. and Pakbaz, A. 2024. Workers physiological/psychological responses during human-robot collaboration in an immersive virtual reality environment. *In*: Computing in Civil Engineering 2023: Data, Sensing, and Analytics—Selected Papers from the ASCE International Conference on Computing in Civil Engineering 2023. https://doi.org/10.1061/9780784485224.056.

Ji, Z., Liu, Q., Xu, W., Yao, B., Liu, J. and Zhou, Z. 2023. A closed-loop brain-computer interface with augmented reality feedback for industrial human-robot collaboration. International Journal of Advanced Manufacturing Technology. 124(9): 3083–3098. https://doi.org/10.1007/s00170-021-07937-z.

Jost, J., Kirks, T., Gupta, P., Lünsch, D. and Stenzel, J. 2018. Safe human-robot-interaction in highly flexible warehouses using augmented reality and heterogenous fleet management system. *In*: 2018 IEEE International Conference on Intelligence and Safety for Robotics (ISR). 256–260. https://doi.org/10.1109/IISR.2018.8535808.

Kalatzis, A., Prabhu, V.G., Stanley, L. and Wittie, M.P. 2023. Effect of augmented reality user interface on task performance, cognitive load, and situational awareness in human-robot collaboration. *In*: 32nd IEEE International Conference on Robot and Human Interactive Communication, RO-MAN 2023. IEEE Computer Society. https://doi.org/10.1109/RO-MAN57019.2023.10309468.

Khamaisi, R.K., Prati, E., Peruzzini, M., Raffaeli, R. and Pellicciari, M. 2021. UX in AR-supported industrial human–robot collaborative tasks: A systematic review. NATO Advanced Science Institutes Series E: Applied Sciences. 11(21): 10448. https://doi.org/10.3390/app112110448.

Kopp, T., Baumgartner, M. and Kinkel, S. 2021. Success factors for introducing industrial human-robot interaction in practice: An empirically driven framework. International Journal of Advanced Manufacturing Technology. 112(3): 685–704. https://doi.org/10.1007/s00170-020-06398-0.

Kötter, D., Wiedon, G., Meierkord, D., Trinh, M., Petrovic, O. and Brecher, C. 2023. Development of an augmented reality user interface for collaborative robotics in quality inspection for manufacturing. *In*: 2023 5th International Conference on Control and Robotics, ICCR 2023. https://doi.org/10.1109/ICCR60000.2023.10444814.

Kusiak, A. 2018. Smart manufacturing. International Journal of Production Research. 56(1–2): 508–517. https://doi.org/10.1080/00207543.2017.1351644.

Kwok, A.O.J. and Koh, S.G.M. 2021. COVID-19 and extended reality (XR). Current Issues in Tourism. 24(14): 1935–1940. https://doi.org/10.1080/13683500.2020.1798896.

Lanzoni, D., Cattaneo, A., Vitali, A., Regazzoni, D. and Rizzi, C. 2023. Markerless motion capture and virtual reality for real-time ergonomic analysis of operators in workstations with collaborative robots: A preliminary study. Lecture Notes in Mechanical Engineering. https://doi.org/10.1007/978-3-031-15928-2_103.

Legler, F., Trezl, J., Langer, D., Bernhagen, M., Dettmann, A. and Bullinger, A.C. 2023. Emotional experience in human–robot collaboration: Suitability of virtual reality scenarios to study interactions beyond safety restrictions. Robotics. 12(6): 168. https://doi.org/10.3390/robotics12060168.

Li, S., You, Y., Zheng, P., Wang, X.V. and Wang, L. 2024. Mutual-cognition for proactive human–robot collaboration: A mixed reality-enabled visual reasoning-based method. IISE Transactions. 1–13. https://doi.org/10.1080/24725854.2024.2313647.

Liu, C., Zhang, Z., Tang, D., Nie, Q., Zhang, L. and Song, J. 2023. A mixed perception-based human-robot collaborative maintenance approach driven by augmented reality and online deep reinforcement learning. Robotics and Computer-Integrated Manufacturing. 83: 102568. https://doi.org/10.1016/j.rcim.2023.102568.

Liu, Y., Caldwell, G., Rittenbruch, M., Teixeira, M.B.F., Burden, A. and Guertler, M. 2024. What affects human decision making in human-robot Collaboration? A scoping review. Robotics. 13(2): 30. https://doi.org/10.3390/robotics13020030.

Lunding, R.S., Lystbæk, M.N., Feuchtner, T. and Grønbæk, K. 2023. AR-supported Human-Robot Collaboration: Facilitating Workspace Awareness and Parallelized Assembly Tasks. *In*: Proceedings—2023 IEEE International Symposium on Mixed and Augmented Reality, ISMAR 2023. https://doi.org/10.1109/ISMAR59233.2023.00123.

Lunding, R.S., Lunding, M.S., Feuchtner, T., Petersen, M.G., Grønbæk, K. and Suzuki, R. 2024. RoboVisAR: Immersive authoring of condition-based AR robot visualisations. *In*: Proceedings of the 2024 ACM/IEEE International Conference on Human-Robot Interaction. 462–471. https://doi.org/10.1145/3610977.3634972.

Macciò, S., Shaaban, M., Carfì, A., Zaccaria, R. and Mastrogiovanni, F. 2023. RICO-MR: An Open-Source Architecture for Robot Intent Communication through Mixed Reality. https://doi.org/10.1109/RO-MAN57019.2023.10309471.

Maragkos, C., Vosniakos, G.-C. and Matsas, E. 2019. Virtual reality assisted robot programming for human collaboration. Procedia Manufacturing. 38: 1697–1704. https://doi.org/10.1016/j.promfg.2020.01.109.

Matour, M.-E. and Winkler, A. 2023a. Development of a Platform for Novel Intuitive Control of Robotic Manipulators Using Augmented Reality and Cartesian Force Control. https://doi.org/10.1109/ETFA54631.2023.10275598.

Matour, M.-E. and Winkler, A. 2023b. Intuitive robot path planning through augmented reality. *In*: 2023 27th International Conference on Methods and Models in Automation and Robotics, MMAR 2023—Proceedings. https://doi.org/10.1109/MMAR58394.2023.10242522.

Memmesheimer, V.M. and Ebert, A. 2022. Scalable extended reality: A future research agenda. Big Data and Cognitive Computing. 6(1): 12. https://doi.org/10.3390/bdcc6010012.

Milgram, P. and Kishino, F. 1994. A taxonomy of mixed reality visual displays. IEICE Transactions on Information and Systems. 77(12): 1321–1329. https://search.ieice.org/bin/summary.php?id=e77-d_12_1321.

Moletta, M., Wozniak, M.K., Welle, M.C. and Kragic, D. 2023. A virtual reality framework for human-robot collaboration in cloth folding. *In*: IEEE-RAS International Conference on Humanoid Robots. https://doi.org/10.1109/Humanoids57100.2023.10375184.

Moya, A., Bastida, L., Aguirrezabal, P., Pantano, M. and Abril-Jiménez, P. 2023. Augmented reality for supporting workers in human–robot collaboration. multimodal technologies and interaction. 7(4): 40. https://doi.org/10.3390/mti7040040.

Nakamura, K. and Sekiyama, K. 2023. Robot symbolic motion planning and task execution based on mixed reality operation. IEEE Access. 11: 112753–112763. https://doi.org/10.1109/ACCESS.2023.3322933.

Omidi, M., Van de Perre, G., Kumar Hota, R., Cao, H.-L., Saldien, J., Vanderborght, B., et al. 2023. Improving postural ergonomics during human–robot collaboration using particle swarm optimization: A study in virtual environment. NATO Advanced Science Institutes Series E: Applied Sciences. 13(9): 5385. https://doi.org/10.3390/app13095385.

Page, M.J., Moher, D., Bossuyt, P.M., Boutron, I., Hoffmann, T.C., Mulrow, C.D., et al. 2021. PRISMA 2020 explanation and elaboration: Updated guidance and exemplars for reporting systematic reviews. BMJ. 372, n160. https://doi.org/10.1136/bmj.n160.

Pettersson, J. and Falkman, P. 2023. Intended human arm movement direction prediction using eye tracking. International Journal of Computer Integrated Manufacturing. 1–19. https://doi.org/10.1080/0951192X.2023.2229288.

Pilacinski, A., Pinto, A., Oliveira, S., Araújo, E., Carvalho, C., Silva, P.A., et al. 2023. The robot eyes don't have it. The presence of eyes on collaborative robots yields marginally higher user trust but lower performance. Heliyon. 9(8): e18164. https://doi.org/10.1016/j.heliyon.2023.e18164.

Polic, M., Car, M., Petric, F. and Orsag, M. 2021. Compliant plant exploration for agricultural procedures with a collaborative robot. IEEE Robotics and Automation Letters. 6(2): 2768–2774. https://doi.org/10.1109/LRA.2021.3062301.

Prasad, D. and Jayswal, S.C. 2019. A review on flexibility and reconfigurability in manufacturing system. Innovation in Materials Science and Engineering. 187–200. https://doi.org/10.1007/978-981-13-2944-9_19.

Prati, E., Peruzzini, M., Pellicciari, M. and Raffaeli, R. 2021. How to include User eXperience in the design of human-robot interaction. Robotics and Computer-Integrated Manufacturing. 68: 102072. https://doi.org/10.1016/j.rcim.2020.102072.

Puthenkalam, J., Zafari, S., Sackl, A., Gallhuber, K., Ebenhofer, G., Ikeda, M., et al. 2023. Where should I put my mark? VR-based evaluation of HRI modalities for industrial assistance systems for spot repair. *In*: IEEE International Workshop on Robot and Human Communication, RO-MAN. https://doi.org/10.1109/RO-MAN57019.2023.10309414.

Ratava, J., Penttilä, S., Lund, H., Lohtander, M., Kah, P., Ollikainen, M., et al. 2019. Quality assurance and process control in virtual reality. Procedia Manufacturing. 38: 497–504. https://doi.org/10.1016/j.promfg.2020.01.063.

Rivera-Pinto, A. and Kildal, J. 2020. Visuo-tactile mixed reality for offline Cobot programming. *In*: ACM/IEEE International Conference on Human-Robot Interaction. https://doi.org/10.1145/3371382.3378290.

Schroepfer, P., Gründling, J.P., Schauffel, N., Oehrl, S., Pape, S., Kuhlen, T.W., et al. 2024. Navigating real-world complexity: a multi-medium system for heterogeneous robot teams and multi-stakeholder human-robot interaction. *In*: Proceedings of the 2024 ACM/IEEE International Conference on Human-Robot Interaction. 630–638. https://doi.org/10.1145/3610977.3634932.

Shen, Y.-T. and Hsu, J.-S. 2023. The development of mix-reality interface and synchronous robot fabrication for the collaborative construction. pp 372–381. *In*: Chen, J.Y.C. and Fragomeni, G. (eds). Virtual, Augmented and Mixed Reality. HCII 2023. Lecture Notes in Computer Science, vol 14027. Springer, Cham. https://doi.org/10.1007/978-3-031-35634-6_26.

Si, W., Zhong, T., Wang, N. and Yang, C. 2023. A multimodal teleoperation interface for human-robot collaboration. *In*: 2023 IEEE International Conference on Mechatronics (ICM). 1–6. https://doi.org/10.1109/ICM54990.2023.10102060.

Siegele, D., Steiner, D., Giusti, A., Riedl, M. and Matt, D.T. 2021. Optimizing collaborative robotic workspaces in industry by applying mixed reality. Augmented Reality, Virtual Reality, and Computer Graphics. 544–559. https://doi.org/10.1007/978-3-030-87595-4_40.

Sievers, T.S., Schmitt, B., Rückert, P., Petersen, M. and Tracht, K. 2020. Concept of a mixed-reality learning environment for collaborative robotics. Procedia Manufacturing. 45: 19–24. https://doi.org/10.1016/j.promfg.2020.04.034.

Sonntag, S.D., Hutabarat, W., Prabhu, V., Oyekan, J., Tiwari, A. and Turner, C. 2023. An immersive virtual reality platform for enablement and assessment of human-robot interactions for intelligent asset management. Lecture Notes in Mechanical Engineering. https://doi.org/10.1007/978-3-031-25448-2_10.

Sopon, I., Tincu, C., Ganciu, A. and Burlacu, A. 2023. Mixed reality framework for eye-in-hand collaborative robot-human interaction. *In*: 2023 27th International Conference on System Theory, Control and Computing, ICSTCC 2023 - Proceedings. https://doi.org/10.1109/ICSTCC59206.2023.10308497

Speicher, M., Hall, B.D. and Nebeling, M. 2019. What is mixed reality? *In*: Proceedings of the 2019 CHI Conference on Human Factors in Computing Systems—CHI '19. The 2019 CHI Conference, Glasgow, Scotland UK. https://doi.org/10.1145/3290605.3300767.

Tram, M.Q., Cloud, J.M. and Beksi, W.J. 2023. Intuitive robot integration via virtual reality workspaces. 2023 IEEE International Conference on Robotics and Automation (ICRA), London, United Kingdom, 2023, pp. 11654–11660, doi: 10.1109/ICRA48891.2023.10160699.

Tran, D.L., Yamawaki, T., Fujiwara, H. and Yashima, M. 2024. Variable impedance control using mixed reality for human-robot collaboration. *In*: 2024 IEEE/SICE International Symposium on System Integration, SII 2024. https://doi.org/10.1109/SII58957.2024.10417182.

Tung, Y.-S., Luebbers, M.B., Roncone, A. and Hayes, B. 2024. Workspace optimization techniques to improve prediction of human motion during human-robot collaboration. *In*: Proceedings of the 2024 ACM/IEEE

International Conference on Human-Robot Interaction. 743–751. https://doi.org/10.1145/3610977.3635003.

Weber, D., Fuhl, W., Kasneci, E. and Zell, A. 2023. Multiperspective teaching of unknown objects via shared-gaze-based multimodal human-robot interaction. *In*: Proceedings of the 2023 ACM/IEEE International Conference on Human-Robot Interaction. 544–553. https://doi.org/10.1145/3568162.3578627.

Wilkinson, A., Gonzales, M., Hoey, P., Kontak, D., Wang, D., Sinclaire, A., et al. 2021. Design guidelines for human–robot interaction with assistive robot manipulation systems. Paladyn. 12(1): 392–401. https://doi.org/10.1515/pjbr-2021-0023.

Wozniak, M.K., Stower, R., Jensfelt, P. and Pereira, A. 2023. Happily error after: framework development and user study for correcting robot perception errors in virtual reality. 2023 32nd IEEE International Conference on Robot and Human Interactive Communication (RO-MAN), Busan, Korea, Republic of, 2023, pp. 1573-1580. doi: 10.1109/RO-MAN57019.2023.10309446..

Yang, W., Xiao, Q. and Zhang, Y. 2023. HAR2bot: A human-centered augmented reality robot programming method with the awareness of cognitive load. Journal of Intelligent Manufacturing. 1–19. https://doi.org/10.1007/s10845-023-02096-2.

Ye, Y., Zhou, T. and Du, J. 2023. Robot-assisted immersive kinematic experience transfer for welding training. Journal of Computing in Civil Engineering. 37(2): 04023002. https://doi.org/10.1061/JCCEE5.CPENG-5138.

Zhang, R., Liu, X., Shuai, J. and Zheng, L. 2020. Collaborative robot and mixed reality assisted microgravity assembly for large space mechanism. Procedia Manufacturing. 51: 38–45. https://doi.org/10.1016/j.promfg.2020.10.007.

Chapter 12

VR Environments for Architectural Education: Feasibility, Development, Integration, and Evaluation of VR Prototypes

Anastasia Globa*[1], Kun Lyu[2],
Muhammed Yildirim[3] and Ozgur Gocer[4]

[1,2,3,4]School of Architecture Design and Planning,
The University of Sydney

[2]School of Architecture, Civil and Environmental Engineering, École Polytechnique Fédérale de Lausanne

INTRODUCTION

Interactive Virtual Reality (VR) environments have been increasingly adopted in design and architecture to simulate design proposals and to communicate existing and proposed scenarios to various stakeholders. It is widely acknowledged that VR can provide immersive and interactive experiences that can help understand and explore spaces in ways that

*For Correspondence: anastasia.globa@sydney.edu.au

DOI: 10.1201/9781003581642-12

traditional methods cannot. Recent exploratory studies further expanded the applications of this technology by demonstrating the successful application of VR in the fields of pre-occupancy, and performance and comfort simulation in built environments (Liu et al. 2020, Pas et al. 2017). The advantages of immersive VR technologies leverage the potential to significantly enhance user engagement, provide a tangible sense of physical experience, and offer a more profound comprehension of spatial concepts, particularly when design proposals or sites are only accessible in a digital format both in practice and educational settings (Globa et al. 2022, Kandi et al. 2020).

However, despite these potential benefits, the adoption of VR in architectural practices and architectural education has been hindered by a wide range of significant challenges (Kumari and Polke 2019). From the user's perspective, the prolonged use of VR systems can cause cybersickness which often manifests as feelings of nausea and dizziness due to oculomotor disturbances and disorientation. The use of VR systems can also be less intuitive compared to more conventional media. While ongoing advances in VR technology help to alleviate barriers associated with the user experience, they largely do not address the barriers to VR experience production. From the VR creator's perspective, the development and implementation of VR often involve substantial time and financial investments. The use of gaming engines such as Unity 3D (2024) and Unreal (2024), which are common tools for VR development, requires a high level of expertise and specialised knowledge (Globa et al. 2023). Such applications as Enscape (2024)—a VR plugin for Revit, SketchUp, Rhino, and Archicad, allow for easy-to-use walk-through experiences, otherwise providing limited additional VR functionality and interactions. Certain types of VR hardware can also come at a high cost. These factors have led to a limited uptake of VR systems in architectural design and education to date, significantly reducing its potential accessibility and wider adoption. This study investigated whether the implementation of different VR production software and hardware could help alleviate these VR development barriers in architectural education and wider design practices.

This manuscript presents two key phases of the research project. The initial phase (Globa et al. 2022) described a comparative analysis of alternative prototype development pipelines, one using a gaming engine—Unity 3D (2024), and the other using 3DVista software (2024). During the first stage, we compared the resources and expertise needed to develop a standard architectural VR application using both approaches, outlining their limitations and affordances. The second phase, presented in this manuscript involved rigorous experimental studies on VR applications produced using an easy-to-use approach (tested for 3D Vista 2024). The studies were conducted at the University of Sydney (USYD), Australia in 2023. The experimental study involved 32 participants, primarily postgraduate architecture students. The objective of this phase was to evaluate the advantages and limitations of the approach and validate the developed VR applications within an architectural context. We detail the adopted research methodology for assessing interactive VR systems, applying standard evaluation techniques and metrics from the Extended Reality (XR) fields to the realm of architecture. The manuscript presents the user-testing process and details the results of the user study and data analysis methods.

This research adopted a commercially available VR tour creation software—3DVista (2024) as a time and cost-effective alternative method for VR development (Globa et al. 2022). For this study, three VR environments were created and subsequently implemented in a design studio setting for the core unit of the Bachelor of Architecture Environments program at the University of Sydney. The first VR experience was a walkthrough environment designed to familiarise students with the existing site context. The second VR experience presented qualitative evaluations of spaces by students who had visited the site in person. The third VR experience offered an immersive exploration of students' final design projects placed within the virtual site. To evaluate and contrast different hardware output scenarios, all VR environments were tested on a desktop VR application, a Smartphone VR headset (Shinecon 2024), and a Meta Quest 2 VR headset (Meta 2024).

The study aims to provide empirical evidence on the benefits and limitations of VR environments implemented using this application for different architecture-specific VR scenarios, testing different VR hardware outputs: (a) Desktop VR—a non-immersive VR option, (b) Smartphone VR—semi-immersive VR option, and (c) standalone HMD system (Meta 2024)—fully-immersive VR output.

The findings provide valuable insights into the practical implementation of VR software and hardware in architectural education. The manuscript presents a robust methodology for designing user studies and evaluating interactive VR environments for architectural applications.

BACKGROUND AND LITERATURE REVIEW

This section reviews the state of the art in the application of VR in architectural practice and education, along with methods to evaluate the effectiveness of VR systems for these purposes.

DEVELOPMENT OF VR ENVIRONMENTS

VR technology immerses users in a digital environment that simulates a real or imaginary world, where users explore and interact with it through a human-machine interface using a variety of display devices as if they were physically present there. Generally, VR technologies can be classified into three primary groups depending on their degree of immersion: non-immersive VR, semi-immersive VR, and full-immersive VR (Di Natale et al. 2020). Non-immersive VR experiences are often realised through a desktop computer with limited interactivity and sensory engagement. Semi-immersive VR technologies refer to large display screens/projection systems (e.g., CAVE) with a room-scale interaction that offers partial realism, immersion, and a sense of presence in the virtual world (Zhang et al. 2020).

Full-immersive VR, on the other hand, provides users with deeply immersive and highly interactive experiences through HMDs, spatial audio, motion tracking and various modes of user interactions to achieve a sense of being physically present within the virtual environment (VE). Full-immersive VR devices range from high-end standalone or tethered HMDs, such as Meta Quest, HTC Vive, and Pico, to low-budget HMD devices that use smartphones for video displays and audio, such as Google Cardboard, VR Shinecon, and Samsung Gear VR. In many cases, the "smartphone VR" does not support peripheral vision or spatial sound experiences, and therefore can be attributed to the semi-immersive VR category.

On the hardware front, the field of VR has recently witnessed remarkable advancements in terms of ergonomics, visualisation, and interactions, including lighter and more comfortable headsets, increased resolution, wider field of view, eye-tracking technology, and motion tracking. However, although we interact with our surroundings through multiple senses in the real world, the majority of conventional VR implementations are based on audiovisual feedback, resulting in less convincing and engaging experiences. It is demonstrated that multisensory (e.g., olfactory, thermal, haptic) stimuli in VR systems enrich immersion, realism, sense of presence, emotional engagement, user performance, and enjoyment (Yildirim et al. 2024). Olfactory stimuli have been incorporated into VR experiences by means ranging from aroma dispensers and olfactometers (Sona et al. 2019) to wearable olfactory devices (Yildirim et al. 2024) and electromechanical valves with essential oils (Maggioni et al. 2020). There have also been attempts to include airflow and radiation in VR experiences through heat lamps and fans (Lyu et al. 2023). These technologies hold great potential to deliver a wider range of sensory experiences within virtual settings.

On the software front, VEs are usually produced using popular gaming engines, such as Unity (2024) and Unreal Engine (2024), in combination with 3D modelling software, such as Rhino (2024), Autodesk (2024), SketchUp (2024), and Blender (2024). In addition, a recent paradigm shift has introduced an alternative development workflow, that exploits commercially available virtual tour applications, such as 3DVista (2024), Kuula (2024), and Klapty (2024), that require notably reduced time, effort, and expertise to build immersive VR scenes compared to gaming engines.

VR TECHNOLOGY IN ARCHITECTURE, ENGINEERING, AND CONSTRUCTION

During the last two decades, VR has found numerous applications in various fields, particularly in entertainment, gaming, education, training, automotive, marketing, healthcare, psychology, and architecture. Among these fields, VR has also drawn the increasing attention of researchers and practitioners in the architecture, engineering, and construction (AEC) industry for its diverse applications, such as pre-occupancy evaluation, architectural education, virtual construction, safety/training, and real estate marketing (Zhang et al. 2020). Previous research has demonstrated that VR facilitates architectural design in terms of visualisation, review, and collaboration (Liu et al. 2020, Ventura et al. 2019). VR-enabled design process offers enhanced spatial understanding, iterative design review, and real-time collaboration compared to conventional representations through its capability to facilitate interactive, immersive, and realistic experiences of design with a sense of scale (Zhang et al. 2020). For instance, Kandi et al. (2020) showed that VR-based design reviews led the students to identify a higher number of design mistakes and to have more knowledge of the design compared to design reviews through 2D drawings. In another study, Paes et al. (2017) found that users better understood architectural design and heightened spatial perception when the model was displayed through an immersive projection-based VR system vs a non-immersive computer monitor. Zaker and Coloma (2018) demonstrated that implementing a VR-based workflow in conjunction with Building Information Modelling (BIM) promoted an efficient collaboration and decision-making process between stakeholders from a wide range of disciplines, resulting in better project quality.

THE USE OF VR TECHNOLOGY IN ARCHITECTURAL EDUCATION

Architectural education has also significantly benefitted from the recent advances in VR technology. Previous research has shown that VR, with its capacity to construct realistic experimental environments, might function as a powerful teaching tool to address the constraints of current learning methods (e.g., in-person lectures, site visits, online education) and improve learning outcomes. For example, Bashabsheh et al. (2019) found that employing VR to assist in the delivery of a building construction course enhanced students' performance significantly with a high level of enjoyment. In their study, Maghool et al. (2018) presented the potential benefits of a VR prototype comprising materials to facilitate experiential learning of building processes and architectural detailing by simulating a sense of being on a construction site using a flexible, interactive, and immersive environment. Chan et al. (2022), on the other hand, demonstrated that the integration of VR within the framework of remote teaching in an architectural history course, specifically to virtually visit the historical building Pantheon, led to a notable improvement in student learning outcomes.

The transformative integration of VR into sustainable education programmes goes beyond traditional classroom methods, allowing learners to witness the real-world consequences of environmental issues and explore sustainable practices in a controlled VE. Badilla-Quintana and Sandoval-Henríquez (2021) have explored the transformative potential of VR in teaching and learning, emphasising its role in innovating traditional and online education for a more sustainable and accessible learning experience (Lee and Hwang 2022, Hou et al. 2023).

VR implementation within the metaverse can further improve learning practices, emphasising the cultivation of technological readiness and the development of critical 4Cs—Critical Thinking, Creativity, Collaboration, and Communication (Lee and Hwang 2022). Hou et al. (2023) emphasises the efficiency of VR in simulating real-world scenarios, providing an immersive and constructive learning environment. In summary, the diverse studies collectively emphasise the advantages of VR in sustainable education. These extend from increased student engagement to the cultivation of essential skills, thereby highlighting the transformative impact of VR, enabling more effective and impactful teaching and learning applications in architecture and beyond.

EVALUATION METHODS FOR VR APPLICATIONS

Several research efforts have been made to evaluate the effectiveness, quality, and user experience of VR applications. User experience surveys with standardised questionnaires have a crucial role in this regard to quantify user opinions on aspects including presence, engagement, usability, realism, and immersion. Presence in the context of VR is described as the experience and sense of being spatially present in the VE (virtual environment) rather than in the immediate physical environment (Weber et al. 2021). Many questionnaires have been proposed to measure the sense of presence in VEs, including Slater et al. (1994) and Schubert et al. (2001). Igroup Presence Questionnaire (IPQ) (Schubert et al. 2001) is a widely used instrument for measuring the sense of presence in a VE with three subscales: spatial presence, involvement, and experienced realism. System usability is also an important characteristic of VR applications. Usability is defined as the extent to which a system can be effectively and easily used by its intended users to achieve their goals in a particular context (ISO 2018, Kamińska et al. 2022). Several researchers have attempted to develop standardised usability questionnaires, including Chin et al. (1988), Kirakowski and Corbett (1993), and Brooke (1996). System Usability Scale (SUS) (Brooke 1996) is the most widely used questionnaire for measuring perceived usability. Engagement, on the other hand, is defined as the level of emotional, cognitive, and behavioural connection to the VE (Czarnek et al. 2020). However, few standardised questionnaires are available that specifically focus on measuring the level of engagement within the VE. Game User Experience Satisfaction Scale (GUESS) proposed and validated by Phan et al. (2016) has been adopted in several VR studies to measure user engagement with VR applications. Tcha-Tokey et al. (2016) have developed a User eXperience (UX) questionnaire that considers various aspects of user experience in a VE, including presence, engagement, immersion, flow, usability, skill, emotion, judgement, experience consequence, and technology adaptation. Apart from standardised questionnaires, qualitative feedback on other dimensions, such as content, interaction, and hardware, collected through interviews and open-ended questions, provides an enriched context to quantitative data. Such methods provide valuable inputs to develop a user-centred paradigm by identifying the strengths and weaknesses of VR applications.

METHODS

To investigate the applicability of VR in architecture and design education, this research adopted a mixed-method approach based on a case study. The case study revolved around: (1) architectural site exploration—existing context, (2) qualitative and quantitative site evaluation, and (3) integration of proposed design intervention into existing site context with subsequent design evaluation. These VR scenarios were tested for a range of different VR hardware outputs from non-immersive VR to fully immersive VR options: (a) desktop VR, (b) smartphone VR, and (c) standalone HMD system.

The evaluation procedure and methods were based on established research protocols in the XR field. This includes a series of validated surveys, such as IPQ (Schubert et al. 2001), SUS (Brooke 1996), and UX (Tcha-Tokey et al. 2016). In addition, an open-ended interview was administered to research participants after each VR experience.

PARTICIPANTS CHARACTERISTICS

Thirty-one participants (Mean age = 25 ± 6; Gender distribution: male = 22, female = 9; previous VR experience: 'Yes' = 12, 'No' = 19) undertook the experiment. Most of the participants were postgraduate students in the fields of architecture, design, and urbanism. The experiments were conducted in an indoor office room where the ambient environmental conditions were controlled by the HVAC system. The research protocol was approved by the ethics committee at USYD, Australia (Approved Human Ethics Protocol Number: 2019/709).

EXPERIMENTAL SET-UP AND PROCEDURES

Three VEs are constructed using a combination of 360 images and 3D models. For 3D model applications, 3D Vista allows control over cameras, lighting, shadows, animations, and textures. It also enables the integration of gamification features such as questions or quizzes, scoring systems, and Learning Management System (LMS) integration. Despite all these features and functionalities, possible outputs and simulation scenarios of 3DVista are undoubtedly much more limited compared to both Unity and Unreal Engine.

Hypothesis #1 posed that by utilising a simpler and more intuitive software application for VR development, we could bypass major obstacles to VR development and implementation while still providing an appropriate range of VR interactions and experiences covering key types of architecture-specific VR experiences.

Hypothesis #2 posed that even with low-cost VR hardware (such as smartphone VR) higher levels of immersion would lead to higher levels of engagement and satisfaction.

The proposed VR experiences were integrated into VR activities within the Design Communication course, a core unit of the Bachelor of Architecture Environments program at the University of Sydney (USYD). The students were assigned a project to design a "study space for two students" in Cadigal Green, an outdoor urban park situated in the Camperdown Campus of USYD. As per the approved Human Ethics Protocol, to avoid potential conflict of interest, the evaluation of the VR environments was conducted with the 32 students who were recruited externally, on a voluntary basis. All recorded data was anonymous and unidentifiable.

Three types of Virtual Scenes (VS) have been developed and implemented as a part of a design studio (Figure 12.1). VS1 was designed as a simple walkthrough environment to provide students with an understanding of the existing site context (Figure 12.2). The development of the VR experience was achieved by using 360 panoramas captured on-site with the Theta Z1 camera (Ricoh, 2024). This VR scene is then paired with site map navigation functionality, to give students an overview of the site (Figure 12.2).

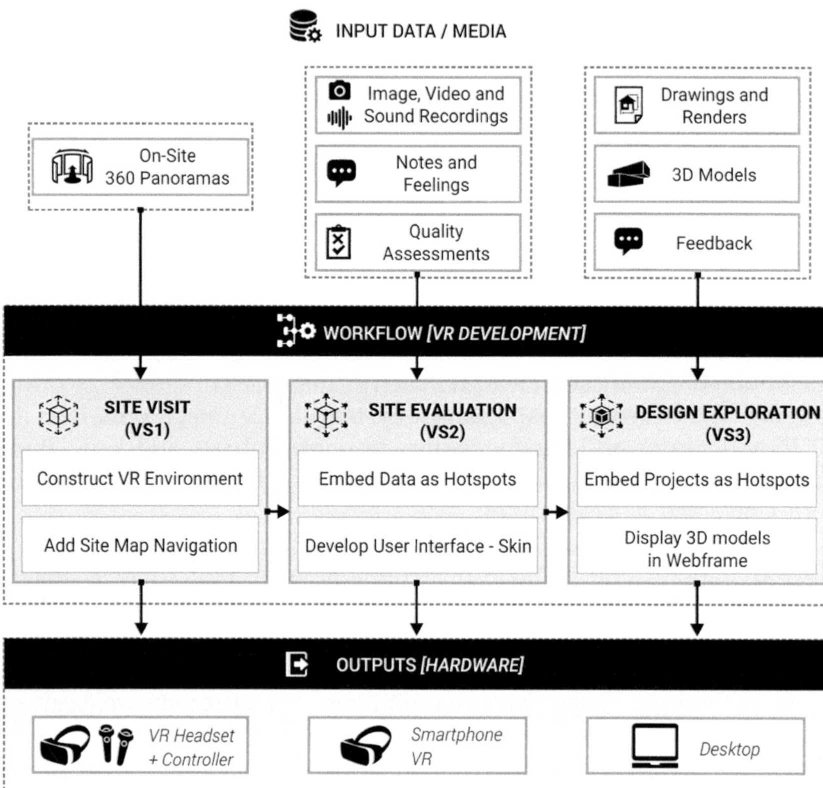

Figure 12.1 Input data and development workflow for virtual scenes (VS).

VS2 development followed the site evaluation exercise that students conducted on-site. Students visited the Cadigal Green site in person and collected data that included assessments of visual, audio, thermal, and air quality, subjective feelings, photographs, and audio/video recordings. These materials were then populated in their corresponding locations on the VR site as hotspots, which included soundscape recordings, images, and multisensory environmental assessments of each zone (Figure 12.3).

Figure 12.2 VS1 allows exploration of the existing site context + map teleportation navigation.

Lastly, VS3 was designed to facilitate immersive explorations of students' design proposals. This is achieved by placing drawings, renders, 3D models, and physical models of students' projects within the chosen location on site as hotspots. External Webframes and built-in albums are then used to display these projects in a VR site context (Figure 12.4).

In the experiment, the presentation order of each VR experience (VS1, VS2, and VS3) to participants followed the 1–3 sequence to represent the actual scenario in design studios (Figure 12.5). The use of different VR hardwear (non-immersive, seme-immersive, and fully-immersive VR) in each VS was randomised and counterbalanced to eliminate the influence of the presenting sequence on the results. Figure 12.5 shows the entire timeline of the experiment. The experiment started with an introduction of the procedure and was followed by a survey

Figure 12.3 VS2 mapping qualitative site analysis data into VR scene.

Figure 12.4 VS3 allows exploration of the final design project placed in a VR site context.

of participants' demographic information (age, gender, occupation, and cultural backgrounds). After that, three VR experiences were presented consecutively. Questionnaires regarding their user experience were administered to participants after each VR experience. Specific activities were targeted to each VR experience. In VS1 and 2, participants were asked to explore the VSs following a specific route and identify their choice of the location. In VS3 where information about exemplar design proposals was introduced, participants were instructed to find the top 3 best projects in terms of quality on project design, graphic presentation, and 3D digital, and physical modelling. Upon finishing the experiments, an interview was conducted consisting of open-ended questions regarding participants' subjective experience in the VEs in terms of VR content, hardware, and human-VR interaction.

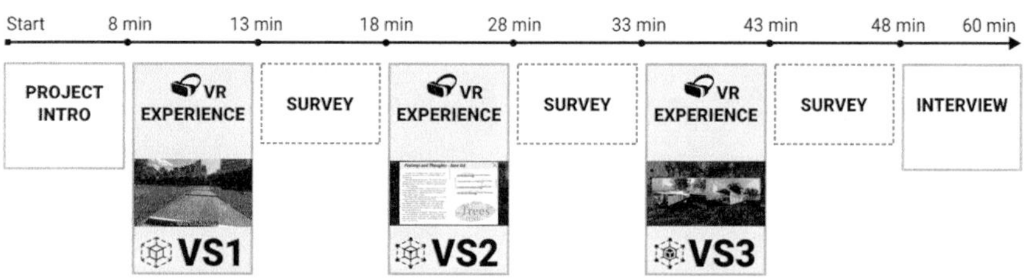

Figure 12.5 User-study procedure and timeline.

All VR environments are tested on: a desktop VR application (non-immersive VR), a smartphone + VR headset (semi-immersive VR), and a standalone untethered HMD (fully-immersive VR) (Figure 12.6). The desktop VR application was included in the study to test the application scenario, where participants might not have access to or funding that is necessary to purchase the VR headsets. It is also aimed to accommodate the user population that might be prone to dizziness and nausea when using VR. The standard 27-inch (686 mm) desktop display was used in the study. The smartphone VR was produced on the SamsungS20 that was placed into the VR Shinecon headset (2024). This headset allowed the use of the screen, audio, and processing power of the smartphone to deliver an immersive VR experience (Figure 12.6). We did not use any handheld controllers for this VR output as it was not possible to achieve with 3DVista software, which imposed considerable limitations on the VR interactions. The third, fully immersive VR output was achieved using a Meta Quest 2 Headset and handheld controllers (2024). Out of the three outputs, this hardware has the most superior VR performance in terms of visual, audio, and interaction experience. However, in terms of availability, this output might not be as feasible to implement en-masse, for schools or design offices due to potential cost considerations.

Figure 12.6 VR site outputs: (1) Desktop, (2) Smartphone VR, (3) Meta Quest 2 Headset.

QUESTIONNAIRE AND INTERVIEWS

In this study, participants' experience in the VE was assessed for usability, presence, and engagement. The SUS (Brooke 1996) was administered to measure the perceived usability of the developed VR prototype. The SUS is a standardised usability questionnaire, including 10 statements rated on a 5-point Likert scale, ranging from "strongly disagree" to "strongly agree", where higher scores represent better usability. Regarding presence, the IPQ (Schubert et al. 2001) has been employed to assess the sense of presence experienced in the VE. IPQ comprises 14 items categorised into three subscales, namely spatial presence, involvement, and experienced realism. Specifically, six of these items have been selected and adapted into the context of this study, focusing on the spatial presence and the sense of being physically present in the VE. These included: a sense of "being there", reality level, being elsewhere, VR as a place visited, memories of experience, and VE awareness level. As for engagement, the UX questionnaire (Tcha-Tokey et al. 2016) has been utilized to evaluate the level of engagement within the VE. UX encompasses 82 items with ten subscales: presence, engagement, immersion, flow, usability, skill, emotion, judgement, experience consequence, and technology adaptation. In this study, specific items (3, 6, 9, 37, and 45) falling under the categories of engagement and emotion have been chosen and incorporated. The interview themes included: (1) user experience, (2) interactions and VR output options, (3) limitations and opportunities for VR applications for architecture, and (4) VR use in the architectural education context.

DATA ANALYSIS METHODS

Quantitative Analysis

Statistical tests were performed to analyse participants' VR experience. Differences between device types and VSs in SUS, IPQ, and Engagement were compared using ANOVA, Shapiro tests ($p < 0.05$), Friedman tests and Post-hoc analyses depending on the data characteristics. Multiple linear regression analyses were conducted to examine the associations between *presence*, *engagement*, and *usability*. The quantitative analyses were performed using *R Studio* (Posit Software 2024) and visualised with the Tidyverse Package (Wickham et al. 2019). The significance level for all statistical tests was set to 0.05 ($p < 0.05$).

Qualitative Analysis

The interviews were recorded and then transcribed for subsequent qualitative examination. The "word cloud" approach was utilised to assist with the quantitative assessment of the keywords based on their diminishing frequency in the responses to open-ended inquiries. The word cloud visualisations were created using the open-ended remarks using an online word cloud generator (Zygomatic 2024). The recurrence of keywords validated the uniformity of the responses from the participants. Quotes from various participants, presented in italics in the Results section, were employed to elucidate their assertions, experiences, and emotions under different conditions.

RESULTS

This section presents the results of the user study, including a quantitative analysis of participants' responses to the questionnaires, as well as a qualitative analysis of their VR experiences and opinions on enhancing VR immersion.

QUANTITATIVE RESULTS

Usability Across Device Types

Due to non-normality as indicated by Shapiro tests ($p < 0.05$), Friedman tests are performed to examine the effects of device type on usability scores. There were statistically significant differences in System Usability Scores in the dimensions of system preference, technical assistance, consistency, cumbersome to use, and confident usage depending on the device types (Table 12.1). Post-hoc analyses using the Wilcoxon Signed-Rank Test with Benjamini-Hochberg p-value adjustment were conducted to identify pairwise differences in individual usability dimensions across device types.

HMD VR headset was the most preferred VR device compared to *Desktop VR* (Median difference = 1, $p < 0.05$) and *Smartphone VR* (Median difference = 1.5, $p < 0.01$). *Smartphone VR* was the least preferred VR device with almost half of the participants preferring not to use it. Participants found the *smartphone VR* more cumbersome to use than *desktop VR* and *HMD VR headset* (Median difference = 1, $p < 0.05$). Similarly, *smartphone VR* was considered less consistent than HMD VR headset (Median difference = 1, $p < 0.05$). Although the *HMD VR headset* was among the most preferable and consistent systems, participants felt less confident using it and indicated needing more technical support.

For the overall usability rating, calculated as the mean score of the individual dimensions, repeated measure ANOVA indicated the significant effects of device types on the overall usability rating ($F[2, 90] = 3.50$, $p = 0.03$). Post-hoc analysis with Benjamini-Hochberg p-value adjustment indicated that both Desktop VR and Meta Quest outperformed Mobile VR ($p < 0.05$) (Table 12.1, Figure 12.7).

Table 12.1 Friedman test statistics of differences in usability between device types

Usability Item	Sample Size (n)	df	Chi-square	p
System preference (Q1)	31	2	15.1	<0.001***
Complexity (Q2)			1.53	0.47
Ease of use (Q3)			3.04	0.22
Technical assistance (Q4)			9.61	**<0.01****
System Integration (Q5)			4.29	0.12
Consistency (Q6)			6.95	**<0.05***
Rapid learning (Q7)			5.15	0.08
Cumbersome to use (Q8)			6.94	**<0.05***
Confident usage (Q9)			9.06	**<0.05***
Prerequisite Knowledge needed (Q10)			0.659	0.72

ENGAGEMENT AND PRESENCE

The repeated measure ANOVA tests indicate that there were significant differences between device types in the *engagement* ($F[2, 90] = 7.32$, $p = 0.001$) and presence *ratings* ($F[2, 90] = 14.26$, $p < 0.001$). Post-hoc analysis with a Benjamini-Hochberg adjustment indicates that the *HMD VR headset* provided a greater sense of *presence* to participants, *the sense of being there in the virtual environment*, compared to *smartphone VR* (mean difference = 0.57, $p < 0.05$) and Desktop VR (mean difference = 1.42, $p < 0.0001$). As shown in Figure 12.8, participants felt more engaged when using an *HMD VR headset* than *smartphone VR* (mean difference = 0.75, $p < 0.05$) and *desktop VR* (mean difference = 1.12, $p < 0.001$).

There was a significant association between the sense of *engagement* and *presence* for all device types ($\beta = 0.75$, $p < 0.001$, $R^2 = 0.52$) (Figure 12.9). This may help explain the reason why desktop VR received a lower engagement score than smartphone VR and Meta Quest. Although Desktop VR was user-friendly, it was not able to provide a sufficient sense of presence for the users and had limited capacity to engage with the users.

QUALITATIVE RESULTS

The survey included 17 open-ended inquiries designed to capture the depth of participants' perspectives. These prompts encouraged respondents to articulate their emotions concerning their overall VR experience, assess their interaction and engagement levels with various devices, and suggest strategies for future improvements.

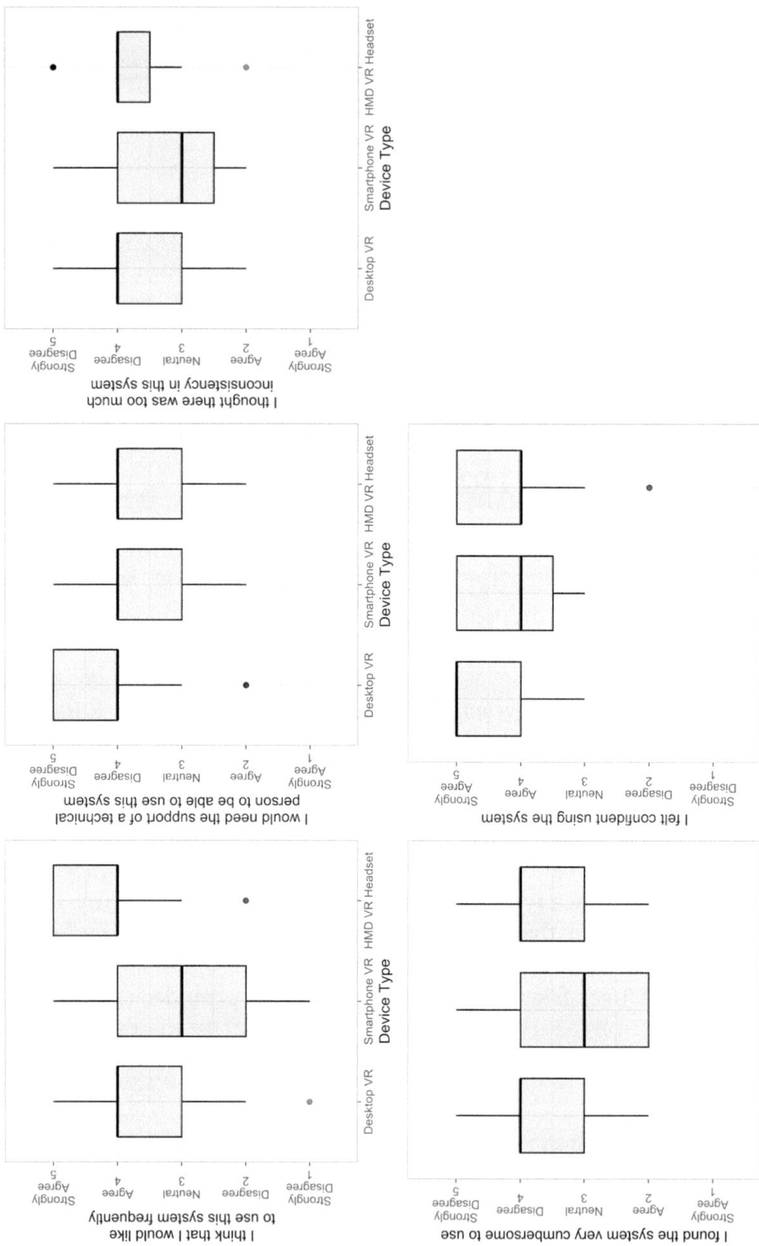

Figure 12.7 Results: Usability scores across VR output devices.

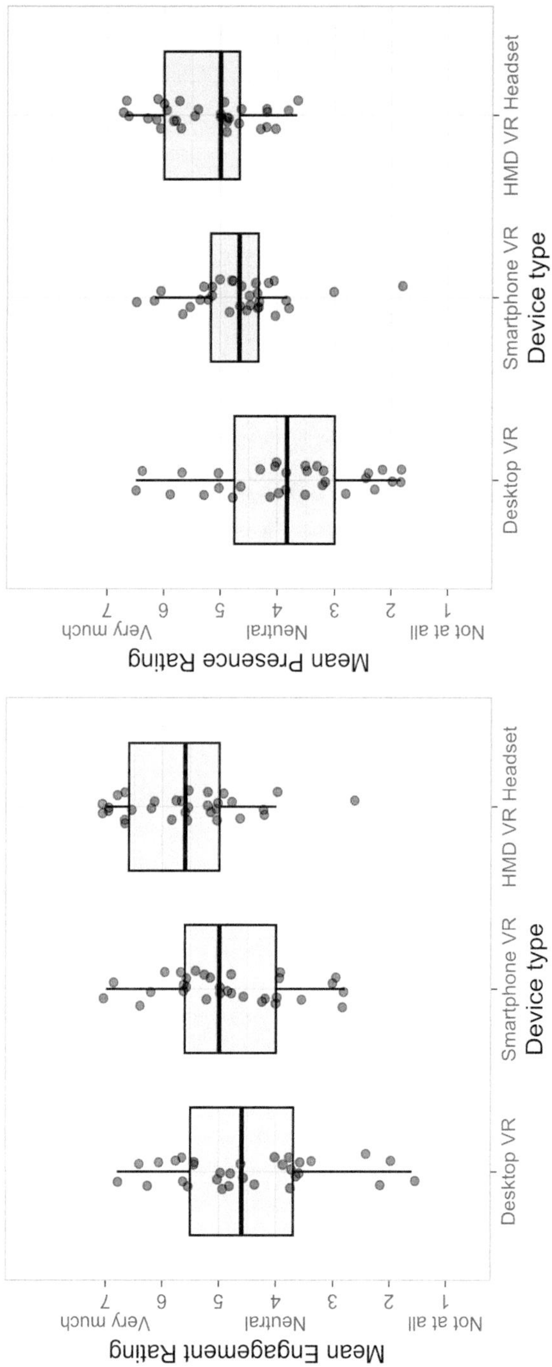

Figure 12.8 Results: Levels of engagement and presence across VR output devices.

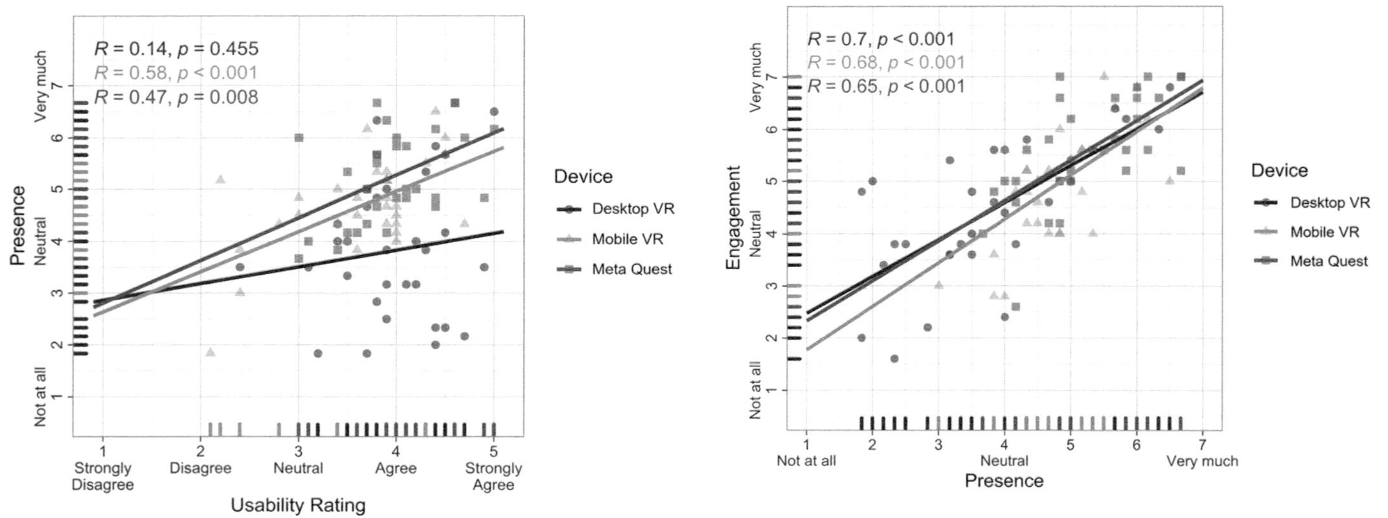

Figure 12.9 Results: Correlation between engagement and presence, and usability and presence across device types.

OVERALL VR EXPERIENCE

A notable finding, as depicted in Figure 12.10, underscores a pervasive positivity characterising the participants' overall VR experiences. This positive sentiment appears to be independent of the participant's familiarity with the technology, encompassing both seasoned users and those engaging with VR for the first time. The visual emphasis on these positive expressions underscores a theme of satisfaction, enjoyment, and positive opinions within the textual data. In this visualisation, the words 'good', 'like' 'okay', 'enjoyed', and 'pretty' stand out prominently. The prevalence of positive terms suggests an overall positive tone in the underlying content.

Figure 12.10 Word cloud analysis of VR experiences of participants.

Interestingly, within the context of the overall VR experience, there emerges a nuanced aspect related to the duration of VR exposure. Participants, as articulated by the statement from Participant 7, implied a potential correlation between prolonged engagement with VR and fatigue: *"Overall, it was a good experience, but it may be exhausting if I keep using it."* This prompts compelling reflections on the unfavourable effects of prolonged VR usage on the user experience and indicates potential directions for additional exploration and mitigation strategies.

Participants generally perceived the desktop VR scenario to exhibit a strong resemblance to Google Maps, as highlighted by Participant No: 12, who described it as *"almost like playing with Google Maps".*

Participant No: 3 conveyed their experience with Meta Quest 2, stating, *"It's smooth, I mean, it feels like you're moving there."* Similarly, Participant No: 10 drew a comparison between the desktop and Meta Quest 2 experiences, expressing, *"We can see, move around, and feel everything, including sound, compared to when we only saw these on Google Maps."*

The elevated popularity of Meta Quest 2 experiences in comparison to other VR platforms can be attributed to heightened levels of immersion, presence, and engagement, as articulated by participants:

- Participant No. 27 highlighted the seamless integration of the camera with head movement in HMDs, emphasising, *"the camera moves with the way your head moves. So, it does feel like you're in the moment. For the controllers, you just have to look at a space for a couple of seconds and it was really easy".*
- Participant No. 6 provided insight into the contrasting experiences, noting, *"It felt more immersive, and the computer one (Desktop) felt more disconnected."*

Furthermore, the profound *"sense of being there"* associated with fully-immersive VR is underscored by Participant No: 17's reflection, *"I can feel … essential emotion sense of being there."*

ENGAGEMENT WITH VR ACROSS DEVICE TYPES

The majority of participants conveyed dissatisfaction with the usability of smartphone VR, citing discomfort arising from issues such as eye strain due to low-resolution quality and the cumbersome weight/ergonomics of the smartphone VR headset. Participant No. 8 elaborated on these challenges, stating, *"Engaging with it was not particularly easy, as I mentioned, given the device's considerable weight. Consequently, I found myself physically holding the device, leading to fatigue after a mere 5 or 10 minutes."* Echoing this sentiment, Participant No. 20 raised a similar concern about the headset's weight, noting, *"I found myself needing to continuously support it with my hands."*

In contrast, respondents expressed markedly more positive feelings regarding their interaction with Meta Quest 2, lauding the hardware's attributes such as being 'responsive', 'realistic', "easy to navigate", 'immersive', and 'comfortable'.

IMPROVEMENT STRATEGIES FOR A MORE IMMERSIVE EXPERIENCE WITH VR

Participants were also queried on ways to enhance the VR experience, with their proposed strategies encompassing a multi-sensory approach. These suggestions included incorporating additional sensory elements such as smell, temperature, and sound, and providing more information about the social and cultural context. The following quotations highlight the participants' perspectives on these proposed improvements:

- Participant No. 9: *"I want to see these components in virtual reality. Because right now, you don't smell anything, but if you're in real places, you smell the rain, the trees, flowers, or if it rains, you feel it."*
- Participant No. 6: *"I think there was enough data, but it would be pretty cool if you could add the feelings of temperature."*
- Participant No. 7 articulated the importance of expanding sensory input in VR, remarking, *"Maybe in person, you have the experience to get information from all the senses, but here it was just visual and auditory. Yes, it's a little bit more immersive and less realistic. Yes, I feel like if I couldn't access it in person, it is still helpful, other than just looking at pictures online."*

USE OF VR IN ARCHITECTURAL CONTEXTS

When participants were asked, "In what situations do you think you would use the prototype?", many participants expressed a strong interest in using VR for virtual site visits, particularly when physical access to a location is challenging or impossible, such as during international projects, remote learning, or in situations where travel is restricted. The ability to revisit sites, understand the scale of design proposals in an immersive environment, and engage with spaces in a way that surpasses traditional images or videos was seen as beneficial. For example, Participant No. 3 stated, *"Virtual site visit is actually a pretty good application for this, especially when you're doing it remotely."*

The analysis of participants' responses to the usefulness of the VR prototype and virtual content in understanding architectural spaces and sites reveals a generally positive reception, with key suggestions for further improvements. For instance, Participant No. 2 expressed their feelings as, *"It was a good way to walk through the site and get a sense of the space. I can get a lot of information about the sun's path, move in a different direction, and in just a few seconds, see what the wind is like and how space feels like without going there."* While the VR prototype was deemed highly useful, participants expressed a desire for additional features that would make the virtual experience even more representative of real-world conditions and more informative for architectural decision-making. A common suggestion was the inclusion of different weather conditions, seasons, and times of day to provide a more comprehensive understanding of the site. Respondents also noted the importance of adding historical context, animated elements, and interactive features, such as moving people and objects, to enhance the realism and educational value of the experience.

Many participants emphasised the immersive, multi-sensory experience that VR offers, which allows users to 'feel' the space in a way that is not possible with traditional two-dimensional media. Moreover, participants noted that VR can consolidate various forms of information—such as images, videos, and technical data—into a single, cohesive experience, enhancing the effectiveness of communication.

DISCUSSION AND CONCLUSIONS

The wider field of education is witnessing an escalating interest in the application of interactive VR technologies, to enhance the learning process. Multiple studies reinforce the idea that VR technology can significantly enrich the teaching-learning process (Kharvari and Kaiser 2022), by immersing students in spatial interactive experiences, thereby providing a more engaging learning environment (Agirachman et al. 2022). The challenge of integrating VR systems and experiences into architectural design practice and education is underlined by the need for expert knowledge in VR application creation and the cost of software and hardware. With the growing ubiquity of VR headsets in recent years, the price and availability of these devices may become a less significant barrier for larger/better-funded architectural practices and educational institutions. However, the production and integration of VR systems still impose considerable challenges.

This study demonstrates that it is indeed feasible to create engaging VEs using relatively simple software for architectural VR production, such as 3DVista (2024), as opposed to more complex gaming engines such as Unity (2024) or Unreal (2024) that are usually utilised for VR development. Despite 3DVista's limited functionality and navigation, this type of software proved its potential to serve as a practical substitute for creating virtual site visits, site evaluations, and project presentations in the realm of architectural practice and education. The results of our study clearly show that the use of relatively simple VR development tools can feasibly deliver immersive experiences with high levels of engagement, providing meaningful benefits to learning and design contexts in architecture. The collected user feedback indicates that all three tested VR scenarios delivered a suitable range of functionality, interactions and experiences required for (VS1) building or site visit, (VS2) site analysis, and (VS3) design evaluation/exploration (Hypothesis #1). The illustrated positive user experience paves the way for future research and provides valuable insights for VR use in educational contexts. The research methodology detailed in this manuscript provides a robust framework for future experiments and user studies in this field.

The current study did not find a significant effect of VR content and functionality (VS 1, 2, and 3) on presence and engagement. This is potentially due to a sequential effect of the presentation of each VS. Future studies may include more content scenarios with a randomized research design. This study is based on a controlled experimental setting, the applicability of VR, including its impact on students' learning outcomes, in architectural education can be further tested in actual design studio educational settings. Future studies can also explore personal factors underlying individual differences in user experiences of VR hardware and contents. The evaluation methods used in this study can be further developed into a standardized protocol for future studies around similar topics to create a database of VR user experiences.

Furthermore, benchmarking studies between immersive VE and real physical environments should be conducted to validate the applicability of this method to the architectural field. The potential influences of cultural backgrounds, previous experience with VR technologies and gender on the user experiences of different VR devices can be further explored in the future.

In the context of our study, one of the primary objectives was to evaluate and compare practical VR tools developed for architectural context, testing their usability, presence, and engagement, comparing across a range of VR hardware outputs and design activity contexts. We particularly focused on testing easy-to-use software and its ability to reliably produce a range of architecture-specific VR scenarios that can be output to non-immersive VR (desktop VR), semi-immersive VR (smartphone VR), and fully immersive VR (Meta Quest 2 HMD). Hypothesis #2 stated that the low-cost (and subsequently limited functionality) VR hardware such as smartphone VR can deliver higher levels of engagement, immersion, and satisfaction compared to the desktop application of VR technology.

Experimental results show that smartphone VR was reported to be the least user-friendly and most uncomfortable hardware by all participants. In fact, almost half of the participants preferred not to use it. Surprisingly despite all that, the desktop VR was still found to be significantly less engaging than any other tested VR hardware outputs (even compared to the smartphone VR). This insight implies that if an individual or an organisation lacks the resources to procure more sophisticated VR headsets for their architectural VR experiences (Meta, Pico, HTC Vive, etc.), the use of smartphone VR (headset + smartphone) might be a viable option, in those cases where the user engagement is an important consideration. Our study shows that regardless of how user-friendly desktop VR is –it might never be able to deliver architectural experiences as engaging and satisfying compared to HMD VR.

The findings of our study contribute to the knowledge of the alternative easy-to-use VR development pipelines fostering future implementation of VR in the field, broadening the scope of VR's potential impact on education and wider architectural practices.

REFERENCES

3DVista. 2024. Professional Virtual Tour Software. 3DVista, España S.L., Granada, SPAIN.

Agirachman, F.A., Shinozaki, M., Koerniawan, M.D. and Indraprastha, A. 2022. Implementing affordance-based design review method using virtual reality in architectural design studio. Buildings. 12(9): 1296.

Autodesk. 2024. 3D Design Engineering and Entertainment Software. (3ds Max/ Maya), Autodesk Inc., California, USA.

Badilla-Quintana, M.G. and Sandoval-Henríquez, F.J. 2021. Students immersive experience in initial teacher training in a virtual world to promote sustainable education: Interactivity, presence, and flow. Sustainability. 13(22): 12780.

Bashabsheh, A.K., Alzoubi, H.H. and Ali, M.Z. 2019. The application of virtual reality technology in architectural pedagogy for building constructions. Alexandria Engineering Journal. 58(2): 713–723.

Blender. 2024. Free and Open 3D Creation. Blender Foundation, Amsterdam, Netherlands.

Brooke, J. 1996. SUS-A quick and dirty usability scale. Usability Evaluation in Industry. 189(194): 4–7.

Chan, C.S., Bogdanovic, J. and Kalivarapu, V. 2022. Applying immersive virtual reality for remote teaching architectural history. Education and Information Technologies. 27(3): 4365–4397.

Chin, J.P., Diehl, V.A. and Norman, K.L. 1988. Development of an instrument measuring user satisfaction of the human-computer interface. *In*: SIGCHI Conference on Human Factors in Computing Systems. 213–218.

Czarnek, G., Strojny, P., Strojny, A. and Richter, M. 2020. Assessing engagement during rescue operation simulated in virtual reality: A psychophysiological study. International Journal of Human-Computer Interaction. 36(5): 464–476.

Di Natale, A.F., Repetto, C., Riva, G. and Villani, D. 2020. Immersive virtual reality in K-12 and higher education: A 10-year systematic review of empirical research. British Journal of Educational Technology. 51(6): 2006–2033.

Enscape. 2024. Realtime Rendering and Virtual Reality. Enscape GmbH, Karlsruhe, Germany.

Globa, A., Wang, R., Tokede, O. and Khoo, C.K. 2022. Pre-Occupancy evaluation of buildings in VR: development of the prototype and user studies. Architectural Science Review. 65(5): 407–419.

Globa, A., Yildirim, M., Lyu, K., Gocer, O. 2023. Evaluation of interactive VR environments for architecture. CAADRIA 2023, Gujarat, India: CAADRIA.

Hou, H., Lai, J.H. and Wu, H. 2023. Project-based learning and pedagogies for virtual reality-aided green building education: Case study on a university course. International Journal of Sustainability in Higher Education. 1308–1327.

International Organization for Standardization. 2018. Ergonomics of Human-system Interaction—Part 11: Usability: Definitions and concepts (ISO Standard No. 9241-11: 2018. https://www.iso.org/standard/63500.html.

Kandi, V.R., Castronovo, F., Brittle, P., Mastrolembo Ventura, S. and Nikolic, D. 2020. Assessing the impact of a construction virtual reality game on design review skills of construction students. Journal of Architectural Engineering. 26(4): 04020035.

Kamińska, D., Zwoliński, G. and Laska-Leśniewicz, A. 2022. Usability Testing of Virtual Reality Applications: The Pilot Study. Sensors. 22(4): 1342.

Kharvari, F. and Kaiser, L.E. 2022. Impact of extended reality on architectural education and the design process. Automation in Construction. 141: 104393.

Kirakowski, J. and Corbett, M. 1993. SUMI: The software usability measurement inventory. Journal of Educational Technology. 24(3): 210–212.

Klapty. 2024. Virtual Tour. Klapty Inc. Switzerland.

Kumari, S. and Polke, N. 2019. Implementation issues of augmented reality and virtual reality: A survey. *In*: International Conference on Intelligent Data Communication Technologies and Internet of Things (ICICI) 2018. 853–861. Springer International Publishing.

Kuula. 2024. Virtual Tour Software. Kuula Inc. Bratislava, Slovak Republic.

Lee, H. and Hwang, Y. 2022. Technology-enhanced education through VR-making and metaverse-linking to foster teacher readiness and sustainable learning. Sustainability. 14: 4786.

Liu, Y., Castronovo, F., Messner, J. and Leicht, R. 2020. Evaluating the impact of virtual reality on design review meetings. Journal of Computing in Civil Engineering. 34(1): 04019045.

Lyu, K., Brambilla, A., Globa, A. and de Dear, R. 2023. An immersive multisensory virtual reality approach to the study of human-built environment interactions. Automation in Construction. 150: 104836.

Maggioni, E., Cobden, R., Dmitrenko, D., Hornbæk, K. and Obrist, M. 2020. SMELL SPACE: Mapping out the olfactory design space for novel interactions. ACM Transactions on Computer-Human Interaction (TOCHI). 27(5): 1–26.

Maghool, S.A.H., Moeini, S.H.I. and Arefazar, Y. 2018. An educational application based on virtual reality technology for learning architectural details: Challenges and benefits. Archnet-IJAR: International journal of architectural research. 12(3): 246.

Meta Quest, 2024. Meta Platforms Technologies, Irvine, California, USA, Retrieved 9 September 2024 from https://www.meta.com/au/quest/

Paes, D., Arantes, E. and Irizarry, J. 2017. Immersive environment for improving the understanding of architectural 3D models: Comparing user spatial perception between immersive and traditional virtual reality systems. Automation in Construction. 84: 292–303.

Phan, M.H., Keebler, J.R. and Chaparro, B.S. 2016. The development and validation of the game user experience satisfaction scale (GUESS). Human Factors. 58(8): 1217–1247.

Posit Software. 2024. The most trusted IDE for open-source data science. https://www.posit.co/

Rhino. 2024. Rhinoceros 3D. Robert McNeel & Associates TLM, Inc. Seattle, USA.

Ricoh Theta Z1. 2024. 360° Camera. Ricoh, Tokyo, Japan.

Schubert, T., Friedmann, F. and Regenbrecht, H. 2001. Igroup presence questionnaire. Teleoperators Virtual Environ. 41. 115–124.

Shinecon. 2024. Immersive Experience Virtual Reality Headsets, Dongguan Shinecon Industrial Co., China.

Slater, M., Usoh, M. and Steed, A. 1994. Depth of presence in virtual environments. Presence: Teleoperators and Virtual Environments. 3(2): 130–144.

SketchUp. 2024. 3D Design Software. Trimble Inc. Colorado, USA.

Sona, B., Dietl, E. and Steidle, A. 2019. Recovery in sensory-enriched break environments: Integrating vision, sound and scent into simulated indoor and outdoor environments. Ergonomics. 62(4): 521–536.

Tcha-Tokey, K., Christmann, O., Loup-Escande, E. and Richir, S. 2016. Proposition and validation of a questionnaire to measure the user experience in immersive virtual environments. International Journal of Virtual Reality. 16(1): 33–48.

Unity. 2024. Real-Time Development Platform. Unity Technologies, Austin, USA.

Unreal Engine. 2024. 3D Computer Graphics Game Engine. Epic Games Inc, Cary, North Carolina, USA.

Ventura, S.M., Castronovo, F., Nikolić, D. and Ciribini, A.L. 2019. A framework of procedural considerations for implementing virtual reality in design reviews. *In*: Proceedings of the 2019 European Conference on Computing in Construction. 442–451.

Weber, S., Weibel, D. and Mast, F.W. 2021. How to get there when you are there already? Defining presence in virtual reality and the importance of perceived realism. Frontiers in Psychology. 12: 628298.

Wickham, H., Averick, M., Bryan, J., Chang, W., McGowan, L.D., François, R., et al. 2019. Welcome to the Tidyverse. Journal of Open Source Software. 4(43): 1686. https://doi.org/10.21105/joss.01686.

Yildirim, M., Globa, A., Brambilla, A. and Gocer, O. 2024. Multisensory design in VR: Implementing digital smell technologies for architecture. CAADRIA. 3: 449–458. Hong Kong.

Zaker, R. and Coloma, E. 2018. Virtual reality-integrated workflow in BIM-enabled projects collaboration and design review: A case study. Visualization in Engineering. 6(1): 1–15.

Zhang, Y., Liu, H., Kang, S.C. and Al-Hussein, M. 2020. Virtual reality applications for the built environment: Research trends and opportunities. Automation in Construction. 118: 103311.

Zygomatic. 2024. World Cloud Generator. [Online Software]. https://www.wordclouds.com

TRPG story-worlds are usually inspired by genre fiction, which provides players with familiarity with the game's setting before even the game starts. So much so, since the release of *Advanced Dungeons and Dragons: Dungeon Masters Guide* (Gygax 1979), publishers have encouraged players to consume various kinds of genre fiction and media for easier immersion into game worlds. TRPG publishers present their own original game worlds to gamemasters and players through descriptive and assistive texts in the form of rulebooks, sourcebooks, and adventure modules (Harrigan and Wardrip-Fruin 2007). Usually, they each provide a different type of information and may even target different actors participating in a game (Nikolaidou 2018). As the name suggests, rulebooks mainly describe how game mechanics work but also provide fictional background information for the actions these rules enable. While a core rulebook presents all the information required to understand the setting and play the game, supplemental rulebooks may introduce new types of infrastructures for interactions, i.e., seafaring in a fantasy TRPG. While the terminology may change from publisher to publisher, sourcebooks are usually complementary publications containing new information players can use to enhance or extend the game without introducing any new major rule sets beyond what may be needed to engage with the new concepts, i.e., new warrior classes with unique skill statistics. As rulebooks and sourcebooks generally target both players and gamemasters, they may include short stories depicting action scenes and sometimes ending with cliffhangers, which act as inspirational pieces for players. Showcasing how new concepts may affect the game world, they functionally resemble design fiction short stories. In contrast to rulebooks and sourcebooks, adventure or campaign modules are mainly aimed at gamemasters. These provide materials to create scenarios to be enacted during game sessions, including new locations, characters, goals, mysteries, and possibilities for players to explore, i.e., a treasure hunt on a mysterious island. While some adventure and campaign modules present highly structured events for gamemasters to follow, others may only provide loose materials for them to use as building blocks for their own adventures. These and other types of texts and props, like maps, monster guides, miniatures, random encounter tables, and so on, describe the game world both on a fictional level and through formal rules managing it. Dormans (2006) argues that such texts collectively constitute a simulation of the setting, which is only activated during play sessions. In this regard, according to Jara (2013), these texts should be described as "generic framing devices" for TRPGs, which not only shape the reception of a game world but also incite the production of collective narratives by the participants.

As Cook (2012) points out, story-world databases must cover a wide range of topics in detail since players may decide to explore or attempt to use any aspect of the game world they encounter. Similarly, Borgstrom (2007) argues that extensive story-world databases should help players explore narrative threats without imposing any expectations. In this regard, as Schallegger (2018) points out, TRPG publications are specifically designed with narrative gaps and adaptation options to be filled by player interactions. Even if a large section of the possibilities offered by official publications is not implemented by the players in a session, they do contribute to the overall worldbuilding of a game. In other words, as world infrastructures, by describing nature, cultures, languages, technologies, mythologies, and philosophies, rulebooks, sourcebooks, and adventure modules enhance the verisimilitude of imaginary game worlds. Through each interaction with these rule-supported descriptions, players learn the mechanisms of the world, which they later re-construct and use to manipulate the fictional reality as they play (Jara 2013). Therefore, even though they cannot provide a complete analysis of how specific technologies are experienced by players in TRPGs, the analysis of official publications will present the possibilities imagined by designers.

TRPGs AND CRITIQUE OF EMERGING TECHNOLOGIES

Many science-fiction-themed TRPGs have in-game items utilizing XR technologies. The near future space exploration TRPG 2300AD (Mongoose 2022) features a "clothing automat" visually scanning customers' bodies, presenting options on them, and then 3D printing garments. The science fantasy TRPG *Starfinder*'s "mimic imager" (Paizo 2023) functions both as an image scanner and a holographic projector. Consistently introducing new ocular augmentations, autonomous imaging machines, VR, and XR experiences, one specific sub-genre, cyberpunk TRPGs, has been urging players to critically engage with various types of XR since the 1980s.

Cyberpunk, as a literary genre, attempts to make sense of the scale, pace, and patterns of technological developments and their influence on human affairs (Shurin 2023). Discussing the evolution of the cyberpunk TRPGs, Carbonell (2020) notes that the genre has gone through a transformation in its representation of possible future technologies since its emergence in the mid-1980s. Paralleling a similar shift in literature and film, the late 20th-century postmodernism portrayed in early cyberpunk TRPGs by flesh and metal cyborgs and parallel virtual worlds, evolved into the posthumanism of the early 21st century by the integration of elements such as genetically engineering, nano-machines, and the ability to transfer both natural and artificial consciousness' from one body to another. Bordering the fantastic, this expansion of transformative options gave players the ability to create characters with limber plasticity, capable of merging information technology with biotechnology, robotics with genetics, and cognitive science with nanotech in any number of boundary-crossing splices. Carbonell (2020) argues that this shift can be observed in the differences between the world buildings of the seminal TRPG series *Cyberpunk* (R. Talsorian Games 1988-2020) and the transhumanist *Eclipse Phase* (Posthuman Studios 2009), as well as in transformation of the *Shadowrun* series which has been published uninterrupted since the late 1980s and combines a grounded speculative vision successfully with fantasy elements like dragons and magic.

Considered one of the most popular cyberpunk-themed TRPGs, *Shadowrun* was first published by the *FASA Corporation* in 1989 and has evolved into a transmedia franchise over the years, spreading to comics, novels, and video games (Appelcline 2014). Despite the changing ownership of the IP, new editions of the game have been continuously in circulation, with its current sixth edition being launched in 2019 by *Catalyst Game Labs*. Translated into multiple languages, the game has also been adapted to various international settings, leading to the publication of local editions with unique content in France, Hungary, Japan, and most prominently in Germany (Hamelmann and Lonsing 2005). Set approximately 60 years in the future, in the 2050s in the first edition and 2080s in the current sixth edition, the game utilizes many cyberpunk genre tropes to depict a technologically advanced, corporate-run world, with high levels of socio-economic inequality and diminishing personal freedoms. While sharing several worldbuilding aspects with the *Cyberpunk* series, the setting differs itself in its integration of fantasy elements. The imaginary future of *Shadowrun* is not only shaped by advances in technology and devastating global events, but also by the awakening of the supernatural in the 2010s. Thus, in this fictional world, multinationals run by dragons, elves developing AI, and magicians merging with software are common sights. As a gameplay feature, magical attributes can be used by players either as alternatives to technology or as abilities compatible with it in a balanced manner, with each having its own advantages and disadvantages. Mechanically, this balance is achieved through the so-called "essence attribute", which limits the number of cybernetic implants a player character can have. Depending on the edition, essence loss may also affect the social interaction options provided to the players. According to Cameron (2020), the writing style of the official publications seamlessly integrates these fantastic elements into the conspiratorial cyberpunk future of the game world, without breaking its perceived verisimilitude. This techno-fantasy world gives players a wide range of options while building their characters as 'runners', or freelancers performing various illegal or covert operations such as theft, espionage, or sabotage for various clients.

Describing the worldbuilding of *Shadowrun* as a critique of global capitalism and constant technological surveillance, Schmidt (2012) argues that the game presents success as the avoidance of these dominant forces. Thus, machine vision and XR technologies play a significant role in the *Shadowrun* game world as tools for surveillance, control, and combat. Corporations, governments, criminal or religious organizations, and individuals use various forms of AI-integrated XR technologies to get the upper hand against each other. According to Schmidt (2012), one of the key factors contributing to the relevance of the world of *Shadowrun* to each new generation of players has been its reflections on real-world technological developments. Each new edition adapts and integrates contemporary trends and inventions into the game setting and explores their probable uses as narrative and gameplay elements. In this regard, *Shadowrun*'s various versions can be seen as commentaries on the potential of XR technologies as they evolve over time.

XR AS A NOVELTY

Set in the 2050s, the first (1E) and second (2E) editions of *Shadowrun* featured innovative XR and machine vision technologies, some of which became genre staples or even ubiquitous applications over time. The 1E and 2E Core Rulebooks (FASA 1989, 1992a) listed ocular implants and drones with visual sensors amongst other equipment and cyber-augmentations available to players. Reflecting the novelty of the technology at the time of publication, the *Corporate Security Handbook* (FASA 1995a) even explained in detail how closed-circuit television (CCTV) systems worked and how runners could use or manipulate them. *Shadowtech* (FASA 1992b) and *Cybertechnology* (FASA 1995b) sourcebooks provided further details on ocular implants called 'cybereyes', which could provide basic XR functions such as a retinal clock and an image display capable of making video calls. Upgrading their cybereyes, players could enhance their characters' vision beyond the visible spectrum and thus gain new skills for engaging their environment and enemies. In mechanical terms, such updates would apply modifiers to players' perception dice rolls, and from a role-play perspective give them new options such as receiving private calls during a negotiation. While they would be updated in later editions like the rest of the game, the general mechanics managing how players use XR during the gameplay would remain as the application of situational modifiers for dice rolls linked to visual actions, or to use them as diceless mechanics enabling certain actions. Any use of XR which does not require some form of gameplay challenge would be experienced as a descriptive dialog between the players and the gamemaster.

Combining the enhancement and surveillance aspects of machine vision, the imaginary simulated-sensory experience technology, or 'simsence' introduced in the first edition, allowed player characters equipped with neural implants to perceive sensory inputs originating in machine sources as their own. Building on this concept, the *1E* and *2E Rigger* sourcebooks (FASA 1991a, 1997) covered how characters with these implants could become the brains of cybernetic systems and see through cameras, which gave them the ability to command drones, control vehicles as extensions of their own bodies, or function as the center of larger surveillance systems with enhanced situational awareness. Characters who took these roles, however, could only focus on one action or sensory input at a time and would experience synchronous data coming from other sensors only as bodily sensations, limiting the effectiveness of the systems they control on a fictional level while also balancing the gameplay. These player characters would also be immobile in the physical world, usually requiring some type of protection for their bodies.

The simsence technology was also mentioned in the *1E* and *2E Virtual Realities* (FASA 1991b, 1995c) sourcebooks, which explained how so-called 'deckers', or hacker analogues in the *Shadowrun* universe, could immerse themselves into the VR network called "the Matrix", an Internet analogue. While the rulesets were updated between editions, the internal data architecture of the Matrix and the ways players navigated and manipulated it has been a key component of *Shadowrun* over the years. While these details are beyond the scope of this study, focusing on the representations of XR, it should be noted that these data structures had to be considered by the players while acting in the Matrix. Visually early sourcebooks depicted this version of the Matrix as an abstract neon-lit spatial representation of data, much like the visualizations of VR in science fiction films of the period, like *The Lawnmower Man* (Leonard 1992) and *Johnny Mnemonic* (Longo 1995). Using attributes specifically designed for the Matrix, players could move within this space and interact with data objects, transforming hacking into a spatial puzzle experience set in a universe with alternate physics leading to a complex dice play. While not directly exploring the broader social and economic implications of the Matrix as a VR system, these sourcebooks did present evocative concepts embedded in heist or espionage scenarios, such as isolation and sensory overload in VR or the emergence of early artificial intelligence within hidden data pockets in the VR.

XR and machine vision technologies in these early editions of *Shadowrun* reflected the novelty of the concept and emphasized human control over information processing and decision-making. Cybereyes or CCTV were only as effective as the person using them. Some of the rare exceptions were tactical 'headware' covered in the *Corporate Security Handbook* (FASA 1995a). If connected to cybereyes they were capable of tracing and predicting movements of selected targets for players during combat. 'Autonavigation' and "remote piloting" introduced in *Rigger* sourcebooks also described how vehicles or drones could act semi-autonomously while executing a command. Despite their limitations, these early representations of AI-integrated XR formed the basis of later imaginary devices and technologies in future iterations of the game.

TRANSFORMATIONS AND SOCIAL IMPLICATIONS

Released in 1998 and set in the 2060s, the third edition (3E) of *Shadowrun* presented a major overhaul of the game's existing representation of XR technologies and introduced new concepts with broader social implications. First, the widespread uses of commercially available surveillance technologies by governments and corporations, as well as individuals such as journalists, for security and investigation purposes were summarized in the *3E Core Rulebook* (FanPro 1998). The *3E Rigger* sourcebook (FASA 2001) also covered more advanced and diverse versions of the previously covered XR and machine vision technologies, such as self-driving vehicles, automated traffic control systems capable of recognizing license plates, and autonomous drones with visual sensors designed for non-violent utilitarian purposes like house cleaning or as pets providing companionship. Thus, players could encounter AI-integrated XR in previously impossible scenarios and had to consider its capabilities in their decision-making. Yet, these publications also noted that humans, or metahumans, were still the ones watching and analyzing audio-visual feeds originating from machine vision systems using either screen-based or VR systems, thus human perception still played a key role in their effectiveness.

The third edition upgraded the game's representation of VR y as well, not only by introducing more complex rules for actions and movement in the Matrix but also by enhancing worldbuilding. Instead of focusing on the novelty of the technology, *Target: Matrix* (FASA 2000) sourcebook depicted the titular platform as a worldwide VR network akin to a metaverse, resembling its conceptualizations in science fiction and by contemporary tech companies in the early 2020s (Mystakidis 2022). Corporations, governmental agencies, and other organizations had their own interconnected virtual 'realms' in the Matrix, each providing different services, which interestingly aligns with the contemporary visions of a fragmented future XR structure with dispersed ownerships as well (Bolter et al. 2021). In *Shadowrun*'s version of the future, these virtual spaces were visited regularly by millions of users for business, entertainment, education, and other social activities. While doing so they could present themselves using various realistic or fantastical avatars and explore different identities. The sourcebook also described underground communities and gangs formed in the Matrix, some of which did not have any physical counterparts. Meaning, instead of being a type of visualized data space as in the earlier versions of the game, this upgraded VR system was envisioned more like an extension of or an alternative to physical reality. In this regard, it provided a space for players to explore the potential social consequences around the value of VR objects, or in Aarseth's (2024) terms, the social norms of post-reality in VR. In fact, the closing campaign of the third edition, *System Failure* (FanPro 2005A), provided a scenario for the players just to do that, as it depicted the crash of the Matrix and featured post-crash characters who had lost all their VR assets and had to adapt to the physical reality financially and psychologically.

Overall, what characterized the fictional XR technologies featured in the third edition of *Shadowrun* was their growing importance in everyday activities. To some extent, they provided a conceptual framework for a potential metaverse and the opportunities and risks it represents. While extremely immersive, these technologies were not yet completely ubiquitous at all stages of life. On a positive note, they were also not fully capable as mechanisms of overarching control. They were, however, indispensable for the users who wanted to be properly functioning members of a space and society run by corporations.

Set in the early 2070s, the 2005 fourth edition (4E) of *Shadowrun* represented a major shift in the portrayal of XR technologies, especially in the conceptualization of the Matrix. Reflecting on the rising use of Wi-Fi networks at the time of the publication (Schmidt 2012), the fourth edition *Core Rulebook* (FanPro 2005B) introduced the "Matrix 2.0", which was a wireless network replacing the earlier Matrix after the global crash concluding the previous edition. The new Matrix 2.0 was based on MR and a complex Internet of Things (IoT), which shaped the data architecture of the network as well. Gone were the days of jacking in on a chair. Accessed through devices like smart glasses or ocular implants, the new MR of *Shadowrun* consisted of networked objects and users as data nodes. Camera feeds, object and facial recognition software, and geotagging also supported the XR system. Images in the *4E Core Rulebook*, depicted the Matrix 2.0. as a spatial experience enhanced by over-layered digital visuals and virtual objects, some mobile, others attached to specific physical locations, objects, or users. In other words, the new Matrix offered a new type of ever-present spatial computing experience.

In terms of gameplay, this new model provided multiple new options and offered a more infused experience for individual players and parties, as the division between activities and players in and outside of the Matrix disappeared. For example, a player could use the technical schematics of a device as an overlay while working on it and thus apply dice pool modifiers for the action success roll. One could have multiple active AR windows during combat, feeding in tactical data like maps or real-time sensor readings, which could be translated into a certain type of contextual bonus by the gamemaster, like having an extra stealth action option. However, the *4E Core Rulebook* also warns against the gameplay challenges of AR. If a player is engaged in multiple parallel AR activities in an unsafe location, they may not be able to notice someone or something sneaking behind them in the physical world. The constant cacophony of personal and spatial data could lead to unexpected outcomes and cooperative role-play as well since every player could experience the same location in different ways. Overall, many actions and experiences previously limited to immobile deckers have become accessible for most players all the time.

Introducing multiple new scenarios involving machine vision and spatial computing, this iteration carried *Shadowrun*'s focus on the spatial and immersive characteristics of digital media to the next level (Murray 1997). While VR still had its core immersive appeal for certain activities like gaming, most users preferred the omnipresent interactive AR and MR services in their daily lives. *The Unwired* (Catalyst Game Labs 2008) rulebook described the networked MR as the main mode of all social and economic activities in the game world: Virtual offices and remote working became the norm, reducing costs for corporations and increasing work hours for employees. Education also shifted to AR, with schools being replaced by teacher bots for the poor, and elites being tutored by experts from all over the world in virtual campuses. Even religious rituals were moved to the Matrix. The Muslims regularly attending collective virtual prayers on Fridays choose to perform their rituals at a time synchronized to Mecca time in AR instead of congregating at local mosques where prayer schedules were traditionally aligned to local time, which represented a major shift in the religious dogma.

Recording and analyzing user data through multiple tools, including biometrics and facial recognition, the new Matrix 2.0. was also conceptualized as a surveillance system, which was much more capable compared to the old Matrix of the previous editions. It was utilized by companies to target individuals with personalized virtual advertising embedded in their daily routines. The *4E Core Rulebook* describes how the same empty physical surface could show different brands to different users and how these could change thanks to guerrilla marketing tactics. AR adverts could direct users to specific products in the nearest stores as they enter a street. In terms of gameplay, this could be beneficial if the players were looking for the advertised products or stores, but being bombarded with commercial messages in AR could also be a hindrance while chasing someone, which would be translated into some kind of movement or perception penalty by the gamemaster. Surveillance integrated into augmented reality was also used by authorities to control personal freedoms, for example, by limiting players` characters` access in certain neighborhoods unless they followed instructions. Such actions were linked to the data architecture model of the game, where each person was also a data node that could have multiple privacy settings. Not giving corporations access to one's personal data or using some type of privacy screen in corporate controlled environments could lead to confrontations.

According to the *4E Core Rulebook*, besides the socio-economic changes, MR-enhanced products also affected how individuals in the game world perceived and represented themselves on a personal level. Using virtual filters attached to these products, anyone on the Matrix 2.0 could change how they appeared to other users or decorate their homes with virtual overlays, as long as they could afford to buy them from corporate providers or were ready to take the risks of using illegal versions. In other words, while creating a rift between the physical and augmented realities, these filters also acted as signifiers of self-identities, group memberships, and economic status. In terms of gameplay, the concept introduced multiple new disguise options as well.

The ubiquitous and widespread MR system of the fourth edition of *Shadowrun* introduced multiple themes within its fictional setting. Some of these became discussion points within the context of real-world XR and machine vision technologies in the following decades. Depictions of virtual offices in the fourth edition bore similarities to commentaries on remote working and the decline of employees' rights (Donnelly and Johns 2020). Commercial and oppressive uses of the Matrix 2.0 for both manipulating and limiting character behaviors were extreme versions of the commodification of user data in surveillance capitalism (Zuboff and Schwandt 2019) and restrictions on social lives through surveillance-driven social credit systems (Yang 2022), respectively. Scenarios of AR-enhanced appearances of products and individuals could be seen as fictionalized accounts of uses and abuses of image filters on social media (Bakhshi et al. 2021), and the social impacts of cosmetic items in virtual worlds (Fennimore 2020). Furthermore, the virtual development of urban environments in the game preceded the contemporary legal and commercial conflicts faced by the owners of physical spaces geotagged with AR experiences (Bolter et al. 2021). Overall, the game presented a broad societal scenario in which the digital divide between haves and have-nots merged with the physical world due to the omnipresence of MR and IoT. Official *Shadowrun* adventures utilizing these themes positioned players as runners trying to escape, manipulate, destroy, or benefit from futuristic XR and machine vision systems, and pushing them to their imagined limits. All in all, the ways the fourth edition represented imaginary XR technologies were innovative, complex, and cynical, if not critical. The focus was not only on action and combat but also on the broader implications of XR being at the center of all socio-economic activities at all levels. Enhancing the verisimilitude of the game world, the story-world database provides gamemasters with multiple narrative elements to convey to players what it could feel like to live in such a society. In other words, the story-world database of the game was written to provide plausible contexts for multiple possible scenarios about opportunities and challenges of XR, which could emerge from the interactions between gamemasters and players.

In terms of representing XR technologies as narrative and gameplay elements with potential critical undertones, the fourth edition of *Shadowrun* can be seen as a milestone in providing a stable framework for later editions. The fifth (5E) and sixth (6E) edition *Core Rulebooks* (Catalyst Game Labs 2013, Catalyst Game Labs 2019) did not introduce new ground-breaking XR concepts fundamentally reshaping the game world while being set in the mid-2070s and early 2080s, respectably. They built on existing themes, shifted world-building elements like corporate control levels to create challenges, elaborated on XRs' various uses for specific purposes in conjunction with other technologies and magic, as in the use of AR in creating artworks, and modified the mechanics of interacting with XR gradually over time. Publications like the in-universe fictitious newspaper *MegaPuls*, released by the German publisher of *Shadowrun* as online supplements to be used as in-game handouts, did provide glimpses of evocative themes in the form of news articles and adverts. *MegaPuls* presented topics like data security concerns linked to VR pets (Pegasus Press 2018) or exploration of gender identities in the Matrix (Pegasus Press 2024) as daily topics of the game world. These short pieces not only contributed to the world-building of the game but also provided potential adventure seeds for the players, and thus gave them the option to tackle the technologies behind them. In this regard, while their intended uses were quite different, *MegaPuls* did share many characteristics of a design fiction piece written in the form of a newspaper. Overall, it can be argued that while the latest two editions of *Shadowrun* did not introduce major changes to the game series` representation of XR technologies, by utilizing them as an almost mundane element of the game world, they created spaces for potential discussions and criticism.

The *Shadowrun* series provides a broad historical overview of how the popular understanding of XR has changed and how ideas around it evolved. Positioning this new emerging technological spectrum not as a pool of products that must have benefits for the users, but as a mundane element of a technology-driven world with both benefits and risks, which can be amplified by commercial, cultural, and social power struggles, the series gave players the opportunity to experiment with it, mainly for fun but also through critical lenses if they wish to abide the genre conventions of cyberpunk.

CONCLUSION

This chapter investigated the representation of the XR spectrum in the TRPG series *Shadowrun* since the 1980s, mainly in its world-building but also in its game design. Throughout this period, each iteration not only evolved in terms of its mechanics and systems but also adapted its world-building to the technological advances in the real world. This parallel relationship resulted in a speculative vision which preceded the popularization and commercialization of XR in the real world. Building on taxonomical studies analyzing science fiction texts to recognize patterns and variations of the design fiction approach, the study recognizes two historical periods in the worldbuilding of the *Shadowrun* series. The first one reflects upon the novelty aspect of XR applications and aligns with mainstream science fiction tropes. The second period presents a world where XR technologies have become ubiquitous either in the form of a metaverse or as an MR built on an ever-present IoT and experienced through spatial computing applications. The study has shown that multiple social impacts of XR depicted in the second period predicted contemporary and emerging challenges. In this regard, the *Shadowrun* series exemplifies how informed worldbuilding can provide sound speculative scenarios for emerging technologies in the long run. Studies on other established science fiction TRPG franchises can provide further historical perspectives exposing our relationship with emerging technologies and how the ways we perceive them change over time when the novelty aspect fades away.

This study argues that speculative games can be utilized to explore critical perspectives towards the future both in their worldbuilding and during play. A long-running series such as *Shadowrun* can provide a corpus for taxonomical studies, which can expose the historical evolution of technological visions and social reactions and expectations towards them. While not the focus of this study, comparative analysis of games with international versions and specials can also offer broader views. Speculative games can also be approached as text resembling second-order design fictions. Official TRPG publications provide potential space for various actions and approaches as a database of possibilities parallel to second-order design fiction. Both provide problems and complex contextual data to trigger speculations and action. In other words, they present evocative glimpses of a fictional world with the intent of generating provocations. However, since the study did not investigate play sessions or retellings, any comments on player actions refer to the assumptions given in official publications. Further studies are needed to investigate the parallels between TRPGs and design fiction in terms of how they shape players' speculative creativity. The chapter presents a case for speculative gaming. Even if they prioritize fun, games can present grounded speculations on the future without being tied to the logic of promotion. Studying depictions of fictional XR technologies, applications, ecosystems, and their effects on society in speculative games can be beneficial in understanding the complex web of relationships around the spectrum and preparing for it on a conceptual level.

REFERENCES

Aarseth, E. 2024. Back to reality: The case against ludo-fictionalism. pp. 13–22. *In*: Kissel, A. and José Ramirez, E. (eds). Exploring Extended Realities: Metaphysical, Psychological, and Ethical Challenges. Routledge.

Appelcline, S. 2014. Designers and Dragons: The '80s. Silver Spring: Evil Hat Productions.

Arnaldi, B., Guitton, P. and Moreau, G. 2018. Virtual Reality and Augmented Reality: Myths and Realities. John Wiley & Sons.

Bakhshi, S., Shamma, D., Kennedy, L. and Gilbert, E. 2021. Why We Filter Our Photos and How It Impacts Engagement. *In*: Proceedings of the International AAAI Conference on Web and Social Media. 9(1): 12–21.

Baur, W. 2012. Worlds and technology. pp. 63–69. *In*: J. Silverstein (ed.). The KOBOLD Guide to Worldbuilding. Kirkland Open Design Llc.

Bleecker, J., Nova, N., Girardin, F. and Foster, N. 2023. The Manual of Design Fiction. Venice Beach: Near Future Laboratory.

Bolter, J.D., Engberg, M. and MacIntyre, B. 2021. Reality Media: Augmented and Virtual Reality. The MIT Press.

Borgstrom, R. 2007. Structure and meaning in role-playing game design. pp. 57–66. *In*: Harrigan, P. and Wardrip-Fruin, N. (eds). Second Person: Role-playing and Story in Games and Playable Media. The MIT Press.

Bowman, S.L. 2010. The Functions of Role-playing Games: How Participants Create Community, Solve Problems, and Explore Identity. Jefferson: McFarland & Co.

Cameron, H. 2020. Shadowrun (Case Study). pp. 209–215. *In*: McFarlane, A., Schmeink, L. and Murphy, G. (eds). The Routledge Companion to Cyberpunk Culture. Routledge.

Carbonell, C.D. 2020. Tabletop roleplaying games. pp. 200–208. *In*: McFarlane, A., Schmeink, L. and Murphy, G. (eds). The Routledge Companion to Cyberpunk Culture. Routledge.

Catalyst Game Labs. 2008. Unwired. Catalyst Game Labs.

Catalyst Game Labs. 2013. Shadowrun: Core Rulebook. Catalyst Game Labs.

Catalyst Game Labs. 2019. Shadowrun: Core Rulebook. Catalyst Game Labs.

CD Projekt Red. 2020. Cyberpunk 2077. CD Projekt.

Clements, P.J. 2019. Dungeons and discourse: intersectional identities in dungeons and dragons. PhD, Bowling Green State University. https://scholarworks.bgsu.edu/acs_diss/105.

Cook, M. 2012. Different kinds of worldbuilding. pp. 13–16. *In*: J. Silverstein (ed.). The KOBOLD Guide to Worldbuilding. Kirkland Open Design Llc.

Cross, K.A. 2012. The new laboratory of dreams: Role-playing games as resistance. WSQ: Women's Studies Quarterly. 40(3&4): 70–88.

Donnelly, R. and Johns, J. 2020. Recontextualising remote working and its HRM in the digital economy: An integrated framework for theory and practice. The International Journal of Human Resource Management. 32(1): 84–105.

Dormans, J. 2006. On the role of the die: A brief ludologic study of pen-and-paper role-playing games and their rules. Game Studies: The International Journal of Computer Game Research. 6(1). https://api.semanticscholar.org/CorpusID:846875.

Dunne, A. and Raby, F. 2013. Speculative Everything: Design, Fiction, and Social Dreaming. The MIT Press.

FanPro. 1998. Shadowrun: Core Rulebook. FanPro.

FanPro. 2005a. System Failure. FanPro.

FanPro. 2005b. Shadowrun: Core Rulebook. FanPro.

FASA Corporation. 1989. Shadowrun. FASA Corporation.

FASA Corporation. 1991a. Rigger. FASA Corporation.

FASA Corporation. 1991b. Virtual Realities. FASA Corporation.

FASA Corporation. 1992a. Shadowrun Second Edition. FASA Corporation.

FASA Corporation. 1992b. Shadowtech. FASA Corporation.

FASA Corporation. 1995a. Corporate Security Handbook. FASA Corporation.

FASA Corporation. 1995b. Cybertechnology. FASA Corporation.

FASA Corporation. 1995c. Virtual Realities 2.0. FASA Corporation.

FASA Corporation. 1997. Rigger 2. FASA Corporation.

FASA Corporation. 2000. Target: Matrix. FASA Corporation.

FASA Corporation. 2001. Rigger 3. FASA Corporation.

Fennimore, J.J. 2020. Are They Really Just Cosmetic? The Impact of Cosmetic Items on Fortnite's Gameplay and Game Design. University of Wisconsin-Milwaukee, MA Thesis, https://dc.uwm.edu/etd/2494.

Fry, T. 2022. Writing Design Fiction: Relocating a City in Crisis. Bloomsbury Publishing.

Garcia, A. 2017. Privilege, power, and dungeons and dragons: How systems shape racial and gender identities in tabletop role-playing games. Mind, Culture, and Activity. 24(3): 232–246.

Gibson, W. 1984–1988. Sprawl Trilogy. Gollancz.

Graves, E.K. 2024. Extended Reality Technologies in the Media. Routledge.

Gygax, G. 1979. Advanced D&D Adventure Games Dungeon Masters Guide. Random House.

Hackl, C. and Cronin, I. 2024. Spatial Computing: An AI-Driven Business Revolution. John Wiley & Sons.

Hamelmann, T. and Lonsing, C. 2005. Die sechste Welt. Fantasy Productions.

Harrigan, P. and Wardrip-Fruin, N. 2007. Tabletop systems. pp. 1–4. *In*: Harrigan, P. and Wardrip-Fruin, N. (eds). Second Person: Role-playing and Story in Games and Playable Media. The MIT Press.

Jara, D. 2013. A closer look at the (Rule-) books: Framings and paratexts in tabletop role-playing games. International Journal of Role-Playing. 1(4): 39–54.

Kawitzky, F.R. 2021. Magic circles. Performance Research. 25(8): 129–136.

Kuusniemi, T. 2018. Dungeons & Discourses: A nexus analytic case study of negotiating competence and identity in table-top role-playing games. MA, University of Oulu. http://jultika.oulu.fi/Record/nbnfioulu-201805312343105.

Legiedz, R. 2024. XR Demystified: Separating Facts from Fiction. https://www.youtube.com/watch?v=IWxyuvf310Q.

Leonard, B. 1992. Lawnmower Man. New Line Cinema.

Longo. R. 1995. Johnny Mnemonic. 20th Century Fox.

Mochocki, M. 2021. Role-Play as a Heritage Practice: Historical LARP, Tabletop RPG, and Reenactment. Routledge.

Mongoose Publishing. 2022. 2300 AD. Mongoose Publishing.

Murray, J.H. 1997. Hamlet on the Holodeck: The Future of Narrative in Cyberspace. Free Press.

Mystakidis, S. 2022. Metaverse. Encyclopedia. 2(1): 486–497.

Nikolaidou, D. 2018. The evolution of fantastical storyworlds: A study of tabletop role-playing settings. Ex-centric Narratives: Journal of Anglophone Literature, Culture, and Media. S.l.(2): 218—229.

Paizo Inc. 2023. Starfinder RPG: Starfinder Enhanced. Paizo Inc.

Pegasus Press. 2018. MegaPuls 31.12.2080. https://shadowrun6.de/index.php/ingame-material-2/novapuls.html.

Pegasus Press. 2024. MegaPuls Zoom 05.02.2083. https://shadowrun6.de/index.php/ingame-material-2/novapuls.html.

Pirandello, S. 2021. A Journey into artworks: Storytelling in augmented reality and mixed reality. Cinergie –Il Cinema E Le Altre Arti. 10(19): 135–145.

Posthuman Studios. 2009. Eclipse Phase. Catalyst Game Labs.

Ramirez, J. and Kissel, A. 2024. Through a glass virtually: On the future of extended realities. pp. 213–236. *In*: Kissel, A. and José Ramirez, E. (eds).

Exploring Extended Realities: Metaphysical, Psychological, and Ethical Challenges. Routledge.

Rettberg, J.W., Gunderson M., Kronman, L., Solberg, R. and Stokkedal, L.H. 2019. Mapping cultural representations of machine vision. *In*: Proceedings of the 30th ACM Conference on Hypertext and Social Media. 97–101. Association for Computing Machinery.

Rettberg, J.W., Kronman, L., Solberg, R., Gunderson, M., Bjørklund, S.M., Stokkedal, L.H., et al. 2022. Representations of machine vision technologies in artworks, games, and narratives: A dataset. Data in Brief. 42: 108319. doi:10.1016/j.dib.2022.108319.

Riccitiello, J. 2022. Getting Beyond the Fiction and Seeing the Reality in the Metaverse. https://www.youtube.com/watch?v=hnWzVN42uP0 [Last Accessed 20 June 2024].

Roddenberry, G., Hurley, M., Berman, R., Piller, M. and Taylor, J. (Executive Producer). 1987–1994. Star Trek: The Next Generation [TV series]. Paramount Domestic Television.

R. Talsorian Games. 1988–2020. Cyberpunk. R. Talsorian Games.

Schallegger, R. 2018. The Postmodern Joy of Role-playing Games: Agency, Ritual, and Meaning in the Medium. Mcfarland.

Schmidt, D.N. 2012. Zwischen Simulation und Narration: Theorie des Fantasy-Rollenspiels. Peter Lang.

Shurin, J. 2023. Introduction. pp. xiii–xx. *In*: J. Shurin, (ed.). The Big Book of Cyberpunk. Vintage Books.

Solberg, R. 2023. Playing posthumanism: A study of machine vision and tensions of human-machine relations in digital games. PhD, University of Bergen. https://bora.uib.no/bora-xmlui/handle/11250/3039103.

Spielberg, S. 2002. Minority Report. Twentieth Century Fox.

Stephenson, N. 1992. Snow Crash. Bantam Books.

Steinicke, F. 2016. Being Really Virtual. Springer.

Tromp, J.G. 2022. Extended reality and the backbone: Towards a 3D mirrorworld. pp. 193–228. *In*: Alcañiz, L.M., Sacco, M. and Tromp, J.G. (eds). Roadmapping Extended Reality: Fundamentals and Applications. John Wiley & Sons.

Wachowski, A. and Wachowski, L. 1999–2003. THE MATRIX Trilogy. Warner Bros.

Wolf, M.J.P. 2013. Building Imaginary Worlds: The Theory and History of Subcreation. Routledge.

Yang, Z. 2022. China just announced a new social credit law. Here's what it means. MIT Technology Review. https://www.technologyreview.com/2022/11/22/1063605/china-announced-a-new-social-credit-law-what-does-it-mean/.

Zagal, J. and Deterding, S. 2018. Definitions of "Role-Playing Games". pp. 19–51. *In*: J. Zagal and S. Deterding (eds). Role-playing Game Studies: Transmedia Foundations. Routledge.

Zuboff, S. and Schwandt, K. 2019. The Age of Surveillance Capitalism: The Fight for a Human Future at the New Frontier of Power. Profile Books.

Chapter 14

Enhancing Earthquake Preparedness and Awareness: A Virtual Reality Serious Game for Residential Interiors

Merve Öksüz*[1], Özge Cordan[1] and Güven Çatak[2]

[1]Department of Interior Architecture, Faculty of Architecture, Istanbul Technical University (TR)
Email: cordan@itu.edu.tr

[2]Digital Game Design Undergraduate Program, Faculty of Communication, Bahçeşehir University (TR)
Email: guven.catak@bau.edu.tr

INTRODUCTION

Human, natural, or hybrid disasters cause death, injuries, and damages (Shaluf 2007). Earthquakes, which are among the natural disasters, have devastating effects on human life and property. Studies carried out to ensure the safety of human life and property before, during, and after an earthquake focus on both theoretical and practical studies.

Human and property losses caused by earthquakes are based on structural and non-structural factors. Research and applications for

*For Correspondence: oksuz19@itu.edu.tr

DOI: 10.1201/9781003581642-14

non-structural elements and damages that concern the discipline of interior architecture and interior architects are important before, during and after an earthquake. Ertaş Beşir and Dereci (2021) emphasize that nonstructural elements have the potential to threaten life safety during an earthquake if the necessary precautions are not taken. The Federal Emergency Management Agency (FEMA 2023) divides nonstructural components into three categories: architectural (such as chimneys, partitions, interior walls, trim, and ornamentation); mechanical-electrical equipment and plumbing (such as generators, distribution systems, heating and cooling systems); and furniture, fixtures, and equipment.

Moved/overturned furniture and falling objects can cause many deaths and injuries during and after an earthquake and delay or prevent safe escape by blocking evacuation routes (Kaneko 2012). Garip et al. (2023, p. 251) classified components in residential indoor areas that may present life- safety risks, including fixed and mobile furniture, objects, non-structural elements, electrical appliances, technical equipment, and lighting fixtures, and stated that the studies mostly focused on fixed furniture and non-structural elements. The principal risks are "fixed furniture involves tumbling, breaking, and blocking escape routes due to the falling or pulling of structural elements". They also stated that these studies mostly focused on fixed furniture and non-structural elements.

Sarı and Aktar (2017) highlight the importance of implementing protective measures, such as securing, locking, or fixing mobile furniture to walls or floors (that may prevent evacuation and rescue). Additionally, Karamanoğlu and Ulay (2017) recommended using lightweight materials for mobile furniture manufacturing. Doğan (2020) suggested reducing risks by integrating shelves and drawers into the structure and concealing them.

In addition to strategies aimed at preventing disasters and reducing damage and hazards, interior space organization is essential for loss of life, security, and safety. The Chamber of Interior Architects of Turkey (TMMOB) (2023) states that interior space organizations should not have any effects that weaken escape routes or pose risks to earthquake safety. Furthermore, active and passive protective measures should be taken indoors. As Garip et al. (2023) stated it is crucial to prevent the damage caused by earthquakes by taking measures in the interiors of buildings, and it is of great importance to develop collective awareness of this fact.

While evacuating buildings after an earthquake is a basic strategy (Lovreglio et al. 2017), "drop-cover-hold on", which features protective actions during an earthquake, is also vital (FEMA 2023). In addition to theoretical studies on pre-earthquake, earthquake, and post-earthquake in the literature, virtual reality (VR) and/or augmented reality (AR) and mixed reality technologies (MR), which have been developing rapidly since the 2000s, have come to the fore with practical studies focusing on education and training studies on simulated disaster scenarios.

Liang et al. (2018) conducted a VR-based earthquake simulation, allowing participants to interact with objects through training and education. Integrating VR/AR/MR technologies into educational game environments facilitates learning by doing, trying and experiencing. Lovreglio et al. (2017) also state that VR and serious games (SG) represent new and effective ways of training people for emergencies such as earthquakes.

This study aims to enhance earthquake preparedness and awareness to prevent and reduce injuries, fatalities, and property loss. It presents a beta version and single-player VR SG for minimizing earthquake hazards and evacuation caused by non-structural factors in residential interiors.

BACKGROUND

In the Cambridge Dictionary (2022), 'play' refers to participating in a game or organized activity, while 'game' is defined as an entertaining activity, sport, or equipment. Dörner et al. (2016) expressed the difference between the concepts of play and game: "Playing is a purposeless, intrinsically motivated human activity without explicit rules, whereas gaming is a purposeless, intrinsically motivated human activity based on explicit rules." (Dörner et al. 2016, p. 8). According to Ohler and Nieding (2005), play is not merely a random activity chosen to alleviate boredom; instead, it is a deliberate and purposeful action that supports developmental processes (as cited in Ritterfeld and Weber 2005). Aarseth (2007) stated that games focus on player behavior and their primary purpose is entertainment, while Stenros (2016) stated that in the operational game tradition (Stenros 2016), the goal is to reach a solution to a posed problem. It includes simulations "where people interact to aid in decision-making and planning" (p. 503).

Games that use some kind of computing machinery (e.g., a personal computer, a smartphone, or a piece of electronics dedicated for playing games such as a video game console) are called *digital games* (Dörner et al. 2016, p. 2). Games present players a fun and/or social medium in which to pass time or interact with other users. Video/digital games, primarily designed for entertainment, are often discussed for their educational potential as well (Oksuz and Cordan 2022). A *serious game* is a *digital game* that uses the medium of games to deliver a message, teach a lesson, or provide an experience (Michael and Chen 2006, p. 23). Likewise, Djaouti et al. (2011) define serious games as the combination of a non-entertaining purpose (serious) with a video game structure (game) through software. On the other hand, the feeling of fun is described as positive feedback that encourages the repetition of player actions (Michael and Chen 2006). While it is debated whether the fun factor in serious games is a necessity or merely a preference, it is undeniable that this element is essential for player engagement. At this point, the ability to make something enjoyable becomes an integral part of the mission of the design and development team in creating serious games (Michael and Chen 2006).

Dörner et al. (2016, p. 9) highlight the characterizing goals of serious games, which are associated with various domains of competence: "The characterizing goals of *serious games* can be matched to competence domains, e.g., cognition and perception, emotion and volition, sensory-motor control, personal characteristics, social attitudes, and media use." Educational games, a subgroup of serious games, address dedicated education institutions, ranging from primary school to higher education, vocational training, and collaborative workplace learning, with a focus on formal learning (Dörner et al. 2016, p. 9). These games should, in general, motivate the player to achieve the defining goal by providing an engaging player experience through appropriate methods and using appropriate interaction technologies (Caserman et al. 2020). Lovreglio et al. (2017) also state that VR and serious games (SGs), in their various forms, prioritize education as the primary goal.

VR SG focusing on earthquake scenarios also aims to provide training and education for people in emergencies (Lovreglio et al. 2017). "FEMA Earthquake School Hazard Hunt Game" (2021), "Earthquake Simulator VR (2018)", and "Drill" (2023) are earthquake-related games in which scenarios are simulated with serious games for disaster preparedness education and problem-solving. Therefore, players are trained to identify and mitigate potential risks, take appropriate precautions for damages, and respond effectively in the event of an earthquake.

DEVELOPING A VIRTUAL REALITY SERIOUS GAMES

The game provides a beta version of single-player VR SG for minimizing earthquake hazards and evacuation caused by non-structural components in residential interiors. In the design process of the game developed in three stages, an empirical and bottom-up design model (Brooks Jr. 2010) was followed: In the conceptual design process, which constitutes the first phase, decisions were made about the purpose of the game and the target audience, as well as the rules, the VR/game environment, the actions that the player should (and should not) take to achieve the desired goals, the interaction model and degree of the game before the first idea was realized. In the second phase, the production and development phase, the game interface and system(s) were tested by the researcher (designer) and the game developer, and necessary corrections and additions were made. In the third and final phase, the experimentation phase, the design students experienced the earthquake simulation game through a workshop.

Study Participants

The participant group consisted of 12 volunteer undergraduate students, 11 from the Department of Interior Architecture at Istanbul Technical University and one from the Department of Digital Game Design at Bahçeşehir University. The rationale for selecting participants from third and fourth-year students is that they have attained a defined level of professional knowledge, skills, and competencies. In contrast, the level of mastery and technical expertise concerning VR environments and tools was not considered when selecting the experimental group. The objective is to ascertain the ease or difficulty of employing VR technology as a prospective learning environment and educational instrument.

Game Environment and Dynamics

In the workshop, students were encouraged to consider active and passive safety measures in residential indoors before, during, and after an earthquake, considering that structural performance is secured, and what interventions could be for prevention and mitigation.

The game presents three different problems for the participant/players to solve:

- Planning the selection and layout of furniture and equipment to mitigate non-structural damage before an earthquake,
- Safe spot/place selection during an earthquake,
- Providing evacuation and rescue when the shaking stops.

The player is expected to solve the design problems while choosing (right or wrong) among the alternatives presented to him/her. A single playthrough is not enough if the player wants to see the results of different choices; the game must be played more than once.

Preparation Phase

A flow diagram was constructed to provide a more detailed insight into the player experience and gameplay and to assist the game developer during the development phase (Figure 14.1).

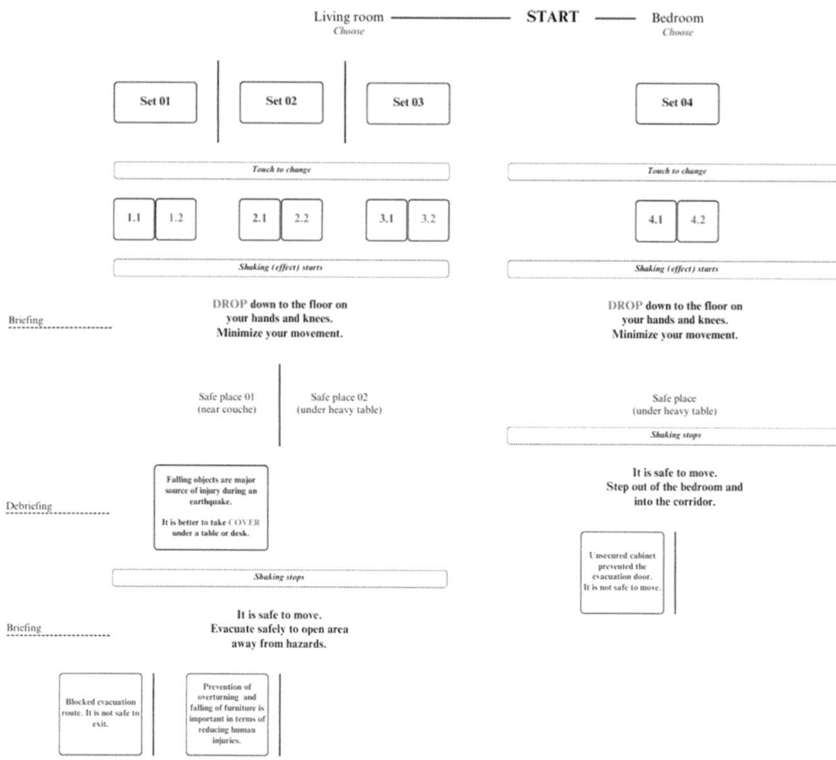

Figure 14.1 Flow chart for the game developer.

The plan that serves as the foundation for the learning environment and is transferred to the virtual domain is a generic plan for a reinforced concrete structure with a one-bedroom apartment. The housing plan combines a kitchen and living area, with an entrance hall leading to a bedroom and bathroom. Built-in appliances (extractor fan, dishwasher, oven, and hob), bathroom cabinet, television unit, and sanitary ware are the fixed furnishings in the interior. Before transferring the existing plan diagram (Figure 14.2) to the virtual environment, several non-structural alterations were made.

The initial alteration involves the removal of the sliding door that previously separated the residential space from the rest of the dwelling. This modification was implemented due to the sliding door's potential to prevent or hinder evacuation. Another alteration is the reduction in the window dimensions near the refrigerator. The aim is to take precautions against the potential for glass breakage and other similar situations (Kaneko 2012) that may occur due to the overturning or falling of furniture placed by a window. The proposed changes to the furniture selection and layout in the existing generic plan include a wall-mounted TV instead of the television unit and a fixed seating unit/sofa to prevent overturning, falling, or moving during an earthquake. The kitchen table, mobile furniture in the existing plan, is designed as an extendable dining table that works with the kitchen cabinets in the new solution proposal. This table also acts as a divider between the kitchen and the living area. Thus, the kitchen has been separated from the living space, as it is a storage area for items and objects that are prone to overturn or movement during and after an earthquake, posing human injury (Kaneko 2012). The refrigerator's location was rearranged to prevent any obstacles during an evacuation. As a result, the pathway from the living area to the exit, identified as the evacuation route, was cleared of heavy and tall furniture (Figure 14.2).

Figure 14.2 The existing generic plan (left) and the plan developed within the scope of solutions and regulations for mitigating non-structural damages in the residential interior (right).

Two distinct wardrobe options were proposed for the bedroom, one with hinged and the other with sliding doors. The desk was removed from the window and moved next to the wardrobe. They were securely fixed together and walled to reduce the overturning. Furthermore, to analyze the behavior of different lighting types during an earthquake, two lighting fixtures were recommended alongside the ceiling-mounted pendant light: a floor and wall lamp (Figure 14.3).

On the start screen, the game presents two distinct scenarios to the players/participants: the living room (Scenario 01) and the bedroom (Scenario 02) (Figure 14.4).

In the living area, three experience sets were designed: the kitchen and dining table (Set 01), the television unit (Set 02), and the lighting fixture (Set 03). Two sets (Set 04) were developed in the sleeping area, each featuring different wardrobe and desk configurations.

Figure 14.3 The axonometric perspective of virtual environment including correct applications.

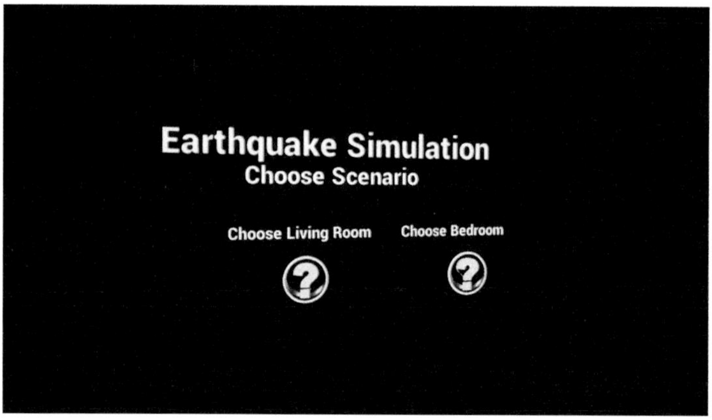

Figure 14.4 Game start screen.

Each set presents one correct and one incorrect application, focusing on minimizing injuries and preventing damage (Figure 14.5). Even if the player selects the incorrect option within each set, they can still progress to the next stage. Utilizing the hardware's real-time motion tracking capability, the player can adjust their viewpoint and direction within the virtual environment by looking around or leaning, while also modifying their position by walking or using the teleportation feature.

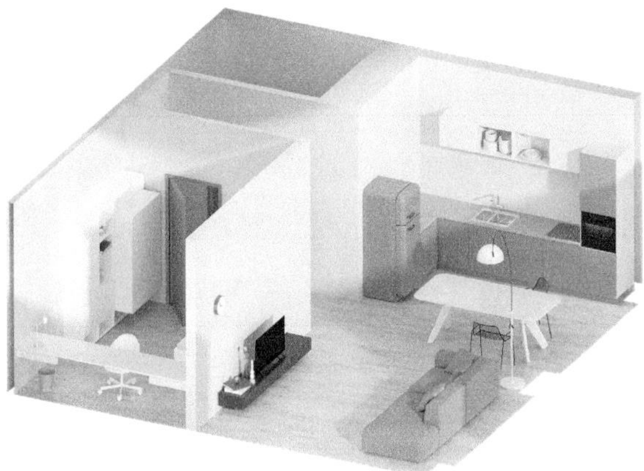

Figure 14.5 Axonometric perspective of virtual environment including incorrect applications.

EXPERIENCING THE GAME

To ensure users have a safe experience, the first step involved defining the activity/movement area within the physical environment, and removing any items or objects that were not part of the interaction. In the second step, the play-area borders were defined using the *Guardian* feature. The *Guardian* boundary helped users remain within the designated play area during the game/experience and prevented collisions with objects in the physical environment. At the beginning of each session, participants were instructed and shown how to wear, adjust, and use the virtual reality headset to ensure a comfortable experience and achieve the best visual quality. During the session, verbal guidance was provided by the workshop facilitator to help participants acquire basic usage skills and understand the interaction range of the game. This guidance included:

- How to navigate or move within the virtual environment and adjust their perspective or orientation,
- What changes they could make within the virtual environment and the number of options available to them for such changes,
- How to interact with virtual objects—for instance, select, modify, or trigger actions (e.g., simulating an earthquake).

To familiarize participants with the interface, the gameplay began in the bedroom—a more limited space with fewer interactions than the living area—serving as the initial testing environment (Figure 14.6). Additionally, participants were guided through feedback, explanations, and suggestions provided by the system in response to their in-game choices and actions, whether correct or incorrect.

Figure 14.6 Participant (K3) experiencing the bedroom scenario, downing on their knees until the shaking (effect) stops.

The most effective and immediate action to reduce injuries and losses during an earthquake and to ensure survival is "drop, cover, hold on". When shaking starts, the first step is to drop to the ground onto your hands and knees to prevent falling, cover your head and neck to protect them, and maintain your position by taking shelter under a sturdy table or desk (if available) to avoid exposure to hazards until the shaking stops.

During the earthquake simulation, the player can choose one of the safe spots/places and remain there until the shaking stops. Alternatively, they may relocate based on feedback received in response to their actions (Figures 14.7 and 14.8).

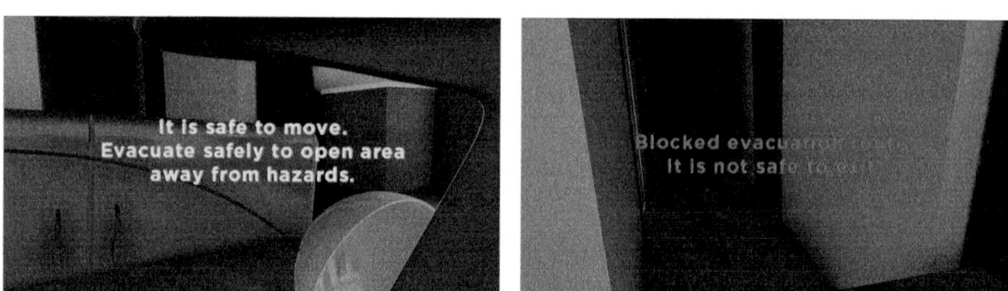

Figure 14.7 Brief explains that the player can safely evacuate the space/area once the shaking has stopped (on the left) and feedback is provided in response to the player's incorrect decision (on the right).

Figure 14.8 Brief that instructs the player to drop down to the floor when the shaking begins (on the left), and the highlighted safe spot (on the right).

Materials and Methods

Ethics committee approval was obtained from the authorities. Each participant/player was also informed about the aim and method of the study and signed a consent form before experiencing the game in the workshop held on March 4, 2023 in Studio 134 on the ground floor of the Taşkışla Building, Faculty of Architecture at Istanbul Technical University.

AutoCAD and the 3D modeling software 3ds Max were employed during the VR SG's design, production, and visualization phases, while Unreal Engine 5, featuring a visual scripting language, was utilized in the development phase.

The setup comprised a VR headset (Oculus Quest 2), a link cable, and two touch controllers to facilitate real-time interaction between the player and the (virtual) learning environment, including game objects. Furthermore, a laptop (Dell G15) was used as the data source, given the application's need for a computer processor.

Each participant was allocated a 30-minute session based on the planned gameplay duration.

In the workshop's data collection phase, quantitative and qualitative research methods and techniques were employed, including visual methods and surveys. Within this framework, participants' narratives and behaviors during the game experience were observed and documented by the researcher using participant observation techniques (Zeisel 2006). To ensure detailed and comprehensive data on behaviors and processes, each participant's experience was recorded through photographs, video, and audio (Sanoff 2016). Additionally, a two-stage survey was implemented as a data collection tool to address the research questions related to the virtual reality game. The survey, created via Google Forms, consisted of 25 questions, including open-ended, multiple-choice, nominal (e.g., yes-no, age, educational background, profession), and rating (Likert scale) questions. The first stage of the survey was conducted online one day before the experiment to capture participants' existing ideas, opinions, behaviors, and tendencies regarding earthquake awareness. In this stage, participants were asked eight questions in addition to providing personal information (gender, age, educational background, and profession). The second stage, comprising 12 questions, was administered online after the experiment to gather participants' feedback, opinions, and suggestions about their gameplay experience.

In the analysis of visual data, participants' narrative data were examined using content analysis (Strauss and Corbin 1990), while behavioral observation data were analyzed with the aid of annotated diagrams (Zeisel 2006).

RESULTS

Among the participants, 58.3% were male, and 41.6% were female. The age range of the participant group was between 18 and 31 years. Except for one individual, all participants were undergraduate design students. The game offered participants two scenarios: *living room* and *bedroom*. Both scenarios included experiential sets designed to demonstrate correct and incorrect practices regarding the organization, selection, and layout of non-structural elements within residential interiors. The living room scenario featured three experiential sets, while the bedroom included one.

During the gameplay phase, participants' behaviors were observed to collect data on their actions, gestures, facial expressions, and informal conversations while experiencing the game.

Participants with limited familiarity with virtual reality environments, tools, and technologies exhibited more anxious behaviors during gameplay. For instance, Participant K1 firmly gripped the touch controllers and, driven by an instinct to protect their head, placed their hands on both sides of it, which inadvertently caused the headset to shift and extend its gameplay duration. Similarly, Participant K12 frequently looked down at their feet during the initial stage, driven by a need to check where they were stepping. As a result, the researcher guided them to adopt a perspective that would allow for better spatial awareness. Participant K5, while attempting to interact with a marker required to modify an experiential set, encountered the virtual boundary (Guardian) and questioned, "I think that's outside the boundary, isn't it?" In response, the researcher reminded them about the 'teleportation' feature that could be used as a travel technique that allows users to move around. Participants unfamiliar with VR tools, environments, and technologies often replicated physical-world body movements to navigate or reposition themselves in the virtual environment. Consequently, they did not utilize the features and capabilities offered by the interface and hardware.

During gameplay, participants provided feedback regarding the game's mechanics. For instance, Participant K1 asked, *"Why do I need to change these objects?"* after being informed about which objects could be modified and how. Another participant, K7, after experiencing the bedroom scenario, questioned the researcher while engaging with the living room scenario, asking, *"Can I use a clue from the previous scenario?"* This reflected their inquiry into whether the practices they had encountered earlier would be applicable or effective in a different context or process. Similarly, Participant K2 expressed a deliberate approach to their choices and actions in the living room scenario, stating, *"I made my selection because I anticipated that the TV or refrigerator would overturn."*

Participants shared both positive and negative feedback regarding their experiences in the game. Among those with positive experiences, Participant K4 stated, *"It was amazing! I've never tried this (virtual reality) before. I completely forgot about this place (the physical environment)!"* Another participant, K9, expressed surprise at the earthquake effect and overall satisfaction with the experience, describing it as *"Very fun!"* and *"Highly impressive!"* For participants unfamiliar with virtual reality, the game created a sense of curiosity. For example, Participant K3 expressed interest in the virtual environment and the gameplay options, saying, *"Let it collapse a bit; I want to see that."* Another participant, K4, questioned whether they could move within the virtual environment. Similarly, Participant K11 explored their surroundings during the earthquake simulation to understand what was happening while maintaining their position. They also changed locations by crawling on their knees, minimizing movement during the shaking. However, some participants expressed anxiety about the earthquake simulation. For instance, Participant K10 commented, *"Right now, beside the couch feels safer than under the table. The table—it could be the model—doesn't seem very sturdy to me, so I prefer to stay here (Safe Zone 01)."* This reaction highlighted the need to establish a sense of environmental safety. Participant K1 reflected on prior knowledge, stating, *"I read somewhere before that you should never go under a table."* Similarly, Participant K6 said, *"I'm trying to figure out which is safer. If this (Set 4.1) falls on me, I think I can lift it, so I'm choosing this one,"* emphasizing their search for a safe zone. Another participant, K8, in the bedroom scenario, opted to move after selecting furniture, choosing to crouch in a location they perceived as safer—a corner away from the outer walls of the room and heavy, tall furniture. These indicate that participants internalized their actions and choices as tasks, actively engaging in problem-solving to stay safe and addressing challenges they encountered during the game.

As part of the study, a two-stage survey was administered to participants to collect data.

In the first part of the survey, participants were asked questions about their familiarity with VR tools and environments before experiencing the game. This section was conducted online before the gameplay session. The questions aimed to assess whether participants were familiar with VR tools and environments, the reasons for their familiarity, and their proficiency levels. The data revealed that 41.6% of the participants were familiar with VR tools and environments, while the majority (58.3%) had no prior experience. Those familiar with VR technologies had gained this familiarity through activities such as gaming, exploring virtual spaces, content creation, and attending virtual exhibitions.

This indicates that participants' familiarity with VR tools, environments, and technologies largely stemmed from personal interests and preferences. Among participants familiar with VR equipment (e.g., headsets, touch controllers), approximately 50% demonstrated moderate proficiency. This suggests that while a small number of participants had prior exposure to VR technologies, their experience and usage were relatively limited.

In the second part of the survey, participants were asked about their earthquake awareness, including whether they had previously experienced an earthquake, how such events made them feel, their knowledge of precautions to take before and during an earthquake while indoors, and the sources of this information.

A significant majority, representing 75% of participants, had experienced an earthquake before. One participant described their feelings during an earthquake as follows: *"Mostly fear and panic, along with a sense of not knowing what to do at that moment."* (K7). Another shared: *"Panic, chaos, uncertainty."* (K6). A different participant, (K1), reflected: *"Since it happens so suddenly, you're left unsure of what to do. Not knowing what to do is the hardest part."* Most participants emphasized the panic they felt during the earthquake, highlighting the anxiety, fear, and chaos caused by their lack of knowledge and experience about what actions to take during such an event.

Regarding their understanding of precautions, 66.6% of participants considered themselves sufficiently informed about what to do before and during an earthquake while indoors. Participants reported that they primarily obtained this information from video-sharing and social media platforms (75%), websites (66.6%), television and radio (50%), and printed materials such as magazines, newspapers, books, brochures, or ads (50%). These responses indicate that participants predominantly rely on social media and web-based communication tools to acquire earthquake-related knowledge. However, despite possessing this information, the panic, fear, and anxiety they described suggest that their knowledge does not translate into confidence or effective action during an earthquake. In other words, the lack of experiential learning prevents participants from internalizing this knowledge, creating a barrier to problem-solving in such critical situations.

In the online post-experiment survey, participants were asked to share their opinions, thoughts, and suggestions regarding the game experience. The survey included questions about the game's features, how it differs from other games, challenges encountered during gameplay, and for improvement.

All participants unanimously agreed that the game was educational. A significant majority found the game intriguing (92%), and half (50%) reported it as an engaging experience. Additionally, some participants described the game as entertaining (33%).

The responses indicate that the game was not only perceived as educational but also highly engaging, particularly because it allowed participants to experience earthquake scenarios and responses through technology that facilitates both theoretical learning and experiential engagement.

Participants noted that the game's real-life connection, educational and experiential nature, and ability to raise awareness distinguished it from other games (66.6%). One participant, (K1), summarized this sentiment: *"It's both educational, fun, and raises awareness."* Another, (K4), remarked: *"...Experiencing ideas that might not be feasible in a real situation was both enjoyable and highly effective in providing preliminary knowledge, thanks to features like shaking offered by the VR headset."* A third participant shared: *"It felt less like a game and more like being in an educational simulation."* (K12).

These statements emphasize the game's distinctiveness for students, arising from its ability to offer practical engagement with a phenomenon through an exploratory environment and technology. This aligns with the principles of serious games, as the proposed game demonstrates educational objectives, structured rules, and processes designed to facilitate learning through experience while fostering awareness. The participants' feedback highlights these characteristics as distinguishing features, suggesting that the game successfully achieves its intended goals of experiential learning and raising awareness.

The majority of participants (66.6%) reported that they did not encounter difficulties while playing the game. However, one participant shared their challenge during gameplay: *"Although there were some guiding texts, I had to listen to the instructions provided during the experience to figure out what to do the first time."* (K9). Another participant, (K1), reflected: *"It was a bit difficult as I was introduced to a new technology, but I am very pleased to have learned,"* expressing both the difficulty and the value of the experience. These responses indicate that the verbal instructions provided by the researcher during the game were perceived positively by some participants but were less effective for others. Additionally, familiarity and proficiency with virtual environments, tools, and technologies emerged as factors positively influencing the gameplay experience.

While 66.6% of participants believe the game should be improved, their feedback can be classified into three categories: narrative, performance and optimization, and interaction level.

Narrative

One participant, (K6), suggested: *"Instead of external guidance, the game itself could guide the player, maybe through a small meta-scenario. For instance, a storyline where due to increased earthquakes, people have technology enabling them to select furniture alternatives moments before the quake."* Another participant, (K6), proposed: *"There could be more furniture alternatives, and scenarios branching out based on those choices. For example, if a piece of furniture falls on us, the game could continue with a scenario where we're trapped under the debris."*

Performance and Optimization

A participant, (K10), mentioned encountering bugs that impacted their decisions and overall experience, while another, (K7), pointed out shadow issues with furniture changes and suggested improvements in textures and materials.

Interaction Level

One participant (K4) highlighted the accessibility of the interface: *"The interface is simple enough for even a beginner to enjoyably complete the (learning) process. Many people memorize written information but forget it, postponing necessary precautions. This makes the game a valuable effort to address such issues."*

Participants acknowledged the game's educational nature (K10), its facilitation of active learning (K4), ease of use (K4), and ability to raise awareness (K8). Suggestions for further development included adding a narrative (K3, K6), including different locations simulating earthquake scenarios (K11), diversifying the plot and scenarios (K2, K9, K10), improving the game's technical infrastructure (K2), expanding the play area (K5), enhancing the variety of objects and situations for interaction (K8), increasing the game's reality to better reflect possible earthquake scenarios (K2, K7). The participants' feedback underscores the game's potential as a serious game with an educational focus while providing directions for enhancing its functionality, engagement, and overall impact.

FINDINGS

The findings of the study, based on the analysis and evaluation of data obtained through visual methods, informal conversations, and surveys related to the VR game experience and feedback, are categorized under two main headings: "findings on earthquake awareness", and "findings on game experience".

Findings on Earthquake Awareness

The primary sources of information for participants regarding earthquake awareness are websites, video-sharing and social media platforms, and other web-based communication tools. Considering that the participants are between the ages of 18 and 31, it is evident that the majority of the group (91.6%) belongs to the younger generation. Given young people's remarkable demand for and inclination toward technology in education, it is crucial for educators to incorporate new technologies into educational environments and systems. Adopting more visual and interactive methods to facilitate quick and easy access to information is particularly significant. In this context, Mayer's (2009) argument that active, effective, and lasting learning can be achieved by integrating multimedia (text, sound, and images/graphics) into educational processes with the support of technology further supports these findings.

Findings on Game Experience

During the gameplay phase, participants provided significant feedback regarding the game's purpose, narrative, gameplay, level of interaction, and performance and optimization. According to participants, the standout features of the virtual reality experience were its educational and curiosity-invoking aspects. As a serious game, the primary objective of the application is to educate. Nevertheless, using VR technology and environments to simulate earthquake scenarios and behaviors introduces an innovative and exploratory medium for teaching and learning, making the experience both exciting and engaging.

Sherman and Craig (2019) describe the concept of physical (or sensory) immersion, which distinguishes VR from other media types, as "the feeling of being in an environment" (p. 10). Immersion measures how much attention the player gives to the game or how deeply they are engaged with the virtual world (Bostan 2021, p. 208). Atiker (2021) connects the level of immersion to the concept of flow, noting that as players become more familiar with this synthetic environment, their awareness of the medium decreases. One participant (K9) stated that listening to external instructions diminished their connection to the game, highlighting that interventions from outside the VR experience can disrupt or interrupt the gameplay. This suggests the importance of incorporating a 'tutorial' or 'briefing' phase into the game, as well as embedding gameplay tips and feedback within the software itself. These elements are critical for ensuring a seamless and engaging user experience while enabling players to become familiar with the VR interface and equipment.

In digital games, players are generally informed about how to make their choices through controllers (Salen and Zimmerman 2004). Players may use various mechanisms to perform their actions, with the critical factor being that these choices influence the game's narrative on a micro and/or macro level. Feedback on the outcomes of these choices provides context for the player's subsequent decisions, thus enabling the system to function effectively (Salen and Zimmerman 2004). Through the options or preferences presented within the game, the player or participant can alter the fictional world and/or diversify their actions within the narrative; all of this contributes to the interactive storytelling experience (Bostan 2021, p. 84). In this context, participants' suggestions to enhance the sense of realism in the game (K2, K6, and K11) are significant. In the developed game proposal, the number of micro-level choices in the narrative, or the objects, environments, or situations with which the player interacts is limited. Therefore, to make the fictional world more vivid and realistic, it is necessary to elevate the expected level of interaction to a macro scale and thoroughly analyze how and in what ways the player engages with different elements. Similarly, participants' remarks, (K6 and K8), regarding the potential for varied choices and scenarios in the game confirm the need to elaborate on the narrative—specifically, to diversify the available options and their consequences.

According to the survey, the majority of participants (58.3%) had no prior experience with VR tools or environments. However, throughout the experiment, guidance provided by the researcher regarding the actions to be performed within the VR/game environment helped participants develop basic interface and hardware usage skills. As a result, each participant could complete their experience within the anticipated playtime (or even in less time). On the other hand, feedback from one participant, emphasizing that the game would be more engaging if it guided users independently rather than relying on external instructions (K6), is particularly noteworthy. It appears that the in-game hints and guidance within the user interface were insufficient to keep players immersed in the context and maintain a continuous flow. This aligns with Atiker's (2021) assertion that "The continuity of flow is directly proportional to isolation from real-world space and time" (p. 330). Additionally, technical issues related to performance and optimization—such as bugs and problems with lighting and shadows—emerged as critical feedback, highlighting the need for improvements to the game.

In the context of residential interiors, the study emphasizes the educational use of video games and related hardware for arranging, selecting, and positioning non-structural elements (specifically furniture, equipment, and lighting fixtures) in living and sleeping areas during earthquakes, based on two distinct scenarios and different experience sets. This aligns with Lovreglio et al.'s (2017) focus on the application of games for educational purposes.

Serious games, known for their educational value, particularly among young people and children (Binark et al. 2009), have proven effective in helping participants—design students in this study—understand and experience real-life situations. However, the findings also highlight the need to reorganize the constructed narrative to make it more realistic, and inclusive. This includes diversifying scenarios to encompass various situations/processes, expanding the level of interactions, and ensuring the player experience remains uninterrupted.

CONCLUSION

This study focuses on non-structural elements in residential interiors where the likelihood of encountering an earthquake is significantly high. It aims to promote earthquake preparedness and awareness by reducing and preventing potential damage. The risks posed by these elements during and after an earthquake, as well as measures to mitigate these risks, are specifically examined in the context of furniture, equipment, and lighting elements.

Findings from the study suggest that serious games can foster societal awareness of disasters like earthquakes. VR tools and environments can simulate the dynamics of such events and processes, offering an interactive and inclusive platform for the organization, design, and implementation of non-structural elements in residential interiors. These characteristics make VR a highly effective and lasting medium for teaching and learning.

By refining the game's narrative and scenarios to immerse the player, addressing both technical and informational disruptions that could interrupt the game flow, and incorporating additional features and alternative scenarios, the game can become a broader platform for raising awareness and disseminating knowledge. Serious games used for educational purposes enable participants/players to experience, interpret, and learn by doing in realistic scenarios. This method could raise awareness and educate society on mitigating adverse conditions before, during, and after earthquakes through experiential learning.

Future research could expand the participant profile and group size to explore different contexts (e.g., hospitals, schools, shopping malls, or open spaces) and processes. This approach would measure how the proposed educational tool achieves its learning goals. Given the diversity of disasters, scenarios can be developed for different target groups or situations. Multiplayer learning environments could also be introduced. Additionally, integrating tutorial or briefing phases more cohesively into the game could enhance user adaptation to virtual tools and technologies, sustaining engagement for longer periods.

This study highlights the importance of interdisciplinary collaboration in developing new teaching and learning methods for educators. It supports students in solving design problems through experiential learning via video games. Moreover, it contributes knowledge and methodologies for preparing for earthquakes (and other disasters), disaster resiliency and a culture of preparedness and risk mitigation. The research has significant economic and political implications, aiming to create a resilient and disaster-ready society. Furthermore, by fostering internalized learning, it seeks to prevent individuals from responding to adverse conditions with panic, anxiety, or chaos.

Ultimately, this study is expected to assist experts, institutions, and organizations in identifying more effective and lasting ways to raise social awareness of disasters like earthquakes.

ENDNOTE

[1] This study was produced from the unpublished thesis titled *A Virtual Reality Experience Proposal for Raising Public Awareness in Earthquakes* by Merve Öksüz, under the co-advisory of Prof. Dr. Özge Cordan and Assoc. Prof. Dr. Güven Çatak.

ACKNOWLEDGMENTS

This study was supported by the Istanbul Technical University Research Project within the scope of the Performance Based Research Project with project number 44095. We would like to thank Bahcesehir University BUG LAB for providing their facility for experiencing case study games. We also would like to thank Zeynep Burcu Kaya for contributing to the realization of the game of the study, and ITU Interior Architecture and BAU Game Design undergraduate students for participating in the experimental phase of the study.

REFERENCES

Aarseth, E. 2007. I Fought the Law: Transgressive Play and The Implied Player. Kopenhag: Authors & Digital Games Research Association (DIGRA).

Atiker, B. 2021. Artırılmış Gerçeklik Oyunları. pp. 307–335. *In*: E. Süngü and B. Barbaros (eds). Dijital Oyunlar 1.0 Oynanış ve Anlam. Nobel.

Binark, M., Bayraktutan, G. and ve Fidaner, I.B. 2009. Dijital Oyun Rehberi. Kalkedon.

Brooks Jr, F.P. 2010. The Design of Design: Essays From a Computer Scientist. Addison-Wesley Professional.

Bostan, B. 2021. Dijital Oyunlar ve İnteraktif Anlatı (1b). The Kitap.

Caserman, P., Hoffmann, K., Müller, P., Schaub, M., Straßburg, K., Wiemeyer, J., et al. 2020. Quality criteria for serious games: Serious part, game part, and balance. JMIR Serious Games. 8(3). https://doi.org/10.2196/19037.

Doğan, C. 2020. Hareketli Mekân Tasarımındaki Ergonomik Faktörlerin Deprem Bölgesi Konutlarına Uygulanması. Journal of Architecture and Life. 5(2). doi: https://doi.org/10.26835/my.803977.

Dörner, R., Göbel, S., Effelsberg, W. and Wiemeyer, J. 2016. Serious Games Foundations, Concepts, and Practice. Cham, Switzerland: Springer International Publishing.

Ertaş Beşir, S., and Dereci, Ş. 2021. Deprem sırasında konut i-ç mekânlarında yapısal olmayan elemanların yarattığı riskler ve alınabilecek önlemler. International Social Mentality and Researcher Thinkers Journal. 7(42): 350–360. doi: http://dx.doi.org/10.31576/smryj.818.

FEMA. https://www.fema.gov/sites/default/files/2020-07/fema_earthquakes_reducing-the-risks-of-nonstructural-earthquake-damage—a-practical-guide-fema-e-74.pdf>, erişim tarihi 10.01.2023.

Garip, S.B., Garip, E., Birgönül, Z. and Güzelci, H. 2023. An analytical approach to identify design criteria for reducing earthquake risks in residential interiors. ITU A|Z. 20(1): 47–264.

Kaneko, M. 2012. Fixing and layout of furniture and fixtures. *In*: The Japan Institute of Architects (JIA), & Japan Aseismic Safety Organization (JASO) (eds). Earthquake-resistant Building Design for Architects. Shokokusha.

Karamanoğlu, M. and Ulay, G. 2017. Deprem Riski Yüksek Binalarda İç Mekan Düzenlemelerinin İncelenmesi (Tosya Örneği). Journal of Foresty Faculty. 186-193.

Liang, H., Liang, F., Wu, F., Wang, C. and Jian Chang. 2018. Development of a VR prototype for enhancing earthquake evacuee safety. *In*: VRCAI '18: Proceedings of the 16th ACM SIGGRAPH International Conference on Virtual-Reality Continuum and Its Applications in Industry, Tokyo, Japan. 1–8. https://doi.org/10.1145/3284398.328441.

Lovreglio, R., Gonzalez, V., Amor, R., Spearpoint, M., Thomas, J., Trotter, M., et al. 2017. The need for enhancing earthquake evacuee safety by using virtual reality serious games. *In*: Procceedings of Lean and Computing in Construction Congress (LC3). Volume I. pp. 381–438. Heraklion, Crete, Greece. https://doi.org/10.24928/JC3-2017/0058.

Mayer, R.E. 2009. Multimedia Learning (2b). New York: Cambridge University Press.

Michael, D. and Chen, S. 2006. Serious Games: Games That Educate, Train, and Inform. Boston: Thomson Course Technology.

Oksuz, M. and Cordan, O. 2022. Using video games for design education: An example of developing earthquake scenarios for home environments. Journal of Design Studio. 4(2): ICMEK-5 Rethinking. 65—73.

Ritterfeld, U. and Weber, R. 2005. Video games for entertainment and education. *In*: P. Vorderer and J. Bryant (Dü) içinde, Playing Video Games-Motives, Responses, and Consequences. 399–413. New Jersey: Lawrence Erlbaum Associates.

Salen, K. and Zimmerman, E. 2004. Rules of Play: Game Design Fundamentals. MIT Press.

Sanoff, H. 2016. Visual Research Methods in Design. Routledge Revivals. doi:10.4324/9781315541822.

Sarı, O. and Aktar, E. 2017. Deprem Sonrası Yapılan/Yapılacak Binalarda Engelli ve Yaşlılara Dönük Düzenlemelere İlişkin Uygulayıcıların Görüşleri: Van İli Örneği. İnsan ve Toplum Bilimleri Araştırmaları Dergisi. 6(1): 482–499.

Sherman, W.R. and Craig, A.B. 2019. Understanding Virtual Reality: Interface, Application, and Design. Morgan Kaufmann.

Shaluf, I.M. 2007. Disaster types. Disaster Prevention, and Management, an International Journal. 16(5): 704–717. https://doi.org/10.1108/09653560710837019.

Stenros, J. 2016. The game definition game: A review. Games and Culture. 12(6): 499–520. doi:https://doi.org/10.1177/1555412016655679.

Strauss, A.L. and Corbin, J. 1990. Basics of Qualitative Research: Grounded Theory Procedures and Techniques. Sage.

TMMOB İçmimarlar Odası. 2023. March. TMMOB İçmimarlar Odası Deprem Bildirgesi. https://www.icmimarlarodasi.org.tr/haber_detay/270.

Zeisel, J. 2006. Inquiry by Design: Environment/Behavior/Neuroscience in Architecture, Interiors, Landscape, and Planning. New York: W.W. Norton & Company.

Chapter 15

Regenerating a Memory Place in the Virtual World: Taşkışla

Demet Arslan Dinçay
Department of Interior Architecture, Faculty of Architecture,
Istanbul Technical University (TR)

INTRODUCTION

It is fascinating how virtual environments have opened up new possibilities for experiencing space. As Tuan notes, movement and experience are vital factors in determining the meaning of a physical space. When these experiences are collective and continuous, a space becomes a cherished memory place (2001). From this point of view, creating a memory space in a virtual environment requires a multidimensional process. A memory place is perceived by memories and cultural values by the users in the physical environment, so it is also expected to reflect these meanings in the virtual world.

The use of immersive technologies such as virtual reality (VR), augmented reality (AR), and mixed reality (MR) in the field of cultural heritage is growing and attracting user attention. These technologies benefit the documentation, preservation, and conservation of cultural environments, and provide great convenience for tourism.

For Correspondence: dincayd@itu.edu.tr

DOI: 10.1201/9781003581642-15

With the help of immersive technologies, many people can explore heritage sites and historic buildings from a distance without any physical effort. Unlike the physical world, where our senses of touch, sight, and movement play a critical role in how we perceive a place, digital environments offer innovative perceptual experiences through immersive technologies. According to El-Hakim et al. (2004), Virtual Heritage reconstruction has several motivations, including documenting, reconstructing, creating educational resources for history and culture, visualizing scenes from viewpoints impossible in the real world due to size or accessibility issues, interacting with objects without risk of damage, and providing virtual tourism and virtual museum exhibits (El-Hakim et al. 2004). To achieve these aims, several heritage places have been modeled with immersive technologies (Foni et al. 2002, Vlahakis et al. 2001). Memory places also regenerate in the virtual world with similar aims.

Existing research on immersive technologies in cultural heritage primarily focuses on tourism, with some applications positively impacting tourists' perceptions while others have adverse effects, according to the authors (Merkx and Nawijn 2021, Wei et al. 2019). Besides, regenerating cultural sites virtually is crucial for preserving and conserving heritage materials and is attractive for the first experience of spaces.

Immersive technologies have recently enhanced immersion in user experiences by combining physical and virtual settings, primarily centered on cognition and emotions (Flavián et al. 2019). A place in the physical world is defined by the experiences that people have been there. These experiences build up over time and create a collective memory unique to that particular space. Although digital technologies have made it possible to recreate a place in the virtual world in realistic views, it is important to note that the experience of the virtual memory space has to include different components that enhance the user perception. Addison notes a lack of perception in the digital experience since heritage is as much about the living and evolving place, people, and environment as any static monument or landscape (2000).

This study aims to explore how users perceive virtual memory spaces in terms of user experience and sense of presence. Specifically, the study seeks to answer the questions of whether virtual space is regarded as a novel experience or merely a reminder of physical space, and what is the role of individual memories in physical spaces in shaping perceptions of virtual space. To achieve these goals, the study was structured around a theoretical framework, a case study, and a survey. The theoretical framework examined the themes of space, place, and presence in both physical and virtual environments. The case study focused on designing Taşkışla Digital, an AR-based virtual memory space, and at the end the study presented the results of a survey that measured user perception in terms of experience and sense of presence.

CONCEPTUAL FRAMEWORK FOR PHYSICAL/ VIRTUAL SPACE EXPERIENCE

To make sense of the concept of virtual memory space, it is necessary to define the themes that make up the physical space and the concepts of physical memory space. Space experience in the physical world encloses physical, sensitive, and perceptual assets in general. Yi Fu Tuan (2001) determined physical space and the dynamics of its experience. For Tuan, space is just limited to geographical location and its contours. As we start to interact in space, it becomes more familiar to us and turns into place. Through our movements and experiences in space, we construct meanings and create places (Tuan 2001). As per Heidegger's philosophy, spaces do not come into existence through the mathematical grasp of space but through the human experience of place (Sharr 2007). Similarly, Lefebvre (2007) introduces the concept of space by using "abstract and social" definitions. All these basic definitions are related to interaction and movement in physical space. Based on the fact that what makes a space into a place is the users' experience. The continuity and collectiveness of the spatial space experiences, transform the space into a memory space. When it comes to virtual worlds, there are significant differences in terms of space experience. Virtual worlds are immersive environments designed to simulate the experience of being in a physical space. These environments allow users to interact with objects, spaces, and even other virtual characters. Unlike the real world, which we experience through our senses, virtual worlds rely entirely on technology to create a sense of immersion (Skulmowski and Rey 2018).

The term 'presence' is used to describe the experience of being in and perceiving a virtual world. The concept of presence is related to embodiment wands as emphasized by Merleau-Ponty (2010) in his philosophy embodiment. He refers to how the body shapes and is shaped by our perception and experience of the physical world. Ponty argues that the body is not just a passive tool or biological entity through which we engage with the outside world but rather an active participant in processes of perception and understanding and a source of significance. Our bodies serve as both the vehicle through which we interact with the outside world and how we express ourselves and interact with others. For him, the body is crucial to our subjectivity and understanding of the world (Ponty 2012). The concept of the embodiment has also been discussed with the presence of virtual environments. It refers to the psychological and emotional connection that users establish with a virtual environment and the sensation of being in a place. Space interaction is enabled by sensory immersion in virtual worlds to make up for the deficiency of the body's sensation. Research has shown that having a virtual body in immersive VR can contribute to the sense of being in a virtual location. The embodiment has three subcomponents: the sense of self-location, the sense of agency, and the sense of body ownership (Kilteni et al. 2012).

Sensory immersion refers to the realistic experience of sensory stimuli in a virtual environment, including sound and touch. Spatial immersion refers to the believability of the virtual space as a real, three-dimensional location that the user can navigate and interact with. Cognitive immersion refers to the level of engagement and absorption the user experiences while interacting with the virtual environment and performing tasks or activities (Cummings and Bailenson 2016). The reality of the virtual space affects the user's perception. Various Immersive technologies have different assets to create a realistic world.

VR can create a strong sense of immersion and presence by creating a realistic and believable virtual environment and engaging the user's senses and cognitive processes. The sense of presence is influenced by both physical and cognitive factors and can be affected by both the virtual environment and the user's state of mind (Teras and Raghunathan 2015). Although Presence is closely associated with VR rather than AR, AR can offer a form of presence when digital elements seamlessly merge with the real world, providing an engaging MR experience with distinctions from typical VR experiences (IxDF 2023).

Virtual Memory Place Experience

The meaning of a place is derived from the actions and presence of individuals within it. Our experience of space is closely linked to how we move within it. This creates a unique space that is associated with physical presence and memory. Therefore, a place in our memory should encompass the time spent there, our movements, and all tangible and intangible communication forms. However, transferring this physical correlation to virtual space will inevitably result in significant differences.

Memory place can be described as a familiar place that is mapped in an individual's memories. According to Raymond Williams (1983), landscape/space has a different quality for those who remember it. When it's a case of communities instead of individuals, the concept of a collective memory comes to the agenda. Spaces that have similar meanings for a community such as Heritage sites may also define the memory places, through their impact on collective memory. In other words, the value of a cultural heritage lies in individual and collective memories, and a place becomes meaningful when linked to memories. The process of collective memory is constantly evolving and influenced by social, cultural, and political factors. It is commonly associated with physical space that is perceptible with sensations. A public building like a castle, palace, or theater, which has witnessed life in it and surrounds it for generations, is a cultural heritage site and a memory place.

According to Tuan (2001), if a sculpture is an image of feeling, a successful building is an entire functional realm made visible and tangible. Tuan reveals the time and place relation with their approaches: time as motion or flow and place as a pause in the temporal current; attachment to place as a function of time captured in the phrase, "it takes time to know a place"; and place as time made visible, or place as a memorial to times past. Similarly, Merleau-Ponty maintains that perception is not an event or state in the mind or brain but an organism's entire bodily relation to its environment (2012). It's possible to say that time is the crucial component for place perception, and each visit to a space/ memory space creates a unique perception in an individual's mind. Similarly, Trigg notices that past and present experiences retranslate memory and place and are always at odds. How we experience a place in the present is never the same experience of that place. Body and cognition respond to the environment to create and remember a place, defined as lived spatiality and an expression of being in the world (Ponty 2012). The correlation between movement, time, and social interaction within a space will create a completely new perception

When it comes to experiencing a memory space in the virtual world, there are two distinct experiences of the same place with different dynamics. The virtual representation of the physical space is a new expression process that keeps the memory of the physical space alive. Lombard and Ditton (1997) reviewed a broad body of literature related to the presence and identified six different conceptualizations of presence: realism, immersion, transportation, social richness, social actor within a medium, and medium as social actor. This approach can be explanatory in terms of classifying the concept of presence in a virtual memory space.

Memory space is created through social relations, and exists not only in an individual's perception but also in collective perception. Expect personal spaces, most memory places may also define a cultural heritage example. From this point of view, much research in the virtual heritage field can shed light on virtual memory space studies. According to Addison (2000), virtual heritage can be a bilateral tool and its successes are related to technological opportunities and the ability of the appliers. Although some 3D presentations and immersive technologies offer innovative experiments for a cultural heritage place via high virtual technologies and realistic models, some virtual worlds remain static and lifeless (Addison 2000). According to Whirt et al.'s research (2007), media's immersive capacities make users believe they are personally and physically "present" in the displayed environment). If the media provide highly immersive technologies, humans may respond with feelings of Spatial Presence. However, immersive impulses are not provided by the media product; internal processes, for example, imagination, can compensate for that deficit in external stimulation—at least to a certain degree.

An increasing number of researchers are beginning to view the virtual world as a blend of meaningful components, symbolic representations, human activity, and dynamic interaction (Champion and Dave 2007). According to Pujol and Champion (2012), Presence is an umbrella term with specific sub-definitions for different context domains. To them, the widespread use of VR in cultural heritage has implicitly introduced the concept of Cultural Presence.

Thus, when we talk about cultural heritage places and/or memory places, it's essential to consider not just the physical presence of the place, but also its deeper meaning, cultural value, and also the impact of past experiences and memories in it. Similarly, Riva et al. (2002) noticed that presence will be enhanced if the content is realistic and relevant in terms of social or cultural factors (Riva et al. 2002). For a memory place the relevant social and cultural factors may define the practices in the space. As Trigg (2012) observed each memory is associated with certain practices in a physical space. Moreover, each experience could form a new structure in the user's mind for the same place (Trigg 2012). In this point of view, the practices in a memory space are based on action patterns that are often repeated or unique experiences that belong to an individual's memory. Thus while creating a virtual memory place, providing interactive experiences that augment users' memories and power of imagination as the key factors. Therefore, the success of a virtual space is related to the regeneration of these memories or actions.

STUDY METHODOLOGY

The study is based on the evaluation of virtual space experience and the following research questions:

- How can the effect of the representation of a physical memory place in a virtual environment on the user be defined?
- Is this experience new or familiar to the user?
- How does the virtual experience interact with physical space in memory?
- Can memories affect a user's perception in an experience of virtual memory space?

The Taşkışla building, which is a memory space, was modeled in a virtual environment and used as the research setting for this study under the name Taşkışla Digital. As a first step, former users who have strong ties with the physical building were allowed to experience the virtual space. For the second stage, a survey measuring UX and PRESENCE dimensions was presented to the users. The research questions were evaluated according to the survey results.

Research Setting: Taşkışla Digital

This study includes an evaluation of Taşkışla Digital as a virtual memory place in terms of user experience. The original building, dated the 19th century, was designed by English architect William James Smith. A Neo-Renaissance style is predominant in the facades and architectural elements. Taşkışla was built to provide the Medical School with modern equipment in a brand-new masonry building. In 1849, the building was converted into military barracks while construction works continued. Taşkışla was a military hospital for French soldiers during the Crimean War (1853-56). During the Balkan Wars, Taşkışla was again used as a hospital and was finally allocated to Istanbul Technical University in 1944. Since 1944 building has been used as an architectural faculty with a significant role in the professional development of designer candidates (Overview Taşkışla).

This place holds significant historical value and has contributed greatly to the city and it has been a collective memory space for decades in many designers' and Istanbulities' minds. Memory Places are physical embodiments of shared memory, connecting people with the past, honoring essential figures and events, and facilitating a greater appreciation of our collective heritage. For the concept of collective memory and place relationship, French sociologist Maurice Halbwachs observed that every collective memory is formed within a spatial framework (Halbwachs 1992). This framework may include a country, city, buildings, and squares. According to Halbwachs, spatial frameworks serve as protectors that help us preserve our impressions and understand the past. Pierre Nora (1989) further explains that collective memory sites around specific attachment points to the past, which develop into symbolic figures. These sites of memory, be they material or immaterial, such as buildings, places, events, acts, books, and people, become icons that shape our understanding of the past. In other words, these sites are significant because of their meaning. They convey rather than their material presence. From this point of view, Taşkışla is a crucial memory space for their users in physical and symbolic ways. It has been an education building and a habitat for the users for decades (Figure 15.1).

Figure 15.1 Taşkışla, İTÜ Faculty of Architecture, Taşkışla Building (author's archive).

Taşkışla Digital is an AR-based virtual space created during the 2020 pandemic time. The model's original intention was to create a virtual exhibition, but it has evolved to something greater—a virtual representation of Taşkışla. The primary goal is to virtually capture the deep bond that its graduates, former and current users share and the building.

Taşkışla Digital was developed with Unity and complied with WebGL. The front view, entrance hall, and two main corridors of Taşkışla were modeled based on plans, sections, and photos. The colors and textures of the interior were also closely matched to the original.

Additionally, courtyard photos were incorporated into the Model to provide a sense of the interior-exterior spaces. Once the virtual space was created, the Digital Exhibition team prepared the students' projects in jpeg format and displayed them on grid boards, mimicking the physical setup. The aim is to keep the application's hardware requirements to a minimum so that anyone who wants to enter the exhibition can access it.

At the beginning of the project, some principles were determined:

1. The Model should be as close to reality as possible. (Realistic Model)
2. Render and shaders should focus on a realistic appearance rather than a stylistic one. (Realistic Material and Render)
3. The Model's polygon count should be at a level that can run on older computers. (Low Polygon)
4. It should be able to display approximately 3,000 sheets.
5. It should load quickly.
6. It should be interactive. Exhibition materials sheets should be viewed and examined in detail with tools such as Zoom and Pan.

A Sketchup model was created for the first stage, using the ground floor plan and facade drawings in DWG format. However, due to issues with shading and reflection, the Blender software used to create the model experienced difficulties. The advanced animation and modeling tools in Blender have improved the success of the Taşkışla model (Figure 15.2).

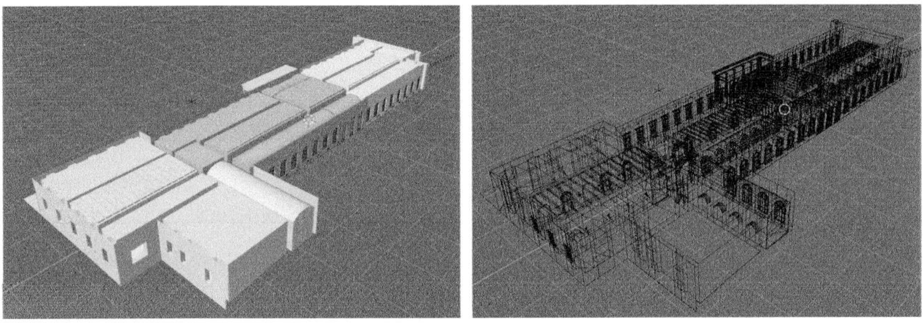

Figure 15.2 Partial model of Taşkışla (author's archive).

The Blender model only includes the exhibition area in Taşkışla. These restrictions reduced the polygon count and saved time. The most challenging part of the modeling process was producing surface textures. After the main textures were created, additional normal maps were generated to enhance the lighting and shadows on the surface. Textures called roughness maps were prepared to make the reflections more realistic during the modeling of the windows. These textures allowed for the creation of dusty surfaces on the windows. Highly realistic visuals were produced by avoiding homogeneous reflections when light hits the windows.

After the modeling and material production stages were completed, the production of realistic scenes in Unity began. Due to solving the restrictions of Unity, light mapping was used. Instead of calculating lighting hundreds of times per second, performance was optimized by using light textures. All lights, reflections, and shadows are pre-calculated in the current application. Reflections in specific areas are captured in advance using a reflection probe method.

Cummings and Bailenson (2016) suggest that the level of presence experienced by users has a significant impact on their engagement time, interaction capacity, and cognitive load. The degree of presence is considered a measure of the system's effectiveness, and it depends on several elements that influence the user's sensation of presence. To enhance the user's presence level, exact details of the interior space, color, texture, and lighting conditions are transferred, along with the significant symbols of living in Taşkışla, such as cats.

For the last stage, exhibition materials were added to the application as sheets. The number of materials is approximately 3,000 sheets for each semester. Each sheet is around 5 MB, so the total file size would be around 15,000 MB. A Photoshop macro was created to ensure each student's files have the same size and extension.

Figure 15.3 Scenes from Taşkışla Digital (https://mim.itu.edu.tr/blog/2021/03/17/webgl/).

Since the end of the 2020 fall semester, students and faculty members have had access to the Taşkışla Digital Exhibition. Users with strong connections to the building provided favorable feedback for the application, especially during the pandemic. Digital Exhibition, planned to update the application by replacing the sheets and one datasheet without building and compiling it using Unity for each new semester. In other words, the application has been made dynamic.

Design of the Survey

With the scope of this study, a survey was created to measure the user experience for Taşkışla Digital as the virtual memory space. The survey involved 23 participants (14 female and 9 male); aged between 24 and 46, with an average age of 23.5. All of them were graduates who received education in Taşkışla for a period of 4–8 years. According to their self-reported statements, all participants had a strong connection with the building, although they had not used it for quite some time.

The survey is composed of three parts: user's profile, user experience, and presence experience. The first part's questions aim to reveal the users' profile such as age, gender, connection with the building, and familiarity with the virtual environments. The questions about familiarity are rated on a Likert scale of 1 to 5, where 1 indicates strong disagreement and 5 indicates strong agreement in this part.

For the second and third parts of the survey, employees are expected to rate virtual memory space through the study's main objective.

The second part was about User Experience (UX). To measure UX, the AttrakDiff2 questionnaire (Hassenzahl et al. 2003) which is based on the two-component model (pragmatic and hedonic subjective quality perception), was used. At the beginning of the survey, employees are expected to rate their virtual space experience due to the Likert scale. Then, they are asked to choose between the word pairs that they think will fit the virtual place best for them. This part consists of both hedonic stimulation (dull-captivating; ordinary-novel) and attractiveness (unpleasant-pleasant; bad-good) components.

The third part of the survey is centered around the concept of spatial presence. Hartmann et al.'s research was utilized to create the questionnaire. According to Hartmann et al. (2015), there are several scales for measuring spatial presence. Some of them and the main principles are:

The Presence Questionnaire (PQ) by Witmer and Singer (1998) is used to assess the quality of various inputs and experiences provided. The PQ not only aims to assess the intensity of spatial presence as a state but also strives to assess contributing factors (Witmer and Singer 1998).

The Igroup Presence Questionnaire (IPQ) by Schubert (2003) and Schubert et al. (2001) aims to measure spatial presence as a sense of "being there" in interactive virtual environments. The IPQ measures three potential subcomponents of presence (Schubert 2003): spatial presence ("being surrounded by the virtual environment, directly interacting in it…, and a sense of transportation to another place"; involvement ("focusing on the virtual environment instead of focusing on the real world"), and realness ("how real the virtual environment is judged to be").

Having its origins in MEC-SPQ (Vorderer et al. 2004) The Spatial Experience Scale (Hartmann et al. 2015) is proposed as an alternative measure of presence with two subdimensions: Self-Location and Possible Actions. Self-location part about feelings of "being there" or "being physically present" in the media environment. Self-location may also imply that users feel like they have departed from their real environment and feel like they have stepped into another place. On the other hand, the possible action part deals with users' subjective impression that they would be able to carry out actions in the environment. (Hartmann et al. 2015). In the light of these studies, for the third part of the survey, PQ and SPES scales were interpreted and used in ten different questions. In addition to rating questions, surveys also include open-ended questions to gather personal feedback about virtual spaces.

Results of the Survey

At the beginning of the survey, participants were expected to rate their relationship with the building and their interest in immersive technologies and virtual spaces on a Likert scale of 1 to 5. All of them rated their relationship with Taşkışla as very strong. They rated their interest in immersive technologies and virtual space as very high or high at 63%. The rate of those who have previously experienced a virtual environment is 62%.

In the scope of the UX part, 75% of the participants gave Taşkışla Digital (5-4) points for the general evaluation. Participants found the exhibition materials reachable and the Model attractive overall. Questioners who rated their familiarity with immersive technologies and virtual heritage as very high (5) found the space more attractive than the exhibition materials. These participants also added that they prefer the physical experience to the virtual one. On the contrary, participants who rated their familiarity with immersive technologies as low (1–2) defined exhibition content as attractive.

Participants chose between the word pairs that they think will fit the virtual place best for the UX part of the survey for the spatial presence part. They rated Digital Taşkışla as pleasant at 35%; good at 39%; ordinary at 13%; captivating at 9%; and dull at 4%; (Figure 15.4).

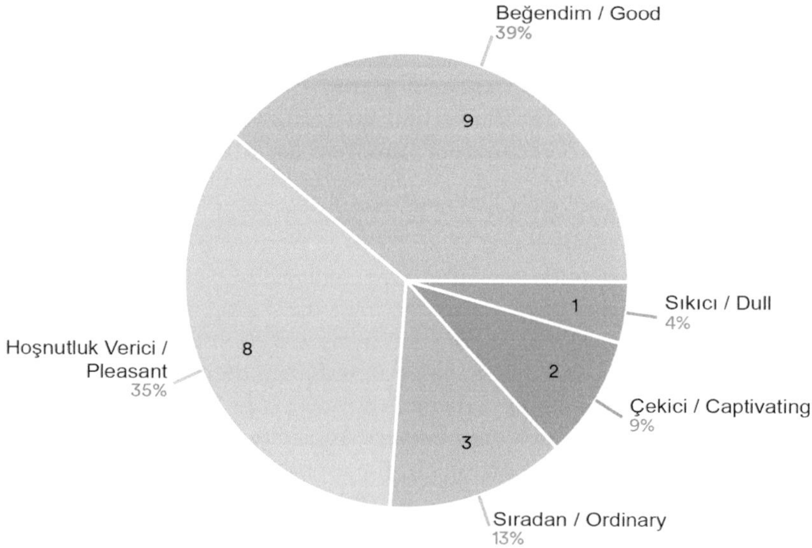

Figure 15.4 Digital model rates due to UX.

According to the adjective pair choices of the questioners, it was seen that the virtual place created positive emotions at a rate of 83% and left a negative impact at a rate of 17%. As seen in the resulting survey graphic (Figure 15.5), 92% of the participants (familiar or not with the immersive technologies) indicated that the digital space experience regenerated their memories in Taşkışla in different expressions.

For the following question, 34% of the participants noted that the experience was reminiscent of Taşkışla and 25% of them noted that the experience made them want to revisit Taşkışla. 30% of the participants mentioned that it was not a substitute for physical experience on the contrary 11% of them expressed that they felt as if they visited the Taşkışla. (Figure 15.6). 63% of respondents said they liked *Taşkışla Digital* since it provides an innovative technological experience.

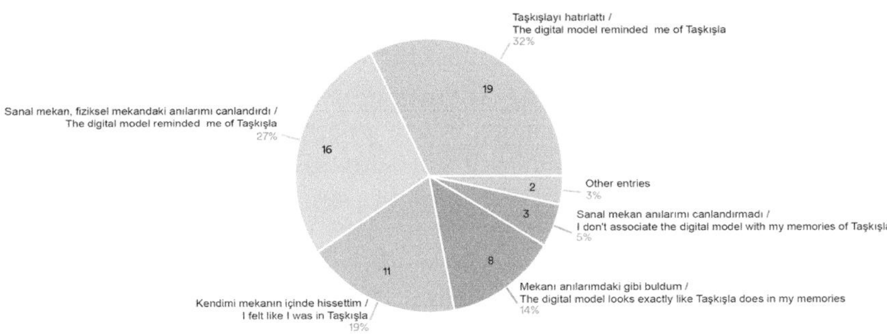

Figure 15.5 Relationship between memories and the digital model.

The responses to the questions about presence were mainly about the experience of the physical building. The answers revealed that users perceive virtual space in their minds, with memories linked to the physical building. In the comments section, 70% of respondents stated that they were particularly attracted to features of the building, such as the courtyard, lighting elements, and resident cats. These elements had already been incorporated into the virtual environment because they are vital to the Taşkışla community's life in the physical world.

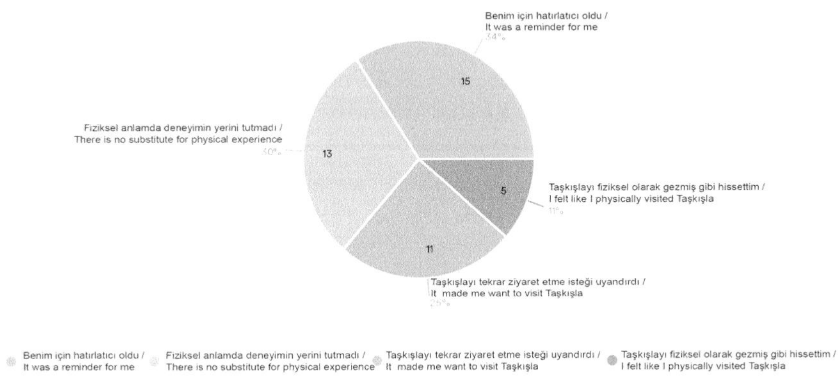

Figure 15.6 Evolutions about presence questionnaire.

There were some criticisms due to the limited space modeled in open-ended questions. Some participants specified they would also like to experience the studios and courtyard of the Taşkışla in the digital model. There was a negative comment for the background music of the Taşkışla Digital. Some of the participants reported that it was not a good match since there is no music in the Taşkışla building in real life. The survey findings indicate that the expectations from the virtual memory space are first of all an exact model of the physical space and basic reminders for the atmosphere of the building overall.

CONCLUSION

Virtual spaces are becoming increasingly important, particularly in preserving cultural heritage. More people can access them by documenting and preserving cultural sites in the virtual world and using them for tourism. These techniques are also important for the sustainability of cultural heritage. Immersive technologies allow us to experience these sites spatially and provide information about them. The effectiveness of a virtual environment is directly related to the presence of realistic perspectives and technically flawless scenes. However, there is still a need to focus more on virtual memory space aspects.

Exploring a virtual heritage site or building can have different impacts on users' minds due to their familiarity with the actual structure. Some users may have personal memories associated with the real building, while others may be unfamiliar with it. For users who are unfamiliar with a building, a virtual experience can provide them with basic information. However, for places/buildings that hold dear memories for people, the perception of the virtual space is much deeper. This study released the assets of virtual memory spaces with the help of a case study that contains a visual experience and a survey that measured user experiences. The case study findings showed that the experience of virtual memory places depicts an integrated perception linked to the current moment and recalling past physical experiences. Unlike other virtual spaces, virtual memory prioritizes physical reality and memory details over digital techniques. Thus, user experiences in physical spaces can be the starting point of creating a virtual memory space, rather than measuring the final product.

In this respect, a virtual memory space may be defined in one aspect as a trace or a reference, of physical spaces similar to Ruchatz's definition of photography (2008). When virtual memory space refers to the physical one not as its representation but as its product, it functions as a reminder that triggers or guides remembering. While virtual memory spaces offer new experiences and highly digital technologies, they are also expected to present deeply realistic scenes, which are the real sources of memories.

As the further study hypothesis; can interactivity use a theme for virtual memory spaces? Can the user personalize the virtual environment with their memories? Can Interactive memory spaces be much more satisfying to the users? These questions may open a new perspective on the user experience of virtual memory spaces.

ACKNOWLEDGEMENTS

Thanks to Yusuf Işık (Game designer) for creating the virtual space; and to Salih Özdemir, and Yasemin Coraklı (Rest. Asst., ITU) for their valuable contributions to the study.

REFERENCES

Addison, A. 2000. Emerging trends in virtual heritage. IEEE Multimedia. 7(2): 22–25.

A3 Digital Sergi arch.itu.edu.tr. https://mim.itu.edu.tr/blog/2021/08/16/2020-2021-bahar-yariyili-a3-ogrenci-projeleri-sergisi-dijital-ortamda/.

Champion, E. and Dave, B. 2007. Dialing up the Past. *In*: F. Cameron and S. Kenderdine (Eds). Theorizing Digital Cultural Heritage: A Critical Discourse. 333–348. The MIT Press.

Cummings, J.J. and Bailenson, J.N. 2016. How immersive is enough? A meta-analysis of the effect of immersive technology on user presence. Media Psychology. 19(2): 272–309.

El Hakim, S., Beraldin, J., Picard, M. and Godin, G. 2004. Detailed 3D reconstruction of large-scale heritage sites with integrated techniques. IEEE Multimedia. 24(3): 21–29.

Flavián, C., Ibáñez-Sánchez, S. and Orús, C. 2019. The impact of virtual, augmented, and mixed reality technologies on the customer experience. Journal of Business Research. 100: 547–560.

Foni, A., Papagiannakis, G. and Magnenat-Thalmann, N. 2002. Virtual Hagia Sophia: Restitution, visualization, and virtual life simulation. In: The Proceedings of UNESCO World Heritage Congress.

Halbwachs, M. 1992. On Collective Memory. Chicago: University of Chicago Press.

Hartmann , T., Wirth, W., Schramm, H., Klimmt, C., Vorderer, P., Gysbers, A., Bet al. 2015 . The spatial presence experience scale (SPES). Journal of Media Psychology Theories Methods and Applications. 1(–1): 1–15. https://www.researchgate.net/publication/272427353_The_Spatial_Presence_Experience_Scale_SPES.

Hassenzahl, M., Burmester, M. and Koller, F. 2003. AttrakDiff: Ein Fragebogen zur Messung wahrgenommener hedonischer und pragmatischer Qualität. Mensch & Computer 2003: Interaktion in Bewegung. 187–196.

IxDF (Interactive Design Foundation). 2023. What is Presence in Virtual Reality? https://www.interaction-design.org/liatarature/topic/presence.

Kilteni, K., Groten, R. and Slater, M. 2012. The sense of embodiment in virtual reality. Presence: Teleoperators and Virtual Environments. 21(4): 373–387.

Lefebvre, H. 2007. The Production of Space. Blackwell Publishing. 229.

Lombard, M. and Ditton, T. 1997. At the Heart of It All: The concept of presence. Journal of Computer-Mediated Communication. 3(2). http://dx.doi.org/10.1111/j.1083-6101.1997.tb00072.x. [Accessed Apr 08 2024].

Merkx C. and Nawijn J. 2021.Virtual reality tourism experiences: Addiction and isolation. Tourism Management. 87: 104394.

Merleau-Ponty, M. (2010). Phenomenology of Perception (D. Landes, Trans.; 1st ed.). Routledge. 159–162. https://doi.org/10.4324/9780203720714.

Nora, P. 1989. Between memory and history: Les Lieux de Mémoire. Representations. 26: 7–24.

Overview Taşkışla. arch.itu.edu.tr. https://mim.itu.edu.tr/tarihte-ve-kultur-3/.

Pujol, L. and Champion, E.M. 2012. Evaluating_Presence_in_Cultural_Heritage_Projects. International Journal of Heritage Studies. 18(1): 83–102. www.researchgate.net/publication/233296232_ [Accessed Apr. 08 2024].

Riva, G., Castelnuovo, G., Gaggioli, A. and Mantovani, F. 2002. Towards a cultural approach to presence. *In*: Proceedings of the 5th Annual International Workshop on Presence. 305–309.

Sharr, A. 2007. Thinkers for Architects/Heidegger for Architects. Routledge. 53.

Skulmowski, A. and Rey, G.D. 2018. Embodied learning: Introducing a taxonomy based on bodily engagement and task integration. Cognitive Research: Principles and Implications. 3(6). https://doi.org/10.1186/s41235-018-0092-9.

Taşkışla Digital. https://mim.itu.edu.tr/blog/2021/03/17/webgl/

Teras, M. and Raghunathan, S. 2015. Big data visualisation in immersive virtual reality environments: Embodied phenomenological perspectives to interaction. International Journal on Soft Computing. 5(4): 1009–1015.

Trigg, D. 2012. The Memory of Place: A Phenomenology of the Uncanny. Ohio University Press. 5.

Tuan, Y.F. 2001. Space and Place: The Perspective of Experience. Minneapolis: University of Minnesota Press. 164–179. ISBN: 9780816638772.

Wei, W., Qi, R. and Zhang, L. 2019. Effects of virtual reality on theme park visitors' experience and behaviors: A presence perspective. Tourism Management. 71: 282–293.

Williams, R. 1983. A Vocabulary of Culture and Society, 2nd Ed. Oxford. University Press.

Wirth, W., Hartmann, T., Boecking, S., Vorderer, P., Klimmt, C., Schramm, H., et al. 2007. A process model of the formation of spatial presence experiences. Media Psychology. 9: 493–525. https://doi.org/10.1080/15213260701283079.

Witmer, B.G. and Singer, M.J. 1998. Measuring presence in virtual environments: A Presence Questionnaire. Presence. 7(3): 225–240.

Vlahakis, V., Karigiannis, J., Tsotros, M., Gounaris, M., Almeida, L., Stricker, D., et al. 2001. Archeoguide: first results of an augmented reality. *In*: The Proceedings of Mobile Computing System in Cultural Heritage Sites, Virtual Reality, Archaeology, and Cultural Heritage International Symposium, Glyfada, Nr. Athens, Greece.

Vorderer, P., Wirth, W., Gouveia, F.R., Biocca, F., Saari, T., Jäncke, F., et al. 2004. MEC Spatial Presence Questionnaire (MECSPQ): Short Documentation and Instructions for Application. Report to the European Community, Project Presence: MEC (IST-2001-37661). Online. Available from: http://www.ijk.hmt-hannover.de/presence.

Index

A

AR-aided design 162, 194
AR assistance assembly 193, 195, 196, 198, 199, 201, 202, 203, 204, 207, 208
ATC Training 112, 115
Augmented Fabrication 196, 197, 198, 212, 213
Augmented Reality (AR) 2, 3, 5, 9, 15, 22, 24, 81, 103, 104, 111, 171, 193, 205, 218, 221, 245, 246, 298, 310, 318, 339
Avatar Creation Interface 42, 48, 52
Avatar Customization 42, 52, 55
Aviation 9, 103, 104, 105, 106, 107, 108, 109, 110, 111, 112, 113, 114, 115
Awareness 14, 23, 24, 42, 47, 112, 141, 142, 159, 208, 212, 250, 252, 253, 256, 283, 306, 318, 319, 327, 328, 330, 331, 332, 333, 335, 336

B

Blended Learning 80

C

Custom Manufacturing SME, 193, 196, 212
Cyberpunk 300, 303, 304, 312
Cybersickness 7, 12, 14, 23, 24, 25, 26, 271

D

Design Education 81, 82, 83, 99, 276
Didactic Systems 165
Distance Learning 99

E

Earthquake 317, 318, 319, 320, 321, 323, 325, 326, 327, 329, 330, 331, 332, 333, 334, 335, 336
Education 11, 23, 27, 61, 62, 63, 76, 81, 82, 83, 96, 99, 100, 111, 150, 153, 155, 156, 157, 158, 165, 167, 218, 243, 271, 272, 274, 275, 276, 283, 292, 293, 294, 299, 308, 309, 319, 320, 333, 345, 348
Experimental Study 272
Extended Reality 1, 2, 3, 4, 11, 75, 103, 171, 178, 243, 244, 246, 272, 298

F

Flight Simulators 10

G

Gamification 63, 64, 65, 76, 277
Gender Identity 41, 42, 43, 45, 46, 47, 48, 51, 55

H

Hand-tracking 64, 72, 74, 124, 125, 132, 133, 135, 142
Human-Computer-Interaction (HCI) 9, 218, 219
Human-Robot Collaboration (HRC) 205, 219, 220, 222, 237, 244, 245, 246, 261

I

Interaction design 61, 65, 68, 72, 73, 74, 156
Interactive Art 61, 71
Interactive Experiences 270, 273, 292, 344

L

Letterpress 80, 81, 82, 83, 85, 87, 88, 90, 93, 95, 96, 97, 98, 99, 100

M

Machine vision 298, 299, 300, 305, 306, 307, 309, 310, 311
Mechanic 20, 24, 65, 67, 70, 74, 75, 111, 124, 125, 126, 127, 129, 130, 131, 132, 139, 140, 141, 142, 300, 302, 305, 311, 312, 318, 328
Mixed Reality 2, 3, 4, 26, 103, 104, 143, 171, 174, 176, 189, 195, 200, 245, 246, 298, 318, 339
Model-Based Systems Engineering 170, 189
MRO 105, 110, 111, 114
Multimodal Design 153

N

Natural interface 143
Numerical Simulation 61, 62, 65, 66, 67, 70, 72, 74, 75

P

Pilot Training 105, 110, 114
Presence 2, 3, 4, 12, 14, 19, 20, 21, 22, 25, 26, 46, 49, 73, 112, 114, 148, 149, 158, 171, 179, 180, 182, 187, 253, 273, 275, 276, 282, 283, 285, 287, 288, 290, 293, 340, 341, 342, 343, 344, 345, 347, 348, 349, 350, 351, 352

Q

Quantum Games 65
Quantum Physics 60, 61, 62, 65, 66, 67, 70, 71, 72, 73, 76

R

Research methods 190, 272, 293, 327
Robotic manufacturing 218, 222

S

Serious Games 63, 319, 320, 331, 335
Shadowrun 301, 304, 305, 306, 307, 308, 309, 310, 311, 312
Sketching 223, 225
Social VR 17, 26, 40, 41, 42, 43, 44, 45, 46, 47, 48, 49, 50, 51, 52, 55, 56
Spatial Computing 103, 104, 109, 114,
Storytelling 61, 62, 63, 65, 74, 75, 76, 334
Systems Engineering 170, 171, 172, 179, 189
Systems Modeling Language 171

T

Tabletop role-playing games 300
Technology acceptance 12, 14, 18, 19, 24
Transgender Studies 40, 41, 42, 43, 44, 45, 46, 47, 48, 49, 50, 51, 52, 53, 54, 55, 56, 57, 58, 59

U

Usability 11, 12, 14, 15, 16, 17, 18, 19, 23, 26, 83, 85, 86, 94, 95, 96, 97, 98, 99, 100, 112, 125, 126, 127, 129, 133, 135, 139, 141, 142, 143, 171, 179, 180, 183, 188, 189, 250, 261, 275, 276, 282, 283, 284, 285, 286, 288, 290, 293
User experience 4, 11, 12, 14, 15, 17, 18, 19, 22, 23, 26, 70, 83, 88, 162, 165, 171, 179, 181, 184, 188, 189, 207, 233, 260, 261, 271, 275, 276, 281, 283, 290, 293, 333, 340, 342, 345, 348, 352

V

Virtual memory space 340, 341, 343, 344, 348, 351, 352
Virtual Reality (VR) 2, 3, 4, 9, 15, 23, 24, 26, 40, 42, 60, 62, 72, 97, 103, 104, 111, 113, 124, 125, 134, 149, 150, 151, 153, 156, 158, 160, 161, 163, 167, 171, 174, 176, 189, 245, 246, 270, 291, 298, 318, 320, 325, 327, 328, 329, 333, 336, 339
Visual Narrative 62, 63, 65, 68, 74
Visualization 5, 10, 60, 66, 68, 71, 72, 73, 74, 113, 153, 154, 160, 173, 174, 176, 177, 189, 218, 219, 221, 222, 227, 233, 306, 327
VR Development 50, 51, 52, 53, 54, 55, 270, 271, 277, 278, 292
VR Evaluation 12, 13, 14, 17, 23, 25, 26, 27
VR for Education 22, 23, 61, 62, 81, 271, 275, 276, 283, 294
VR in Architecture 276

W

Workload 20, 21, 250, 252, 253, 260
Worldbuilding 64, 301, 303, 304, 305, 307, 312

About the Editors

Özge Cordan is a full-time Professor at Istanbul Technical University (ITU), Department of Interior Architecture. She was the national coordinator of the International Masters of Interior Architectural Design Program (IMIAD) between 2008-2018 and the international coordinator of the IMIAD Program between 2010-2015 and the deputy head of the Interior Architecture Department between 2008-2010. She currently serves as the department head. She worked as visiting scholar at College of Design, Architecture, Art, and Planning (DAAP), University of Cincinnati between 2007 and 2008. She has supervised many completed and ongoing master's theses and teaches in both undergraduate and graduate programs. Her main research focus includes gamification and design, interior architecture and education, and inclusive design. Besides her research projects regarding interiors, she completed an EU Erasmus+ project (PUDCAD- Practicing Universal Design Principles in Design Education through a CAD-based Game) with Demet Arslan Dinçay in 2020. She is one of the editors of the "Game + Education" proceedings volume.

Mehmet İlker Berkman is a faculty member at Communication Design Department in Bahçeşehir University (BAU), is actively engaged in research related to human-computer interaction. His expertise lies in user-centered design methods and interactive media design. He specializes in psychometrics in order to develop research tools for subjective assessment of user experience. Dr. Berkman holds an M.A. in interactive media design, an M.Sc. in information technologies, and a Ph.D. in computer engineering. His recent research focus centres around games user research, with a particular emphasis on virtual reality gaming with head-mounted displays.

Demet Arslan Dinçay is an associate Professor at Istanbul Technical University (ITU), Department of Interior Architecture, where she also serves as the coordinator of the International Masters of Interior Architectural Design Program (IMIAD). She was the vice dean of the ITU Faculty of Architecture between 2020-2022. She has been in the USA, Auburn University College of Architecture, Design, and Construction 2018-2019 academic year. Her research interests include interior design, cinematic spaces, and inclusive design in interior architecture. Currently, she is working on the application of virtual environments, as well as virtual and augmented reality, in interior architecture and the integration of AI-generated models in interior design education. In 2020, as co-coordinator with Ozge Cordan, she completed an EU Erasmus + project (PUDCAD-Practicing Universal Design Principles in Design Education through a CAD-based Game) that connected her major interests in inclusive design and virtual environments. She is one of the editors of the "Game + Education" proceedings volume.

Güven Çatak is a full-time Associate Professor at Bahçeşehir University (BAU). He's head of the Department of Digital Game Design and the Game Design Graduate Program coordinator. He's also founder director of the BAU gaming structure, "BUG Lab". His main research areas are serious games, social impact games and cinematography and new techs in gaming. He worked in various gaming related EU Erasmus+ projects as a researcher and producer. Dr. **Çatak** holds an M.Arch and Ph.D. in architecture and computational design.